Music!

Its Role and Importance in Our Lives

Charles Fowler

Contributing Writers

Timothy Gerber   Vincent Lawrence

Glencoe
McGraw-Hill

New York, New York   Columbus, Ohio   Woodland Hills, California   Peoria, Illinois

Meet the Experts

Author

Dr. Charles Fowler celebrates 40 years of professional contributions to music education with the publication of this textbook. He has spent his lifetime as an educator, author, and spokesperson, championing the right of students to acquire an understanding of their musical heritage. For this text he has created a broad and engaging structure and assembled an impressive team in order to produce a set of educational materials that will open the study of music to many more high school students.

Contributing Writers

Dr. Timothy Gerber, associate professor of music at The Ohio State University in Columbus, helped create the student activities and assemble the popular and jazz components of the text.

Dr. Vincent Lawrence, professor of music at Towson State University in Maryland, developed the scope of learnings and the glossary for the text, and helped create the student activities in classical music throughout.

Contributing Specialists

Native American Music
Mr. Edwin Schupman

African-American Gospel Music
Dr. Barbara Baker

Sub-Saharan African Music
Dr. Barbara Lundquist
Mr. Salomão Manhica

African Music and Its Influence
Dr. Christopher Waterman

Arabian Music
Dr. Virginia Danielson

Chinese Music
Dr. Terry Liu

Hispanic Music
Dr. Daniel Sheehy

Indian and Pakistani Music
Dr. Greg Booth

Indonesian Music
Mr. Benedict Lim
Dr. Harold Kacanek

Japanese Music
Dr. James Reid

Laotian and Tibetan Music
Ms. Katherine Bond

Reviewers

American and Western Music
Dr. Anne Dhu Shapiro

African-American Music
Dr. James E. Mumford

Jazz, Pop, and Rock
Dr. Robert Myers

Ethnic Music
Dr. William M. Anderson

Specialists

Swing Music
Mr. Robert T. Bryan

American Folk Music
Mr. Robb Goldstein

The Music of Louis Moreau Gottschalk
Dr. John Doyle

Music Education
Mr. George DeGraffenreid

Assessment
Ms. Andrea Kay

Send all inquiries to:

Glencoe/McGraw-Hill
21600 Oxnard Street, Suite 500
Woodland Hills, CA 91367

ISBN 0-02-642121-6

8 9 10 11 12 13 14 15 16   003   04 03 02 01 00 99 98

Contents

Music!...
To Tell Us
Who We
Are

~

Chapter 1
Music in Our Culture

Chapter 2
Music in Other Cultures

Music in Our Culture

Objectives

By completing this chapter, you will:
- Understand how the variety of music performed in America reflects the diverse cultural backgrounds of its people.
- Become familiar with many different styles of music.
- Begin to identify a wider range of musical styles.
- Learn how to describe and compare contrasting musical compositions.
- Begin to develop a descriptive vocabulary to describe musical characteristics.

Musical Terms

classical music
concerto
culture
homophony
jazz
jitterbug
musical style
perceptive listening

4

$\mathcal{M}$usic is one of the great pleasures of life.
It has the power to command our attention and inspire us.
It speaks to our spirit and to our inner feelings.
It provokes thoughts about the mysteries of life such
as why we exist, the vastness of the universe, and our
purpose on earth. Music reaches deep into our nature
to console us, to reassure us, and to help us express
who and what we are as human beings.

Who We Are

As Americans, we are part of a culturally diverse group of people. Immigrants came to America from every part of the globe. Your classmates, neighbors, and community members probably represent a mixture of racial or ethnic backgrounds. How do you feel about people whose backgrounds are different from yours? Perhaps you interact little with these people. Then again, perhaps you go to school together, understand each other, and get along well.

One way to relate with others is by sharing your culture. **Culture** is *the customs, ideas, tastes, and beliefs acquired from a person's background. It is the sum total of one's lifestyle.* Your culture may be your most personal and important possession. Sharing your culture is the greatest gift you can give others.

One of the most revealing ways that people share their culture is through the arts. The arts radiate the lifestyle of the people who created them. This helps define their culture. Music, perhaps more than any other art form, reflects the diverse cultures of our population. Music is as varied as the cultures that create it. All these different musics define who we are as a nation.

Our Affinity for Music

All people, from the earliest recorded history, have created music. Humans, like birds and whales, have a natural tendency for making sounds and responding to them. When music is pleasurable, it says something to you. It communicates a feeling or conveys a message. It speaks to your inner being.

Teenagers have a strong affinity for music. According to the A. C. Nielsen Company, teens between the ages of 12 to 17 years old watch television 23 hours a week or more than 3.2 hours each day. The time they spend listening to and participating in music may rival that average. Obviously, the amount of time you devote to listening to music will vary according

---

PROJECT

Compare Listening Habits

Gather data on your own music listening habits for three consecutive days. Find out precisely how much you listen to music each day. Maintain an accurate record for three full days. At the end of each day, write down the total time you spend listening to music. On the fourth day, bring your data to class and calculate the average listening time per day. Compare your listening time to that of your classmates.

to your interests and schedule, but the amount of time you actually spend is a clear indication of how much you enjoy music. If you are like most teenagers, you probably enjoy listening to music because you are getting something in return. It is saying something to you that you want to hear.

Preference of Musical Styles

The kind of music you prefer tells something about who you are and what you know. Your likes and dislikes—your musical preferences—express your personal taste. They reveal something about you. Music helps define who you are. This may be one of the reasons it is valued so highly.

As a human being, you have the option to narrowly or broadly define your musical preferences. For example, you may consider yourself a rapper, a rocker, and/or a classical enthusiast. Your musical preference often reflects your lifestyle.

Variety of Styles

As humans, we can be more than one-dimensional. We can stretch our likes and understandings beyond the narrow range of one type of music. In so doing, we define ourselves more broadly and probably more completely. People need not be limited in their musical likings, any more than they need to limit the hairstyles they admire or the kinds of food they enjoy. We are as narrow and limited as we choose to be, or as broad and all-encompassing.

Like all forms of communication—speech and written language, scientific symbols, graphics, visual arts, and gestures—music must be learned. If you want to fully understand and respond to its power, you have to study it. By paying careful attention to music, you can come to know it better and can broaden and deepen your range of understanding and your ability to respond to it.

▼*Activity:* **Radio Scan**

What kind of music do you like?

When you scan radio stations to find the music you like, you hear many different musical styles. If you are like most people, you quickly skip over several stations until you find your musical preference. This process raises some questions about how you define yourself musically. For instance:

1. How long must you listen to one station to know if it is playing what you like?
2. Why is there such a wide variety of music available on the radio?
3. Is this variety important?
4. Are your musical choices different when you are alone?
5. Under what circumstances would you spend more time listening to a station that is unfamiliar to you?

Listen to the musical selections and pretend that each comes from a different radio station. Indicate your reactions to each example by writing down how long you would listen to each station.

▲ Your personal taste in music helps define who you are and usually indicates the kind of group with whom you associate. What do your musical preferences "say" about you?

Different music serves different purposes, different moods, and different human needs. You may find that you are less tolerant of a new type of music. Unfamiliar music may make you suspicious, just as you are cautious when meeting a stranger. This course and this text will help you open your ears to new kinds of music so that you can broaden your musical tastes. By studying music you will be able to stretch your likes and deepen your understanding.

Music differs in the way it is composed and performed. Different types of music have different characteristics—different styles. **Musical style** refers to *the distinct manner or character of musical expression.* This is best understood when qualities between one piece of music are compared to those of another piece of music. For example, just as you learn to recognize different models of cars, you can learn to distinguish between different styles of music and develop a vocabulary—"descriptors"—to define them.

The musical world contains an enormous variety of musical styles. This variety helps to characterize and document what we are like and who we are as a society. Some of these styles are broad categories that cover a wide range of music. For example, the term popular music refers to commercial music that the general public uses for dancing and entertainment. Subcategories under pop might include rock, heavy metal, top 40, rap, and reggae, to name a few. The categories and names of different types of music are numerous and sometimes confusing.

Cooperative Learning

Research Listening Time
How much time do you spend listening to music?

Find out the average time American teenagers spend daily in contact with music. Is it more or less than the time they spend viewing television? How much time per day would you imagine students in your school actually spend in contact with music? Include listening to or making music, attending concerts, or watching music videos.

Working in small groups as a research team, establish a hypothesis about the amount and quality of music listening habits. First, choose one of the hypotheses below (either A or B). Then, estimate the average amount of daily contact with music your classmates actually have over a three-day period, keeping track in hours and minutes. Write down your research group's estimate of the average amount of daily musical contact that students in your class have.

Hypothesis A: Students in my class spend more time in musical contact than in ordinary television viewing (more than the average 3.2 hours per day).

Hypothesis B: Students in my class spend less time in musical contact than in ordinary television viewing (less than the average 3.2 hours per day).

Cooperative Learning

Identify Musical Styles
How many musical styles can you name?

Working in your research team, list all the different styles of music you know. Your style list may contain broad categories and smaller subgroups. Name all the different kinds of music that you can.

▶ Most radio stations become noted for playing only one particular style of music. By listening to a variety of radio stations, you can broaden your exposure to a wider range of music.

▼*Activity:* **Musical Style Check**

How broad is your aural knowledge of musical styles?

How familiar are you with the many styles of music heard daily in the United States? As you listen to the short musical examples, try to identify and match the style. Discuss: (1) What percent of this music are you familiar with? (2) How does this music define America?

Jazz and Classical Music

One of the ways to distinguish the many styles of music is by comparison. Jazz and classical music, for example, are easy to distinguish because they have very different characteristics.

Jazz, *an African-American invention, is a popular style of music that developed in New Orleans during the late 1800s and early 1900s.* It was instrumental music of exuberant spirit, sometimes improvised (invented) on the spot. It most likely emerged from the rhythmic music played during lively street parades and funeral processions. Among those who cultivated jazz were Joseph "King" Oliver and Louis "Satchel Mouth" Armstrong. A simple, heartfelt music, intended for small audiences and for participation, jazz was the kind of music that set feet tapping. Jazz was dance music.

As jazz developed in the early 1940s, people danced the **jitterbug,** *the term jitters referring to the fast acrobatic movements that accompanied swing music.* Jazz ensembles, which consist of rhythm, brass, and reeds, set the entire body—feet, arms, hips, back, head, and hands—in motion. In the rhythm of jazz you can hear the echoes of African tribal drums, but the use of certain instruments—piano, trumpet, clarinet, saxophone, and trombone—is definitely a European and American characteristic.

In music, the term classical has two meanings: **classical music**, in its broadest sense, refers to *a style of "art" music as distinguished from folk, jazz, or popular music.* More specifically, **classical music** refers to *European music of the Classical period; that is, music composed from about 1725 to 1810 by composers such as Franz Joseph Haydn and Wolfgang Amadeus Mozart.*

The Classical period was a time when musicians and other artists looked back to the simple, stately, uncluttered, classical architecture of ancient Greece. It was a time in which revolutions overthrew the old social order in France, and when American independence and democratic rule began. People were searching for a sense of order. The result was a trimmer, clearer music. Instead of many melodies occurring simultaneously, as in the preceding period, Classical composers opted for a more transparent style in

P R O J E C T

Classify Musical Styles

Find out how musical styles are classified and categorized in record stores. Take your completed musical styles worksheet to the most comprehensive audiotape or CD store in town or at the mall. On a separate sheet of paper, develop a complete list of both broad categories and subcategories. Make a note of (a) any styles that you did not list on your worksheet, and (b) those styles you listed that the audio store does not use. Answer these questions:

1. How does the audio store solve the problem of large versus smaller subcategories?
2. How does your team's list compare with the way the audio store classifies the variety of musical styles?

◀ Like the fancy costumes of the day, the music of the Classical period (c. 1750 to 1825) was highly ornamented, giving melodies a flashiness and dazzle.

Louis Carmontelle. *Mozart's Father and His Two Children.* c. 1763–64. Museé de la Ville de Paris, Museé Carnavalet, Paris, France.

which one melody sang out, while the other parts provided a simple accompaniment. This form of music is known as **homophony,** *a single melody with chordal accompaniment.* This new homophonic style projected a sense of aristocratic elegance. Like the fancy attire of the day, the music was highly ornamented, giving the melodies flashiness and dazzle. Moods changed freely, and composers used dramatic changes of soft and loud, fast and slow, and high and low to make the music expressive and full of interesting surprises.

Classical composers explored new instrumental combinations. The **concerto** (con-CHAYR-toh), *a composition usually written in three sections or movements featuring the interplay between one or more soloists and an orchestra,* became a popular vehicle for showing off the skill of an instrumental soloist accompanied by the newly formed symphony orchestra. Strings, woodwinds, and brass instruments were combined and contrasted to create a whole new world of musical expression.

▼*Activity:* **Compare Musical Styles**

How would you describe two different musical compositions?

Listen to the following compositions that represent two different styles of music from different historical periods.

- Allegro movement from Concerto in D Major for Trumpet and Orchestra by Michael Haydn (performed by Wynton Marsalis).
- "You'd Be So Nice To Come Home To" by Cole Porter (performed by Ella Fitzgerald).

As you listen, write down the musical similarities and differences you hear. What can you tell about these pieces just by the verbal clues—the names of the composers, the performers, and the titles of the musical selections? Use your notes to discuss these comparisons in class.

PROJECT

Analyze Musical Preferences

Try to describe the music your classmates like. Bring to class the one recorded piece of music that you believe is the very best musical composition you own. Select any performing artist, style, historical period, or performing media, but make sure your selection is appropriate for classroom discussion. Avoid song lyrics containing language or subject matter that could be considered offensive. Share your musical preference with your classmates. Analyze and describe each of the compositions your peers bring to class.

What We Like

This text invites you to explore many different forms of music. It does not present one type of musical style as best or ask you to like a particular kind of music. You may like all of it, some of it, or none of it. That is your choice. However, you are asked to develop the ability to substantiate your musical opinions based on your analysis of the music itself.

Do not be fooled, either, into thinking that every piece of music you will hear in this course is of equal value and importance. Even though you will hear outstanding examples of music from many cultures, you will find some may be more profound than others, some may be more imaginative, and some may be more difficult to comprehend. Value them accordingly. The goal of this text is to expand your horizons. The skill you acquire in analyzing music and learning to listen to it perceptively will enable you to make musical choices and to know why you made them.

Profile

Wynton Marsalis
American Trumpeter
1961–

WYNTON MARSALIS

Although he was born in New Orleans, the birthplace of jazz, Wynton Marsalis did not play jazz as a youngster. Marsalis picked up the trumpet when he was 12, and quickly learned and excelled in classical music. Encouraged and guided by his musician father, Marsalis was a member of the New Orleans Symphony Orchestra at the age of 14. By the age of 17, he impressed audiences by playing concertos written by Haydn and Bach. It was at the prestigious Juilliard School of Music in New York that Marsalis first became exposed to jazz.

Once interested in jazz, Marsalis voraciously sought out and studied anything pertaining to it, going to libraries, museums, and clubs. His mentors introduced him to local and visiting jazz musicians. Motivated by his love for traditional jazz and fortified by his classical virtuosity, Marsalis's inspired playing allowed him to become a recognized recording artist by the time he was 20.

Since collecting Grammy awards in both jazz and classical categories in 1984, Marsalis has committed himself to advancing the art of jazz. His popular and artistic success has helped create a new generation of jazz fans and inspired other musicians to explore this art form. His versatility in both jazz and classical music has established him as a major force in American music.

▲ There are as many different kinds of music in the United States as there are different peoples. This variety of musical styles helps define who we are as a nation.

Why We Like It

The old Latin expression, *De gustibus non est disputandum* ("There is no disputing taste") seems to suggest that differences in taste cannot be substantiated. For some people, "I like it" or "I don't like it" are sufficient explanations. However, understanding why you like or dislike something is important, if only to validate your perceptions to yourself. Then, too, you may want to be able to persuade others.

Before you can fully and fairly judge whether you like a new piece of music, you have to be certain you hear what the sounds are doing. You have to know what you are hearing and become familiar with the characteristics of the music. This implies a willingness to listen, even if the sounds do not readily appeal to you. You have to give unfamiliar music a chance, which may mean giving it your attention more than once in order to feel comfortable with it.

▼*Activity:* **Listen Perceptively**

How much can you tell about music by listening with greater focus?

Listen again to the compositions by Michael Haydn and Cole Porter. See if you can discover more distinguishing characteristics. As you listen, try to make some musical observations based on the following:

1. Determine the musical means (the source of sound and the size of the group for each piece).
2. Describe the musical expression (the rhythm, melody, and mood).
3. Determine each piece's order or organization (the amount of repetition and contrast that is used).
4. Determine the possible origin (the where, when, and by whom the music was created).
5. Characterize the use of the music (its function or purpose, and its intended audience).

Perceptive listening is *the ability to discern musical characteristics and describe them.* These characteristics are both internal (dealing with sound) and external (dealing with the social aspects). In its sound, every piece of music uses a distinctive *means* (the source of sound), *expression* (feeling), and *order* (organization).

In its social aspects, every musical piece has a distinctive *origin* (the where, when, and by whom the music was created) and *use* (function or purpose). To develop the capacity to listen perceptively, you must analyze what you hear. You need to perceive the internal and external characteristics of the work and develop the ability to describe them. For this purpose you may have to acquire some new vocabulary, or "descriptors." This new vocabulary will permit you to communicate your likes and dislikes persuasively.

Profile

Cole Porter
American Composer
1893–1964

COLE PORTER

Cole Porter was a remarkable man who had a special genius for creating brilliant lyrics and memorable melodies. Yet, it is a near miracle that he ever got into the music business. Cole Porter was born into wealth; his grandfather, a speculator in West Virginia coal and timber, was determined that Porter would become a lawyer. When Porter was at Yale, he wrote student shows and two of Yale's great fight songs, including the "Yale Bulldog Song." Later at Harvard Law School he switched to the School of Music!

Porter never won his grandfather's blessings. His first Broadway score was such a flop that he ran off to North Africa and joined the French Foreign Legion. Fortunately, after World War I, his first hit song, "An Old-Fashioned Garden," paid off so well that he lived royally in Europe. His grandfather's will soon made him a millionaire, and he married a beautiful lady who was even richer! The two of them associated with the famous, gave lavish parties, and toured the world.

If you had that much money would you work? Porter did. In fact, few people could ever say they worked harder. Porter composed Broadway shows one after the other, sometimes two a year, and most of them became smash hits. In 1937, both of Porter's legs were crushed when the horse he was riding fell and rolled over him. Although Porter could not walk again, he continued to write. His many fine songs include: "Love for Sale," "Night and Day," "I Get a Kick Out of You," "Begin the Beguine," "What Is This Thing Called Love?" and such motion picture songs as "I've Got You Under My Skin" and "Don't Fence Me In."

Summary

Music is one of the ways in which we define who we are as individuals and as a society. Through music and the other arts, we express our cultural lifestyles as Americans. Multiculturalism is what American life is all about. Rather than argue over our differences ("My music is better than your music!"), we can learn to celebrate our diversity. Our pluralistic society and its pluralistic tastes give us a rich and unique heritage. Our culture is no longer a melting pot in which cultures blend and lose their identity.

As a people, we are not one-dimensional and neither is our music. As you have heard through the musical activities in this chapter, a broad diversity of musical styles is available to all Americans. We are not confined to one kind of music or to one taste. We can learn to savor the great variety that surrounds us. All we have to do is open our ears and our minds. We can learn to appreciate the great variety that surrounds us by becoming perceptive listeners.

We can acquire new sources of musical pleasure and understanding if we are willing to pay attention to the other cultures that are around us. Today these different cultures are easily accessible. Much of their music is available on radio and television, on recordings, and through live performances. Immigrants have come to our shores and brought their instruments, their songs, their dances, and their love of music with them. Music is part of their roots. It is a memory of the best of their homeland. Such cultural memories are a very personal and precious part of these people. That is why sharing that culture is such a generous gesture. That is why living in a country in which we share so much of the world's music is such a privilege.

CHAPTER 2

Music in Other Cultures

Objectives

By completing this chapter, you will:
- Assess your familiarity with music of other cultures.
- Understand how music can allow a person to develop empathy for people of different cultures.
- Begin to associate musical styles with their place of origin in the world.
- Recognize music from cultures represented by American citizens who are of African, Mexican, and Chinese descent.
- Understand how these cultures express themselves musically.
- Recognize how different cultures use music for a variety of purposes.

Musical Terms

anthropologist
empathy
ethnomusicologist
heterophony
Lali
mariachi
mestizo
Peking opera
timbre

*D*o you realize that much of the music you hear in
the United States comes from other countries? Most people
who immigrate to America gradually adapt to and acquire
much of the lifestyle of their new homeland. However,
they do not generally give up their music. Their musical
tastes may be influenced and adjusted, but they will
continue to like, and perhaps even favor, the music of
their original homeland. Eventually, as they hear new
sounds that attract their attention and listen to the new
music often enough, they may begin to prefer it.
But rather than give up the music of their heritage,
their tastes stretch to accommodate new types of music.

Discovering New Soundscapes

As Americans, we collectively embrace the larger world of sound represented by our multicultural society. We all have some affinity for rhythm and blues, gospel, jazz, or other musical traditions given to us by African Americans. We can hear Chinese music when we visit Chinatown or attend a Chinese New Year's celebration. When we eat in ethnic restaurants, we are apt to hear music from countries such as Germany, Italy, Japan, or Mexico. You are probably familiar with a wider variety of the world's music than you think!

Although different kinds of music come from different countries, people have not always had the opportunity to enjoy music from other lands. Prior to Thomas Edison's invention of the phonograph in 1877, the only way to hear music was to experience it live. If you wanted to hear music of other lands, you had to travel to the place where it was being performed. The phonograph changed this. It made music from around the world easily accessible to everyone. Perhaps without even being aware of it, you have learned to associate certain sounds with certain cultures.

As you listen to music from around the world, you will probably notice that there are vast differences in the way various peoples make music. There is no one absolute way. As a matter of fact, if all the world's composers had one motto, it might be: "There are many ways to do one thing correctly."

Regardless of the musical style or the origin, almost all music shares several common elements: melody, rhythm, and **timbre** (TAM-bur), *the quality of the sound.* When you listen to music from various countries, consider

> **P R O J E C T**
>
> ### Music in Your Community
>
> Working in small groups, find out where you can go in or around your community to hear music of other cultures. Are there musical performances from other countries at a nearby university? in a concert hall or auditorium? on the radio? sponsored by social or religious groups? Which countries are featured? Make a list of all these places. Call or investigate them. Share your list with the class.

the type of melody, the type of rhythm, and the type of timbre. Think of descriptive words such as "lively" or "dancelike" to associate with the various musical styles.

▼Activity: *Discover Music from Other Countries*

How familiar are you with the music of different countries and cultures?

Listen to musical examples that represent the musical traditions of people from Africa, Asia, Europe, Central America, and North America. Rate your familiarity using a scale of 0–3 (0 = no familiarity; 1 = little familiarity; 2 = some familiarity; 3 = great familiarity). Can you identify the example recorded in Africa? In the United States?

Who They Are

▲ The restored Harp of Ur now appears as a boat-shaped harp of thirteen strings. The string pegs of these harps were made of precious metals while each string arm terminated in a cap of gold or silver. What do these artifacts tell you about earlier civilizations?

Harp of Ur. 2600–2350 B.C. from the Royal Cemetery at Ur (restored). The British Museum, London, England. Reproduced by Courtesy of the Trustees of the British Museum.

Throughout history, people have always engaged in the creation of art. Magnificent cave paintings and carvings from the late Ice Age revealed that early people did not simply make tools; they decorated them. They had a sense of craftsmanship and design. Their artifacts give us an indication of how these people lived, thought, and conducted their lives.

In Mesopotamia, around the ruins of Babylon, archaeologists uncovered rattles, flutes, and harplike instruments dating back to almost 2000 B.C. The purported splendor of King Nebuchadnezzar's hanging gardens leads us to envision magnificent entertainments as well. Ancient people were fascinated with music.

Just as your musical preferences help define who you are, the music of other people and cultures helps to define who they are. The use of musical instruments by ancient people tells us that they were not that different from us. They, too, had dreams and found ways of coping with the human struggle. They, too, were sensitive and considered the arts important in their lives.

Try to imagine the music of these people. What did they sing when they were victorious in battle? What were their love songs like? How did they dance? If we knew, we would know much more about them. But their music was not written down; in fact, a system for writing music was not developed in Western Europe until about the ninth century A.D., and the recording of music has only been possible for a little more than 100 years.

From the standpoint of being able to hear the music of other peoples, we have accessible to us only about 1,000 years of written music. We can become acquainted with some of the unwritten cultural traditions through examples of music that were recorded "in the field" by **anthropologists,** *scientists who study the physical and cultural characteristics and social customs of a group of people,* and **ethnomusicologists,** *professionals who study the music of different cultural groups.*

Developing Empathy

Through familiarity with and understanding of the music of other cultures comes **empathy**, *the ability to look at the world from another person's perspective.* Empathy gives us an understanding of someone else's viewpoint. Music gives us an indication of how other people express themselves and communicate their feelings. It invites us to know other people and to be empathetic towards them.

What makes music universal is its capacity to speak to our inner being. It touches our feelings and expresses the rituals of our lives. Music is a richness of knowing people and of exploring the world of humanity, past and present.

▲ To share music between cultures is to explore the world of humanity. It is the way people express and communicate their cultural heritage.

Crossing the Cultural Chasm

Having easy access to the wonder of sound created by all the peoples of this world does not mean that you are going to readily like or understand all of it. There are vast differences in the ways various cultures express themselves musically. These chasms may be difficult to cross, because our ears tend to get stuck in our own culture, or music of other people may not readily communicate its message to those outside the culture. In spite of the difficulties you may have in breaking out of your musical comfort zone, exploring music that is exotic and strange can be highly rewarding. It's like making new friends.

To grow in your tolerance of music from other cultures, all you have to do is be willing to explore what is unfamiliar. The more you are willing to listen, the more rapidly you can accustom yourself. It is like sampling food from foreign countries. At first you may not like it, but then you begin to savor it because it is different. If you can find out what music is trying to communicate and how it is intended to be used, you will have some basis for understanding it.

The first taste of another culture is usually the most difficult. Initially, you may not like what is unfamiliar and different. You may be uncomfortable. However, exposure leads to familiarity. You have to experience it to accommodate yourself to it. You have to adjust your musical expectations. The second and third listenings can make it more palatable. In these ways, foreign music will become less strange. Through such explorations, you may discover a new sound to treasure.

Finding Similarities

It is not important that you like the music of other cultures and peoples equally, but it is important that you recognize that people from all cultures value music. Even though "musical language," or the way people use sounds, may be vastly different, music serves many of the same purposes—ceremonial, religious, and social—in different cultures. Similarities in the use of music throughout the world indicate that human beings are far more alike than different. You may discover that music that sounded very strange at first has familiar aspects.

To begin your exploration of music of other cultures, you will be introduced to music from three cultural traditions that are well represented in the American population: African (Cameroon), Hispanic (Mexico), and Asian (China). For each culture, you will be provided with background about the country, the people, and the musical traditions. Then, in that context, you will be asked to listen to typical examples of the music.

Cameroon (Africa)

Cameroon is a republic in west central Africa. Its two official languages, English and French, help people from more than 150 ethnic groups, with many different languages and dialects, communicate with each other. In 1472, Portuguese sailors visited the coast of what is now called Cameroon and enjoyed eating the prawns they caught in the Wouri River. They called this river *Rio dos Cameroes,* or "River of Prawns," and the name "Cameroon" soon identified the entire country.

Cameroon lies on a volcanic belt that separates west and central Africa. This double chain of volcanic peaks rises to an elevation of 13,350 feet (4 069 meters) at Mt. Cameroon, the highest point in West Africa. The terrain in Cameroon is diverse. The hot, humid coastal plain that extends inland from the Atlantic Ocean to the slopes of these mountains is among the wettest places on earth. The central Adamawa Plateau has a relatively cool, pleasant climate with little variation in annual temperature. It is an ideal place to live and is heavily populated. This plateau is the home of the Bamileke (Bah-mee-LAY-KAY) people, who live in neighborhoods of family homesteads. The Bamileke people are divided into chiefdoms, subgroups that have some distinct traits within the overall common culture.

The Music of Cameroon

The Bamileke people perform **Lali** (LAH-LEE), *a warrior dance.* The example you will hear was performed by the Menne (me-NAY), a subgroup of the Bamileke people. Lali is a music of great rhythmic energy and subtlety. In the sub-Sahara, warrior dances served preparatory and celebratory purposes. These male dances expressed bravery, virility, and brotherhood. They celebrated prowess (ability and skill) in battle, self-confidence, and manliness. But they served other, perhaps even more important, purposes.

From the fifteenth through the early twentieth century, colonialism—the imposed rule of a European power—stripped many African peoples of their independence. Warrior dances were viewed by colonial rulers as a symbol of self-assertion. They became a metaphor for local pride and revolution. In her studies of these dances, Judith Hanna observes that "throughout Africa, warrior dances were usually crushed as were other dances that might loosen the colonial grip through their expression of communal life." Such expressions were widely prohibited. Missionaries often feared them because of the sense of solidarity they proclaimed.

▼ The Bamileke people, like their Cameroon neighbors the Kwifon (shown here), perform dances that symbolize tribal unity and pride.

Members of the *Kwifon* society.
The Metropolitan Museum of Art, New York, New York. The Robert Goldwater Library, Paul Gebauer Collection. Photograph by Paul Gebauer at Nkwen.

Today, these dances still symbolize tribal unity and pride. The Bamileke present these dances now as musical performances expressing these sentiments, rather than as expressions of war. Lali was originally danced by members of a secret society. In all probability, the performers wore ceremonial masks that are typical of this region. The iron bells heard in this music are now used in other music of Cameroon.

▼*Activity:* **Discover When the Pattern Changes**

See if you can detect when the two-tone woodblock changes its initial pattern.

Listen to Lali performed by the Bamileke-Bamoungoun percussion ensemble from Cameroon and "air perform" with your index fingers the following pattern of eight pulses, high-low, high-low:

Determine when it changes. Do you hear other changes in the woodblock?

How many of the following instruments can you hear?

- Four two-tone bells of different sizes. (How many pitches can you distinguish? Can you hear more than six?)
- *N'to* (n-TOH), a medium-sized tubular drum that is open on one end.
- *N'ket* (n-KET), a large closed drum with a carved-out base on which it stands. (Can you hear its low tones?)
- Three rattles that seem to be playing the following pattern:

Can you tap the rattles' pattern along with the recording? Can you detect how the other instruments also repeat their rhythms and vary them subtly? Is there an underlying sense of shared rhythm throughout? When are the parts occasionally silent?

Mexico

Mexico is a large country with many regions. As in the United States, people in these regions differ in dialect, foods, clothing, and music. Although the country is largely mountainous, more than half the work force engages in agriculture. Industry and commerce are growing. The official language is Spanish, but sizable minorities speak Indian tongues.

For many centuries music has had a special place in the lives of the Mexican people. Before Hernán Cortés and his Spanish conquistadors arrived in what is now Mexico in 1519, both religious and social music were important to the Indian civilizations. The Spaniards introduced a rich musical heritage, including a wide variety of music and instruments. African slaves and Caribbean immigrants also influenced Mexican music. The cross-fertilization and blending of the Spanish, Indian, and African cultures produced a rich **mestizo** (mes-TEE-soh), *mixed culture*, and a musical life that has been envied and enjoyed by people around the world.

▲ The festive atmosphere, traditional attire, and lively music create a special musical "feel" unique to the Mexican culture. The dancers stamp a foot pattern on the floor. This percussive sound, along with the instruments, contributes to the communal spirit.

The Music of Mexico

In today's Mexican music, the legacy of the past has been reworked through centuries of creativity into strikingly different, yet in some ways similar, regional forms of music. These separate traditions have original musical forms and compositions, but they also share Spanish-derived instruments such as the folk harp, violin, and guitar-type instruments, as well as a special musical feeling that is unique to Mexico.

Visit any Mexican town and you will hear music. Mexicans use music to celebrate events such as baptisms, birthdays, weddings, anniversaries, funerals, civic ceremonies, and religious holidays. The people like music and they show it. They sing along with the musicians and burst out with enthusiastic yells, laughter, clapping, and dancing.

Two types of regional music popular throughout Mexico are from the states of Veracruz (in the east) and Jalisco (in the west). Typically, Veracruzan music is performed on four instruments: a 35-string harp called *arpón* that plays both melody and bass; a four-string guitar called *requinto jarocho* (reh-KEEN-toh hah-ROH-choh) that provides melody; a thin guitar called *jarana* (hah-RAH-nah), and a six-string guitar—both of which provide rhythmic and harmonic accompaniment. Traditional songs are called *sones* (SOH-nehs) *jarochos*. One of the most famous sones jarochos is "La Bamba."

▼ Activity: **Participate**

Listen for the repeated rhythmic and chordal patterns in "La Bamba." Clap the bass rhythm played by the low strings of the harp.

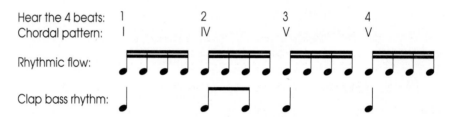

| Hear the 4 beats: | 1 | 2 | 3 | 4 |
| Chordal pattern: | I | IV | V | V |

Rhythmic flow:

Clap bass rhythm:

Can anyone in the class play the chordal pattern of the bass rhythm on a guitar, piano, or another instrument (Key of C)?

Listen to the four different instruments and add a fifth. Can you distinguish the four stringed instruments? Often a fifth instrument is added—the feet of a dancer stamping on the floor while dancing. Can you stamp the following rhythmic pattern along with the repeated cycle above?

Rhythm of feet:

Foot pattern: l   r - l   r   l - r
(l=left, r=right)

Music from Jalisco is usually played by the **mariachi** (mah-ree-AH-chee), *a musical group with several violins, two trumpets, a bass guitar called guitar-rón (ghee-tah-ROHN), a short five-string rhythm guitar called vihuela (vee-WAY-lah), and a six-string guitar.* The mariachi plays many types of music. Two of the most popular are the *son jalisciense* (hah-lee-see-EN-seh), a type of *son* from Jalisco, and the *canción* (cahn-see-OHN) *ranchera*, a country song. "La Negra" ("The Dark Woman") is the most well-known of the *sones jaliscienses*.

◀ This Veracruzan-style jarocho ensemble now performs in the United States. The instruments from left to right include: six-string guitar, harp, *requinto jarocho*, and *jarana*.

▼Activity: *Experience the Difference*

Sense the rhythmic shifting from a feeling of three to a feeling of two in the son jalisciense "La Negra."

Feeling of three:

Count: 1 & 2 & 3 &

Tap: [● · ● · ● ·]

Feeling of two:

1   2   3   4   5   6

[● · · ● · ·]

Try tapping four verses in the pattern of three, then four verses in the pattern of six. Can half the class tap in three and half the class tap in six while counting together?

Now follow the *guitarrón* (bass) line and hear it when it plays in three:

1 & 2 & 3 &   1 & 2 & 3 &

[● | ● | ●]   or   [(rest) | ● | ●]

It also plays the following tricky pattern in six.

1 & 2 & 3 &

[| ● | | ● |]

To get the feeling of the constant flow of six beats and how the guitarrón line fits in, pair up so that one person claps a repeated cycle of 12 while the other claps on 2, 5, 9, and 11:

1 2 3 4 5 6 7 8 9 10 11 12

[| ● | | ● | | | ● | | ● |]

Start slowly, then speed up until you are going as fast as this music.

Cooperative Learning

Listen for the Meaning

What is there about the performance of "La Negra" that makes it right for celebration?

Working in small groups, describe how the rhythm, pace of the music, variations in loudness or softness, and verbal expressions communicate emotions. Which emotions are communicated?

China

China, one of the world's largest countries, has mainly a temperate climate. Even though it is one of the world's largest mineral producers, its economy is primarily agricultural. Many great rivers, among them the Yangtze and the Yellow, still serve as important arteries of transportation. China's ruling dynasties extended from about 2,000 B.C. to the early twentieth century. Today, The People's Republic of China is ruled by a communist government that was established in 1949.

The long history of the Chinese people is rich in literature and the arts. Chinese arts, often expressions of religious belief, are among the oldest in the world. In religion, the Chinese practice a mixture of Confucianism, Buddhism, and Taoism. Early writings include the works of Confucius, a philosopher and teacher of court officials. Confucius believed that only by learning justice, self-sacrifice for the good of all, and correct behavior could one achieve peace. Appreciation of the best music was part of one's development.

▶ Up until this century, male actors played the female roles in Peking opera. Two of the customary female roles in Peking opera include a refined lady with elaborate costume and long sleeves, and a beautiful warrior woman.

The Music of China

During the sixth century A.D., a new, wealthy middle class developed a combination of music and theater called Chinese opera. Soon there were public performances of opera throughout China. Hundreds of different styles developed. In the seventeenth century, a number of these styles were combined in the capital city of Peking. This style of opera became known as **Peking opera,** *an art form that combines an orchestra with speaking, singing,* *acrobatic martial arts, and pantomime*. The vocal range of singing is generally higher than in Western opera. Whereas European and American opera singers resonate sound in their chests, Chinese opera singers make the sound vibrate in their head cavities, producing a shrill tonal quality.

The accompanying instrumental ensemble sits to the right of the stage in full view of the audience. Loud cymbals, gongs, a bright sounding drum, and a wood clapper (the latter played by the ensemble leader) accompany the actors' movements. Singing is accompanied by stringed instruments. The *jinghu* (jing-who), a small two-stringed bowed lute, accompanies male roles; a larger one, called *jing erhu* (jing AR-who), accompanies female roles. A round plucked lute, called *yuegin* (you-ay chin), accompanies both. The musical texture is heterophonic. **Heterophony** occurs *when everyone sings or plays the same melody, but each in its own appropriate way, according to the instrument*. Melodies and rhythms serve the mood of the drama. Generally, the stories are taken from Chinese history or folklore.

Chinese opera is performed wherever there are large Chinese communities. In China, nearly every city has at least one well-attended theater and opera company, despite other forms of popular entertainment such as movies and rock music. Audiences are avid fans! They are familiar with the stories and know the songs by heart. They clap and shout *"hao!"* (how) when a song or aria is sung especially well.

Even though Chinese opera developed as a form of entertainment, the Confucian values of patriotism, loyalty, fidelity, and respect for elders and those in authority remain embedded in it. The cast of a Chinese opera is made up of a number of characters: ancient bearded men, flirtatious girls, aspiring students, women warriors, and others symbolizing various aspects of society. Generals and kings with distinctive costumes are presented in a larger-than-life manner. Common people are portrayed by clowns. In symbolic plots, these characters entertain and educate their audiences.

◀ A string ensemble performs at a hotel in Dongguan in South China's Guangdong Province. From left to right there are two *erhu*, a type of bowed lute; then a *yangqin* (yahng-CHIN), a hammered dulcimer; a *ruan* (roo-AHN), or plucked lute; and finally a *pipa* (PEA-pah), or pear-shaped lute. The group performs in heterophony—everyone playing essentially the same melody.

Cooperative Learning

Compare Peking Opera with Western Opera

What are the basic similarities and differences between Peking opera and Western opera?

Listen to a selection from a Peking opera and an excerpt from a Western opera. As you listen to each excerpt, write down a description of the following characteristics: source of sound; size of group; variety of sound; degree of blend; rhythm; melody; mood; dynamics; texture; repetition/contrast; the function of this music; and the intended audience. Discuss your answers.

The Story of White Snake

One well-known Peking opera, *The Story of White Snake,* tells the story of two goddesses, White Snake and Green Snake, who decide to visit the mortal world. They each assume a woman's form. Soon White Snake meets, falls in love with, and marries a mortal man, Xu Xian (sue see-EN). The antagonist or opponent Fa Hai (fah high), religious leader of the town, knows the true identity of White Snake. He convinces Xu Xian to make White Snake drink wine, revealing her as a snake. Xu Xian shrieks and falls dead with fright.

White Snake dashes back to heaven, fighting her way through the heavenly guards to obtain an herb that will save her husband's life. She returns and saves him, and eventually bears his child. Still Fa Hai makes Xu Xian frightened of her, and Xu Xian leaves for the monastery. In a final meeting on a bridge, White Snake, whose love is as real as it is immortal, forgives Xu Xian. Her friend Green Snake is ready to skewer the cowardly man. As White Snake lets down her guard, a monk uses his power to imprison her and Green Snake in a pagoda for 10,000 years.

This story contains everything that Chinese audiences love: beautiful ladies, wonderful costumes, a wide range of emotions, acrobatic martial arts, and animal gods and goddesses. The Chinese audiences know that there are lessons to be learned here. Marriage is an important institution in Chinese society. Most Chinese believe that marriage and a stable family are the basis for social order. Love is a powerful emotion that all people feel, but like many tragic lovers, White Snake and her husband sacrifice their love because of rigid social conventions. The established ways of religion, represented by Fa Hai, do not permit true love in unusual circumstances. So, the kindhearted White Snake loses everything in the end. Chinese audiences leave the world of the theater with much to talk about, as they return to the real world where the strict ways of society prevail.

▼*Activity:* **Experience Peking Opera**

Listen to the excerpt from the Peking opera, and try to understand how it expresses heartbreak and forgiveness.

In the scene White Snake is heartbroken to learn that Xu Xian, her husband, is leaving her to enter a monastery. However, she understands his fear and forgives him because her love for him is so strong.

Try to perceive the themes of heartbreak and forgiveness, and how the Chinese depict emotions in this musical example. Listen carefully and think about this particular moment in the story. Then listen again to the excerpt and answer the following questions:

1. How many different sources of sound can you distinguish? Do they blend or contrast?
2. Do the two instruments (*yuegin* and *jing erhu*) that accompany White Snake play totally independent parts and melodies that contrast with her melody, or do their parts relate to hers?
3. Do we have any forms of expression in the United States that ask us to "suspend reality" and accept the unreal in order to get the meaning?

◀ In Peking opera you will see larger-than-life portrayals of generals and kings played by men with mask-like painted faces, who wear elevated shoes and move like giants.

Summary

Musical traditions must be viewed in the context of the culture from which they come. When you hear music with some understanding of how and why it was developed, and you know something about its use and meaning, then you can begin to relate to it. You have to hear it enough to become accustomed to its musical conventions before it can speak to you emotionally. Then you can feel empathy for the people who created and shared the expression.

People become knowledgeable in the ways of this world by discovering and experiencing a larger universe. One way is through music. Musical expression comes from the depths of who and what we are as humans. It is a way that we share our inner being with others. To know the music of other people is to know something very important about them—their spirit and their feeling.

Apply What You Have Learned
Chapter 1

Match the music with the environment.

Often we associate different environments with different types of music. Look at the photographs. For each photo, answer the following questions:

- What is the environment or place?
- What style of music is being performed?
- What is the source of sound? (Describe the means.)
- What is the function of the music? (Describe the use.)
- Who is the intended audience?

When you have finished, discuss your answers. Are there times when other music might be heard in the same environments?

1.

2.

3.

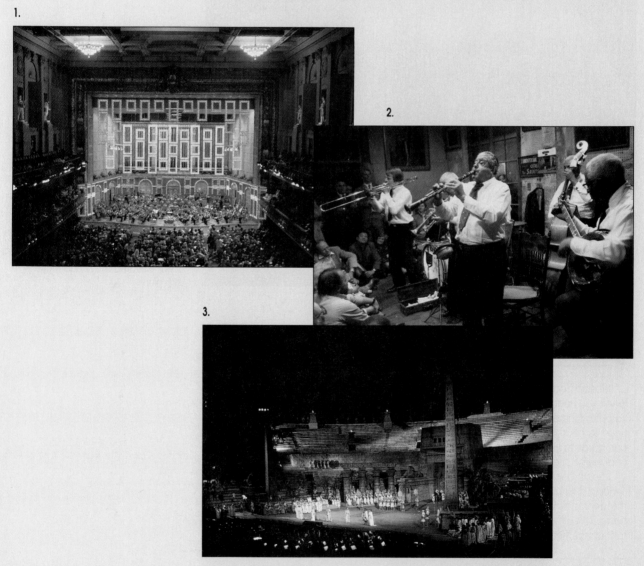

4.

5.

Apply What You Have Learned
Chapter 2

On the basis of (1) what you have learned about African, Mexican, and Chinese music, and (2) clues that you identify in the music, determine which broad culture the music represents.

    Listen to the musical examples and make notes on as many of the musical characteristics as you can. On the basis of your analysis of each of the three pieces and what you know about music of other cultures, place each work in its proper cultural context. Be prepared to discuss the reasons for your choices.

Music!...
To Invite Us
To Move

~

CHAPTER 3

Interpreting Rhythm Through Movement

Objectives

By completing this chapter, you will:

- Use movements of your body (tapping, clapping, and so forth) to understand rhythm in music.
- Differentiate between "felt" time and "real" time in music.
- Become familiar with tempo designations, pulse, meter, and accent.
- Learn to improvise rhythms.
- Become acquainted with some rhythmic aspects in the music of India.
- Create syncopation and polyrhythms.

Musical Terms

accelerando
accent
a tempo
"felt" time
improvisation
meter
polyrhythms
rhythm
rhythm cycle
ritardando
syncopation
tempo

*M*usic progresses through time. Like a film, a play, or a speech, a musical work has a beginning, a middle, and an end. If it is well conceived, it provokes our interest. It teases us and catapults us along from its start into its interior and on to its finish. To hold our attention, it presents us with a series of events—surprises or revelations, frustrations and satisfactions—that stir our excitement and draw us into deeper involvement. And it promises a conclusion or resolution—and delivers it.

The Momentum of Music

If the music is effective, it will provoke expectations. It commands our attention by making new sounds occur in a driving force—a momentum—so compelling that it pulls us along with it. We begin to anticipate what is coming and delight in the surprising turns along the way. When we are excited and engaged in a film, play, speech, or piece of music, we feel that time flies by; when we are bored, we are aware that time seems to drag. This sense of time has little to do with real, or clock time. It is "felt" time. Music seems to stretch and expand time, condense it, or make us forget it altogether.

▼ *Activity:* **Discover "Felt" Time**

Without looking at your watch, try to determine which of these two contrasting musical pieces is longer.

You will hear (1) the *Adagio for Strings* by Samuel Barber and (2) the "Badinerie" from the *Orchestral Suite No. 2* by Johann Sebastian Bach. As you listen, decide which of the following words describe the character of each selection. Make a list that fits each composition.

slow	hurried	strong pulse	fast
calm	detached	tension	weak pulse
spirited	short sounds	repose	smooth sounds

1. Which of these words, or "descriptors," characterize both selections?
2. Which piece seems longer?
3. Discuss how your choice of words reflects the sense of "felt" time embodied in the music.

PROJECT

Create a Story Line

Working alone or in small groups, create a title and a one-page story line for an imaginary film that would use either the *Adagio for Strings* or the "Badinerie" as the musical soundtrack. Try to make use of the experience of "felt" time in order to add a dimension of meaning to your story. Be prepared to read your title and story line over the recorded musical example you have chosen as if it were a one-minute-long radio advertisement for the film.

Cooperative Learning

Designate Tempo Markings

Select what you think would be an appropriate tempo marking (in Italian) to describe the pace for each of the following situations:

1. Your high school track team is competing in the state championships. Final victory depends on your winning the short-distance running competition. What tempo marking reflects how you should run?
2. You have been sent to the principal's office. You are sitting looking at the clock. It seems to be moving at what tempo?
3. You are attending a rehearsal for your high school graduation ceremony. What tempo marking would describe the speed of the processional march?
4. You are running down the hall late for class. You meet the principal and are reprimanded for running. The principal turns the corner, and you dash ahead again. What tempo marking could be used to describe your resumed pace?
5. You are taking the road test for your driver's license. From a complete stop you accelerate to a speed of 40 miles per hour before slowing to a complete stop at the next traffic signal. What two tempo markings describe your movement?

▶ Around 1900, people in the South danced the cakewalk, an elaborate strut full of rhythmic energy. The dancers, sporting their finest clothing, competed for the prize of a cake.

George Luks. *Cake Walk*. 1907. Delaware Art Museum, Wilmington, Delaware. Gift of Helen Farr Sloan.

Rhythm

Rhythm *is the way music paces itself and moves through time.* Like a stream, music can flow gently or forcefully, smoothly or roughly. It might move in a trickle or broadly and majestically. The movement can be rapid or slow, deliberate or tentative, powerful or timid, depending upon what the composer wants to express.

Tempo *is the pace with which the music moves.* The pace of music is one of its most expressive elements. Rapid music may convey excitement or violence. Slow music may convey peacefulness, impending threat, or sadness. Tempo is the pace of the steady beat. This "pulse" or "pulsation" is like a heartbeat, which speeds up or slows down according to our activity and mood. There are many gradations of tempo. In classical music, these are often expressed in Italian terms:

Largo	*Adagio*	*Andante*	*Allegretto*	*Allegro*	*Presto*
very slow	slow	moderately slow (walking)	moderately fast	fast	very fast

- **Accelerando** (aht-cheh-leh-RAHN-doh): *gradually growing faster.*
- **Ritardando** (ree-tar-DAHN-do): *gradually growing slower.*
- **A tempo** (ah TEM-poh): *in normal time, or a return to the preceding rate of speed.*

Music can change pace. In this way our interest is sustained. Changing the pace means varying the tempo (and usually the mood, since the two are practically inseparable). Change can be abrupt or gradual. Abrupt change might be from *adagio* to *presto* or vice versa. Gradual change might move from slow to fast (*accelerando*) or from fast to slow (*ritardando*).

Profile

JOHANN SEBASTIAN BACH

Johann Sebastian Bach
German Composer
1685–1750

An orphan at 10, Johann Sebastian Bach was raised by an older brother who tutored him in music. By the age of 15, Bach's talents had earned him a scholarship to St. Michael's School in Lüneburg, Germany, where his musical ability matured.

Bach composed an astonishing amount of music in almost every category then known: instructional pieces for students; virtuoso keyboard works; instrumental sonatas, suites, and concertos; works for harpsichord and organ; and much sacred music of the highest caliber. While director of music for the town of Leipzig and the Church of St. Thomas, Bach composed numerous sacred vocal and instrumental compositions called cantatas for the Sunday services. Often he provided a new cantata each week, composing more than 200 in all.

Although few of Bach's compositions were published during his lifetime, most of his works (more than 1,000) have survived to this day. A masterful organist and improviser, Bach surpassed all other composers in the art of writing contrapuntal music.

▼*Activity:* **Answer with Your Ears**

Listen to the musical selections listed below, and on a piece of paper assign what you think would be an appropriate tempo marking in Italian for each.

As you listen a second time, match the titles of the compositions with the selections. Consider (1) the title (verbal clue), (2) tempo, (3) style of the music, and (4) possible uses of the music. The titles are listed in random order:

- "Trio" from *Pomp and Circumstance, March No. 1* by Sir Edward Elgar
- "Little Train of the Caipira" from *Bachianas Brasileiras No. 2* by Heitor Villa-Lobos
- "Cripple Creek" (American Folk Dance)
- "Flight of the Bumblebee" from the opera *Tsar Saltan* by Nicolai Rimsky-Korsakov
- "Ase's Death" from *Peer Gynt Suite No.1* by Edvard Grieg
- "The Strings of God's Lute Are in My Body" (Islamic music from Pakistan)

Discuss the relationship between the title you assigned for each and the Italian term you used to describe the tempo.

Pulse

The pulse gives music much of its energy, excitement, and drive. More than any other factor, it is the tempo of the pulse that conveys **"felt" time**—*the space that music appears to carve out for itself.* Dance and drama—the other performing arts—also exist in time (unlike the visual arts, which can be experienced in totality at one time). Similarly, poems, short stories, and novels appear to unfold as we read them. In the course of a novel or drama, we may feel that we have lived through several years of action in what is actually a short span of real time. But do not make the mistake of

PROJECT

Create a Film Soundtrack

Working alone or in small groups, create your own film soundtrack by selecting recorded music that will express the tempo marking assigned to two of the five situations listed in the cooperative learning activity, page **34**. Decide how music can be used to express the pace of each situation. Include dynamics (loud and soft) to reinforce the expression and heighten the intensity. Use music of any style you think would fit. Be prepared to share these musical choices and interpretations in class.

equating the pace of the action with interest: fast is not necessarily more interesting, nor slow necessarily boring. The quality of the "felt" time that the artist creates depends on many factors, not just activity but the tension that is created and then resolved.

The pulse moves by steady beats, some of which are accented to create strong and weak beats. An **accent** is *the emphasis placed on a beat.* These stressed and unstressed pulses usually fall into groups of twos or threes. Being aware of this rhythmic organization helps us to be more conscious of how the music is moving forward. We have to be aware of the beat when we are marching or dancing. In march or dance music, some beats are deliberately accented so that people can easily move "in time," that is, in coordination with the rhythm. The beat is exaggerated, but it is important to be able to feel the pulse of the music even when it is not overstated.

▶ People throughout the world use rhythm in their music. These Moroccan dancers accompany their movements with percussion instruments.

▼Activity: *Feel the Beat*

See if you can internalize the steady pulse.

While you listen to the musical selection, count out loud from one to eight while you perform the following:

> First 8 beats: Snap fingers on each beat
> Second 8 beats: Snap 7 beats, clap 1 beat
> Third 8 beats: Snap 6 beats, clap 2 beats
> Fourth 8 beats: Snap 5 beats, clap 3 beats
> Continue until you clap on all 8 beats.

Now repeat the sequence but count silently and only perform the claps! Now you are thinking the beats. Can you do this in reverse? (Clap 8; then clap 7, snap 1; clap 6, snap 2; and so forth.)

▼*Activity:* **Accent the Beat**

See if you can accent some of the beats.

While you count eight beats evenly, perform the following patterns of accented (●) and nonaccented beats (•) by clapping on the accented beats and snapping on the others. Be sure to count out loud.

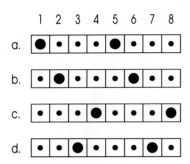

Can the class get all these patterns going at once?

See if you can coordinate hands and feet.

Now tap the steady beat with your left foot while you think the count, then perform each of the patterns by clapping just on the accented beats while the other beats remain silent. While you listen, perform two sets of each pattern.

We often respond to a musical beat by tapping our feet or clapping our hands. Usually the beats are grouped, and the groups are distinguished by a stressed or accented beat. It is the accented beat that tells us how the beats are grouped:

Beats grouped in twos:

Beats:	•	•	•	•	•	•	•	•	•	•
Accent:	>		>		>		>		>	
Count:	1	2	1	2	1	2	1	2	1	2

Beats grouped in threes:

Beats:	•	•	•	•	•	•	•	•	•	•	•	•
Accent:	>			>			>			>		
Count:	1	2	3	1	2	3	1	2	3	1	2	3

Meter

These repeating patterns of beats create what is called **meter**, *a rhythmic measure of a certain number of beats.* The first meter above is duple, the second triple. The first beat in each measure is accented. Hearing that accent helps us establish the meter. To determine the meter, feel where the accented beat is and call it "one." Then count the beats in between until you hear another strong beat, which is "one" again.

▼*Activity:* **Practice and Determine Meters**

Perform duple and triple meter, then determine the meters in the musical example.

As you listen to the music, perform this duple-meter pattern by clapping on the accented beat (●) and snapping on the others (•). Note that the vertical bars mark the measure.

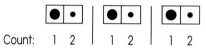

Count: 1   2   1   2   1   2

As you listen to the music, perform this triple-meter pattern by clapping on the accented beat (●) and snapping on the others (•).

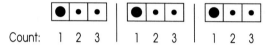

Count: 1   2   3   1   2   3   1   2   3

Show that you can hear the changes in meter by clapping and patting to the meter of the music: "Procession of the Nobles" by Rimsky-Korsakov.
What is the order of the meters in this music?

The regular, recurring beats in music require musicians to exercise rhythmic control. You may have noticed that in tapping a steady beat, you have a tendency to speed up. Musicians have to concentrate to keep the beat steady. This exactness can be learned through practice.

Musicians also have to learn how to keep more than one rhythm going at one time. While they keep a steady beat, they may perform one or more complex rhythms with it. For example, a pianist might play one rhythmic pattern in the right hand, and another in the left. An organist might add yet another rhythmic pattern with both feet on the pedal board. At some time you probably have demonstrated your coordination by rubbing your stomach with one hand while patting your head with the other. This type of psychomotor challenge is very similar to what all good keyboard artists and drummers do. Their hands, arms, and feet have to work independently.

▼*Activity:* **Count and Coordinate Rhythmic Patterns**

Can you get your right hand, left hand, and left foot to perform different rhythms simultaneously?

Try to imitate the skills of a fine trap-set drummer. Follow these three steps:

1. Listen to the recording and establish the accent on beat 1. Tap this accent with your left foot every time you hear it.
2. While your left foot continues to tap on 1, use your left hand to tap regular pulses of four. Tap these four even beats on your desk. Make sure you accentuate the first beat.

3. While you continue to tap your foot on 1 and use your left hand to tap regular pulses of four, use your right hand to double the speed of your left hand so you are playing eight even beats. Use your pencil as a drumstick, holding it lightly as you tap these eight beats on your desk. In your head, think the eight beats by counting to eight silently as you play. Do not speed up!

Play all three rhythms with the recording.
In a musical score, what you are doing looks like this:

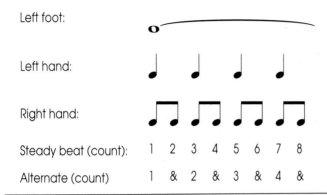

Left foot:

Left hand:

Right hand:

| Steady beat (count): | 1 | 2 | 3 | 4 | 5 | 6 | 7 | 8 |
| Alternate (count) | 1 | & | 2 | & | 3 | & | 4 | & |

Improvisation

Music is not something fully created that has to be passed on and learned as is. When we learn music, we bring to it something of our own talent, feeling, and personality. But music also invites us to invent. We may find ourselves humming or whistling our own tune or tapping a rhythm that we make up. This kind of *spontaneous musical invention* is called **improvisation**. The improviser is both a composer and a performer simultaneously.

Do improvisers do anything they want? Not usually. Most musical improvisation is done within certain boundaries that help to reduce the number of choices, making it easier. The improviser might elaborate upon—or embellish—a familiar melody, adding tones and altering rhythms to enhance a particular feeling. In the seventeenth and eighteenth centuries, for example, opera singers improvised impressive ornaments in their melodies, sometimes to the liking of the composer, sometimes not. More recently, a jazz clarinetist or trumpeter might "take" a solo—that is, improvise—while the other musicians in the band provide an accompaniment. Rendered on the spot, these improvisations add an element of expectation and surprise for the audience. In live performance, improvised music is never the same old thing.

Improvisation is an art with a technique. It is a way of making music a form of direct self-expression. However, improvisation is risky. It requires musicians to take chances. They have to think ahead to where the music is going and how they want it to sound, then be able to perform what they want to hear. They have to be careful not to out-think their technique or they will stumble in their performance.

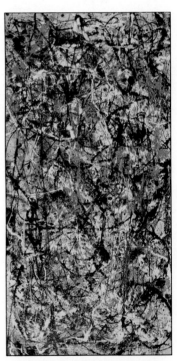

▲ American artist Jackson Pollock invented an abstract style of painting by spontaneously dripping paint on the canvas. He improvised, making up his effects as he went along.

Jackson Pollock. *Cathedral.* 1947. Dallas Museum of Art, Dallas, Texas. Gift of Mr. and Mrs. Bernard J. Reis.

▼*Activity:* **Improvise**

Try your hand and mind at improvising different rhythms and creating a rhythmic ostinato, a clearly defined rhythmic pattern that is persistently repeated.

A master drummer is frequently used to keep an African musical ensemble together. Working in a group of four, have one person assume the role of the master drummer while the others improvise individual rhythmic patterns on other percussion instruments. The objective is to create a group composition that is musically interesting.

The master drummer should set a steady tempo and play all eight beats in the 8-beat pattern. The first improviser should think a pattern of sound, selecting a combination of those beats, for instance, 1, 3, 6, and 7. Try to hear the pattern (in your mind) before you play it. Repeat the pattern four times (for four counts of 8); then if you are satisfied that this is what you want, write the numbers down so you do not forget them. Improvisers two and three then take their turn, creating their own individual patterns and writing down the numbers. Now put the whole composition together with each person entering after a repetition of two 8-beat counts. Once everyone is playing, keep this rhythmic ostinato going for eight counts of 8. After this is going smoothly, switch roles and start again inventing new patterns.

When writing down the patterns you have invented, use a dot (●) on beats to be played and a blank for silence, as in this example:

Counting Pattern:	1	2	3	4	5	6	7	8
Master Drummer:	●	●	●	●	●	●	●	●
First Improviser:		●		●		●	●	

Rhythm and Improvisation in the Music of India

With a population of over 800 million people (three times the population of the United States!), India is the world's largest democracy. In all aspects of life, contrast and variety prevail. There are huge cities and over half a million tiny villages, sophisticated factories and small family farms, automobiles and elephants, richness and poverty. The people speak 14 languages and many more dialects. Although the majority of Indians are Hindus, five other religions, including Christianity, are common.

Indian music is as varied as this land of snake charmers and filmmakers. Take a walk down any street in India and you will probably hear Western pop music played on trumpet, saxophone, guitars, and drums; but you will also encounter quite different music. From a Hindu temple you might hear people singing with a pump organ, string instruments, Indian drums, and cymbals. Dancers in a colorful wedding procession making its way through the streets to the bride's home move to the shrill music of Indian *shahnai* ("oboes"), or to the music of a brass band! In the evening, you might come across an outdoor concert of classical music taking place under a huge tent or by a river. Traditional Indian instruments give you the feeling you are in another world.

▼*Activity:* *Compose a Rhythm Score*

Invent a four-measure rhythm score for two parts: one for your left hand, the other for your right hand.

Write a rhythm composition that you can practice and play yourself. All you need is a pen, paper, two pencils to serve as drumsticks, and a table top. Compose a composition that is four measures in length: that is, four sets of the 8-beat framework. Make the composition as rhythmically interesting (but still playable!) as possible. The first two measures of your "score" should look something like this:

Count:	1	2	3	4	5	6	7	8		1	2	3	4	5	6	7	8
Left hand:	●	●	●	●	●	●	●	●		●	●	●	●	●			
Right hand:	●		●		●		●			●		●		●		●	

Practice your composition so you can perform it in class as a solo. Challenge your friends or members of your small group to sight read your piece.

▲ The music of India is as varied as the country itself. Walking down a typical urban street you might hear arrangements ranging from Western pop or brass marching bands to traditional Indian music.

▶ Making music together, this Indian family group plays classical Indian music using the following instruments (from left to right): *tabla tampura, swara mandal,* and *harmonium.* Each string of the *swara mandal* is tuned to match notes of the scale, but all the strings are strummed together for accompaniment rather than being plucked for melody.

Indian instruments include a number of strings or "cordophones," such as the *sitar, sarangi, vina,* and the *tambura.* The tambura supplies the drone, the much needed tonal support to all sorts of performances from vocal to dance. Just as important is the pair of small drums called *tabla.* The bigger (lower pitched) drum is made of metal and shaped like a small kettle drum, while the smaller (higher pitched) drum is made of wood and is more cylindrical in shape. The tabla are played with the hands and fingers. When played, this simple looking instrument can produce an astonishing variety of sounds or timbres. Tabla players develop the skill of moving their hands and fingers very rapidly.

Indian music is performed to a basic beat, but the beats are not grouped into regularly recurring patterns of two, three, and four as in much of our Western music. The tabla player, for example, performs in a rhythm cycle that may be anywhere from seven to 104 beats in length! A **rhythm cycle** *is a fixed number of beats in a series that repeats itself over and over* (similar to the continuous 1-2-3-4, 1-2-3-4 pattern in a march). When audiences in India listen to music that includes tabla, they sometimes use a series of hand motions to keep track of their place in the rhythm cycle. One of the most popular rhythm cycles—tintal (TEEN-tal)—is 16 beats long. In Hindi, *tin* means "three" and *tal* means "clap"—a reference to the three claps used in following this cycle.

▼*Activity:* **Challenge**

Learn to use your hands and fingers to keep your place in the tintal cycle.

As you count beats 1 through 16 of the tintal cycle, mark groups of four beats with the following movements of your hands and fingers:

1. Clap beat 1 bringing your right hand down onto your up-turned left palm.
2. Mark beats 2, 3, and 4 by bringing the fifth, fourth, and third fingers of your right hand, one after the other, onto your left palm.
3. Repeat step 2 for beats 5 through 8.
4. Use a small hand wave rather than a clap on beat 9 and continue with fingers on beats 10, 11, and 12.
5. Repeat clap and fingers on beats 13, 14, 15, and 16.
6. Begin the pattern all over again.

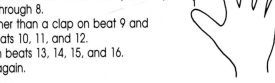

Keeping track of 16 beats in a tintal cycle

Beats:	1	2	3	4	5	6	7	8	9	10	11	12	13	14	15	16
Hands:	clap				clap				wave				clap			
Fingers:		5	4	3		5	4	3		5	4	3		5	4	3

When you have learned to keep your place in the tintal cycle, use the hand and finger movements while listening to the tabla play the cycle six times. Can you find a musical reason for the wave segment that begins on beat 9?

Now see if you can clap tintal, just as a knowledgeable Indian might, while you listen to a sitarist and tabla player improvise. Can you hear the bass drum pattern? The sitarist's melodies are also connected to the pattern.

Indian drums can make a wide variety of sounds: from low to high and from mellow to bright. Over the centuries, Indian drummers devised a way to keep track of all these different sounds. They gave a name to each distinct sound or drum stroke, creating what we might describe as a drum language. Tabla players are able to sing or recite their drum music the same way we might sing a melody. When students learn the tabla, they learn this drum language.

All drums can make at least two sounds: a deep booming sound that is made by playing close to the center of the head and letting the sound ring, and a dry sharp sound made by playing close to, or on the edge of, the head or rim and "damping" the sound by leaving one's fingers on the head. The word *dum* (doom) refers to the center stroke; the word *te* (tay) refers to the rim stroke. These are two words from the Indian drum language. Indian drummers sometimes make up compositions that simply sound good when they are spoken. They enjoy organizing sounds into different rhythmic patterns just for the fun of it.

▼*Activity:* **Perform an 8-beat Indian Rhythm Cycle**

Learn to speak and play an Indian drum composition.

Practice the 8-beat hand and finger pattern called "Adi Tal":

Beats:	1	2	3	4	5	6	7	8
Fingers:		5	4	3				
Hands:	clap				clap	wave	clap	wave

When you can clap the pattern easily, recite the drum pattern with it using the two words *dum* and *te* from the drum language:

Beats:	1		2		3		4		5		6		7		8	
Words:	dum		–	dum	–	–	te	te	te	te	te	te	dum	–	–	–

Recite this until you are sure of it, then increase the tempo.

Now try transferring this pattern to a drum or tambourine. While part of the class recites the rhythm cycle with fingers and hands, play the *dum* in the middle letting the sound ring; play the *te* on the rim holding the fingers down. Recite the composition as you play it. This form of counting permits musicians to coordinate their performance and stay together.

Working in pairs, have one person recite the rhythm cycle with fingers and hands while the other practices making variations for the composition in Indian drum language. This is the way Indian drummers improvise. Some of these variations might look and sound like this:

Beats:	1		2		3		4		5		6		7		8	
Words:	dum	te	dum	te	dum	–	te	te	te	te	te	te	dum	–	–	–

Beats:	1		2		3		4		5		6		7		8	
Words:	dum	dum	te	dum	–	dum	te	dum	te	te	te	te	dum	–	–	–

Beats:	1		2		3		4		5		6		7		8	
Words:	dum	te	dum	–	–	dum	te	dum	–	–	te	te	dum	–	–	–

Beats:	1		2		3		4		5		6		7		8	
Words:	te	te	dum	te	dum	–	–	te	dum	–	te	te	dum	–	–	–

Try reciting these variations, then change places with your partner. Can you play these on a drum?

▼*Activity:* **Improvise**

When you are familiar with these variations, try creating your own.

Have a classmate clap and count while you recite or play your new rhythmic ideas. For more variety, experiment by beginning your improvisations with *te* or *te te*, or by using spaces (silence) in places where they might not be expected. If you feel very adventurous, begin your improvisation with a space on the first beat. Try playing your improvisations on a drum.

◀ Together these people are leading a religious procession in southern India. The musician on the left is playing an oboe-like instrument, called a *nadhaswaram* (nah-dah-SWAH-rum), which has extra reeds and religious medallions hanging from it. The other musician uses a stick and his hand to play the drum-like instrument called a *thavil* (TAH-veel).

Syncopation

If music were simply a progression of steady beats with regularly recurring accents, it would hardly be as exciting as it is. Once the ongoing, steady pulse is established, accents can be shifted from the strong to the weak beats and even between the main beats. This is called **syncopation,** *deliberate shifts of the accent so that it goes against the steady beat, conflicts with it, and tries to upset the steady pulse.* Syncopation emphasizes the weak beats and denies the strong beats their usual stress. This creates a feeling of imbalance, a kind of teasing and thwarting of the steady recurrence of beats and accents. Syncopation is something unexpected, and that is a good part of its pleasure.

Ragtime, an American music full of syncopation, was a dance form that appeared in the nineteenth century and became popular during the first decades of the twentieth century. While jazz, at first, was primarily improvised, ragtime was usually written down. This may account, in part, for its popularity. Amateurs could buy piano rags in sheet music and play them, note for note, like the great rag pianists and composers—Scott Joplin, Jelly Roll Morton, and Eubie Blake. When Scott Joplin's "Maple Leaf Rag" was published in 1899, it quickly sold a million copies.

These rags were popular because they had a catchy, syncopated melody set against a moving bass that emphasized a steady beat in duple meter. From that collision of accents came a new musical feeling—exuberant and infectious. Soon people could play the syncopated strains of ragtime on piano rolls in penny arcades and hear rags performed on the pianos that accompanied the silent films in nickelodeons. American popular music and show music would never get over the feeling.

Profile

Scott Joplin
American Composer
1868–1917

SCOTT JOPLIN

Called a forgotten genius when his *Collected Piano Works* were finally published in 1971, Scott Joplin has enjoyed a long-overdue revival. During the early part of the twentieth century, Joplin was in the forefront of American popular music, composing "rags" that established one of the influential dance styles of the period—ragtime. His music was original and immediately likeable.

Around 1900, Americans were cakewalking to his rags, while the rest of the world took notice. But the terms rag and ragtime were not meant to be complimentary. On the contrary, they were derisive terms cast by racists. Joplin called these names "scurrilous" and considered them as grossly abusive.

Nevertheless, Joplin's rags were enormously popular, even though the classical music snobs of the day would have no part of them. With Joplin's death on the eve of World War I, ragtime fell out of favor and was completely overshadowed by American jazz. It was not until the film, *The Sting* (1973) and its theme song, Joplin's rag "The Entertainer," that Americans were reawakened to his music. Since then, Joplin's music has reemerged triumphantly after more than half a century of neglect. His works—including more than 40 rags, waltzes, and marches for piano—are now regarded as American classics.

Joplin also wrote a number of songs and the opera *Treemonisha* (1911), an African-American folk opera about a young black girl who rises through hardship and trial to become a leader of her people.

▶ When "Maple Leaf Rag" was published in 1899, almost every home had a parlor (called a living room today) with a piano. People could buy the sheet music for ragtime and play it themselves, which may account, in part, for its popularity. The term "rag" referred to the "raggedy" rhythms that were associated with black musicians.

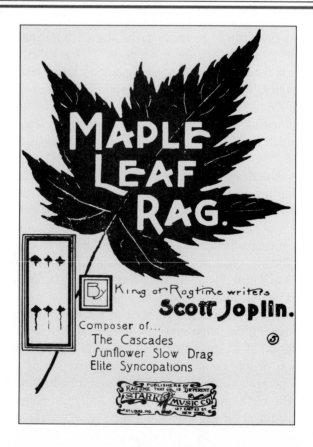

▼*Activity:* **Create Syncopation**

Can you feel and play syncopated rhythms?

To feel syncopation, you have to know where the steady beat is because you are dealing with two rhythms. To understand this, divide the class in half and try tapping the following rhythms together, beginning with the steady beat (1) and adding the syncopation (2):

Now listen to the opening section of Scott Joplin's "Maple Leaf Rag" and see if you can hear this same steady beat in the left hand (lower part) and the syncopation in the right hand (upper part or melody). The main syncopated notes have been colored blue to correspond with the above example.

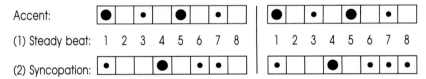

A different syncopated pattern is used in the trio section of the rag. Again, try tapping the two rhythms together, beginning with the steady beat (1):

Follow the score as you listen for these syncopated notes (blue):

Now listen to the entire rag and try to recognize the familiar syncopations and identify the new ones in the middle or "B" section of the composition.

▲ Jelly Roll Morton (shown in the picture above), Eubie Blake, and Scott Joplin were great ragtime pianists and composers of the early twentieth century.

Polyrhythms

Syncopation creates rhythmic energy, excitement, and interest by juxtaposing two conflicting rhythms in the same meter. **Polyrhythms** *are two or more independent rhythms sounding together*. Unlike syncopated music, however, polyrhythmic music generally combines rhythms that appear to have different basic meters, such as duple in one part and triple in another. These combinations can sound complex to our ears. The device is highly developed in West Africa where drums and other percussion instruments —instruments that must be struck, shook, or scraped to produce sound— weave a number of contrasting and repeated rhythmic patterns into a quilt-like fabric of sound.

Polyrhythms create cross rhythms in which accents in one part conflict with accents in other parts. The effect can be hypnotic and exotic to ears that are used to just the simple, regular-recurring accents common to much Western music, both classical and popular. Polyrhythms take the rhythmic dimension of music to a new level of complexity, sophistication, and expressiveness.

▼*Activity:* **Create Polyrhythms**

Use your experience with various rhythms to create a polyrhythmic texture.

You can create polyrhythms by stacking one meter on top of another so that two different and conflicting meters are superimposed. First set the basic beat of 12 with accents on one and seven, then superimpose a triple rhythm, then a duple (in four). Be careful to accent the first beat:

Basic beat: 1   2   3   4   5   6   7   8   9   10   11   12

Triple meter: 1   2   3 │ 1   2   3 │ 1   2   3 │ 1   2   3

Duple meter: 1   2   3   4 │ 1   2   3   4 │ 1   2   3   4

Try this in faster tempos. Transfer it to percussion instruments. Can you hear the cross rhythms?

Now try shifting the patterns one beat and keep repeating:

Basic beat: 1   2   3   4   5   6   7   8   9   10   11   12│1

Triple meter: 1   2   3 │ 1   2   3 │ 1   2   3 │ 1   2   3   etc.

Duple meter: 1   2   3   4 │ 1   2   3   4 │ 1   2   3   etc.

These polyrhythms can have a "jazzy" effect because they suggest, or give a feeling of, syncopation.

▼*Activity:* **Take Rhythmic Dictation**

Can you write down the rhythms you hear?

Many musicians are able to listen to a rhythm and write it down in musical notation. This is a skill that can be learned. Using the 8-beat measure, first practice replicating the one-measure rhythm you hear by clapping it back (like echoes). Then, listening to the rhythms your teacher dictates, circle only the numbers (1–8) on which a sound is heard.

◀ Van Gogh's brush strokes create rhythms by repetition. The quick beats of the wheat field contrast with the more deliberate rhythms of the rocks and cypress trees and the broader rhythms of mountain and sky. This painting produces a polyrhythmic feeling. The expressive result: we can "feel" the wind and turbulence.

Vincent van Gogh. *Wheat Fields and Cypress Trees.* 1889. The National Gallery, London, England.

Summary

Rhythm is much of the excitement and fun of music. It conveys a good deal of the spirit we feel. The variety of moods it can establish is infinite—from slow and languorous to rapid and robust. But it has other important functions. It is rhythm that gives music its sense of movement, its energy, its drive, and life. Rhythm provides music with its sense of continuity—the feeling that it is cut from one piece of cloth. But its most important function may be the underlying structure it provides so musicians can perform together even when each is doing something different. It is rhythm that pulls us along through the music, that gives us a sense of time and space, and that carries us out of the real world and into a world of imagination and mystery.

Rhythms That Dance

Objectives

By completing this chapter, you will:

- Understand how different rhythms create different dances.
- Learn the rhythms of a variety of dances.
- Become acquainted with Tex-Mex and Native American dance.
- Realize some of the basic differences in music for popular, folk, theatrical, ballet, and modern dance.
- Become familiar with the instrumental suite.
- Differentiate between the minuet as a dance and the minuet as a movement of a symphony.
- Recognize how composers have incorporated dance rhythms in their instrumental works.
- Become acquainted with the work of American composers Louis Gottschalk and William Grant Still.

Musical Terms

minuet
reggae
samba
suite
tango
waltz

*D*ance has been part of the life of every tribe, society,
and culture. It is one way of expressing our essence:
who we are and what life is about. In primitive societies,
people danced to celebrate a marriage, a birth, a successful
hunt, a good crop, or a victory. They danced to ward
off evil spirits, to prevent sickness and danger, to
bring good fortune, to ask for rain, and to cope
with the other mysteries of life. Dance was, and is,
a communal form of solidarity.

Dance in Our Heritage

Dance is more than mere physical movement. It is expression. It uses the human body as a musical instrument. Music generally serves as the springboard to dance, imbuing it with much of its expressive power. Because it can be sensuous, dance has been forbidden by some religious sects. Today, dance is accepted as a pleasant and popular diversion, and as an expressive art form.

Music and dance burst with energy. Rhythm is both the source of this energy and the means for regulating it. Dance has been called organized energy. Humans have a built-in rhythmic impulse that is transformed through dance. By giving "voice" and order to the energy within us, dance uplifts the human spirit.

Popular Dance

Dances are popular because of their distinctive rhythms. In fact, American dances often have such distinct personalities that they characterize their social period. The Charleston, for example, evokes the 1920s just as disco characterizes the 1970s.

The Latin Influence

The dance music of Latin America and Cuba became popular in urban centers of the United States during the 1930s and 1940s. The conga, an Afro-Cuban dance, gained popularity because of its catchy rhythm and because it was easy and fun to dance. Later, the cha-cha, rumba, mambo, calypso, samba, tango, and reggae were among the new Latin-American dances that captivated America's dance craze.

The roots of many of the exciting dance rhythms in Latin-American and Caribbean music can be traced to Africa. The music of these cultures is generally inseparable from dancing. Throughout the Americas, dance music

PROJECT

Choose Either A or B

A. Analyze Dance Music

Analyze your favorite piece of dance music (whether you have danced to it or not). Identify the title and the performer of the work, and briefly describe its overall style and character. As you listen to it, list as many characteristics of this music as you can.

B. Compose a Dance Melody

In the style of the Viennese waltz, compose a 16-measure dance melody. Work with a partner to create two 4-measure answers to the waltz phrases written on the waltz worksheet. Keep your melody in C major (limited to the white keys on a keyboard) and the rhythm in 3/4 meter (three beats to a measure). Experiment on any melody instrument (keyboard, mallet percussion, recorder, etc.) while you compose.

shares some basic features: highly syncopated rhythms, improvised drumming, and a variety of percussion instruments. The delightful mixture of African and Latin-American rhythms has become the primary international influence on social dancing in the world today.

▼Activity: **Perform the Dance Rhythms**

Listen and then learn to perform the characteristic rhythmic patterns of an Argentine tango, Brazilian samba, and Jamaican reggae.

Working in small performing ensembles of four people, follow these instructions for each dance you hear:

1. Listen to the rhythm. Tap even quarter notes, four beats to the measure.
2. Listen a second time. Tap out an improvised, syncopated rhythm that fits the music.
3. Assign the various rhythmic parts in each dance to the members of your group. Try to read and perform these rhythmic patterns. First count and then tap each of the rhythms. After you have mastered them, transfer your tapping to instruments or into distinctive sounds using your hands, feet, or voice.
4. Try to play your rhythm section along with the recording. Your group may want to perform for the class or join with other groups in playing these characteristic dance patterns.

The Tango

The **tango**, *a Latin American dance of Afro-Cuban origins, is performed at a moderately slow, walklike tempo in 4/4 meter.* The primary accents on beats 1 and 3 mean this dance has no backbeat (accents on 2 and 4). Each pattern below is one measure long and should be repeated throughout. Try an improvisation every second measure based on the first measure.

▲ The tango, an urban Argentine dance with long gliding steps and dips, became popular as a ballroom dance in Europe and the United States after World War I.

Numeric Counting Guide With Steady Eighth Notes	1	2	3	4	5	6	7	8	

BASS

CLAVES

ACCORDION

GUIRO (optional)

The Samba

The **samba** is *an Afro-Brazilian dance that is faster and jazzier than the tango*. Although you may count the samba in a fast 4/4 meter, you should feel it in strong two-beat groupings. Like the tango, the samba uses no backbeat, but it is more syncopated. The rhythmic pattern is two measures long. Bring out the guitar line because it distinguishes the typical samba rhythm. Add improvisation where you think it will fit.

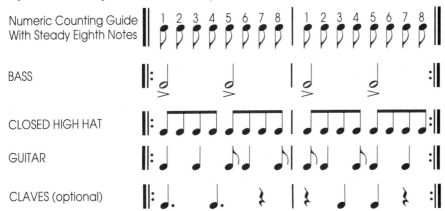

◀ During the 1930s and 1940s, Spanish band leader Xavier Cugat (1900–1990) and his orchestra popularized Latin American rhythms, instruments, and dances throughout the United States. He is shown here with his wife, the singer Abbe Lane.

Reggae

Although **reggae** *presents an interesting mixture of African and Caribbean rhythms, it is primarily attributed to the musical creativity of Jamaican musicians.* Reggae's undeniably happy sound comes from the combination of backbeat (accents on beats 2 and 4) with syncopated "afterbeats" often played on rhythm guitar. The other significant feature is a syncopated and quickly moving melodic bass line. Can you hear the frequent improvisation in this bass melody?

Tex-Mex Music

Although dance is almost universally practiced among all peoples, it is not performed in the same way. One of the traditions of the Southwest is *conjunto*, a dance music created by Texas-Mexicans. It is often called "Tex-Mex" music, since it is derived from the unique Texas-Mexican cultural mix.

Three influences shaped conjunto music: (1) several kinds of dance music, especially the polka and the waltz were brought to Mexico from European countries in the nineteenth century; (2) Germans, Czechs, and Poles, for whom these dances had special importance, immigrated to southern Texas and continued to play and dance them; and (3) around 1900, these immigrants brought to Texas and popularized the button accordion. Influenced by their new European neighbors, *tejano* (teh-HAH-noh), or Texas-Mexican, musicians created a body of music in which the polka is still the most important dance, and in which songs in polka rhythm are by far the most popular.

Conjunto music, one of the most notable forms of traditional music created in the United States, is dance music in a one-two, one-two polka rhythm. The central musical instrument of the conjunto is the button accordion. It is accompanied by a 12-string Mexican guitar, called *bajo sexto* (BAH-hoh SEX-toh), on which is played fast bass runs and a chordal accompaniment; an electric bass guitar; and a drum set. The Spanish lyrics are often sung in the typically Mexican style of close harmony in parallel thirds.

◄ Before 1836 most of what is now Texas was part of Mexico. This Mexican heritage lives on in Texas, but the cultural mix has caused Texas-Mexicans to invent their own musical styles.

▼Activity: *Test Your Ears*

Can you differentiate among the four instruments of the conjunto tejano?

Listen to "Ay te dejo en San Antonio" and identify the four instruments: the button accordion, electric bass, *bajo sexto* (playing bass runs and chordal offbeats), and drum set.

Can you identify the refrain in each of the three *strophes* or stanzas of the song? The text of the refrain is "*Te gusta mucho el baile, y bailas al compas, te vas hasta Laredo, y quieres mas y mas*" ("You like dancing a lot, and you dance with the beat, you go over to Laredo, and you want more and more"). Can you sing along with it?

Native American Dance

Although there are more than 300 different Indian tribes in North America, each with its own culture, every tribe has its own music and dance, its own purposes for performing, and its own musical styles. Within this diversity are some general musical characteristics that are shared by many of these tribes. To the Native American, music and dance have always been essential parts of life, expressing the mystical elements of religion, love, birth, death, hunting, war, and celebration. Tribal dance is functional, ceremonial, and participatory. It is never used as merely passive entertainment.

Native American music is primarily sung. It is a tradition with rich and varied uses of the voice by both men and women. Drums and rattles are the main types of musical instruments, and they come in many different sizes, shapes, and materials. Rattles, for example, are made out of gourds, turtle shells, carved wood, leather, baskets, coconuts, cocoons, cow horns, rattlesnake rattles, bird beaks, animal bones, and seashells.

Some tribes used various types of flutes, and one tribe, the Apaches, played a type of one-string fiddle. The making of musical instruments is often a highly regarded vocation in the Native American world because of the social responsibilities and artistic talents it requires. Some of the instruments are beautifully crafted works of art.

Most American tribal languages do not contain a word for music. If they did, its meaning would be quite different than a European or Western definition of music. The notion of a composer sitting at a piano or some other instrument and attempting to create a work of art does not exist. For the Native American, one of the most traditional and valued means of acquiring new songs is through dreams or visions. Spiritual guidance often indicates how the music is to be used. Music is a gift from the Creator or other spiritual sources. It is sacred. Songs are imbued with a power to help people meet their needs.

Befitting their sacred quality, songs are treated with respect and reverence, and governed by strict rules of when, under what circumstances, and by whom they can be performed. New songs are occasionally composed, but only in permissible genres and for specific situations. Because songs have such value within the society, they are occasionally traded or sold as property, or given away as gifts of great significance and meaning.

There is another basic difference. Native American music is not performed to provide an aesthetic experience for the listeners, such as we expect when attending a concert. Instead, music is generally one component of an event that fulfills a function within the society—a religious ceremony, a healing ritual, the honoring of an individual, or ensuring a successful hunt or crop.

Like traditional music in other parts of the world, Native American music is not written down. It is committed to memory and passed on orally (or aurally) from generation to generation—creating an unbroken strand of performance practice that originated in the distant past. This achievement is often impressive, given the extreme complexity of certain ceremonies that last several days and include hundreds of songs. Any individual who becomes a carrier of a musical tradition accepts a huge responsibility within the community. Only trusted and reliable individuals are chosen for such tasks. If the music is forgotten, mistreated, or performed incorrectly, the tradition is corrupted or dies.

Native Americans dance and sing to show their pride in who they are; to honor their families, their ancestors, and their tribes; to assure the continuance of time-honored traditions; and to bring good fortune to their people. On less sacred occasions, social songs and dances are performed.

Lakota Eagle Dance

The Lakota are one of many Native American tribes that people commonly refer to as the "Sioux." The traditional culture of these horsemen and buffalo hunters of the Great Plains has for a long time been popularized in literature and film. Unfortunately, much of what has been depicted of Lakota culture in the past has been incorrect, oversimplified, or stereotypical. The Lakota people still enjoy a rich heritage of traditional music and dance. The singers and dancers you will hear and see come from the Rosebud Reservation in southwestern South Dakota.

▼ Through the Eagle dance, this Lakota dancer gracefully and respectfully honors an animal that holds a great deal of importance to his people. The eagle symbolizes the Great Spirit known as Wakan Tanka.

▼*Activity:* **Listen, Observe, and Answer**

Use your listening skills and powers of observation to find out more about Native American music and dance.

In the video segment, you will see and hear the Lakota Indians tell of some of the significance and meaning that their tribal music and dance holds for them. Then you will see the Eagle Dance. Based on your observations, see if you can answer the following questions:

1. What are the functions of Lakota music and dance?
2. Why is the Eagle Dance performed?
3. What does the whistle imitate?
4. What does the eagle symbolize?

Theatrical Dance

America loves theatrical dance. In the nineteenth-century minstrel shows, dances were commonplace. Operettas in the late 1800s and early 1900s contained ample dancing, as did the vaudeville shows that flourished in the early decades of the twentieth century.

Among the forms of dance that are distinctly American is tap, which has its roots in the African-American community. Tap seems to have originated in the rhythmic dances of African slaves that merged with the fancy footwork of Irish clogging. It made its Broadway debut in the early 1920s in black musicals. The tap craze was sparked by Bill "Bojangles" Robinson, grandson of a slave, who was born in 1878 in Richmond, Virginia. As a young man, Robinson first saw the shuffling dances of the black performers in traveling minstrel shows in Washington, D.C. He used the basics of clogging to develop his own more intricate, energetic, and syncopated style. He soon became a headliner on the vaudeville circuit—"The King of Tap Dancers." Nicknamed "Bojangles," Robinson won America's heart and established a new art form in the process.

In tap dancing, the feet are used as percussive instruments. The shoes, with their bright-sounding metal taps at the toe and heel, become a way of tapping out complex rhythms. Tap dancers improvise elaborate rhythms, shifting their weight nimbly from foot to foot, using their arms for balance, and turning in space. The rhythms are as complex as those of the jazz drummer and include much syncopation.

Dance is an integral part of American musical theater. It is a standard part of any Broadway musical. Jerome Robbins's dances from *West Side Story*, performed to music composed by Leonard Bernstein, are particularly memorable examples, perhaps because they are so integral to the story. Since this show opened on Broadway in 1957, it has been hailed as a landmark of American theater. The plot is a modern-day version of Shakespeare's *Romeo and Juliet* transplanted to New York's West Side. It revolves around the conflict between two street gangs: the Jets who are white, and the Sharks who are Puerto Rican. Tony, a former member of the Jets, meets

◀ American composer Leonard Bernstein (1918–1990) combined Latin dance rhythms, big-band jazz, and expressive love songs in his Broadway musical *West Side Story* to tell a story of racial conflict and doomed love, based loosely on Shakespeare's play, *Romeo and Juliet.*

and falls in love with Maria, a Puerto Rican girl, whose brother is a member of the Sharks. Tony and Maria meet in secret, but their relationship is doomed because of the conflict between these rival gangs.

Bernstein incorporates jazz style to convey youthful vigor and violence, and he uses Latin-American dance rhythms to portray the Sharks. The dances characterize the tension between the gangs. They help to tell the story, so much so, that the dances alone embody the plot. Realizing this, Bernstein made an arrangement of the dances in a separate work for orchestra entitled *Symphonic Dances from "West Side Story."*

▼Activity: *Figure Out*

How do the dances support the dramatic action and story line in *West Side Story?*

Listen to *Symphonic Dances from "West Side Story"* by Leonard Bernstein and determine the order of the story line. Write down the titles of the sections of the composition in the proper order. Use the musical descriptions to help you make your decisions.

Ballet

The art of telling a story through music and movement originated in a style of dance known as ballet, which emerged in France during the sixteenth century. Because ballet is physically strenuous, dance solos or duets (*pas de deux*) normally last from two to four minutes. Dancers need constant breaks to catch their breath so dance stories must be told in many scenes. Consequently, music that is suitable for ballet should be rhythmic and colorful, and full of short, changing, and clearly delineated moods.

In 1910 Igor Stravinsky, an unknown young Russian composer, created his first ballet score, *L'Oiseau de feu* (*The Firebird*). When the ballet premiered at the Paris Opera with dance steps by choreographer Michel Fokine, it caused a sensation and launched Stravinsky's career. The work continues to be performed by ballet companies throughout the world.

The story of *The Firebird* is adapted from several Russian fairy tales. To make certain the music fit the plot, Fokine discussed each element of the story with Stravinsky, explaining how the music and dance should meld. Stravinsky composed a continuous score, even though the story is broken into a number of short scenes in the usual ballet tradition. The intent was to maintain the dramatic continuity through the music. (Breaks often interrupt and stop the flow.)

In *The Firebird*, the curtain rises on the enchanted garden of the wicked wizard, Kashchei. Soon the firebird appears and performs a glorious dance. She is pursued and captured by Prince Ivan Tsarevitch. She pleads for her release, plucking out one of her bright red feathers to give to him. Then 13 enchanted princesses enter and play with golden apples. Suddenly Ivan appears and they dance to a theme Stravinsky borrowed from a Russian folk song. When daybreak comes, the princesses disappear. Kashchei's

▶ This is a scene from the American Ballet Theater's 1977 production of *The Firebird* with music by Igor Stravinsky. Prima Ballerina Natalia Makarova (center stage) dances the role of the firebird.

Profile

Igor Stravinsky
Russian Composer
1882–1971

IGOR STRAVINSKY

Born in Russia, Stravinsky spent much of his life in the United States, settling in Hollywood in 1939 and becoming an American citizen in 1945. When he was 19 and already studying law, he met Nicolai Rimsky-Korsakov, the great Russian composer and orchestrator, and was encouraged by him to pursue the study of musical composition. He later studied with the composer privately.

By chance, the famous impresario Serge Diaghilev heard one of the young man's new works performed in St. Petersburg and commissioned this young "find" to produce music for a new ballet in Paris. The subject was to be a suitable Russian tale. The result was *The Firebird*, the first of a number of ballet masterpieces composed by Stravinsky.

Following this, Stravinsky moved to Paris and teamed up with Diaghilev and the Ballets Russes. He produced *Petrouchka*, and then the primitive and revolutionary modern work *Rite of Spring*, which caused a riot at its first performance! His works continued to reflect his interest in dance. *L'Histoire du soldat* (*The Soldier's Tale*) consists of several stylized modern dances, and *Ragtime* was inspired by American dance rhythms. Stravinsky composed a variety of music, in many styles for different occasions.

guards rush out of their subterranean home and capture Ivan. Kashchei confronts Ivan, but the princesses intercede on Ivan's behalf. Again the firebird appears, casting a spell on Kashchei's subjects and making them dance fiendishly.

Kashchei and his court are put to sleep so that Ivan can seize the egg that contains the secret power of Kashchei. By breaking it, Ivan brings about Kashchei's death. Stravinsky lets us hear the egg break. The prince and princess then marry. The music of the finale is composed in the style of a Russian chorale. Stravinsky alters its accents by changing it from six beats to seven, giving the ballet a triumphal, majestic close.

The music from *The Firebird* is frequently performed in concert halls, in a seven-movement suite that Stravinsky arranged for a very large orchestra. This colorful, descriptive score calls for quadruple woodwinds, an additional trumpet, three harps, 32 violins, 14 violas, 8 cellos, and 6 double basses.

▼*Activity:* **Visualize**

How does the music support the dramatic action?

You will hear the conclusion of *The Firebird* by Igor Stravinsky. All the tensions in the plot are resolved after Ivan breaks the magic egg, putting an end to the evil Kashchei. How does Stravinsky's music convey the drama? How does he let you know that the action is resolved?

► From the beginning, Alvin Ailey (1931–1989) had a vision of creating a company dedicated to the preservation and enrichment of the American modern dance heritage and the uniqueness of black cultural expression. "Revelations" dates from 1960.

Modern Dance

Musical rhythm and movement alone can arouse and convey a wide range and variety of moods. Modern dance, invented by American dancers as an alternative to ballet, is made up of a variety of dance styles unimpeded by the strict traditions of classical ballet. This free expression of a free people was pioneered by Isadora Duncan, Ruth St. Denis, Ted Shawn, and Martha Graham during the first half of the twentieth century and continues to be explored today.

Among those who have contributed to the development of modern dance are African Americans. One outstanding example is Alvin Ailey, who founded the Alvin Ailey American Dance Theater. Ailey translated African-American folk music and jazz into dance forms that capture the soul of his people.

▼*Activity:* **Experience**

What music does Alvin Ailey use to express the biblical theme of "Revelations" in this excerpt from his dance work of the same name?

Look at the movements and listen to the music to determine Ailey's theological interpretation of "Revelations." What is he trying to say to us through this dance and this music?

The Undanced Dance

Dance rhythms carved out a place and a purpose for instrumental music. Vocal music had its message in the texts. In contrast, instruments could deliver a snappy rhythm and make us celebrate with our feet. The sheer delight of dance rhythms inspired the development of instrumental music, and this delight followed the instruments right into the concert hall.

The Suite

During the first half of the eighteenth century, Johann Sebastian Bach and George Frideric Handel arranged the popular dances of their day—the allemande, courante, sarabande, gigue, and so forth—into **suites**, *sets of instrumental pieces each in the character of a dance.* Suites were composed for a keyboard instrument or a small orchestra. Although much of the music of this period—Baroque—incorporated dancelike rhythms, these rhythms were meant more to be played and heard than to be danced to.

▼*Activity:* **Distinguish**

Listen to three movements from George Frideric Handel's *Water Music Suite* and decide which of the three dances he used as inspiration.

Tap or clap the following rhythmic patterns of three eighteenth-century dances observing tempo, meter, and accent:

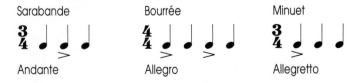

Which dance inspired each movement?

After you have decided the order of the dance patterns, clap the appropriate pattern as you listen to the music. Describe the differences between the three dance styles. Which are similar? How are they different?

Why is Handel's work a stylized use of these dance rhythms and not the actual dances?

Through the suite, composers learned how to make instrumental music expressive. The various types of dances found in the suite permitted composers to change tempos, shift accents, and alter dynamics. They found that instruments could portray affections (feelings) just as effectively as vocal music.

The Minuet

Another dance form that has entered the musical mainstream is the minuet. The **minuet**, *a rather slow and charming old French dance in triple meter, probably originated as a country dance.* It was danced at the court of Louis XIV during the seventeenth century. In the hands of Franz Joseph Haydn (1732–1809) and Wolfgang Amadeus Mozart (1756–1791), the minuet was turned into an art form that epitomized the graceful dignity and elegance of the Classical period. Composers began to include a minuet as a contrasting movement in their sonatas, quartets, and symphonies. As the third (occasionally second) movement in these three- or four-movement works, the minuet often provided a lighthearted contrast to the more serious musical statements that preceded and followed. Even though the minuet became a piece to listen to, it retains its triple rhythm and its catchy charm.

▼ Aristocrats at the court of Louis XIV danced the minuet, a stately old French dance in triple meter. Later, Classical composers such as Haydn and Mozart incorporated the minuet in their multi-movement musical forms, such as the sonata, the string quartet, and the symphony.

Profile

Wolfgang Amadeus Mozart
Austrian Composer
1756–1791

WOLFGANG AMADEUS MOZART

Wolfgang Amadeus Mozart (MOAT-zart) may have been the greatest genius who ever lived. As a child prodigy of eight, he astounded King Louis XV of France, George III of England, and other royalty with his skill at improvisation on the harpsichord. He composed his first symphony when he was 10 and his first opera at 11. At 14 during a visit to Rome, he heard a performance of Gregorio Allegri's *Miserere* in the Sistine Chapel and wrote out all nine parts of the work from memory after a single hearing! He experienced his first operatic success in Milan, where he conducted 26 performances of his new opera. He was not quite 15 years old. In 1772 at the age of 16 he composed seven symphonies and numerous other works.

As a composer, Mozart had incredible facility. He wrote for every medium current at his time in Vienna—masses and other sacred works, marches and dance music, canons, short orchestral works, vocal music, piano sonatas, string quartets and other chamber music, concertos, operas, and symphonies—literally hundreds of works. His music reflects his abundant wit and wisdom. It could express simple slapstick humor, complex nobility, and scores of other moods. Always there is a formal perfection, rich harmony, ingenious coloration, and melodic beauty. Among his operas are *The Marriage of Figaro, Don Giovanni,* and *The Magic Flute,* works still widely performed. Although he was highly regarded in his day, he and his family managed to live only modestly from his commissions, court salary, teaching fees, and income from publications. He died of rheumatic fever at the age of 35.

The Waltz

Like the minuet, the waltz is a dance in triple meter. Both the minuet and the waltz started out as social dances that eventually graduated to the concert hall. Unlike the minuet, the waltz has enjoyed great popularity for nearly 200 years. In the early nineteenth century, it prevailed as the most fashionable and favorite of all dances. At that time, one of the dance halls in Vienna, the Apollo, could accommodate 6,000 dancers.

▼*Activity:* **Answer with Your Ears**

How can you identify the vintage Viennese waltz?

Listen to *The Blue Danube* by Johann Strauss, Jr., and answer the following questions:

1. Using the second hand of your watch or the classroom clock, determine the length of the introduction. That is, precisely how many seconds go by before Strauss begins the main theme? How do you know where the first theme begins?
2. Try to tap three even quarter notes in each measure during the main theme of the waltz. Is the tempo the same throughout the dance? Which of the three beats is sometimes delayed or lengthened? Is Strauss's music actually danceable, or would it be more successful in a concert hall? In what ways is this waltz unlike the dance music of today?
3. Generalizing from your experience in listening to *The Blue Danube,* can you name several characteristics of the Viennese waltz?

Cooperative Learning

Compare Minuets

Describe the difference between two minuets written by Mozart.

Listen to two minuets written by Mozart. One Mozart composed when he was six years old; the other he composed when he was 32 years old. As you listen to the two works, identify the characteristics and describe the differences between the two minuets. Which of the minuets sounds similar to the minuet in Handel's *Water Music Suite?* Which is more stylized? Why? Working in small groups, discuss your answers.

Compared to the stiff and stately minuet, the waltz was unsophisticated and unrestrained. Its fast, pulsating rhythms invited couples to whirl and glide in close embrace. But the sheer physical appeal of waltzing led some nineteenth-century critics to claim it was indecent and immoral. In fact, newspaper accounts in 1899 state that the waltz was actually banned in some parts of Switzerland.

By the mid-nineteenth century, Vienna had become the center of waltz music. Vienna's most beloved citizen, composer Johann Strauss, Jr. (1825–1899), also known as "the Waltz King," composed almost 400 waltzes. *The Blue Danube* reigns as one of his most famous. It was an immediate success at its 1867 premiere and remains a classic example of the vintage Viennese waltz.

The waltz usually begins with an introduction that includes a short announcement of the waltz rhythm before the dance actually begins. Often, the waltz itself is in two parts (16 measures each), and several waltzes (usually five) follow one another in a row with a concluding finale. The waltz is lighthearted, optimistic music, conveying happiness and good feelings.

The waltz was elevated to concert music during the nineteenth century when Frédéric Chopin (1810–1849) and other composers wrote instrumental waltzes that were not meant for dancing. Maurice Ravel (1875–1937), was inspired to write his choreographic poem for orchestra, entitled *La Valse*, in 1920. He imagined this waltz as a fantastic and fatal sort of dervish's dance. (A "dervish" is a member of a Muslim order, some of whom whirl and chant as part of their religious acts.) He initially entitled the work "Vienna" in honor of the waltz capital of the world. A brilliant orchestrator, Ravel created *La Valse* as a glorified tribute to the symphonic waltz style. He considered his exalted orchestral waltz more as a ballet to be choreographed than as a ballroom dance for couples.

▼*Activity:* **Compare Waltzes**

Can you find the similarities and differences between *The Blue Danube* and *La Valse*?

Listen again to *The Blue Danube*, then listen to the beginning of *La Valse* to answer question 1 below. Then listen to its surprising and fantastic ending to answer question 2.

1. At what point can you confirm with confidence that this piece is written in the Viennese waltz style? (Use the second hand of your watch to get an idea of where an identifiable waltz theme begins.) How is the beginning of *La Valse* different from the beginning of *The Blue Danube*?
2. What has Ravel done to the waltz style at the end of *La Valse*? What similarities are there with *The Blue Danube*? How does Ravel convey the image of a "fatal sort of dervish's dance"?

The Use of Latin Dance Rhythms

The highly celebrated American pianist and composer Louis Moreau Gottschalk (1829–1869) was among the first to incorporate exotic creole and black folk idioms into his compositions. He had heard these rhythms and tunes when he was growing up in New Orleans and thought it natural to include them in his works. Gottschalk's open and democratic spirit is notable for the time. As a virtuoso pianist, he performed throughout the world, traveling to Europe, South and Central America, and the islands of the Caribbean. He was fascinated by the local music, particularly the Latin-American rhythms, and he boldly incorporated them in his music. *La Gallina* ("The Hen"), a work for piano, is based on a Cuban contradance (country dance), and his symphony, *A Night in the Tropics*, used Cuban rhythms and native percussion instruments. He was one of the first composers to honor Latin-American music.

While he was visiting Puerto Rico in 1857, Gottschalk heard strolling musicians perform traditional Christmas carols. He freely adapted one of these in composing *Souvenir de Porto Rico*, which he subtitled *Marcha y danza de gibaros* ("March and Dance of the Peasants"). The use of such native folk materials was very daring and innovative in his day. (See Activity: Master on page 68.)

African dance rhythms, have been incorporated in the work of a host of black American classical composers, led by William Grant Still (1895–1978) and Ulysses Kay (b. 1917). In the mid-1940s, a friend brought Still a set of Panamanian dance tunes and asked him to use the new melodies as a basis for composing a string quartet. Still did just that and the result was his *Danzas de Panamá* composed in 1948. The fourth movement of this quartet, written for the customary two violins, a viola, and a cello, bursts with Latin-American dance rhythms. (See Activity: Match the Rhythms on page 69.)

▲ Inspired by Cuban, Puerto Rican, and Latin American rhythms, American pianist and composer Louis Moreau Gottschalk (1829–1869) was one of the first composers to incorporate native folk materials into his classical compositions.

Caricature of Louis Gottschalk. New York Public Library, Music Division. Astor, Lenox, and Tilden Foundation.

Profile

William Grant Still
American Composer
1895–1978

WILLIAM GRANT STILL

One of the most famous African-American composers of classical music, William Grant Still wrote operas, ballets, choral works, and symphonies that have been performed around the world. His *Afro-American Symphony*, composed in 1931, was the first symphony by a black composer to be played by a major orchestra. Still, determined to develop a style of classical music that reflected and expressed Afro-American tradition, incorporated African-American folk song melodies in his work.

Still grew up in Little Rock, Arkansas. His father, a leader of a local band, died when Still was a baby. His stepfather took him to musical events and encouraged his interest in music. In college, he majored in science but eventually changed to music. After graduating, he wrote jazz arrangements for W. C. Handy, the jazz musician and composer who wrote "St. Louis Blues." He then went on to study composition at Oberlin Conservatory, the New England Conservatory, and privately with the French avant-garde composer Edgard Varèse.

Still was also an accomplished oboist. In spite of all his achievements, he remained a gentle, kindly man with a sense of humility. He eventually settled in Los Angeles, where he lived and continued to compose until his death in 1978.

▼*Activity:* **Master**

Learn to perform the complicated Puerto Rican rhythms Gottschalk used in his *Souvenir de Porto Rico*.

First practice tapping each of the measures separately (one and three are alike) counting the pattern of eight. Gradually increase the tempo. Put all four measures together and repeat them until you can tap them easily. Then try tapping the rhythms while you count in two.

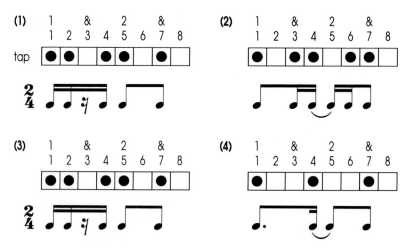

Now listen to Gottschalk's piano work and see if you can hear when this four-measure rhythmic pattern comes in.

▼*Activity:* **Match the Rhythms**

Match the rhythms of William Grant Still's themes to the correct sections of his "Cumbia y Congo," the fourth movement of his string quartet *Danzas de Panamá*.

As you listen to this movement, you will notice that it contains several distinct themes and tempo changes. All four string instruments use a technique called pizzicato (plucking the strings with the fingers). The musicians also tap the wood of their instruments to imitate the sound of native Panamanian drums.

Each of the four sections of this movement—Introduction, Section A, Section B, and the Coda (the last four bars)—uses a different melodic rhythm. Can you match each of these sections with its proper rhythm as notated below?

Summary

Music invites us to move. It calls our rhythmic impulse into action, translating it into the expressive movements we call dance. Rhythm is the underlying organizational pattern that gives music and dance its distinct and expressive order.

Like music, dance is a cultural expression. It springs from the soul of a people. Its rhythms convey the special way people view themselves in relation to the world around them. The music of the dance radiates life. It emits the glow of the human spirit and the vitality of being alive. This rhythmic energy is the basis for much of the expressive quality of all music.

Originally it was dance that gave instrumental music its reason for being. Eventually, instrumental music incorporated dance rhythms into purely musical statements, raising them to a level of art so that they served the mind, not just the feet. The spirited rhythms of real-life dance still fascinate composers and inspire them to incorporate the feeling into their musical expressions. The dance element in music is one of its most attractive and compelling characteristics.

Apply What You Have Learned

Using your knowledge of rhythm, create a rhythm soundtrack and record it.

Put what you have learned about rhythm to the test. Working in a small group of five to seven of your classmates, organize, compose, perform, and record a 32-measure soundtrack for percussion.

Follow these musical requirements:

1. Select percussion instruments whose sounds you like.
2. Use the 8-beat set (measure) as the organizing metric device (1 measure = 8 beats) for the soundtrack.
3. Prepare the composition in four sections of eight measures each. The four sections should have an organizational plan of A A' B A: that is, the A sections should be alike, the B section different. The A' (A-prime) section should be somewhat different from A. (You can introduce some slight variations here.)
4. Develop section B in a different tempo. This section should be improvised.
5. Include regular and syncopated rhythmic patterns in both sections. Incorporate polyrhythms if you can!

Create a score for your work using the count of eight and X's to mark where each instrument should play.

Here is the plan for your soundtrack:

Organizational Plan

Section	A	A'	B	A
Length	8 measures	8 measures	8 measures	8 measures
Rhythms	8-beat sets with synco-pation	sets that are similar to A, but varied	sets in a different tempo and improvised	Exactly the the same as the first A section
Instruments	You decide!			
Tempo	You decide!			
Other expressive ideas	You decide!			

Remember this is one continuous piece; the sections have to connect.

Record your soundtrack. Compare your percussion piece with others in the class.

Apply What You Have Learned
Chapter 4

Summarize what you have learned about rhythm in danced and undanced music.

Check your listening knowledge of types and origins of dance music and their basic metric organization. Respond to the musical examples and identify the type of dance (i.e., waltz). Determine the meter of the dance (i.e., duple or triple). Finally, indicate whether the musical example is best suited for the dance hall or the concert hall.

Pick the correct dance or dance rhythm from the following list:

Minuet	Tap	Charleston
Cha-cha	Ballet	Waltz
Native American Dance	Square Dance	Theatrical Dance
Disco	Tex-Mex Polka	Sarabande
Modern Dance	Tango	Social Slow Dance
Twist	Samba	Hip Hop

▲ Tex-Mex

▲ Ballet

▲ The Waltz

▲ The Twist

Music!... To Let Us Perform

~

CHAPTER 5

From the Performer's Perspective

Objectives

By completing this chapter, you will:

- Find out that you can "think" sound.
- Use your voice to express yourself musically.
- Understand musical communication as a performer.
- Become acquainted with how voices are classified musically.
- Try your skill at the art of interpretation.
- Learn to sing in a style appropriate to the music.

Musical Terms

alto
audiation
baritone
bass
basso profundo
bel canto
coloratura
contralto
countertenor
crescendo
diminuendo
mezzo-soprano
phrase
soprano
tenor
vocal range
vocal register

*T*o live is to be active, to do, to perform. One way
we perform or feel alive is to make music. We make
music because the capacity to think sound is built into
the human mind. We call this capacity **audiation**,
*the ability to imagine or hear in our head the sound of
a melody, a rhythm, various musical timbres,
or a performance.* Most people possess this talent,
not just a fortunate few, as is sometimes believed.

The Art of Performance

Performers use this capacity to think sound in order to hear the music
before they actually play it. They can "hear it with their eyes." Composers
use this ability to think the sounds, then write them down. Some people
think that composers have to work at a piano. This is not true. Although
some do, others prefer to sit at a desk away from any musical instrument.
They can create their musical sounds and alter them—all in their mind.
You, too, have the capacity to think sound.

Music is a basic and unique part of us. Through music we can express
ourselves and communicate with one another. In fact, some of humanity's
most profound thoughts have been expressed through music. By making
our own music—being a performer—music becomes self-expression.
Although being a performer can be exhilarating, it can be very demanding. Musicians must work to develop control and confidence. They have
to be certain they can produce a level of quality on demand. This takes a
great deal of practice, such as going over a musical passage again and again
until it is mastered.

> **PROJECT**
>
> **Interview a Musical Performer**
>
> Interview a performing musician in your community to find out as much as you can about his or her musical background. Consider anyone who plays an instrument or sings classical, pop, folk, or religious music. The performer may be professional or amateur, old or young, a soloist or a member of a group.

▼Activity: *Think the Musical Sound*

Can you "think" a tune without actually hearing the sound waves?

Refining your audiation skills can make you a better musician and listener. You have used this skill when you internalized the basic 8-beat count in the rhythm exercises in Chapter 3. As you learn more about performing music, see how well you can audiate the following:

1. *Audiate a major scale.* Think the syllables of DO RE MI FA SOL LA TI DO as you silently sing the pitches of a major scale, beginning with DO on C. Sing high DO out loud together to see if you have all arrived on the same pitch.
2. *Audiate instrumental timbres.* Can you hear in your mind's ear the sound of an electric guitar and the sound of a violin playing "The Star-Spangled Banner"? How are they different? How are they alike?

3. *Audiate a melody.* Think of the melody for the first line of "America": "My country 'tis of thee, sweet land of liberty, of thee I sing." When you come to the word "sing" (on DO), sing it out loud to see if everyone in the class arrived on the same pitch at precisely the same time.

4. *Audiate a symphonic motive.* You might recognize the following melodic pattern that is heard at the very beginning of Beethoven's *Fifth Symphony*:

Although it is more difficult to think the sound of a full symphony orchestra, can you hear one playing this theme?

5. *Audiate 12 silent measures while counting like an instrumentalist.* Pretend you have to "rest" for 12 measures and come in at the beginning of measure 13. Establish a moderate tempo, then close your eyes and silently count 12 full measures in 4/4 meter. When you get to measure 13, snap your fingers on beat 1. Did everyone in the class arrive simultaneously on beat 1 of measure 13?

▼ Young people throughout the world perform music, expressing their society's character and the values in which they believe. Through musical performance—instrumental as well as vocal—American students convey their community spirit and pride in who they are.

Using Your Voice to Express Yourself

Your voice is one of your most distinguishing characteristics. It is part of your personality, part of what makes you unique. Your voice is like your fingerprint—different from anyone else's. It is the most important means by which you express yourself and convey your moods and beliefs. Your voice gives you enormous power—the power to communicate. You can improve your speaking voice just as you can develop your singing voice. The more you improve your voice, the more effective communicator you will become. Do not make the mistake of thinking that singers require special talent. While great voices are inborn, every person can learn to sing and sing well.

Singing is sustained speech. When we sing, we aim for the vowels, for they support the tone. With the possible exception of *n* and *m*, we cannot sustain or sing consonants. Singers try to develop pure vowel sounds for tonal clarity and beauty. They also strive for an evenness in sound throughout their low, middle, and upper registers, working to eliminate any "breaks" they may have so there is smoothness throughout. Through lessons and practice, the vocal "instrument" is burnished to its ultimate luster. Acquiring this tonal beauty and the ability to use it expressively requires long and serious study. Singing, then, is raised to the level of an art.

▼Activity: *Determine Your Vocal Range*

Which pitches represent the highest and lowest you can comfortably sing?

To find the limits of your comfortable **vocal range,** *the highest and lowest pitches you can sing,* follow these basic steps:

1. As a class, review staff notation. Practice singing the syllable pattern DO RE MI RE DO TI DO on each of several pitches beginning on middle C.
2. Working in small groups of the same gender, gather around a piano, portable keyboard, or mallet percussion instrument that you can use to find the pitches you produce vocally.
3. To find your lower range, sing the pattern DO RE MI RE DO TI DO together beginning on middle C and moving downward one half-step at a time. Find the lowest pitch you can sing comfortably in medium volume. Notate this pitch on your staff paper. Some people in your group may be able to sing lower than others, so you may want to sing the pattern individually in the lower ranges.
4. To find your upper range, go back to middle C and sing the same pattern, this time ascending in pitch one half-step at a time. Keep your voice light and sing as high as you can comfortably without straining. When you have found the highest pitch you can sing easily, notate this pitch on the staff paper.
5. Your high and low pitches represent your vocal range. How wide is it? Compare your range to that of others in your group and write the composite range of your group on staff paper. Be prepared to report your findings to the class so a composite range of the class can be determined.

Learning the Art of Interpretation

For music to communicate, it must be expressive. Performers must become sensitive to the ways a particular musical composition can be rendered. Sometimes composers designate exactly how a work is to be performed; sometimes they do not. Performers must often decide how a piece will be sung or played. They ask:

- What is the most appropriate tempo for the piece?
- What is the most fitting tone quality, or timbre?
- Should the notes be smooth and connected, or short and choppy?
- Where should special emphasis be given?
- What dynamics should be used?

Musical expression is directly tied to interpretation. Figuring out how to interpret a piece of music requires some ingenuity. The performer has to try to understand what the composer is trying to communicate, then tailor the performance to realize that intent. If the mood of a work is essentially carefree and happy, it should be performed differently than if it were a lament for the death of a hero. To establish the mood, we have to assume the desired attitude, color our tone accordingly, and project that feeling in our performance. There is no one way to perform a piece of music. There are usually many acceptable interpretations.

Interpretation requires an attention to detail. Performing music is not just a matter of getting the notes right, it is making every note mean something. The performer has "to phrase," that is, convey the logic of the melodic flow. A **phrase** is *a series of pitches that makes sense.* Composers sometimes mark the phrase by a curved line over a series of notes indicating that they are connected to form a statement. All music breathes. There have to be resting points or places that mark the end of the phrase, or musical thought. Just as there is a natural rise and fall in the way we speak a sentence, there is a rise and fall in the way we perform a musical phrase.

PEANUTS ®   by Charles Schulz

▼*Activity:* **Learn to Interpret**

See if you can sing this old Latin prayer for peace, paying particular attention to the dynamics and phrase markings.

Practice your ensemble so that the entire class is singing and feeling this piece together. Try to agree on the dynamic levels of: *pianissimo (pp)* very soft, *piano (p)* soft, *mezzo forte (mf)* moderately loud, and *forte (f)* loud.

Practice **crescendos** (◁), *a gradual increase in the loudness of the sound;* **diminuendos** (▷), *a gradual decrease in the loudness of a sound,* and ritardando (rit), *a gradual slowing down at the end.* Practice singing each phrase in one breath or by "staggering" your breathing (sneaking a breath in so it cannot be detected). Sing to express a prayer for peace. Make your performance musical; that is, find the meaning in these notes.

There are three Latin words: *Dona* (DOH-nah) *nobis* (NOH-bees) *pacem* (PAH-chem).

Dona Nobis Pacem

Composer Unknown

Musical Communication

Music is an art of communication. Musical communication, like all communication, is a two-way street. We send and we receive. Most often, music is more than self-expression. It is social. It makes connections between people.

Performers bring us music by repeating from memory traditional musical expressions learned "by ear" from others, by inventing sounds from the mind's imagination (audiating and improvising), or by reading and interpreting the notations on a musical score. Can music be made any other way?

American composer John Cage (1912–1992) has tried to bring greater freedom to musical expression. For Cage, music is not limited to sounds we select and organize for communicative purposes. He believes that any kind of sound can be heard as music. According to Cage, if we attend to the sounds around us, we could interpret them as musical expression. To illustrate his point, Cage produced a "piece" entitled *4'33"* (1952) in which no sounds are intentionally performed. Instead, the "performer" sits at the piano for four minutes and thirty-three seconds and does not play a note. The audience listens as usual. The ambient sounds that occur in the room become the musical expression.

Vocal Timbres

The human voice may be our most expressive instrument. Like other instruments, it comes in an almost infinite variety of tonal qualities, or timbres. Every person's voice has its own special sound. When we identify someone by his or her speaking voice, we base our recognition on the tone color or timbre of the voice and on the **vocal register**, *how low or high someone speaks*. Once we are familiar with television personalities, for example, we do not need to see them to identify them. We associate the sound of their voice with who they are. Without being aware of it, we recognize familiar singers the same way—by the distinctive timbre and register of their voices.

▼Activity: *Characterize the Voices*

Try to recognize these pop artists by the tone quality (timbre) of their voices.

As you listen to these distinctive voices, develop a list of descriptors that help identify the tone color and register of each voice. Some terms that might be used to describe tone color are: bright, dark, harsh, heavy, hoarse, husky, light, mellow, melodious, nasal, rich, rough, shrill, smooth, strained, sweet, tense, warm, and so forth. Is the voice high, low, or medium in register? On the basis of their timbre and register, can you determine their identity? What other clues helped?

Compare and discuss your descriptors with those of your classmates.

Profile

John Cage
American Composer
1912–1992

JOHN CAGE

With his innovative use of chance and nontraditional sounds in his music, John Cage helped to direct the course of music and art in the modern era. Cage's compositions challenge listeners with Zen Buddhist concepts such as natural inconsistency and peaceful disarray. Because Cage finds no logic in nature, his works are often made up of many unrelated layers of sound. *Imaginary Landscape No. 4* (1951) involves twelve radios, with two performers at each, one to manipulate volume, the other the stations. Such chance effects reflect his belief that humans should not try to mold nature to their will but adjust to it and discover what is beautiful. His composition *4'33"* exemplifies these beliefs.

Cage was born in Los Angeles in 1912. He was introduced to music by neighbors and relatives. Cage dabbled in the radio business while in high school, then attended Pomona College for two years before deciding to travel in Europe and develop his writing skills. Upon returning to California, Cage submitted samples of his music and writing to local critics. Because his music was better-received than his prose, Cage chose to become a composer, and studied with Arnold Schoenberg for several years. Since then, Cage has applied his innovative musical theories to create dozens of influential works. He has scored numerous dances, lectured widely, and written books on a variety of subjects. Scorned by some, revered by many, Cage has been the most influential American composer of the twentieth century.

▼*Activity:* **Compare Timbres**

Listen to two singers—one from Bulgaria and one from Mali in West Africa, both popular artists in their own land and describe the differences in their vocal coloration.

Make a list of adjectives that describe the vocal qualities of each singer. Answer the following questions:

1. How do these singers differ from one another, particularly in timbre?
2. Which singer comes from West Africa? (Hint: Pay attention to the accompaniment.)
3. Do you think these voices have carrying power? Why might they have to?
4. Are these voices expressive?

The human voice is imperfect. It can sing out of tune and have a breathy or nasal quality. It can lack adequate strength or sustaining power. It can also be highly expressive. The voice naturally projects a humanness because it comes from within. It therefore speaks directly to other people's feelings.

As an instrument, the human voice has a wide range and a variety of timbres. Female voices are usually higher than those of males and vary in range and quality from **coloratura** (col-or-ah-TOO-rah) and **soprano** (so-PRAH-noh), *the higher of the female registers*, to **alto** or **contralto** (con-TRAL-toh) *the lowest female register*. Male voices likewise differ in range and quality from **countertenor** (coun-ter-TEN-or) and **tenor**, *the highest of the adult male voices*, to **bass** and **basso profundo** (BAS-soh pro-fun-doh), *the lowest of the adult male voices*. The intermediate female voice is called a **mezzo-soprano** (or **mezzo**), and the intermediate male voice is called a **baritone**.

▼*Activity:* **Designate Voice Categories**

What are the qualities that determine voice categories?

Match the picture of the artist and the description of his or her voice category with the voice you hear. How would you describe the differences and the similarities between the voices? Which type of voice is the most unusual? Why?

Edita Gruberova—Coloratura soprano
The highest female register with a lightness and flexibility to facilitate rapid scales and trills.
Character: Queen of the Night
Aria: "Queen of the night"
Opera: The Magic Flute (1791) by Wolfgang Amadeus Mozart (1756–1791)

Marian Anderson—Contralto
A low female register with a full, rich, dark, and powerful quality.
Character: Ulrica
Aria: "Queen of the abyss, make haste"
Opera: The Masked Ball (1859) by Giuseppe Verdi (1813–1901)

Alfred Deller—Countertenor
The highest of the adult male voices with a falsetto range and quality and a register in the female alto range.
Character: Oberon
Aria: "Flowers of the purple dye"
Opera: A Midsummer Night's Dream (1960) by Benjamin Britten (1913–1976)

Luciano Pavarotti—Tenor
A high male register with a powerful, ringing quality, capable of heroic expression.
Character: Calaf
Aria: "Nessun dorma" (No one will sleep)
Opera: Turandot (1926) by Giacomo Puccini (1858–1924)

José van Dam—Baritone
A mid-range male register with a lyrical and legato quality.
Character: Figaro
Aria: "Non più andrai" (Life in the army)
Opera: The Marriage of Figaro (1786) by Wolfgang Amadeus Mozart (1756–1791)

William Warfield—Bass
A lower male register with a rich, robust, resonant, and full quality.
Character: Joe
Aria: "Old Man River"
Opera: Show Boat (1927) by Jerome Kern (1885–1945)

Nicolai Ghiaurov—Basso profundo
The lowest male register with a dark, rich, and powerful quality often used to represent kings, high priests, and other persons of dignity.
Character: Boris
Aria: "Farewell aria"
Opera: Boris Godunov (1874) by Modest Mussorgsky (1839–1881)

Profile

Marian Anderson
American Singer
1902–1993

MARIAN ANDERSON

Marian Anderson, one of the great voices of the twentieth century, broke through racial barriers firmly but gently. She considered her voice a gift and a tool for social change. When she was six, she was admitted to the junior choir in her home church in Philadelphia; from there, her voice belonged to the public.

Music sustained Anderson through difficult times. In the late 1920s she went to Europe and established a dazzling career. There, the renowned conductor Arturo Toscanini called Anderson's voice a "voice heard once in a century." She had an incredible talent and a regal bearing that belied America's negative stereotypes of African Americans at that time.

She returned to the United States only to find some doors still closed to her. In 1939 she was refused access to the most prestigious concert hall in the nation's capital because she was black. First Lady Eleanor Roosevelt helped remedy this injustice. Instead of singing at Constitution Hall, her concert was moved to the steps of the Lincoln Memorial. An audience of 75,000 people assembled to hear her. Anderson walked onto the steps, paused to look at Lincoln's statue, then choked with emotion, sang "My country 'tis of thee, sweet land of liberty, of thee I sing . . ."

Thirteen years later, the policy at Constitution Hall was changed, and she sang there the following year (1953). She later said, "I had no bitterness then. I have no bitterness now." Today, the recording of her 1939 concert at the Lincoln Memorial is one of the ten most requested records at the Library of Congress.

▼Activity: *Recognize Parts of a Chorus*

Can you identify the four parts of a chorus when you hear them?

Listen to the first 14 measures of the "Kyrie" from Johann Sebastian Bach's *Mass in B Minor* and see if you can tell when the theme is sung and which section of the chorus (soprano, alto, tenor, or bass) is singing it. Here is the theme:

Ky - ri - e   e - lei - - son, e - lei - son.

Note that the theme is in 4/4 meter and uses several chromatic or half-step intervals. All the voices sing the same text. *Kyrie eleison* is Greek for "Lord have mercy."

Count measures and listen for the four vocal entrances of the theme. The first entrance occurs in the first measure on beat 1. Locate the remaining three entrances of the theme.

Listen a second time to check your answers. Then, as you listen a third time, circle the number of the beat in the measures where each new voice begins singing the "Kyrie" theme. Do all the voices enter on the same beat?

Listen again and label which section of the chorus (soprano, alto, tenor, or bass) actually sings each entrance of the theme. Is there a pattern to the way Bach introduced each entrance?

▲ The use of hue and intensity in painting is like tone colors (timbres) in music. Dark colors suggest a somber or brooding mood; bright colors, a cheerful mood.

Edward Hopper. *Early Sunday Morning.* 1930. Collection of Whitney Museum of American Art, New York, New York. Purchase, with funds from Gertrude Vanderbilt Whitney.

Matching Timbre with Style

If all sounds in the world can be used for expressive purposes, then the variety of sounds available for music is infinite. Which sounds, then, do we select for what purposes? Are some sounds more suitable for expressing certain emotions than others? The particular tonal quality of a sound, its timbre, gives us a reason to make expressive choices. If we want to create a dark and brooding mood, we would probably not choose a trumpet or flute, any more than a painter would use dark green and purple to express joy. To express a variety of emotions in music and to attain maximum impact, we must choose the most suitable timbre.

The voice can be adapted to sing many different types of music and each type has its own appropriate style. The style of the music dictates the style of the singing. You have some idea of the differences in sound that exist between a pop and an operatic singer. Popular singers work to improve and perfect their technique just like operatic singers, but the timbre of their voice is different. A natural, unaffected, easygoing sound best conveys the intimate thoughts and feelings expressed in pop and folk music. In contrast, the more formal, lofty expression of opera suits a tradition of vocal production called **bel canto** (literally, "beautiful singing"), *a style characterized by lyrical and flowing phrases, beauty of vocal color, and brilliant technique.* Just as we probably would not like to hear a country and western singer attempt opera, we most likely would not want to hear an opera singer attempt pop music.

▼*Activity:* **Identify Differences in Musical Styles**

What are the characteristics that make the differences in these musical styles?

Listen to the following arrangements of "Amazing Grace" played in four different musical styles: classical, jazz, gospel, and pop. Sing them in the order presented and identify each style. How is each performance different? To help you decide, jot down your thoughts about rhythm, tempo, dynamics, harmony, and mood for each example.

Sing again the arrangements of "Amazing Grace" and discuss the various styles. Which style seems least appropriate and why?

Amazing Grace

Composed by John Newton
Arranged by Rob Landes

Amazing Grace

Composed by John Newton
Arranged by Rob Landes

A - maz - ing __ grace! How __ sweet __ the __

sound that __ saved a __ soul like __ me! _____ I

once __ was __ lost, but __ now __ am __ found; was __ blind __ but __

now I see. _____

Amazing Grace

Composed by John Newton
Arranged by Rob Landes

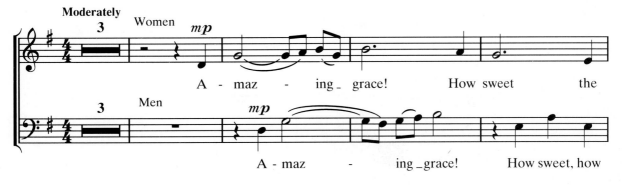

A - maz - ing _ grace! How sweet the

A - maz - ing _ grace! How sweet, how

sound   that saved   a — soul   like   me! _____   I

sweet — the — sound,   that saved,   that saved, that saved a soul, a   soul — like — me!

once _____ was — lost,   but   now _____ am — found;   was

I once,   I   once — was — lost,   but now, but   now — am — found;

blind   but — now   I   see. _____

was blind but   now, but — now I   see. _____

Amazing Grace

Composed by John Newton
Arranged by Rob Landes

Shuffle-feel ♩=102

A - maz - ing — grace! How sweet   the   sound —

— that saved _____ a — soul   like   me! _____   I

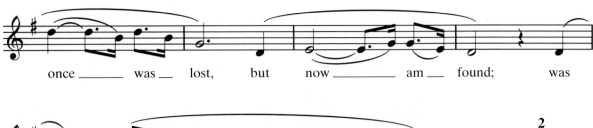

once ———— was — lost,   but   now ———— am — found;   was

blind,   but — now   I   see. ————

Summary

People express themselves musically in many different ways and with an array of sounds—instrumental, vocal, and electronic. The variety of timbres, like a painter's palette, increases the range of musical expression.

Performing music together requires a considerable degree of cooperation and coordination—a sense of togetherness or ensemble. Musical communication requires technique (performing the right sounds, in time, and in tune) and expression (effectively conveying the mood of the music). Musicians perform a piece of music in order to realize its expressive power. Different types of music demand different styles of performance. Performers communicate the meaning of a musical work by paying careful attention to such matters as appropriate tempo, dynamics, timbre (tone color), blend, balance, and phrasing.

Effective communication requires practice and discipline. In music, as in most other human endeavors, performers improve by small degrees. Performers, like athletes, have to persevere in order to polish their technique to brilliance. They learn the more they put into their practicing, the more they get out of it. In this way they discover the meaning of a musical work and bring it to life.

CHAPTER 6

From the Audience's Perspective

Objectives

By completing this chapter, you will:
- Explore the various levels of experiencing music as a listener.
- Become aware of the sources of instrumental sounds.
- Be able to recognize and categorize instrumental timbres.
- Become familiar with how dynamics serve as a powerful expressive aspect of music, and how loudness can be harmful.
- Understand the role of the music critic.
- Begin to develop your own ability to critique music.

Musical Terms

aerophones
authenticity
chordophones
electrophones
idiophones
membranophones
music critic

$\mathcal{W}$e can engage ourselves with music as a creator
(composer), re-creator (performer), or receiver (listener).
As a listener, we respond to music with different levels
of receptivity. We may be very casual about the way we
hear music, paying almost no attention to it. Elevator
or telephone music, for example, is not meant to
be listened to intently. We have all used music as
background sound, a pleasant atmosphere for our own
quiet thoughts. An "easy" listening station can create
a dreamlike haze, and we may deliberately tune out
the music. We are oblivious to the sounds.

Perceptive Listening

There are other times when music is the center of our focus, and we
give it our full attention. This could be in a car, in a church or synagogue,
at a special event, or at a concert. But how are we supposed to listen, and
what are we supposed to listen for? There are different ways to experience
music. Some people let the sounds wash over them like a sonic bath, an
emotional flood. This is the sensuous level. Other listeners respond on a
perceptive or analytical level, delineating the sounds and savoring various
aspects of the music as they unfold. They listen for musical events and
how they accumulate to form an expressive composition. The first level of
attending to music is purely emotive; the second, analytical. The perceptive level raises our awareness. Ideally, we learn to listen more perceptively
in order to increase the emotional impact. Perceptive listening reveals the
expressive power of the work so that we can enjoy it more fully.

How we approach music determines what we get out of it. The more
fully we understand music, the more apt we are to have a heightened
response—a peak experience. The ultimate experience is being so caught
up in the music that we lose ourselves in it. The thrill of music may arouse
goose bumps. Time may appear to stop, and our spirit is transformed. The
following diagram illustrates the various levels of experiencing music:

Levels of Experiencing Music

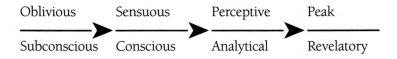

Oblivious	Sensuous	Perceptive	Peak
Subconscious	Conscious	Analytical	Revelatory

▶ American composer John Williams conducts the Boston Pops Orchestra in the premiere performance of his "Liberty Fanfare" on the Fourth of July, 1986, in celebration of the Statue of Liberty's one hundredth anniversary. Williams has composed scores for numerous films, including *Star Wars, Close Encounters of the Third Kind, Born on the Fourth of July, The Witches of Eastwick, Raiders of the Lost Ark, ET,* and *Home Alone.*

Each level of experiencing music is valuable for a different reason. The analytical approach, however, has to be learned. It requires some knowledge of musical events, the elements of music, and what makes music expressive. As an intermediary stage of bringing a musical work to life, the analytical stage can complement the purely emotional response and boost it. This is the approach used in this text. It is the process of paying attention to the details and trying to hear everything that is happening. The reward is emotive revelation.

▼Activity: *Listen Perceptively*

How does this music call attention to itself?

Listen to John Williams's "Liberty Fanfare," a work he was commissioned to write for the one hundredth birthday of the Statue of Liberty. The Boston Pops Orchestra performed this work under the direction of Mr. Williams at the unveiling of the newly restored statue and relighting of the torch on the Fourth of July, 1986.

How does the composer command our attention? Write your thoughts on a piece of paper and be prepared to discuss them.

Now listen again to "Liberty Fanfare." Does an awareness of what is going on in the music help you to get more out of it or increase your enjoyment? Does knowing the purpose for which the piece was created, the function of the music, and the intended audience/occasion increase your response?

▼*Activity:* **Use Your Imagination!**

What are the variables that affect the way we experience music?

With your classmates, simulate the three circumstances described below. Then determine the level at which you are interacting with John Philip Sousa's "The Washington Post March" in each situation. Choose one of these levels: (A) Oblivious (B) Sensuous (C) Perceptive (D) Peak.

1. You are attending a parade celebrating the Fourth of July and sitting in the reviewing stand waiting for the parade to pass by. The crowd around you is talking, and vendors are selling refreshments. You can faintly hear in the distance the band playing Sousa's march.
2. The band arrives at the reviewing stand. They turn, face you, and play the march. You can feel the beat of the drums, and the brilliance of the woodwinds and high brass slice the air. You get goose bumps.
3. While in class, you are analyzing and focusing on the various internal aspects of the march as well as the social function of the music.

Can you imagine a situation in which your interaction with this march might qualify as a peak musical experience?

Being an Audience Member

We often listen to music in the company of other people. We might be listening to the school band, chorus, or orchestra in an assembly, or attending a pop or classical concert. These can be exciting occasions. Performers try to do their best in front of an audience. They work hard to communicate the expressive qualities of the music they are performing.

Listening to music requires personal attentiveness. You have to take an interest in what is going on in the music in order to realize what it is expressing. You have to open yourself to the experience. Music has a way of reaching you, if you are willing to be reached.

How you react to music depends on the type of music, how it is being used, and where you are listening to it. At a basketball game, you probably would not analyze the music being played by the band. At a dance, music appeals to your sense of movement and you react in a sensuous way. Attending a concert, you may try to hear all the details in the music being performed and applaud the performers for their effort and achievement. In a sense, then, the context in which the music is performed dictates what is expected of the listener.

Being part of an audience does not have to be a stuffy or an overly serious experience. Listening to classical music can often be lighthearted and easygoing. This is especially true when a symphony orchestra is performing out-of-doors or in a pop concert. At other times, listening to jazz, concert music, or even folk music can be serious and intense. This is particularly the case if we are determined to hear all the events in the music as they occur.

PROJECT

Instrument Presentation

Select a musical instrument that you can either demonstrate for your classmates or describe in an oral report. The object of this project is to present an informed three-minute presentation that reveals the unique qualities of the instrument, including its classification, history, timbre, range, technical demands, and uses. If you do not play an instrument, use a recording of an instrument or ask a friend who plays one to bring it to class and demonstrate it as you describe its features.

Identifying Instrumental Timbres

As a listener of music, our perception is sharpened when we can delineate the variety of the sounds we are hearing. When we can identify the source of the sound, music becomes more focused. It is like wiping the fog off your glasses. We begin to hear more clearly, more precisely. The human voice is the most primary and natural source of music. You investigated different vocal timbres in the preceding chapter. Many other musical instruments have been invented to serve as sources of sound for making music. Every culture in the world has created musical instruments by using the natural materials of their region—fiber, metal, reed, gut, skin, and even stone—to fashion ways to produce sound. Anthropologists have classified all musical instruments in five basic categories:

Cooperative Learning

Classify Musical Instruments

How would you categorize the musical instruments with which you are familiar using the five basic classifications?

Working in teams of two or three students, make a list of the musical instruments with which you are familiar. Spend no more than five minutes compiling your list. Then classify the instruments into the five basic categories: aerophones, idiophones, membranophones, chordophones, or electrophones.

- **Aerophones,** *instruments that produce sound by a vibrating column of air.* Usually these consist of a pipe made out of wood, metal, or plastic, sometimes with a reed attached. Examples of aerophones include flute, oboe, and clarinet.
- **Idiophones,** *simple, solid instruments that produce sound by being struck, scraped, or shaken.* This includes gongs, cymbals, rattles, and xylophones.
- **Membranophones,** *instruments made by striking or rubbing a skin or membrane stretched across a resonating air chamber.* This category includes conga drums, tabla, or timpani.
- **Chordophones,** *instruments that create sound by striking, rubbing, or plucking a taut string (or chord).* These include a guitar, harp, violin, and string bass. The strings on many of these instruments are attached to a resonating box.
- **Electrophones,** *instruments that generate sound from electricity.* Electronic organs and synthesizers are in this category.

All instruments of the modern symphony orchestra as well as the instruments of the Indonesian gamelan orchestra can be classified in one of the five categories: aerophones, idiophones, membranophones, chordophones, or electrophones. Each of these sources of sound produces a particular tone color, or timbre, that is distinct and clearly identifiable by the ear. As a listener, you can learn to identify the timbre with the instrument that produces its sound. The different timbres and their combinations give music much of its variety, clarity, interest, and expressiveness.

Another way to identify instruments is by their range of audible pitch from very low to very high. While some instruments do not have discernible pitches (a cymbal or rattle, for example), others produce tones that are in the high-, low-, or mid-range. Except in the case of some electrophones, pitch is affected by the size of the instrument. The larger the instrument, the lower the pitch. The smaller the instrument, the higher the pitch. Similarly, the longer the string or pipe, the lower the pitch. Stretching a membrane raises the pitch, while loosening a membrane lowers it. In these ways people have been able to create musical instruments that span the full range of audible pitch.

Approximate Ranges of Orchestra Instruments

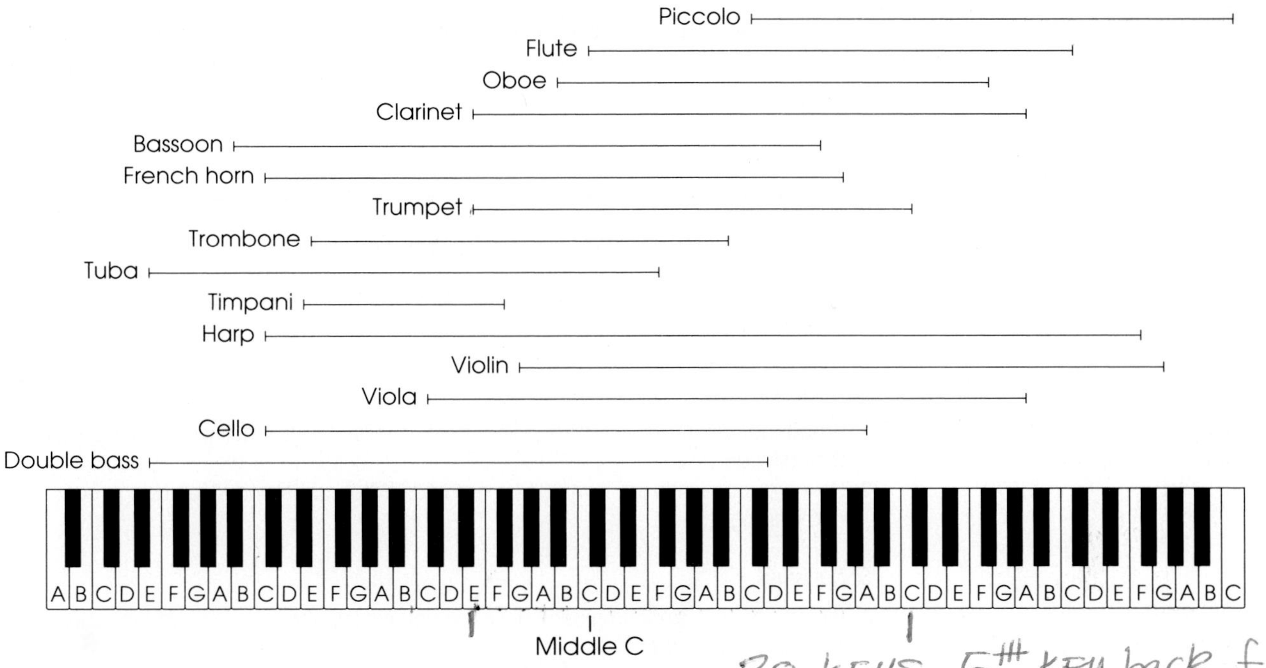

Piccolo

Flute

Oboe

Clarinet

Bassoon

French horn

Trumpet

Trombone

Tuba

Timpani

Harp

Violin

Viola

Cello

Double bass

A B C D E F G A B C D E F G A B C D E F G A B C D E F G A B C D E F G A B C D E F G A B C D E F G A B C D E F G A B C

Middle C

(handwritten annotation:) 20 keys 5th key back from middle C.

▼Activity: *Name the Source*

Discriminate among instrumental timbres that you hear.

Listen to the musical excerpts supplied by your teacher and identify all the timbres and the instruments producing the sound you hear. Then, classify the instruments according to their appropriate category. Hint: All five classification categories are represented.

Listening to Music Alone

Music is frequently listened to in private. Often, recorded music is played for an audience of one. Sometimes we listen to music on the radio by ourselves. In these private situations, we can choose our own level of experience: oblivious, sensuous, or perceptive. If we are fortunate, we may even achieve a peak experience.

Many people enjoy listening to music using headphones. Headphones allow us to escape from the real world and establish our own musical universe. With headphones we can create our own sound space, an environment that shuts out the discordant elements of modern life. One important expressive aspect of music is its volume. As listeners, we want to be able to hear the music being presented. Whether the music is live or recorded, it has to be audible. The capacity to hear music depends on a number of factors: the fidelity or clarity of its sound, its intensity or amplitude; acoustics; and, of course, how well our ears function. The human hearing mechanism is sensitive and can be damaged easily and permanently. The tendency of people to listen to music at high volume levels has alarmed physicians, audiologists, and even social psychologists. Do we really need to listen to music so loudly?

▼*Activity:* **Investigate Volume Levels**

Why do people listen to music at very loud volume levels?

Questions for investigation:

Science and Health Issues

1. Amplitude, dynamics, loudness, and intensity are related but distinct terms. How are they different?
2. How are sound intensity levels (SIL) measured? When are sound levels dangerous and damaging?

Social Issues

3. Why do people like loud music? How can you explain the popularity of the super stereos in cars and trucks?
4. Why do people play stereo equipment (personal stereos or boom-boxes) in public? What are the benefits and liabilities?
5. What are the benefits and liabilities of using personal headphones?
6. What message do people convey when they use a boom-box in public? What message do people convey when they use a personal stereo with headphones in public?

Deciding What You Like

There are many ways to coax the beauty out of music. Some people champion **authenticity**, *performing music as nearly as possible in the way it was performed at the time it was created*. Others apply modern standards and contemporary tastes to reinterpret a work for today's world. The way a work is performed can alter its meaning. When you purchase recordings, you often have different interpretations from which to choose. It is up to you to select the performance that pleases you the most.

On what bases do we make musical choices? For example, if we buy a recording of a particular musical work and there are three different performances to choose from, how do we decide which one is the best? Making a decision depends on comparing the various aspects of one performance with those same aspects in another. But when we are unable to hear the music ourself, as is often the case in an audio store, we have to depend on other people's opinions as expressed verbally or in published reviews. Published reviews are written by the **music critic**, *a person who judges the quality of the performance and the music.*

How's Your Hearing?

Decibels and Deafness:
Pump Up the Volume, Phase Out Your Hearing

by Peter Jaret

In the 1950s, audiologist Samuel Rosen tested the hearing of an African tribe tucked away in quiet isolation on the Sudanese-Ethiopian border, untouched by the roar of traffic or amplified music. Men well into their seventies, he found, could routinely hear sounds as faint as a murmur across a distance the length of a football field.

Few of us will be so lucky. By age 65, one in three Americans suffers hearing loss serious enough to interfere with communication. In one recent study, researchers found that some symptoms commonly blamed on Alzheimer's disease—unresponsiveness and confusion, for instance—can actually be the effects of hearing loss.

Among those fortunate enough to reach their nineties, nine out of ten will have impaired hearing.

And it looks like many of us won't have to wait that long.

The Woodstock Generation

Back in 1969, the summer of Woodstock, audiologist David Lipscomb set about testing the ears of incoming freshmen at the University of Tennessee. Eighteen-year-olds are past the age of childhood ear infections that can dampen hearing but are still too young to be suffering the effects of aging. They should have the most consistently sharp ears around.

Researchers in the 1930s and 1950s had tested 18-year-olds to set the standard for what the human ear can hear. Lipscomb found that, by comparison, the Woodstock generation was in deep trouble. Nearly a third of the students tested showed signs of hearing loss. Among the male students, one in *eight* had damage severe enough to interfere with communication.

Rock-and-roll, most audiologists suspected, was to blame. Live concerts commonly reached sound levels above 120 decibels—louder than a jackhammer or the roar of a chain saw. Until the 1960s, most hearing loss was associated with workplace noise—an occupational hazard. Now, it seemed, people were going deaf just for fun.

And the fun kept getting riskier. In the early 1980s, audiologist Maurice H. Miller of New York's Lenox Hill Hospital was alarmed to hear the noise pouring out of his kids' Walkman-style stereo tape players. So he donned his white lab coat, grabbed a sound-level meter and set off into the streets of New York. Stopping anyone carrying a personal stereo, he measured sounds of 115 decibels and higher pouring out of tiny earpieces directly into vulnerable ears.

"Imagine you're riding a New York subway," Miller told me. "The sound level is about 100 decibels—loud enough to have to shout over. The decibel scale, like the Richter scale for earthquakes, is logarithmic. So 110 decibels is 10 times as loud as that; 120 decibels is *one hundred* times louder than a subway car. That's enough to do permanent damage."

Miller is even more worried about customized car stereos that boast several speakers—and sound levels that reach 130 decibels. "That's roughly the sound of a jet engine at take-off. And believe me, we see the casualties in our clinic all the time—people in their thirties and forties with the kind of hearing loss we used to see only in people past retirement."

Of course, noise-induced hearing loss occurs gradually over time, and few people are willing to admit they're growing hard of hearing—a traditional hallmark of old age. Eyeglasses are stylish; hearing aids are not.

Turn Down That Walkman

What's the best way to save your ears? It's ridiculously simple: Avoid loud noises. "If you have to shout to converse over background noise, it's too loud," Miller said. "And the sound is too loud if someone sitting next to you can hear the music coming out of your Walkman-style stereo." The biggest danger occurs when people turn up the volume in the headsets to drown out the background noise of a subway or airplane. Most have volume settings from one to 10. Four, according to Miller, is as loud as you should ever go.

Noise becomes more damaging the longer it lasts. A food processor spins out about 85 decibels—nothing to worry about for a minute or two. But according to standards set by the Occupational Safety and Health Administration, exposure to sound levels of 85 decibels eight hours a day, five days a week, will eventually cause permanent damage in most people. And each time you add five decibels of loudness, the time it takes to cause lasting injury drops by half. At 120 decibels—rock concert volume—the damage is done in less than half an hour.

The Role of the Music Critic

When the British team of Sir William Gilbert and Sir Arthur Sullivan premiered their comic operetta *H.M.S. Pinafore* in London in 1878, they quivered at the thought of how Queen Victoria would react to this burlesque of the revered Royal Navy and the stiff social class system. She had one curt remark: "We are not amused." Nonetheless, the operetta was a smash success and played 700 performances. (Queen Victoria was not a professional critic.)

▼*Activity:* **Compare Performances**

Which version of Johann Sebastian Bach's Toccata in D Minor do you like better and why?

Compare the original organ version of this work with Leopold Stokowski's transcription for symphony orchestra. Try to substantiate why you think one version is better than the other.

Listen again to Stokowski's version of Bach's Toccata in D Minor and answer the following questions:

1. Bach might have performed his Toccata on the organ of the Church of St. Thomas in Leipzig. This long, narrow, and high building had a reverberation (echo) of 3.5 seconds. How does Stokowski take that phenomenon into account in his orchestral transcription?

2. Bach, who was acknowledged to be the greatest improviser of his day, probably created this brilliant Toccata "on the spot" as a prelude or recessional to the religious service. How does Stokowski's transcription, which was intended for the concert hall, take away from, or add to, the sacred and mystical character of the composition?

PEANUTS reprinted by permission of UFS, Inc. Copyright © June 11, 1989 by United Feature Syndicate, Inc.

More recently, a critic wrote a cryptic review of a new Broadway musical called *Smile, Smile, Smile*. He said, "I didn't, I didn't, I didn't." Most reviews are considerably longer. They delve into and analyze the musical and nonmusical aspects of the performance and the music. A music critic may comment on the performer, the composer, the conductor, the acoustics, the size of the audience and its reaction, or on anything else that relates to the performance.

Music critics can influence public opinion. Because of this, they shoulder considerable responsibility. Depending on how fairly they treat the musical performer, for example, they can make or break a career. For this reason, their views can be controversial. Violinist Isaac Stern has expressed his distress over critics who "are always there 'on the attack.' " He believes the most important quality of a critic "is to be a first-class educator." Some people prefer the term reviewer, rather than critic, because it implies a more objective view and the avoidance of making unsubstantiated personal judgments.

A music reviewer or critic should give you some insight into the music and the performance that you would not otherwise have. From a review, you discover quality and standards of performance, and you can improve your ability to substantiate your own viewpoint. If reviews are to function this way, you must be able to distinguish between fact and opinion.

▼*Activity:* **Investigate Music Reviews**

Can you distinguish between fact and opinion in newspaper columns about music?

Read both newspaper columns supplied by your teacher about Midori, the Japanese-born violinist who was 16 years old at the time. Then answer these questions:

1. Both columns were written by professional music critics. Which one is a music review and which one is a news article?
2. Both columns contain information, but one primarily reports the facts while the other offers opinion. Which does the music review contain? What is the focus of each article?
3. Music critics address topics that include the acoustics, biographical data, conductor, time and place, audience, composer, historical data, performance, audience reaction, audio fidelity, concert setting, music performed, performer(s), and staging. Determine how many of these topics were addressed by the Milwaukee critic.

▲ Shown here at 17 years old, the musical prodigy, Midori, had already been a professional violinist for three years when this photo was taken in 1987. She traveled a great deal, studying her required high school courses on the plane and in her hotel room.

Developing Critical Skills

Critics can be wrong, especially when they offer their personal opinions. When George Gershwin's opera *Porgy and Bess* was first performed in 1935, some critics liked it, others did not. Writing in the now-defunct *New York Herald Tribune*, Lawrence Gilman said "the song-hits which [Gershwin] has scattered through his score . . . will doubtless enhance his fame and popularity. Yet they mar it. They are its cardinal weakness. . . . [Listen] to such sure-fire rubbish as the duet between Porgy and Bess, "[Bess,] you is my woman now." Virgil Thomson, writing in *Modern Music* stated, "I do resent Gershwin's shortcomings. I don't mind his being a light composer, and I don't mind his trying to be a serious one. But I do mind his falling between two stools. . . . [Porgy and Bess] is crooked folk-lore and half-way opera, a strong but crippled work." After a revival of the opera in 1941, Thomson expressed a change of heart and wrote: "After six years George Gershwin's *Porgy and Bess* is still a beautiful piece of music. . . . Its inspiration is authentic, its expressive quotient high. . . . One is inclined to be more than proud of our little Georgie."

We are apt to run into problems when all we have to say is our opinion with nothing to support it. Like most other performers, jazz artist Chick Corea has felt the critic's dart. He believes that negative comments arise from "a need to criticize something." But he thinks that "the more important thing [is] that tastes vary. Music is a very subjective thing. It's a basic human right to like something and not to like something. Criticism should offer some positive solutions to a natural problem. Otherwise you just have someone saying what they think."

All of us are forced to make choices every day. We have to distinguish between good and bad, right and wrong, and make a host of other decisions. When it comes to music, we have a right to exercise our own judgment. As audience members, we can act as music critics for ourselves, making decisions about our likes, dislikes, and preferences. By using perceptive listening skills to improve our understanding of the music, we can develop a descriptive language that permits us to express our judgments and share them.

In making judgments about music, the professional critic can provide a model for us. Critics' comments range from scorn to praise. They use colorful language—descriptive nouns, adjectives, and adverbs—to communicate their reactions and judgments. These descriptive terms help them explain or clarify their points of view, substantiate their claims, and present a fair assessment.

▼ *Activity:* **Analyze Music Reviews**

How do music critics convey their opinions?

Read both reviews supplied by your teacher. The first one critiques a violin recital by Itzhak Perlman. The second evaluates a recording of Wagner's opera *Tristan und Isolde*. Identify all the color words—descriptive nouns, adjectives, and adverbs—words that indicate whether the critic's reaction was favorable or unfavorable.

One review is highly positive, and the other is clearly negative. Make a list of the positive and negative terms these reviewers used. Were both of these reviewers well informed? How do you know?

◄ When George Gershwin's opera *Porgy and Bess* was first presented in 1935, the reviews were mixed. Set in Catfish Row, a crowded tenement in Charleston, South Carolina, this opera tells the story of a disabled man's love for a woman who eventually deserts him. The opera is now hailed worldwide as an American musical masterpiece.

As a listener, performer, or composer, we naturally evaluate the musical sounds we hear, play, or compose. Listeners usually know when a performance is good or bad, although they may not know why. Performers constantly evaluate their own performances—in rehearsal and in concert. Composers continually ask whether the sounds they have composed convey what they intended.

In order to critique music, we must be able to hear what is going on in the music itself. We must understand that performances can usually be viewed in a number of ways. Frequently opinions differ, but if we are going to convince someone that our viewpoint is credible—that it is reliable and believable—we must offer convincing proof. Being a good critic means being able to substantiate our claims. That takes practice.

Summary

We experience music live, on recordings, on the radio, in films, and on television. As listeners we can decide how much attention we give to the music around us. We can ignore it, enjoy the sonic blur, or listen to it intensely. When we give music our fullest attention, we listen perceptively. This combined emotional and intellectual involvement with music may move us profoundly.

As listeners, we are all critics. We make judgments and determine our preferences. To share our likes and dislikes with others, we have to acquire insight into the music and a vocabulary with which to describe it. We learn to substantiate our judgment based upon what we hear. We can also learn something from the professional critics or reviewers by observing how they support their opinions. Like professional music critics and reviewers, we can become more discerning and descriptive. By developing the ability to critique what we hear, we become active participants in the listening process. By awakening our mental antennae, we can experience music more fully.

CHAPTER 7

Virtuoso Performers

Objectives

By completing this chapter, you will:
- Become acquainted with some of the great musical performers of the past and present.
- Learn to recognize and describe characteristics of a virtuoso performer.
- Discover what makes music difficult to master.
- Develop criteria for judging musical performances.

Musical Terms

double bass
musical expression
technique
virtuoso

$\mathcal{W}$hat makes a performer or a performance great? Great performers breathe excitement into music. They captivate the public by making themselves and their art one. Some are superstars, who have extraordinary technical ability, beauty of sound, and personal charisma. Their performances have conviction, and they persuade us that this is the way the music should sound. They make us feel their passion for the music.

The Virtuoso Performer

What is musical virtuosity? The **virtuoso** is *a person with a flawless and brilliant technique, who can seemingly do what no one else can*. Like gold-medal Olympic athletes, virtuosos redefine human ability. They break through established limits and set new standards. They achieve the impossible.

▼Activity: *Discover Musical Virtuosity*

What makes these performers great?

The following artists are regarded as virtuosos. Listen to an excerpt from a performance by each of them and make a list of those qualities that make them unique.

(1) **Louis Armstrong**
   jazz trumpeter and singer
   "West End Blues"

(2) **Andrés Segovia**
   classical guitarist
   "Gavotte en Rondeau"
   from *Partita No. 3 in E Major* (J. S. Bach)

(3) **Maria Callas**
   opera singer
   "Gualtier Maldè! . . . Caro nome"
   from *Rigoletto* (Giuseppe Verdi)

(4) **Jim Walker**
   jazz/classical flutist
   "Caprice"
   (Niccolò Paganini)

(5) **Cho-Liang Lin**
   classical violinist
   Violin Concerto in E Minor
   (Felix Mendelssohn)

(6) **Ustad Alla Rakha**
   Indian tabla player
   Pancham Sawari

(7) **Umm Kulthum**
   Egyptian singer
   "Ana fi intizarak"

▲ Maria Callas (1923–1977), the brilliant operatic soprano, is shown performing the role of Rosina in Gioachino Rossini's comic opera, *The Barber of Seville* (1816). She enhanced her vocal virtuosity with her musically intelligent interpretations, superb sense of drama, and the intensity and authority she brought to every aspect of the roles she performed. The photo above is from a 1956 production staged at the La Scala opera house in Milan, Italy. Baritone Tito Gobbi (right) played Figaro.

▶ Like musicians, artists sometimes exhibit virtuosity. In his painting *Las Meninas (The Maids of Honor)*, the Spanish painter, Diego Velázquez, rendered the sheen and pattern of cloth with finely executed brush strokes. This technical brilliance is comparable to a musician who can improvise with a seemingly flawless flow of expression. In both cases, these artists are supreme masters of their art.

Diego Velázquez. *Las Meninas (The Maids of Honor)*. 1656. Museo del Prado, Madrid, Spain.

Although there have been musical virtuosos throughout history, the nineteenth century spawned a spectacular number, and they are inevitably interesting people. The violin virtuoso Niccolò Paganini (1782–1840), for example, was so gaunt, sallow in complexion, and frightening in appearance that it was rumored that he had made a pact with the devil. How else could he play so brilliantly? And he played the viola just as well! Paganini wrote showpieces for the violin, some of them just to demonstrate that he could play anything, just on the G string.

Certain nineteenth-century performers (Paganini is a good example) have been called legendary. Stories about them abound, and their reputations are fed by news stories of the day. There are no recordings to document the greatness of their performing ability. In Paganini's case, however, we have more than the newspaper accounts. The music he composed and played gives us a good idea of how masterful he had to be to play his own works.

Franz Liszt (1811–1886) was a Hungarian pianist and composer. Like Mozart, he was a child prodigy who composed music and concertized at a surprisingly young age. By the time he was 12 he was dazzling audiences in Europe and in England. At 16, upon the death of his father, he had to fend for himself in Paris. Fortunately, he was able to make a livelihood teaching piano and concertizing. His concert programs often included one or more of his sensational transcriptions, orchestral works such as Rossini's *William Tell* Overture, which he performed on the piano.

Liszt may well have been the Elvis Presley of his day. He drove women wild, not with guitar and voice, but by playing the piano. Wherever he went, women flocked to hear him. Liszt liked their affections and even eloped with a countess. His music was just as romantic. From all accounts he was a virtuoso pianist, perhaps the greatest the world has ever known. It has been said that Liszt could read anything at sight. He could memorize immediately, and he could reproduce a complicated piece of music after hearing it only once. Just as Paganini had composed virtuoso works for the violin, Liszt wrote fiendishly difficult works for the piano—works that no one else at that time could play. He even transcribed some of Paganini's difficult works so that he could show off his own technical sorcery.

The Challenge of Music

Music can be difficult to perform. It can require an extraordinary technical facility on the part of the performer, as well as sheer physical stamina. Rock musicians who perform an entire two-hour concert expend enormous physical and mental energy. Musicians have to be alert and totally

▲ After one of Niccolò Paganini's performances in Italy in 1810, an awestruck critic wrote: "It fairly took one's breath away. In a sense, he is without question the foremost and greatest violinist in the world." Supposedly, according to rumors at that time, Paganini learned all his technical feats while he was in prison. Such fabrications sold a good many tickets.

◀ Musicians often performed for one another in *salons*. Here Franz Liszt plays the piano as his friends listen. From left to right are Alexandre Dumas, Victor Hugo, George Sand, Niccolò Paganini, Gioachino Rossini, and Mademoiselle d'Agoult. In the background are Beethoven's bust and Lord Byron's portrait.

Joseph Danhauser. *Franz Liszt and His Friends.* 1840. Historisches Museum der Stadt Wien. Vienna, Austria.

immersed in their performance. This takes a high degree of concentration. All of their resources of technical ability and expressiveness–their musicianship–have to be brought into play.

What is musical technique? **Technique** is *the facility to perform the music with the correct notes, played (or sung) in tune and in proper rhythm.* This can pose considerable difficulties to the performer. Occasionally a composer will indicate that a piece of music must be played at a tempo so rapid that a performer with only an average technique will not be able to play the notes that fast—at least not without mistakes. Sometimes, for example, Liszt's works call for the pianist to make difficult leaps at high speed, a feat that involves considerable risk of striking the wrong key. Like an ice skater executing a difficult routine, it is easy to slip in spite of all the practice.

▼Activity: *Figure Out*

What makes this music difficult?

Listen to Franz Liszt's piano transcription of Paganini's set of variations on *La Campanella.*

First learn the relatively simple melody that is the basis for this work:

G♯ minor
Allegretto (♩=176)

1. How many times is the melody repeated?
2. What does Liszt do to this melody each time it returns?
3. Why might this be called a variation form?

Mastering technique means that performers conquer the problems of their particular instrument or voice. A piano poses one set of difficulties, a trumpet another, an electronic instrument yet another. A melody of wide leaps, for example, can be difficult to sing but relatively easy to play on a piano or mallet percussion. Fast runs may be fairly simple to play on a violin or flute but extremely difficult on a double bass. A **double bass** is *the largest instrument in the bowed, stringed family.* Moving from pitch to pitch on the long strings of the bass requires a fairly wide and awkward reach between the fingers of the left hand. Then, too, the bass player has to move up and down the full length of the long strings on the instrument to play a scalelike passage. The more physical movement required, the more difficult it is to do it rapidly.

For the musician, playing all the notes correctly and in the proper tempo is just the beginning. Technique itself can be cold, cerebral, and expressionless. In the performance of music, technique must serve musical expression. The performer must capture the spirit of the work and communicate it.

Musical expression is *the feeling the performer brings to the sound.* It is what lies beyond the notes on the page. It is the tasteful choice and combination of tempo, dynamics, tonal shading, phrasing, and musical sense and style that the performer puts into the notes to transform them into sounds that command and stir us. Without musical expression, music would lack the warmth of human emotion. This incredibly important dimension is the performer's creative contribution. Morever, this expression must comply with the intentions of the composer if those intentions have been indicated in the music. If music is not written down, then performers learn it by ear and add their personal touch.

Cooperative Learning

Recognize Virtuosity
Try to recognize virtuosity when you hear it.

Gary Karr, the well-known American double bass virtuoso, has transformed the technique on this instrument, managing to play this instrument as no one has before. Listen to his performance of Edouard Nanny's "Caprice." Working in small groups, discuss the following questions: (1) Is this the timbre you expected from a double bass? (2) Is the double bass capable of musical expression? (3) Can double bass be played as a solo instrument?

◀ Andrés Segovia (1893–1987), the great Spanish guitarist, made his debut at the age of 15. He was soon touring the world, making the first of many visits to the United States in 1928. His mastery at being able to perform the classical repertoire established the guitar as an instrument worthy of serious musical study.

▼Activity: *Experience an Expressive Melody*

What does a fine performer do to convey the expressiveness of a melody?

Listen to Gary Karr perform the spiritual "Deep River" on the double bass.

1. How does he make his instrument expressive?
2. Does Karr do more than simply play the right notes and rhythms?

Profile

Gary Karr
American Virtuoso
Double Bassist
1941–

GARY KARR

"Music," Karr says, "is a voice that communicates how I feel about life." For Karr, that voice is the double bass—also known as the contrabass, bass viol, string bass, and bass fiddle. Just how does he use his instrument to communicate? "When I play for an audience, I want them to use the sounds of my instrument as a window through which they can witness and share my deepest feelings." How does he know when he has communicated? "When the response of the listeners indicates that they have truly perceived my inner world," he says, "I know that I have been successful."

There have been seven generations of double bassists in Karr's family. No wonder Karr studied the bass. It was the first instrument he saw as a child! "It had a sound I liked more than any other," he says. "I called it a 'chocolate' sound because the same adjectives I used to describe chocolate described my bass sound."

From the age of nine, when he began lessons on a small-sized instrument, Karr has practiced a minimum of two to three hours every day. During high school, he played in professional community orchestras. "At one point," he says, "I was playing in seven different orchestras each week!"

At 15½ Karr got his driver's license. "No one ever needed one more," he says. "Up to then, I had to rely on everyone else for rides, and not all cars had room for a bass!" Now, he travels throughout the world giving concerts and playing with many of the world's symphony orchestras.

The instrument Karr plays, made by Niccolò Amati in 1611, is the oldest fully intact bass in the world. (Amati was the teacher of Antonio Stradivari, the great violin maker.) This instrument was presented to Karr as a gift by the widow of the renowned double bassist Serge Koussevitzky (1874–1951). Eventually, it will become part of the collection of musical instruments in the Karr Double Bass Foundation for use by future musicians.

Quality Performance

How can you tell the difference between a great performance and one that is mediocre? What constitutes a virtuoso performance? Perhaps you have attended an extraordinary musical performance that moved you emotionally. Was the music the only factor that contributed to this, or did the setting, the people you were with, or your feeling toward the performer have something to do with the way you reacted? Your frame of mind at the time of the performance can affect the way you receive and perceive music.

While extraneous factors can affect your judgment, a musical performance should be judged on its own merits. However, it takes a wealth of knowledge and experience to distinguish a great performance from a reasonably good one. Being able to judge musical performance depends on a number of factors:

- **Timbre.** The tone quality or timbre, range, variety, appropriateness, and appeal.
- **Expressiveness.** The interpretation, style, and phrasing.

- **Technique.** The performer's skills in bringing the notes to life.
- **Presentation.** The choice and appropriateness of the music, and whether the performance meets our expectations.
- **Impact.** The artist's charisma, the familiarity or newness of what you hear, and, perhaps, how the performance compares with similar performances you have heard.

▼Activity: *Answer with Your Ears*

What qualities make a performance really fine?

You will hear three guitarists who are considered to be virtuosos. (Their names will be revealed later.) Their performances illustrate three types of guitars, as well as the wide spectrum of musical styles the guitar is uniquely able to express:

1. Classical (6-string Spanish guitar).
2. Folk/Jazz Crossover (12-string acoustic guitar).
3. Heavy Metal Rock (6-string electric guitar).

While you are listening to these performances, analyze their quality. Take notes to help you determine why these three guitarists are regarded as virtuosos.

▼ Vladimir Horowitz (1903–1989) was an American pianist who thrilled audiences by playing the difficult works of Franz Liszt and other classical composers with extraordinary speed, power, and expressiveness. He performed with seeming ease, but the strain of public performance took its toll on his health, causing him to alternately retire and re-emerge. In 1986, after his return from two triumphant concerts in his native Russia, he was awarded the Medal of Freedom, the United States' highest civilian honor.

Being outstanding in any human endeavor is a rare achievement that happens around the world, in all races, and in all countries. Recognizing musical greatness when you hear it requires musical knowledge and the ability to discern quality. One of the ways you can do this is by comparing one performance, or one performer, with another. Through comparison you will be able to distinguish subtle differences. Critics and reviewers often use this technique when they compare one recorded performance with another. You, too, can do this.

▼*Activity:* **Evaluate**

How do your critical judgments compare with the judgments of professional critics?

Listen to two performances of the first movement of Beethoven's Symphony No. 5 in C Minor. Both are conducted by world-famous and widely respected musicians. As you will hear, the performances differ in many ways. Apply what you have learned about perceptive listening and about judging quality. (Try to judge the performance, not the quality of the recordings.)

When you have made some judgments, write a short record review in which you compare these two performances, referring to Orchestra No. 1 and Orchestra No. 2. As a critic, which recording would you recommend to the public and why? Make your review approximately two paragraphs long.

When you have completed your review, you will have the opportunity to read the critics' reactions to these same recordings when they were first released.

▶ Some performers simply play better than others. No matter what type of music people play, doing it well requires extraordinary effort and ability. Rock performers work very hard at what they do. Eddie Van Halen is an example of a rock musician who has strived for greatness.

Profile

Arturo Toscanini
Italian-American Conductor
1867–1957

ARTURO TOSCANINI

Arturo Toscanini began his formal musical studies at the age of nine when he enrolled in the Royal Conservatory of Music in his home town of Parma, Italy. By the time he was 13, he was playing cello professionally. When he left the conservatory at 18, he joined a traveling opera company. One evening while on tour in Rio de Janeiro, he left the cello section to conduct from memory Verdi's opera *Aïda*, a feat that caused a sensation and launched his conducting career.

Toscanini challenged the popular Romantic conducting style of the era by performing works as literally as possible. Instead of expressing his own ideas and emotions through a work, Toscanini attempted to convey the spirit of the composer. Scoffing at political and historical interpretations of Beethoven's *Eroica* Symphony, he exclaimed, "Bah! For me it is simply con brio" (full of spirit).

Despite the varying political and musical climates that raged around him (he left Italy when the fascists gained power), Toscanini remained true to his idealistic vision of music throughout his 70-year career. In 1926, during the premiere of Puccini's unfinished opera *Turandot* at La Scala opera house in Milan, Italy, Toscanini put down his baton, faced the audience, and at the point at which Puccini's work ended and another composer's completion of it began, stated, "Here the master laid down his pen." Toscanini also conducted and directed at the Metropolitan Opera and conducted the New York Philharmonic and the NBC (National Broadcasting Company) Symphony.

The success of Toscanini's adherence to literal performance of compositions greatly influenced the direction of European music in the 1900s. No longer were conductors expected to create flamboyant arrangements. No longer was music equated with arbitrariness and interpretation. When Toscanini conducted Debussy or Wagner, it was straightforward and structurally precise.

Summary

We can admire the ski jumper without being able to ski. We can imagine the courage it takes to head down the steep slope and leap into the air. We can see how difficult it would be to maintain control, stretch for distance in the wind, and land with smoothness and ease. Just as we can put ourselves in the place of a skier to sense that achievement, we can assume the viewpoint of a musician to realize musical accomplishment. Understanding the difficulties that must be overcome—the technique that is involved—can help us relate to it and be moved by the experience.

What makes a musical performance great? The more we know about music, the better we will be able to answer this question. We know that a quality performance depends on a performer's timbre, technique, and expressiveness. Does the performer make sense out of the music? Does the performance command our interest and move us? Behind every great musical performance there is the force of a human personality and charisma. Ultimately, it is the humanity that is expressed that reaches out to captivate, enchant, and spellbind us. The performer's personality is one of the intangibles that makes music so fascinating, so surprising, so intriguing, so mystifying. A great performance can be analyzed and explained up to a point; then there is that extra something that can touch us—we know not why.

CHAPTER 8

Alone and Together

Objectives

By completing this chapter, you will:

- Find out how people make music alone and together.
- Discover Native American flute music.
- Become familiar with the basic textures of music.
- Be able to describe the characteristics of the concerto.
- Understand the problem of coordination and how it is solved.
- Conduct in meters of 2, 3, and 4.

Musical Terms

call and response
canon
conductor
counterpoint
imitation
monophony
neumes
polychoral music
polyphony
round
solmization
texture

*M*usic can be a solitary act—a person playing
a guitar or shakuhachi, or singing alone unaccompanied.
You have probably whistled, hummed, sung, or even
played an instrument by yourself, when you had the
privacy to express yourself musically without feeling
the pressure to perform or having the fear of being
criticized. During these private moments, music
becomes a means of personal expression. We speak
through it, and it speaks back to us in a very
intimate way. We can lose ourselves in its magic.

Music as Solo Expression

Throughout the ages and in all cultures, people have been compelled
to make music by themselves. We have an inner need to express ourselves,
to get in touch with our inner feelings and spirit. In this sense, making
music is similar to writing a poem, making a sketch, or dancing alone.

People enjoy expressing themselves through solo musical performance.
The sound of a single voice or instrument can be haunting in its beauty.
There is an intensity about focusing on one timbre and one pitch at a time.

◀ Solo as well as group
performance is common in most
cultures. The kaen, a Laotian mouth
organ, may have six, fourteen, or
sixteen bamboo pipes in a wood
or ivory wind chamber. It comes
in three sizes, the largest of which
has pipes that are 10 feet long.
The player blows into the wind
chamber and elicits sound from
individual pipes by covering
the finger holes. One pipe may
be played alone or several may be
sounded at one time. Instruments
of this kind were first described in
China about 3,000 years ago.

▼Activity: *Identify Expressive Qualities*

Which qualities are unique to a solo performance of a folk song?

Read this famous text "Danny Boy" written by Fred E. Weatherly:

Oh, Danny Boy, the pipes, the pipes are calling—
From glen to glen, and down the mountain side,
The summer's gone and all the roses falling,
It's you, It's you must go and I must bide.
But come ye back when summer's in the meadow,
Or when the valley's hush'd and white with snow,
It's I'll be here in sunshine or in shadow,
Oh, Danny Boy, Oh, Danny Boy, I love you so.

But when ye come, and all the flow'rs are dying,
If I am dead, as dead I well may be,
Ye'll come and find the place where I am lying,
And kneel and say an Ave there for me.
And I shall hear, though soft you tread above me,
And all my grave will warmer, sweeter be,
For you will bend and tell me that you love me,
And I shall sleep in peace, until you come to me.

What one word might describe the emotive meaning of the poem? Discuss the references to the seasons of the year.

Listen to two versions of this famous song. The first version is sung by a professional tenor from England. The second version is sung by a choir. Which version do you think is more expressive? Why?

Native American Flute Music

The flute is the one melodic instrument widely used by Native Americans, and it is always played as a solo instrument. Native Americans use a large variety of flutes of different sizes, shapes, and materials. Most are end-blown with from three to six finger holes to vary the pitch. The flutes are made of various woods, cane, animal bones, and even sawed-off gun barrels!

According to legends the flute was given to the Indian people by the Creator for enjoyment, to ease loneliness, and for other important purposes. Some tribes used the flute as a courting instrument. When a man wanted to attract a woman, he would sit outside of her home and play the flute. If she was interested in him, she would come outside and sit next to him as he played. If she wished to reject his advances, she would remain inside. Other tribes used the flute for quiet, introspective moments.

During the late nineteenth and early twentieth centuries, Native American flute playing nearly became extinct, along with other rich cultural expressions—language, music, dance, art, and knowledge of herbal medicine. Fortunately, many tribes were able to cling to their culture. Today, there is a resurgence of interest among young Native Americans in preserving tribal traditions.

Cooperative Learning

Determine the Mood

In small groups, listen to the following solo instrumental performances, gauge the mood of each, then discuss to see if you agree.

1. The first is a performance of the Japanese *shakuhachi* (sha-ku-HAH-chee), a vertical bamboo flute with five holes (for four fingers and a thumb). The piece is entitled "Hifumi hachigaeshi" (hee-foo-mee ha-chee-gah-eh-see) ("One, two, three, return the bowl").

2. The second is a performance of the *kaen* (can), an instrument in Thailand and Laos that is a cousin of the harmonica. It is constructed of wood and bamboo. It has as many as 16 bamboo tubes, each with a small brass reed set into the wall, so that more than one tone can be sounded at the same time. The piece is "Maeng poo dawn dawk" ("Bees among the flowers").

◀ Flutist John Rainer, Jr., is a member of the Taos Pueblo in New Mexico. His playing, like that of many contemporary Native American flutists, has a lyrical and expressive quality. He enriches the melody with ornaments that suggest bird calls and echoes in deep canyons.

▼ Activity: *Visualize the Melody*

Listen to the performance by John Rainer, Jr., of the traditional Native American song "Northern Plains" and try to visualize the shape or contour of the melody.

This traditional song is normally sung by Native American performing groups called *Drums*. They perform this and other songs at pow wows, particularly among tribes located in the northern plains states. It is an exciting and energetic song and dance, which is adapted for the flute in this recording.

The melody consists of four phrases—A, B, and C—that correspond to the breaths the performer takes (C takes two breaths). Listen to each phrase and try to visualize its contour based on the highness or lowness of the pitches in the melody. Pick out the appropriate general contour for each phrase: (1) descending (moving downward), (2) ascending (moving upward), or (3) level. (*Hint:* Two answers are correct for phrase C.)

On a sheet of paper, draw a line graph to represent the contour of each phrase. Note that the starting pitch of each successive phrase is lower than the previous one.

The tradition of flute playing has been part of this cultural renewal. Native Americans from various tribes now make, play, and sell old-style flutes. The music they perform combines old and new styles. It includes traditional flute songs; tribal songs adapted to the flute; Christian hymns and other non-Native music; and contemporary compositions performed in ensemble with electronic synthesizers, electric guitar, and percussion.

Music as Social Expression

Another important function of music is its use as a form of group expression and social communication. Performing music with other people has its own special satisfactions and rewards. People generally enjoy working together toward a goal that could not be achieved alone. A solo trumpeter, for example, cannot produce harmony or incorporate the expressiveness of another instrumental tone color. That would take another performer. If the goal is to enrich the texture of the music, other people are usually required.

Organizing people to function together in a cooperative and orderly manner is not always easy. To create a unified statement, the group must be thoroughly coordinated. In music, people have managed to achieve this cooperative group expression—called ensemble—in a number of ways. Perhaps the most obvious solution is to have everyone sing the same melody together monophonically, that is, in unison with everyone sounding the same note or octave at the same time.

Another way people make music together is by combining solo and choral response. **Call and response** *follows a simple question-and-answer pattern in which a soloist leads and a group responds.* It is part of the oral tradition—the way music was passed along from person to person and from one generation to the next. Crews on board the old sailing ships had leaders who called out the verses while the others sang the repeated response.

The soloist must know the changing lyrics and be able to sing the more complex melody that sometimes goes with them. The group usually has a simple response that is repeated each time. This way, the group has the part that can be learned rapidly and is easy to remember, enabling them to join in quickly and participate with confidence. The call-and-response form of coordination is found in spirituals and gospel music, and can be heard in the music from Africa and from other cultures. Its influence today can be heard in jazz, blues, rock, rap, folk songs, and backup vocal responses.

Homophonic Texture

Musical **texture** refers to *how the sounds are woven together.* Like fabric, music can be almost transparent, or relatively dense. Generally, the more parts in the music, the more complex and dense the texture.

We can think of music horizontally with different melodies sounding together at the same time, or we can think of music vertically with clumps

---

Cooperative Learning

Create a Call-and-Response Song

Invent your own call-and-response song.

Listen to "Oh Happy Day," a call-and-response gospel song that was made famous in the early 1970s by the Edwin Hawkins Singers. Focus on the alternation of verse and chorus. The first chorus is repeated once before the verse. As you listen to the song, learn the lyrics and try to audiate the responses in answer to Hawkins's call. Then answer these questions:

1. How many responses did you audiate in the first chorus?
2. Are all the responses exact repetitions of the call? If not, where did the divergence occur?
3. Does the verse use call and response?

Listen to this song again so you can use it as the basis for creating your own call-and-response song. In small groups of students, invent a simple call-and-response song that you could sing to the melody of "Oh Happy Day." Use a patriotic theme, or a current topic, rather than a spiritual theme.

of notes accompanying one melody. Much of the music we hear today, including popular music, is of the latter sort. It consists of a melody supported by a chordal accompaniment, that is, homophony ("homophonic" means "same" or "similar" sounding). "Oh Happy Day" is homophonic in texture; one melody predominates, and the voices join together to give that melody a chordal accompaniment.

During the seventeenth century, composers studied the vertical aspects of music closely and discovered certain combinations of notes on each tone of the scale that sounded well together. They called them triads. By using these triads, or chords, to accompany a melody, composers further developed homophonic texture.

Triads in the scale of C major:

This new chordal system gave composers a whole new range of harmonic expression that is still being explored today.

Homophonic or chordal music can be performed on keyboard instruments by solo performers. Usually, a pianist or an organist plays the melody with the right hand and the chordal accompaniment with the left hand. Today, one singer alone can mimic this style of music by recording multiple soundtracks and superimposing them to create a melody and its accompaniment. This can be heard in Bobby McFerrin's 1988 hit song "Don't Worry, Be Happy" in which he wrote and performed all the parts himself. Instead of using traditional instruments for the accompaniment, he simulated their sounds with his voice.

The Concerto

Another way to contrast solo and group performance is in a musical form known as the concerto. In a concerto, a soloist, or a solo group of instrumentalists, is set off against the larger orchestra. Here the skill is in realizing the expressive potential of the lone instrument (or solo group), the orchestra, and their combination. There is much give-and-take between the contrasting forces, including the exchange of themes. Sometimes the orchestra accompanies the soloist; sometimes the soloist plays along with the orchestra; sometimes they play individually. Sometimes they are friends, sometimes rivals, which sets up a tension that can be exciting to see resolved. This conflict and its resolution can be compared to the real-life situation in which an individual struggles for acceptance by the group, or a leader fights to win the support of the people. There are usually three movements in a concerto, so there is ample time to explore the various contrasting textures and timbres. For example, a cello solo might be contrasted with the woodwinds, high strings, or full orchestra.

▼*Activity:* **Map the Forces**

Listen to the first movement of Mozart's Horn Concerto No. 3 and identify the different musical forces as they perform.

As you listen, create a map of the music that shows the basic relationship between the horn soloist and the orchestra. Sometimes each plays alone; sometimes they play together. There is a tension and drama in the interplay between them. Categorize the relationship using the following codes:

A = orchestra alone

B = French horn solo with orchestral accompaniment

C = cadenza, a French horn solo without accompaniment

After you have completed your map, use it to answer the following questions:

1. Are all of the sections of equal length?
2. Can you detect any repetition?
3. Which sections (by number) seem to create the most intensity and drive?
4. Which section was the most different? Use musical descriptors to help define the unique character of this section.
5. What is the basic pattern of the first movement of this concerto?

The Problem of Coordination

The concerto is a good example of how contrasting timbres can be used in one piece of music to create tension and excitement. If we were limited to hearing all our music played on a saxophone (or any other instrument), we would become bored. We need a variety of timbres to maintain our interest.

People were not always able to combine different timbres to make music as interesting or as expressive as it is today. During the early Middle Ages, people had not yet developed a way to coordinate different instruments and melodies. Their music was monophonic (*mono* means "one," *phonic* means "sounds"). Strictly speaking, **monophony** *consisted of a single melodic line without accompaniment.* The underlying rhythmic meter that we take for granted in our music had not been invented. Without it, performers found it difficult to stay together, even when everyone was singing or playing one melody!

Nonetheless, medieval composers were determined to find a way to combine different sounds to broaden the range of musical expression. Since singing and playing together required a way to coordinate the performers, the simplest kind of organization—everyone singing the same tune—was tried first. You can still hear this effect in Gregorian chants. Then they got more adventurous. They tried having one part of the group sing the same melody simultaneously, but at the interval of a fourth above. This early attempt at creating harmony was known as parallel organum.

▼*Activity:* **Go Back in Time**

Given the absence of any formal rhythmic structure, how did a medieval choir deal with the problem of coordination?

As a class, pretend you are members of a monastic choir in the eleventh century. Learn to perform the Gregorian chant (or plainsong) "Hymn to St. John."

1. Practice saying the words of the Latin text until the stresses fall naturally.
2. Play the pitches of the hymn while saying the words. Let the flow of notes follow the flow of the text. Gradually start to sing the words, but resist feeling any steady pulse.
3. Perform together as a class, remembering to stress the first syllable of each line of text as you feel it and sense it together. Performers had to listen very carefully to each other to sense the flow.

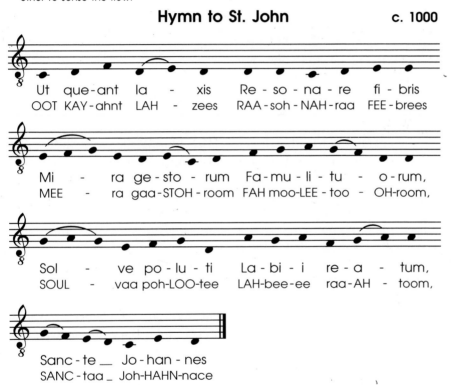

Hymn to St. John   c. 1000

Ut que-ant la - xis   Re - so - na - re   fi - bris
OOT KAY-ahnt LAH - zees   RAA-soh-NAH-raa   FEE-brees

Mi - ra ge-sto - rum   Fa-mu-li-tu - o-rum,
MEE - ra gaa-STOH-room   FAH moo-LEE - too - OH-room,

Sol - ve po-lu - ti   La - bi-i   re-a - tum,
SOUL - vaa poh-LOO-tee   LAH-bee-ee   raa-AH - toom,

Sanc-te __ Jo-han - nes
SANC-taa _ Joh-HAHN-nace

Now perform the hymn in parallel organum. To create a fuller sound, members of a monastic choir added another part, which sang the same melody, four notes higher or five notes lower, or both. The result is parallel organum. Assign half the class to perform the "Hymn to St. John" at the higher (or lower) level. Note that the voices converge at the end.

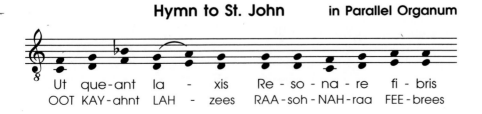

Hymn to St. John   **in Parallel Organum**

Ut que-ant la - xis   Re - so - na - re   fi - bris
OOT KAY-ahnt LAH - zees   RAA-soh-NAH-raa   FEE-brees

Mi - ra ge-sto-rum Fa-mu-li-tu-o-rum,
MEE - ra gaa-STOH-room FAH moo-LEE-too-OH-room,

Sol - ve ___ po-lu-ti La-bi-i re-a-tum,
SOUL - vaa ___ poh-LOO-tee LAH-bee-ee raa-AH-toom,

Sanc-te ___ Jo-han-nes
SANC-taa ___ Joh-HAHN-nace

The chants used in the church services during the early Middle Ages had to be learned by rote. Committing them to memory was a long and arduous process. Sometime during the sixth to the eighth centuries a method of notation was invented that placed **neumes** (*neume* is the Greek word for "sign"), or *marks over the words.* These squiggles showed the singers the direction of the melodic line. The neumes reminded the singers, provided they already knew the basic melody.

The neumes were eventually placed above and below a line that signified a definite pitch. This line provided singers with a general idea of how the pitches related to one another. From this beginning, a four-line staff was developed and, finally, the five-line staff that is still used today. By assigning individual lines and spaces to specific pitches, singers were able to sing unfamiliar melodies from a musical score.

To help his choristers learn to sing more easily, Guido of Arezzo (c. 991–1033), an Italian Benedictine monk and music theorist, devised a system of **solmization**, *a method of sight singing by syllables.* This method forms the basis of our modern DO-RE-MI system of solfège or sight-singing. In order to help his choristers remember the various tones of the scale when singing plainsong, Guido used the well-known "Hymn to St. John" as a memory aid. Since the melody of each phrase of the hymn begins one tone higher than the previous phrase, the corresponding six tones (represented by the syllables UT, RE, ME, FA, SOL, LA) could be extracted from the hymn and applied to the tones of the scale:

UT   RE   MI   FA   SOL   LA

Guido found that by associating these syllables with the scale degrees, people were able to read music. Eventually UT was changed to DO and a seventh tone (SI or TI) was added to create our seven-tone major or diatonic scale. This method of sight-singing was used in monasteries throughout the Middle Ages, and is still taught in schools in the United States and elsewhere. It continues to be one of the basic skills taught to musicians.

Polyphonic Texture

The capacity to notate music and give it a rhythmic structure permitted the development of polyphony in the twelfth century. Polyphony literally means "many sounds." In this style of composition, the voices could sing more than one melody at the same time and even enter at different times! Time was brought into control and music was given order. The various horizontal parts or melodies could be combined, yet still function quite independently, just as threads of different colors can be woven to create a more interesting texture.

The invention of polyphonic music created so many new expressive possibilities that composers explored and continued to develop this way of putting sounds together for the next five centuries! At the height of these developments in the sixteenth and seventeenth centuries, composers throughout Europe and England were composing polyphonic music that was highly expressive and complex. One result of being able to coordinate multiple parts is the elaborate textures that became possible when more than one choir or instrumental group performed together.

▼ The Italian painter Gentile Bellini (1429–1507) painted contemporary life in Venice during the Renaissance. *Procession in St. Mark's Square* contains a choir and a band of instrumentalists. Can you find them? The Basilica of St. Mark dominates the square in the background.

Gentile Bellini. *Procession in St. Mark's Square.* 1496. Academy, Venice, Italy.

Profile

Giovanni Gabrieli
Italian Composer
c. 1553–1612

GIOVANNI GABRIELI

Giovanni Gabrieli was an influential figure in the transition of European music from the Renaissance style to the Baroque style in the late sixteenth and early seventeenth centuries. Gabrieli first composed in a straightforward Renaissance style. However, as he matured, he explored the latest musical techniques and invented many of his own. He was among the first to create vocal works with instrumental accompaniment. He became known for his imaginative polychoral style in which two or more choirs sang in alternating (and often overlapping) dialogue. Many of his large-scale works are published in the multiple volumes of his *Sacrae symphoniae.*

Giovanni Gabrieli was born around 1553 in Venice, where his uncle, Andrea Gabrieli served as the organist at the Basilica of St. Mark. Gabrieli probably benefitted by his uncle's teaching, and in 1575 he accepted a musical position at the court of a duke in Munich. Around the age of 30, he returned to Venice where he competed for, and won, the position of organist at St. Mark's, following in his uncle's footsteps. There, his duties as a composer of ceremonial and religious music allowed him to create musical works of a magnificence befitting the basilica and the bustling port city of Venice, chief link between Europe and Asia. In the early years of the seventeenth century, his instrumental music was the finest of its time.

In the great seaport of Venice, the center of commerce between the East and the West, polyphonic music gave splendid voice to the pageantry and celebration that were so much a part of Venetian life. At the Byzantine Basilica of St. Mark, Giovanni Gabrieli composed **polychoral music**—*music for several choirs singing in answer to each other across the huge recesses of the church.* Substituting instruments for voices, Gabrieli composed music for alternating choirs of brass instruments such as the world had never heard. This new polyphonic dialogue produced grand and dramatic sonorities that matched the splendor and richness of the architecture and the festive atmosphere of the city.

▼*Activity: Visit Venice Around 1600!*

Listen to *Canzon in Double Echo* by the Italian Renaissance composer Giovanni Gabrieli as it might have sounded in the Basilica of St. Mark in the first decade of the seventeenth century.

This work is performed by three brass quintets—15 instruments in all. Each choir consists of two trumpets, a French horn, a trombone, and a tuba. Try to hear how the second and third choirs echo the first.

1. Does Gabrieli's interweaving of many parts create an expressive musical texture?
2. Is there contrast?
3. Why is a steady pulse so important in this music?

The history of European or Western music is primarily an account of the development of various music textures. With the development of musical notation and a common rhythmic system, musicians could finally combine different melodies, rhythms, and timbres. To be sure, they took their steps one at a time and explored these new possibilities thoroughly before venturing further. During the time of Columbus, the explorers, and the development of European trade and commerce, polyphony made music a major form of human expression.

While European composers during the Renaissance created much new and beautiful music, people in other parts of the world were also busy making music. Unfortunately, written history does not provide accounts about music making during this period in Middle Eastern, African, or other major civilizations. It is interesting that the basic idea of **polyphony**, *the simultaneous combination of different melodies and rhythms*, is characteristic of some African music. Polyphony, therefore, could have been practiced in Africa as early as it was in Europe, or even earlier. Obviously, people wanted to combine sounds to form more interesting and more expressive textures, and they found their own ways of doing it.

▼Activity: *Discover Polyphonic Texture*

Can you identify the sources of sound in this African polyphony?

The Ba-Benzele pygmies of the Central African Republic in the equatorial region of West Africa sing this music to accompany a dance in which both men and women participate. Try to hear the principal melody that uses only three pitches, and listen for a variety of other melodies that are sung at the same time. As you listen, answer the following questions:

1. How many different sound sources are there? What are they?
2. Approximately how many singers are performing?
3. How do you suppose the members of this pygmy tribe learned this music? When they perform this piece, does it always sound exactly the same?
4. Why is this music polyphonic?

By the fourteenth century, European composers began to relate the various vocal parts by having them exchange melodies or parts of melodies. When one voice borrowed or suggested the tune of another, that voice imitated the other. The use of **imitation**, *exact repetition or resemblance between the parts*, helped to organize the piece by giving it a sense of consistency and order. One of the most remarkable and ingenious examples of this device of having the different parts share the same melody can be heard in a round or canon. You may have sung the rounds "Three Blind Mice" or "Row, Row, Row Your Boat." In a **round** or **canon**, *the same melody is started at different times and sounded together.* These parts imitate each other exactly. Usually the melody is notated once and the various points of entry are indicated by numbers. The secret of writing a canon is to make it work within itself, and this takes some strict rules. The term canon means rule or law.

▼*Activity:* **Perform a Canon**

Learn to perform the old Latin prayer for peace *Dona Nobis Pacem* as a canon (see page 79).

This melody is actually a canon or round. The same tune can be sung in three parts simultaneously. First try it in two parts by dividing the class in half. When the first part reaches 2, the second part enters at 1. Keep a steady beat so that you can stay together!

Now try it in three parts by dividing the class into three sections. Sing as before; but when the first part reaches 3 and the second part reaches 2, the third part enters at 1.

This is a good example of polyphonic texture—different melodies (in this instance, different parts of the same melody) sounding together.

By the sixteenth century, composers were creating polyphonic music by using **counterpoint**, *a system of countering one note or point against another.* Different melodies were cleverly interwoven to create a uniform texture. To give a work cohesiveness—the quality of making all the parts hold together—composers often made melodic motives that occurred in one part recur in other parts. This technique is known as imitative counterpoint. The highest development of polyphonic or contrapuntal music was attained in the works of Johann Sebastian Bach. Imitation and counterpoint today appear in various guises in all kinds of music. Arrangements of pop music, for example, often incorporate imitation; a melody played by one instrument is taken up later by another.

Conducting

Around the time of Ludwig van Beethoven (1770–1827), when orchestras began to grow in size, it became essential to have someone in front of the musicians to keep them together. This person became known as the **conductor**, *the director of the orchestra, choir, or other performing group.* Conductors do more than just beat time. In addition to maintaining the beat with a baton, conductors interpret the music as it unfolds. They make important musical decisions regarding such expressive matters as tempo, dynamics, spirit, and phrasing. Conductors give visual clues to the performers to help them play as one force and make a unified statement. These gestures often help the audience understand and feel the music as well.

Conductors are the musical leaders of their group. Their instrument is a chorus or an orchestra. They determine the programming, select the music, and rehearse the performers in the repertoire so that there is agreement about how the various works are to be performed. Conductors inspire the group to perform at their highest level and with appropriate feeling. They must exercise sufficient authority and leadership ability to pull all the musicians together and make them perform as one. This means conductors have to know the music very well. The conductor is the key to effective musical communication.

Conducting requires a technique and a superb sense of rhythm. Conductors indicate the meter of the music by beating a pattern that shows the number of beats in a measure and the tempo or speed of those beats. The first beat of each measure (on the count of one) is always straight down—the strongest motion the arm can make. Conductors follow this downbeat with patterns for the other beats (2, 3, 4 or more) ending with an upbeat that prepares them again for the downbeat of one. The patterns are not difficult to learn. The real skill is to beat these patterns and interpret the music at the same time!

▼Activity: *You, the Conductor*

Pretend you are a conductor preparing for an upcoming performance. Rehearse your musicians.

Follow the diagrams and practice beating these patterns:

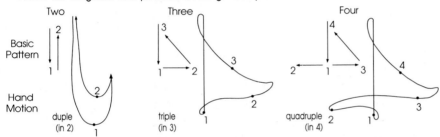

KEEP hand between Your chin AND Waste.

The musical works you will hear are in duple, triple, and quadruple meter. Listen to each example, decide what the meter is, then practice conducting it.

Show differences in tempo (how fast you beat the pattern), dynamics (how big you make the pattern), and articulation (whether the pattern is smooth or clipped—legato or staccato).

Summary

People perform music alone and in groups. A single voice or instrument can be highly expressive and moving. Sometimes a soloist will perform with a group, creating contrast and tension that is dramatic and exciting. The call-and-response form of singing is common in Africa and in the gospel music of African Americans. Another form of it, the concerto, usually features the interplay between a solo instrument and a group of instruments. Putting together a variety of sounds adds impact to our musical expression.

Learning how to coordinate a musical group took a considerable amount of ingenuity. It took hundreds of years and the inventiveness of many musicians and composers to develop a system of musical notation, the concept of an underlying meter, and a means of sight-singing. These systems had to be developed before people could perform different melodies at the same time. Homophonic and polyphonic textures represent two expressive ways we have learned to put sounds together. Today, the conductor plays a major role in this coordination process, helping people perform together with ease and inspiration.

Apply What You Have Learned
Chapter 5

Try to make your vocal style appropriate to the musical style.

Sing the melody and words to "Amazing Grace" in the classical, jazz, gospel, and pop versions (see pages 86–89) with the appropriate vocal style and inflection (changes in tone, dynamics, and modulation of the voice). Decide how the various versions should be interpreted to be consistent with their styles. Note the differences in the melody line and rhythm.

Extra credit: Set up a mini-recording lab with a tape recorder and microphone and record your voice singing in the style of one of the taped accompaniment versions of "Amazing Grace."

Listen to the tape recordings of members of the class. Using the musical descriptors you developed for each of the styles, decide which of the performances is most suitable and appropriate.

Apply What You Have Learned
Chapter 6

How clearly can you express your opinion about a recorded performance?

Here are some basic guidelines for writing your first music review:

1. Select a recording that you believe is particularly good or notably bad. Review the entire recording, describing the variety of music it contains. Highlight the compositions you feel are well performed.
2. Take a stance—either positive or negative. Make it clear to the reader where you stand and why.
3. Refer to the "color words" you listed in your analysis of the Perlman reviews. Use this list as a starting point for your writing. Add words to the list that describe the music.
4. Resist saying what you think. Include some informed opinion and authority in your review.
5. Write a minimum of three paragraphs, but no more than two pages.

Apply What You Have Learned
Chapter 7

Can you distinguish a difference in quality when comparing performances?

In both pairs of performances you will hear, one of the performers is acclaimed to be among the best of his kind, the other is not. Your job is to pick the virtuoso, regardless of whether you like the music or not. You probably will not know the names of the artists or the pieces they are performing. Judge both pairs of performances on the merits of their performance alone.

Comparison 1

Performer A: Recorded in a studio with synthesized sounds
Performer B: Recorded live with a jazz quartet

Comparison 2

Performer C: Lied (song) by Franz Schubert, recorded in German
Performer D: Lied (song) by Franz Schubert, recorded in German

Apply What You Have Learned
Chapter 8

Listen to the musical excerpts and name the textures of these solo and group performances.

The musical examples you will hear are woven together in a number of basic ways:

A. monophonic **E.** polyphonic
B. call and response **F.** parallel organum
C. unison chant **G.** canonic
D. homophonic **H.** heterophonic

Write down the letter or letters for the terms that best describe the music in each example.

Music!...
To Enhance
Expression

~

Chapter 9
The Power of Emotion

Chapter 10
The Beauty of Order

The Power of Emotion

Objectives

By completing this chapter, you will:

- Find out how music stirs our emotions.
- Discover that music, like science and mathematics, is a symbolic system of communication.
- Learn that you can respond to a wide range of music.
- Become familiar with the Balinese gamelan orchestra and the music of the *Barong Dance*.
- Become acquainted with German Romanticism and the music of the Romantic period.

Musical Terms

a cappella
gamelan
Requiem Mass
Romantic period
symphony

$\mathcal{M}$usic and the other arts play a special role in every society providing us contact with the intuitive, mysterious, and emotional realms of life that logic is hard-pressed to explain. In this way, music balances the part of us that is logical, rational, and factual, with the part of us that is imaginative, sensitive, and spiritual.

What Music Expresses

Music is the way we give concrete representation to such inner mental states as love, grief, faith, hope, loss, struggle, loneliness, anxiety, yearning, triumph, jealousy, joy, and a host of other feelings. Music is the way we get our feelings and intuitions outside ourselves in a form in which they can be expressed and communicated. Music permits us to capture, share, and even store perceptions about our feelings or emotions that might otherwise escape us. No art has more emotional impact than music, and none is harder to describe in words. What music conveys to us is largely indescribable. If words could tell us what music expresses, there would be no need for music. Like words, music is a symbolic system of communication completely different from any other. What words can do in music is help us share our insights about it. One thing is certain: music evokes our feelings because we process it intellectually.

◄ The Japanese artist Katsushika Hokusai (1760–1849) created drama and emotion by depicting the frailty of the tiny oarsmen under the threat of a towering, sinister wave. Only Mount Fuji is still. Everything else is in motion, much like music.

Katsushika Hokusai, *Under the Wave Off Kanagawa.* 1823–1829. The Metropolitan Museum of Art, New York, New York. The Henry L. Phillips Collection, Bequest of Henry L. Phillips, 1939.

Analyze Musical Characteristics

Analyze why your favorite piece of music moves you. First make your selection, and then determine how it creates its magic. Answer these questions: (1) What musical characteristics affect you? (2) What other factors influence you? For example: Did you hear and see a performance of this music live or in a music video? Do the words have special meaning? Do you associate this music with a special event? (3) What aspects of the performance and the performers make you react to this music?

A symbol is something that stands for or represents another thing. We can describe an Egyptian pyramid in geometric terms and by giving its mathematical measurements. A photograph or painting of a pyramid might be equally revealing. Each of these forms of representation—mathematical and graphic—are symbolic. They are not the pyramid itself, but rather a representation of it in another form that helps us grasp what it is.

Music is a symbolic system, too. Like numbers, scientific formulas, and words, music represents something else. Science can explain a sunrise; music expresses its emotive meaning. The earth turning on its axis every 24 hours is one part of the truth about a sunrise; the exhilaration we feel at the birth of a new day is another part of the meaning or truth of a sunrise. The British critic Herbert Read once said, "Art is the representation, science the explanation—of the same reality." But the arts and the sciences relate different aspects of that reality. That is why, together, they give a more complete picture than either one alone. We need all these ways to express our understanding of the world because no one way can say it all.

▶ Someone once said, "A picture is worth a thousand words." A sunrise can be described; it can also be captured and interpreted by an artist, in this case, a photographer at Yosemite National Park in California. Music too can convey a sunrise, evoking its emotional aspects—the hope and wonder of a new day.

▼Activity: *Experience a Musical Sunrise*

Listen to the opening "Sunrise" of *Also sprach Zarathustra* by Richard Strauss (1864–1949).

How does this music represent a sunrise? Compare and contrast the following three musical depictions:

1. "Daybreak" from *Daphnis and Chloé* by Maurice Ravel.
2. "Sunrise" from *Also sprach Zarathustra* by Richard Strauss.
3. "Sunrise" from *The Grand Canyon Suite* by Ferde Grofé.

Which setting is the most subtle? Which is the most literal? Why?

As a symbolic system, music permits us to express and communicate the truth of our inner being. It allows us to explore those mysterious, illusive, and imaginative worlds of meaning that we do not fully understand.

Various types of music move us in different ways. Some music is light-hearted; some is more serious, even profound. Some is emotional; some is cerebral. In fact, the emotions expressed through music encompass a range that extends well beyond what most of us experience in a normal day, perhaps even in our lifetime. Music confronts us with feelings that are similar to those we have experienced, and those that are unlike any we have ever known. Through music we can experience certain kinds of feelings for the first time.

▼Activity: *Evaluate Emotional Qualities*

What makes music stir our emotions?

Music makes connections between our head and our heart—between our cognitive, or intellectual, being and our affective, or emotional, state. These two domains work together. Often, they can influence our psychomotor, or physical, state, such as when music makes our heartbeat accelerate or gives us goose bumps or makes us teary-eyed. How does this happen?

Listen to the following three pieces:

1. "Danny Boy," a traditional Irish favorite song sung **a cappella**, *without musical accompaniment.*
2. Second movement of the Piano Concerto No. 21 by Mozart.
3. "The People United Will Never Be Defeated," a Chilean song of solidarity.

For each piece, write down a word or two in the column marked affective that describes the emotions this music brings out in you. Then, in the column marked cognitive, note what you heard in the music that made you react this way. There are no right or wrong answers here. The more attentively you listen, the more powerful you are apt to find this music.

¡El Pueblo Unido Jamás Será Vencido!
By Sergio Ortega

The People United Will Never Be Defeated

De pie, cantar
que vamos a triunfar.
Avanzan ya
banderas de unidad
y tú vendrás
marchando junto a mí.
Y así verás
tu canto y tu bandera
florecer. La luz
de un rojo amanecer
anuncia ya
la vida que vendrá.

Stand up, sing
We are going to triumph.
Flags of unity are advancing now
and you will come
marching together with me.
In this way you'll see
your singing and your flag blossom.
The light
of a red dawn
already announces
the life that will come.

De pie, luchar
el pueblo va a triunfar.
Será mejor
la vida que vendrá
a conquistar
nuestra felicidad.
Y en un clamor
mil voces de combate
se alzarán, dirán,
canción de libertad
con decisión
la patria vencerá.

Stand up, struggle.
the people will triumph.
It will be better
The life that will come
To win
our happiness.
And there will be a clamor
of a thousand embattled voices:
They will speak
a song of freedom.
With determination
the homeland will win.

Y ahora, el pueblo
que se alza en la lucha
con voz de gigante
gritando: ¡adelante!

And now the people
rising up in the struggle
with a great voice
shout "forward!"

La patria está
forjando la unidad.
De norte a sur
se movilizará
desde el salar
ardiente y mineral
al bosque austral
unidos en la lucha
y el trabajo irán,
la patria cubrirán
su paso ya
anuncia el porvenir.

The homeland forging unity
from north to south
will be mobilized
From the fiery salt mine
to the southern forests
united in struggle
and work they will go
They will cover the country,
their step already
announces the future.

De pie cantar
el pueblo va a triunfar.
Millones ya
imponen la verdad.
De acero son
ardiente batallon.
Sus manos van

Stand up, sing
people will triumph
Millions now
impose the truth.
The fiery army
is as steel.
Its hands

Cancionero Canciones Protesta, Bilingual Media Productions.

llevando la justicia	carry justice and reason
y la razón. Mujer	Women with fire
con fuego y con valor	and with courage
ya estás aquí	already you are here
junto al trabajador.	close to the worker.
Y ahora, el pueblo	And now the people
que se alza en la lucha	rising up in the struggle
con voz de gigante	with a great voice
gritando: ¡adelante!	shout "forward!"

Emotion in the Music of Bali

Even when the music of another culture is different from our own, it may communicate its emotional content to us more readily than we might guess. Maybe this is so because, as human beings, we are far more alike than we are different.

The Culture of Bali

Bali is a province of the Republic of Indonesia. Located directly north of Australia, Indonesia stretches east to west for more than 3,000 miles, like a necklace hung from the equator. One thousand of Indonesia's 13,000 islands are settled by 180 million people, making this country the fifth most populated in the world. Bali is approximately 90 miles (145 kilometers) long and 60 miles (97 kilometers) wide with a population of three million people.

The Balinese people are known for their physical beauty and their uniquely ritualistic forms of music, drama, and dance. Although Islam is the predominant religion in Indonesia, the Balinese people are Hindu, and it is their form of Hinduism that inspires all their arts, including music. Males and females of all ages participate in the island's dance traditions. All children learn to dance and sing both in and out of school. Each day, Balinese women prepare elaborate offerings of fruits and flowers to appease the gods. They may decorate the temple grounds for one of the many ceremonies and practice a ballet with the village dance troupe. The life of the Balinese people is simple but artful.

The Music of Bali

Everyone in Bali is an artist. After a busy day in the rice fields, the men gather in the late afternoon to practice with the gamelan orchestra. The **gamelan,** *centerpiece of Balinese music, is an ensemble of 25 performers or more who play on metallophones of several sizes and pitches, gongs of different sizes, cymbals, drums, a flute, and sometimes a simple string instrument.* There are two tuning systems in use on the island, neither one of which corresponds to ours: one divides the octave into seven non-equidistant pitches; the other divides the octave into five evenly spaced tones. Some Balinese metallophones are built in pairs, with one instrument in each pair tuned slightly

▶ In Bali, Indonesia, the Barong is a story told with music and dance. Here men armed with daggers prepare to attack Rangda, the harmful witch-queen, symbol of evil spirits, who is threatening Barong (not shown), the protector of the community and symbol of all that is good. The witch casts a spell that causes the men to turn their blades against their own bodies, but the Barong protects them from inflicting self-harm.

higher than the other. This causes a wavering vibration that is exotic to Western ears. It is said that there are 10,000 orchestras on the island of Bali.

Boys take up the instruments of the gamelan orchestra when they are 10 or 11 and learn "by ear" from the older men. None of the music is written down. Girls take up weaving and continue with dancing. Young men and women dance and act with the gamelan when they have mastered the difficult movements that relate the intricate stories of their religion.

In Bali, there is no dance or drama without music. In the *Barong Dance*, for example, the orchestra accompanies the male and female dancers who portray various animals, humans, and gods. This story, like so many others in the Hindu faith, represents the eternal fight between good and evil. Barong, a mythological tiger played by two men, represents a good spirit, while Rangda, a mythological monkey, represents an evil spirit. For the Balinese, good and evil exist in equal measure in the world. In their drama, good never triumphs over evil. The two are locked in an eternal struggle.

The story of Barong, enacted in elaborate costumes, is told in several acts with many characters—so many, in fact, that the story can become confusing to Westerners. There are many frightening and delightful moments: fights, witchery, sacrifices, marriages, pranks, rescues, and magic. Steeped in these tales from an early age, the Balinese never tire of them. Because of their complexity, there is always something more to learn from them.

▼*Activity:* **Sense the Emotions**

What are the two basic emotions expressed in this music?

Listen to this overture to the *Barong Dance* performed by a gamelan orchestra in a small village in Bali.

- Can you detect two very distinct moods? Can you describe them?
- Is there any repetition?
- How many times does the tempo change?
- What instrument leads the group?

The External Aspects

The external or social aspects of music often help us understand its meaning. Knowing that John Williams's *Liberty Fanfare* was commissioned for the unveiling of the newly refurbished Statue of Liberty on July 4, 1986 (its 100th birthday) helps to put us in the right frame of mind to accept this music on its own terms. Knowing something about the non-musical aspects of the music—the background of the work, the occasion of the performance, the composer, the performer, and so forth—can establish rapport between the listener and the musical work. In this way, historical knowledge enhances our musical understanding.

One of the most electrifying events of the 1980s was the tearing down of the Berlin Wall in November 1989. As the most visible symbol of the cold war between the communist East and the democratic West, the Wall had been an obstruction to freedom for almost three decades. The 29-mile wall around West Berlin was erected by East German authorities in August 1961 to halt the exodus of their citizens to the West. Tearing down the wall was a cause for worldwide celebration: the triumph of freedom over totalitarianism.

◀ On November 22, 1989, the Brandenburg Gate, which marked the division between communist East Berlin and democratic West Berlin, was opened once more. Musicians from both East and West gathered together and performed Beethoven's *Ninth Symphony*, under the direction of Leonard Bernstein, to celebrate the tearing down of the wall that had divided the city for 28 years.

Cooperative Learning

Feel the Emotion

Listen to the fourth movement of Beethoven's *Ninth Symphony*, and imagine it being performed at the Berlin Wall. See if you can understand why it expresses this occasion so well.

Working in small groups, discuss the following:

1. What is there about this music and this theme that is uplifting?
2. Imagine that the singers are people who are celebrating their own newly won freedom. Can you detect their own joy and conviction in the way they perform?
3. Try to follow the text during the performance. Does it help to know the meaning of the words?
4. If possible, listen to the entire fourth movement. Can you sense the tension in the orchestra as it builds to the statement of the "Joy" theme? Does Beethoven alter the "Joy" theme?

To celebrate the overwhelming joy of this event, musicians from East and West assembled in Berlin for a festival of jubilation on New Year's Eve, December 31, 1989. American conductor and composer, Leonard Bernstein, was invited to lead these artists in a performance of Ludwig van Beethoven's *Ninth Symphony* on both sides of the Berlin Wall. The nationalities of the performers reflected the victors and the vanquished in the Second World War (1939–1945), people now united in music to proclaim the harmony of the world.

No other musical work would have celebrated human freedom as well that day. A **symphony** is *an extended work in several movements for orchestra,* but Beethoven added voices. He incorporated Friedrich von Schiller's "Ode to Joy" as the chorale finale of this work. To give special meaning to the occasion, Bernstein had the singers substitute the word *Freiheit* ("freedom") for the term *Freude* ("joy") in Schiller's poem.

The first performance of the *Ninth Symphony* took place 165 years earlier in Vienna in 1824. The four-movement work moves through darkness to light, encompassing the grim and the magnificent, despair and joy. Beethoven, totally deaf when he composed the work, was no stranger to suffering. The fourth movement sings of the triumph of the human spirit over adversity. Beethoven had struggled for months to find the right melody for Schiller's ode. His solution is simple and unforgettable:

The "Joy" theme:

The fourth movement opens with discord. The orchestra appears to be at war with itself, some instruments interjecting with calls for peace. Violence tries to prevail, a strain of the "Joy" theme gently coaxes but is dismissed. It tries to sound again and is rejected. Finally, the theme is stated by the whole orchestra. More rebellion! Then the solo baritone calls for

LUDWIG VAN BEETHOVEN

Ludwig van Beethoven
German Composer
1770–1827

Ludwig van Beethoven, one of the world's greatest composers, was born in Bonn, Germany. He had a childhood of poverty, but from the age of four his father taught him the piano and violin, hoping Ludwig could help increase the family earnings. When he was 17, his mother died leaving him to care for his alcoholic father, his two brothers, and a sister. Fortunately, his talent won him a position in the court orchestra and attracted the support of wealthy patrons. After his studies with Joseph Haydn and others, he became the world's first freelance composer, though his income from his music and teaching barely paid the rent.

Beethoven's artistic output is generally divided into three distinct style periods: the early Vienna years (1792–1802), the middle period (1802–1815), and the final years (1815–1827). In the early years, Beethoven composed music very much in the Classical style. These were also the years that he first noticed his loss of hearing. During the middle period he began to show his true genius, writing some of his most important works, including the *Fifth Symphony*. He showed his great mastery in composing symphonies, sonatas, concertos, and string quartets, although his compositions were the result of great dedication and struggle.

It was during the final years that Beethoven became totally deaf. During this time he wrote the magnificent *Missa Solemnis*, and the *Ninth Symphony*. When he finished conducting his triumphant *Ninth Symphony*, a singer had to tug at Beethoven's shirt sleeve and direct his attention to the audience before he bowed to an ovation he did not hear.

people to join in rejoicing. The basses of the chorus, the solo quartet, and the full orchestra take up the cause. The mood becomes more and more jubilant, rising to shouts of ecstacy—Beethoven's dream of a liberated humanity.

Music permits us to speak with a depth and an emotional power that would not be possible in any other artistic medium. Knowing the external aspects—the historical context of this particular performance and the background of this work and its composer—are the keys that help us unlock the layers of meaning in a musical score. That is why the study of music is so important. Without it, these meanings could not be known or shared.

As exemplified in Beethoven's *Ninth Symphony*, text can add to the emotional impact of music. Words present specific meanings and emotions that are then reinforced by the music. The two, words and music, have to work together if the total expression is to be effective. This is just as true in a simple song as it is in Beethoven's complex symphony. There is an art to the successful marriage of words and music.

All truly effective songs speak from the heart. The words and music meld together to make one unified statement. The performance can make or break this expressive sense of rightness and oneness. A performance should capture this marriage of words and music and make it seem natural and right.

Blind Willie Johnson was born in Texas around 1900. When he was seven years old, he was blinded by his stepmother, who in a fit of rage, threw a pan of lye in his face. Later, as a young man, he survived on the streets of Dallas by his musical talent. However, life was never easy. He had a strong voice, and he learned to accompany himself on guitar by sliding a pocketknife along the strings to create chords. He sang his own blues on the street corners and became a master of slide guitar technique, a way of playing that cut through the clatter on the street. In 1927, Johnson recorded "Dark was the Night." This was at a time in his life when, on a good day, he might earn enough to afford shelter for the night. Otherwise, he slept in the street.

▼*Activity:* **What Makes this Emotional?**

Listen to "Dark was the Night, Cold was the Ground," an early blues song composed and sung by Blind Willie Johnson, and try to grasp its emotional impact.

- Is the spiritual moaning just as effective as words, or more so?
- Does Johnson create empathy for the homeless?
- What does Johnson's slide guitar accompaniment add?
- Does knowing something about Johnson help you to feel the emotion of his music?

The Internal Aspects

When composers want to express themselves, they must choose the particular combination of sounds that will convey their sentiments. These choices include a multitude of musical options—all kinds of melodies, rhythms, and harmonies, plus the voices and instruments to perform them!

The "Dies irae" (DEE-ace ee-RAY) is a Latin medieval poem written sometime during the thirteenth century. The text describes the day of judgment—the terrifying time when life on earth, according to Christian theology, will end and all people will be judged by God for their actions on earth. On this day, humans face either eternal salvation or damnation. This powerful text has served as part of the **Requiem Mass**, or *Mass for the Dead, in the Catholic liturgy.* It has inspired numerous composers, both Catholic and non-Catholic, to capture this ultimate moment in music. The nineteenth-century French composer Hector Berlioz (1803–1869) and the twentieth-century Polish composer Krzysztof Penderecki (b. 1933) were both inspired to create works on this theme using large instrumental and vocal forces. The Berlioz work uses the text to paint a sonic picture of the end of the world, while Penderecki creates a memory of the millions of Jews slaughtered by the Nazis during the Second World War at the concentration camp in Auschwitz, Poland.

▼*Activity:* **Compare**

Listen to the "Dies irae" from Hector Berlioz's *Requiem* (1837) and the "Dies irae" from Krzysztof Penderecki's *Auschwitz Oratorio* (1967). Determine how these composers expressed the Judgment Day theme.

Identify the emotions these works evoke. Specify the musical events you hear that helped to stimulate these reactions. Compare both compositions by answering these questions:

1. In what ways are these works similar musically? In what ways are they different?
2. Do they generate different emotions in the listener?
3. In what ways have both composers made their music reflect the message of a terrifying, final day of judgment?

Romanticism

Music is the language of human feeling. It is always emotive, but during the Romantic period it was especially dramatic and emotional. The **Romantic period**, *which spanned the entire nineteenth century and continued into the early twentieth century, was an era when composers created music that often exploded with emotion.* Composers of this period created supercharged expressions. Romantic music invited the heart to reign.

The Romantic spirit expressed the rise of the middle class, the triumph of the individual. The American Revolution (1776) and the establishment of the new social order in France (1789) affected the entire world. The American Constitution with its appended Bill of Rights and the new French Constitution with its famous preamble, the Declaration of the Rights of Man and Citizen, broke the rule of the old aristocracy. The restraints characterized by the music of Haydn, Mozart, and early Beethoven were cast aside. The feelings, beliefs, and aspirations of the common man would now be heard.

Earlier in the eighteenth century during the Age of Enlightenment, the intellect dominated thinking. We see this in the geometric patterns of the gardens of the Schönbrun Palace in Vienna. Here geometry, not nature, rules. The pattern of every garden and size and color of every tree and plant were planned on paper, then planted. The plants were trained to conform to the perfect order—symmetry and elegance.

While the gardens at Schönbrun Palace are impressive, one can become tired of such rigidity. When rules are strong, humans tend to rebel. The roots of Romanticism lie in just such a revolt against sheer formalism. People sought a more natural order. The design of Central Park in New York City in the nineteenth century illustrates the vast difference in feeling between the Classical and Romantic spirit. There, nature is permitted to assert itself. Romanticism did not impose laws over nature. It set emotions free.

▲ The well-ordered symmetrical gardens of Vienna's Schönbrun Palace, created in the eighteenth century (left), contrast with the freer and more natural treatment of nature in New York's Central Park, created in the nineteenth century (right). They show the difference between the rational thinking of the Classical period and the emotional spirit of the Romantic period.

The problem in the nineteenth century was how far to go with this new freedom. The opposite of complete intellectual rule is complete emotional rule. Both extremes present disadvantages and difficulties. Composers during the nineteenth century reflected their times and gave voice to them. They explored the newly emancipated world of feeling—from delicate and intimate expressions to the most colossal, world-shaking emotional outbursts. (Berlioz's "Dies irae" from the *Requiem* is a good example of the latter.)

Odd as it may seem, with all the freedom to let their hearts speak, Romantic composers were most at home with smaller pieces, usually short descriptive works that allowed them to express their personal feelings. Then, too, longer works presented structural problems that could not be solved very easily without resorting to the ready-made forms of Mozart and Beethoven. But there was another more important reason why Romantic composers chose to write literally thousands of small works. Unlike the composers before them, they were motivated to compose by inspiration. Consequently, they wrote their music on impulse—as quickly as the spirit moved them.

Robert Schumann (1810–1856) was among the first of the new breed of German Romantic composers. In many of his works he created short mood pictures. These highly personal pieces were almost always written for the piano, which he considered the most expressive instrument of the period. His *Carnaval* (*Carnival*) (1834–1835) presents scenes of clowns and dancers interspersed with various masquerading personalities—some imaginary, some real. This work, a suite of character pieces strongly influenced by dance, includes two waltzes, a promenade, and a march. This *Carnaval*, like many real ones, is full of oddities that are not explained; but the imagery can still be felt.

▼*Activity:* **Determine the Character**

What is the character?

Listen to two movements of Robert Schumann's *Carnaval* and try to describe each character the composer is expressing.

1. Describe the mood of "Chopin." It may help to know that Schumann greatly admired the piano compositions of Frédéric Chopin. In this piece, he even imitates Chopin's style.
2. Describe the mood of the characters Harlequin and Colombine. Can you differentiate between the two characters? Can you tell from the music which is the male, and which is the female?

Richard Wagner (VAHG-ner) (1813–1883) was one of the greatest composers of the Romantic period. Success did not come easily for him, and few men have been as vicious to those who offered them help. He rejected the women in his life just as ruthlessly. His was a stormy, egotistical personality, perhaps the epitome of the worst quality of Romanticism: unconstrained emotion. Wagner spent his lifetime borrowing money and eluding his creditors. Despite all his faults, he produced operas—he called them music dramas—of notable power and expressiveness.

One of Wagner's greatest achievements is *The Ring of the Nibelung*, which is based on Nordic legends. This vast work, comprising four full operas, explores just about every human emotion from hate and greed to love and sacrifice—a perfect Romantic tale. Wagner wrote the text of the opera (libretto) as a set of sequels—but backwards! He first wrote the *Death of*

◀ In Wagner's music drama *Siegfried*, the third of the four operas in his *The Ring of the Nibelung*, the young hero slays the dragon and gains possession of the magic ring. The struggle for this ring, which the gods need in order to survive, is the ultimate cause of Siegfried's death in the final opera, *The Twilight of the Gods*. The photo at the left is from the San Francisco Opera's 1984 production of *Siegfried*.

Siegfried, the young hero, which he later renamed *Die Götterdämmerung* (*The Twilight of the Gods*). Then he developed the story that led up to Siegfried's death, which was turned into three other operas: *The Rhine Gold, The Valkyrie,* and *Siegfried.* Wagner created a world where gods and goddesses have all the flaws and feelings that we do—from stealing to falling in love! But these gods have powers and curses and magic that make them super-human. It took Wagner 28 years—from 1848 to 1876—to complete the libretto and the music and to produce the *Ring* cycle.

One of the most dramatic moments in the whole opera is the death of Siegfried. This fearless young man has rescued Brünnhilde from her long sleep by penetrating the ring of magic fire that surrounds her. Later, after drinking a magic potion, he is deceived and falls in love with another woman while pledging Brünnhilde (whom he no longer remembers) to his best friend. By the time his memory is restored, it is too late. Hagen, the evil perpetrator of the scheme, plunges a spear deep into Siegfried's back. Now Brünnhilde understands why her hero betrayed her. As night falls, the servants place Siegfried's body on his shield and carry him in a solemn procession. Wagner's funeral music produces a mighty lament. The moon breaks through the clouds and mist rises from the Rhine river. Toward the end, the bass trumpet and horns sound the stately hero's theme. Gradually the mist engulfs the scene.

Wagner thoroughly explored the expressive qualities of the various instruments of the orchestra. He learned how to wring every drop of expressiveness out of an orchestra, and used the same sense of adventure and determination that the pioneers in this country used as they were exploring the new continent. He was able to portray emotion effectively because he used the orchestra to comment on the action on stage.

▼ *Activity:* **Hear the Timbres of the Orchestra**

How does Wagner use the orchestra to express the death of a hero?

Listen to "Siegfried's Funeral Music" from Wagner's music drama *The Twilight of the Gods* and answer these questions:

1. How does Wagner use instruments to convey Siegfried's good deeds, his heroism, and his tragic end?
2. Is this a real funeral march?

Prior to the First World War (1914–1918), the world turned against the sometimes exaggerated, emotional outpourings of nineteenth-century Romanticism. Reason began to reassert itself. We hear the last expressions of the Romantic spirit in the early decades of the twentieth century in the works of Richard Strauss (1864–1949) and Sergei Rachmaninoff (1873–1943).

◀ Richard Wagner (1813–1883) was one of the nineteenth-century Romantic composers who used new harmonies, soaring melodies, and vivid orchestral colors to express the mystical world of the supernatural. He created music dramas that brought German Romantic opera to its heights.

Summary

Music expresses our emotions in clear and convincing ways. It is not unreasonable to ask whether we could feel the meaning of patriotisim, love, peace, freedom, fear, faith, loss, suffering, and other emotional states as well if we did not have music to express them. In expressing these emotions, music reinforces them, helping us experience them in a more objective way. Music helps to bring our feelings into focus, to intensify them, and to sustain them so that we can grasp their impact fully. A person who has never experienced love, for example, can sense its wonder and joy through music that evokes these feelings.

Because music expresses the feelings of particular peoples, times, and places, it has the power to re-create them. The fact that music is different in the way it speaks to us is just the point. Because of the different ways people express themselves musically, we can begin to grasp what it is like to be Balinese. We can begin to understand Vienna at the time of Mozart and Beethoven. We can visit the Romantic period in the time of Wagner. We can experience, not the reality, but certainly the emotional state of being homeless. Through our feelings we can actually acquire insight and understanding. We can become empathetic and compassionate. The emotional power of music is a window into the very real emotional world of other human beings, past and present.

CHAPTER 10

The Beauty of Order

Objectives

By completing this chapter, you will:

- Gain an insight into some of the ways music is organized.
- Understand how composers use repetition and contrast to create cohesive musical expressions.
- Find out what gives order to popular songs, the Afro-Cuban rumba, the march, and ragtime.
- Understand the forms of the rondo and the sonata.
- Become familiar with the fugue and chance music.

Musical Terms

aleatory music
coda
fugue
hook
motive
ostinato
rondo
scherzo
sonata

*I*nside each of us, there is a constant struggle between
our emotions and our intellect. We may have an urge to
do something, but our judgment may put a damper on
it. Our intuition tells us one thing; reason tells us
another. The reconciliation of these two extremes
takes many forms. Sometimes our emotions
rule, sometimes our intellect rules.

Order in Music

The arts express the resolution of tension between the intellect and the
emotion at any particular time. It is important to remember that emotion
and intellect are always present in all music. During the Classical period,
order and intellect ruled. This does not mean that Mozart's music lacks
feeling. It simply means that emotion is represented in a highly ordered
way. In Wagner's music of the late Romantic period, emotion rules. This
does not mean that his music is thoughtless and lacks order. It simply
means that Wagner made order subservient to his expressive purposes.

Music is more than emotion. It is a representation of thought and
intelligence as well. One of the ways humans bring intelligence into play
is by ordering the sound. Just as there is emotion in all music, so, too, is
there order.

Music is often a model of an ordered world. In general, music stands
in opposition to chaos and anarchy, which are aspects of disorder. Anarchy is lawlessness, disorder, and violence—the antithesis of order. Broadly
speaking, music stands on the side of order, although it represents order
of many different kinds and degrees.

Without some sense of order and agreement, society cannot function as
a community. It would not hold together. Music expresses this social order.
It is logically constructed. It has consistency because its parts relate. Quite
simply, it makes sense.

Orders Based on Repetition

Just as there is a certain ugliness in anarchy and disorder, there is a certain beauty in order and coherence. Even when music expresses disorder,
it uses an underlying structure to do so. How does music express order?
In music, order is expressed through the relationship of the parts. One
musical part relates to another because of its similarities. Musical structure,
or form, is a plan of organization for all the musical events that take place

within the composition. One way that musical forms achieve a sense of order is through the use of repetition. Think of what an automobile would look like if there were no uniformity from one part to another! It would be comical and haphazard. Limiting the look (or sound) of the building blocks and repeating some of them assures unity of design. In music, repetition is a device that uses familiarity to create a sense of order.

Order in American Popular Songs

American popular songs achieve a sense of cohesiveness because of their melodic repetition. You may not have realized that popular music is highly organized. Many songs use a standard 32-bar song form consisting of four sections of eight bars each, in an A A B A pattern. This basic pattern occurs frequently, particularly in jazz and Broadway show tunes.

Composers often use a musical **motive**, *a short, distinctive musical pattern or figure,* as a building block. In popular music, the essence of the song is expressed in the **hook**, or grabber, *the musical motive that generally accompanies the words to the title of the song.* The title is usually sung to a short melodic or rhythmic motive or pattern that is repeated, copied at a higher or lower pitch, or in some altered form (and sometimes imitated). It is the repetition and imitation of this musical motive, or hook, that holds the song together and makes it memorable.

▼*Activity:* **Find the Order**

Listen to the classic 1937 song "My Funny Valentine" by Richard Rodgers (music) and Lorenz Hart (lyrics), and see if you can hear how the song is organized.

This song is composed in A A B A form. Try to listen for the sequence of the repeated melody A-A^1 and the new melodic material B, then the A^2 melody repeated (with a four-measure tag at the end). Did you hear the hook, the musical motive that recurs throughout the piece?

Now look at the melody of "My Funny Valentine" on page 149. You will see the hook is bracketed in black, the A sections are in red, and the B section is in blue.

Analyze the music before you listen to it again. Then answer the following questions:

1. How do measures 1–2 compare with measures 3–4?
2. What is different about the second A section?
3. How do measures 5–6 compare with measures 13–14?

Now study the B section or bridge. Is it organized? Is there repetition? In the final A section, where is the climax? What makes it so stunning?

Song form is generally organized in three sections, that is, in A B A or ternary form even though the first A section is often repeated to form an A A B A structure. There is a comfortable and satisfying symmetry about

My Funny Valentine

Words by Lorenz Hart

Music by Richard Rodgers

▶ In his painting *The Figure Five* (1963), American artist Robert Indiana (b. 1928) created order by the rhythmic repetition of the number five within a five-sided background similar to a road sign. The painting was inspired by Charles Henry Demuth's painting *I Saw the Figure 5 in Gold* (1928), based on a poem about a screaming fire engine—Engine No. 5—tearing through the city streets on a rainy night.

Robert Indiana. *The Figure Five.* 1963. National Museum of American Art, Smithsonian Institution, Washington, D.C.

this arrangement. In the A B A form, the A sections function like bookends enclosing the form and supporting it structurally. Many forms in nature, including the human torso, have this kind of structure, which gives a balance between unity and variety. The music of the repeated sections is set off against the contrast of the middle section. This repetition is a return to the familiar. The repetition can be exact, or it can have some degree of variation or modification.

Musical structure in the Western tradition usually accommodates a progression of feeling from tension, through climax, to repose. It arouses our expectations, causes tension by denying or delaying the satisfaction of those expectations, then soothes and pleases us by fulfilling them. The building of tension and the resulting release is sometimes created by introducing contrasting musical material, then repeating what came before it. The interplay of contrast and repetition is a basic device used in the creation of much

◀ Architecture, like all the arts, is ordered. In the general A B A structure of the U.S. Capitol building, there is a repetition of forms that gives stability at the same time that the central or B section gives added interest and climax. The A B A form is common in all art, including music, because it gives a balance to unity and variety.

of the world's music. Subconsciously, we expect to hear repetition. Most of the musical examples we have heard during our lifetime have led us to expect it. Contrasting material takes us momentarily away from the main theme that has been introduced, and this sets up tension. Returning to the main theme is like greeting a familiar friend. We experience a sense of comfort, repose, and security.

Order in the Cuban Rumba

A large portion of Cuba's population is of African descent. Although Cubans speak Spanish and share many traditions with other Latin Americans, Afro-Cubans maintain a culture with a strong African character. Many retain African tribal identities, practice African religions, speak adapted versions of African languages in addition to Spanish, and preserve forms of music that closely resemble African models. Out of this African heritage, Afro-Cubans have gradually developed new musical forms well suited to modern Cuban tastes. One of these is the rumba.

Rumba is performed with percussion instruments, singing, and dancing. It should not be confused with the ballroom rumba which is a pale, foreign imitation. The most popular of the several types of rumba is *guaguanco* (wah-wahn-COH), a form that has influenced today's popular Latin-American dance music called salsa.

Guaguanco is an original, distinctly Afro-Cuban musical form that is ordered in two important ways. Both ways are common to many types of African music. First, there is a short, repeated rhythm that is played by *claves* (CLAH-vehs), short, round resonating wood bars. This time line serves as a reference point for the rest of the musicians and lends an orderly forward motion to the music. Linked to the time line is a repeated rhythmic pattern of the same length that is played by two *tumbadoras* (toom-bah-DOR-ahs), which are similar to conga drums. Along with this, another drum called *quinto* (KEEN-toh), a higher pitched master drum, improvises, often playing rhythms that mimic or direct the movements of the dancers.

Second, there is a two-part, formal structure that is marked by two singing styles. The initial section has a fixed melody and text, and is often sung in two-part harmony. This is followed by a *montuno* (mohn-TOO-no), a second section that alternates soloist and chorus (refrain). In the montuno, a short, repeated refrain alternates with solo singing of changing, often improvised, verses of text. In this section, the quinto plays more actively, urging the dancers on. Each of the two main sections is preceded by a *diana* (dee-AH-nah), a shorter section of solo singing.

▼ *Activity:* **Test Your Skill**

Perform the repeated rhythm or time line pattern of guaguanco played by the claves.

In a repeated cycle of 16 sixteenth notes, the claves accent the following pulses:

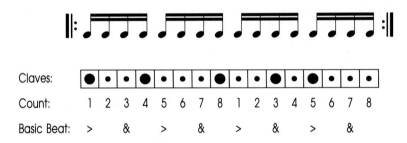

Start by tapping the sixteenth notes, accenting the clave rhythm as indicated. Increase the tempo until you can clap only the accented notes. Try to feel the rhythm.

Now work in pairs with one person clapping the basic beats (four to a measure), while both of you audiate the sixteenth notes. The other person claps the clave rhythm. Note that accents 1 and 5 come on the beat. The second and third accents come just ahead of the basic beat, and the fourth accent comes on "&." Try counting and clapping with a beat of four until you can perform this quite rapidly:

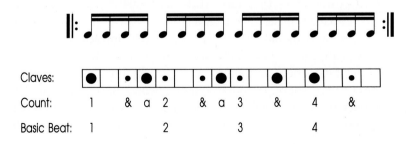

Once you have mastered this rhythm, try tapping along with the claves in "La Negra Sandunguera." Can you hear the pattern of the two tumbadoras?

Perhaps the easiest part of the tumbadora pattern to single out is the following:

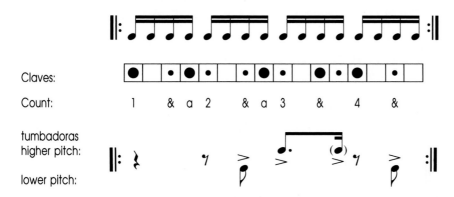

Can you tell when the montuno begins? (Hint: The refrain is "Ay, ay, ay, Que tiene esa negra?" ("Ay, ay, ay, what does that Black woman have?"))

The two-part form illustrated in the guaguanco represents another basic way to organize music. Examples of A B, or binary form, are common. Many dance pieces in the seventeenth and eighteenth centuries are in two sections with each section repeated. This arrangement gives a sense of balance as well as variety within the whole. The repetition of each section gives binary form a familiarity that helps fix it in our memory and create appeal. Nonetheless, three-part (A B A), or ternary form, is more common and perhaps more satisfying.

The Ostinato

As you have heard in the guaguanco, order in music can be established by means of a short musical pattern that is repeated persistently. This pattern might be rhythmic, or rhythmic and melodic. Superimposed upon this recurring pattern is a variety of other rhythms and melodies. The time line rhythmic pattern in the guaguanco is an **ostinato,** *a repeated musical figure that gives stability and uniformity to the composition.* The ostinato gives an underlying unity while still permitting variety in the other parts. It is like wearing the same uniform every day with different accessories.

You have seen how melodic repetition can give order to popular songs and how an ostinato, a constantly repeated musical pattern, gives order to the Afro-Cuban rumba and to some classical symphonic music. This type of repetition almost always occurs at the same pitch in the same part (or instrument). In Baroque music there is often an ostinato—a recurring melody of four-to-eight measures—in the lowest part that is called a basso ostinato or ground bass. The resulting form is sometimes referred to as a passacaglia. Later composers also used ostinatos to organize their music.

▼*Activity:* **Judge the Ostinato Patterns**

How do the ostinato patterns that Georges Bizet (1838–1875) uses in his *L'Arlésienne Suite No. 1* give unity to the work?

Play this ostinato melody during the A section of "Carillon":

(repeat 56 times)

Perform this ostinato rhythm during the B section:

(repeat 89 times)

Play this ostinato melody again during the return of A:

(repeat 39 times)

1. Describe the experience of performing these ostinatos.
2. What is the structural function of these ostinatos? Do they function expressively as well?

Cooperative Learning

Find the Imitation

Listen to the opening of Beethoven's *Fifth Symphony* and recognize the use of imitation.

Remember, imitation can be exact (strict) or inexact (free). Working in small groups, identify all the imitations of the original motive. Identify where and how Beethoven varied the original motive. Which did he keep constant—melody or rhythm?

Imitation

Using a short musical motive as a building block is another way composers give order to their music. To create a feeling of order and relationship, however, repetition does not have to be exact. One outstanding example that you have probably heard is the "dot-dot-dot-dash" motive in Ludwig van Beethoven's *Fifth Symphony*. During the Second World War, this ♪♪♪♩ . . . —pattern, which represents the letter "V" in Morse Code, became the allies' symbol of victory. In this way the allies claimed that Beethoven, the great German composer, was on their side.

Beethoven used this simple pattern to create a movement that expresses conflict with incredible force and emotion. Sometimes, he repeats the pattern exactly. Sometimes, the pattern is imitated—repeated higher or lower, or with some modification. Imitation is the successive statement of identical or nearly identical material in two or more parts. When Beethoven imitates the motive, he sometimes keeps the rhythm the same but slightly changes the melody or vice versa. Even this type of repetition recalls the original pattern and makes it clear that there is a relationship between the two. As a result, the musical statement holds together. It sounds organized and thought-out. It has strength.

The Fugue

Organization in contrapuntal music posed a different challenge. How do you establish a relationship between two or more melodic parts, or voices, when they are sounding together? One technique composers used was to place the same melody in each voice but offset its entrance so that it overlaps and therefore interacts with itself. As you may recall, this is the way the canon is constructed. Another method was to create a **fugue**, by writing *a melody, then imitating it successively in all the parts, building the piece from a series of such imitations.* This chasing of the melody from part to part explains why works created in this manner were called fugues. The term means flight.

Fugue 16

J. S. Bach

Jesu, My Great Pleasure

by J. S. Bach

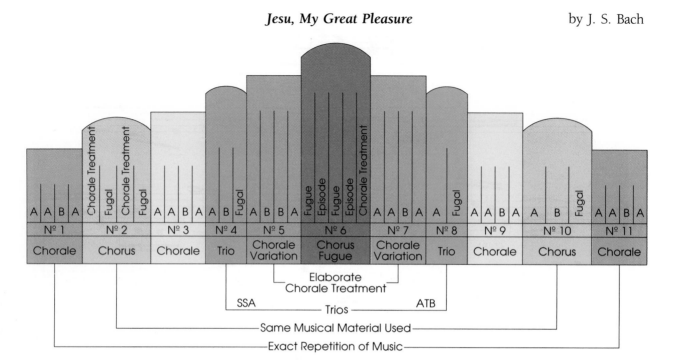

J. S. Bach was one of the great architects of music. In his motet *Jesu, My Great Pleasure* for chorus, diagrammed above, Bach made every other movement a chorale based on the same hymn tune. He designed the 11 movements around a massive fugue (No. 6). On either side he placed a chorale in the same basic form and built on the same theme (Nos. 5 and 7). On either side of these are two trios, one for high voice (No. 4) and one for low voice (No. 8). Moving further out, there are two more chorales (Nos. 3 and 9) and two choruses (Nos. 2 and 10) that are based on the same musical material. To complete the symmetrical structure, he ended the work with the same chorale that he used to begin it (Nos. 1 and 11). The overall design is as complex as the architecture of a cathedral.

Musical works are considered contrapuntal when two or more melodies are sounded together. They are fugal when those melodies exchange the same thematic material. A fugue is an ingenious creation that was brought to its highest perfection by Johann Sebastian Bach in the first half of the eighteenth century. Bach's Fugue No. 16 in G Minor from Book I of *The Well-Tempered Clavier* shows how this exchange of melodic material is accomplished. This fugue has four voices, or parts (melodic lines), though all four are not always in play. For example, the first voice enters with the theme in measure 1; the second voice responds in measure 2; the third voice enters in measure 5; and the fourth voice responds only in measure 12. But when the fourth voice finally enters in measure 12, two other voices are at rest. All four voices sound together for the first time in measure 15. A fugue is not like a canon. While the voices in a fugue share some of the same material, each is quite different, taken as a whole.

The themes that are exchanged among the voices have been color coded so that you can see how they dart from part to part (see page 155). The theme, or subject (in red), is first stated in one voice alone. It is then answered (in imitation) by the second voice at a higher pitch, by a third voice at a lower pitch, and repeated in various sequences throughout. When the answer enters at the end of bar two, the subject continues with a melody in counterpoint with it. This countersubject (blue) is heard throughout the fugue and is also exchanged between the voices. The space between statements of the subject is filled in with freely invented counterpoint, which is often based on melodic motives from the subject and the countersubject. In this way, the entire work is thoroughly integrated in all its parts. Toward the end of some fugues, the subject enters in such rapid succession in various voices that it overlaps itself. This pressing together of the entrances is called stretto, and it can have the grand effect of a series of reverberating echoes.

Fugues can be played by an orchestra or small ensemble, sung by a chorus, or performed on a single instrument such as an organ or piano. The challenge in performing a fugue is to give emphasis to the particular voice that has the subject. Sooner or later all the voices have it, so all the melodic lines are of equal importance—a very democratic kind of music. A fugue is unique because every part interrelates with every other. Composing a fugue is like figuring out a vast jigsaw puzzle. Not many composers had the patience! After Bach, Beethoven composed a number of fugues, but this manner of composition has not been used extensively in the twentieth century.

▼Activity: *Perform and Analyze a Fugue*

Can you determine how every voice in a fugue is treated equally by sharing the subject and the countersubject?

First, learn to play the theme, or subject, of Fugue No. 16 in G Minor from Book I of *The Well-Tempered Clavier* by J. S. Bach. Clap this rhythm as you sing the notes on "ta."

Number the fingers of your right hand, by making the thumb one and the little finger five. Practice crossing your second finger over your thumb to play the G–F#–G.

Perform this 2-measure melody using the rhythmic pattern you clapped and chanted. Now listen to this fugue, and as you follow the score, point to each new entrance of the subject (red). Listen again to the fugue, and as you follow the score, point to each entrance of the countersubject (blue). Listen to the fugue a third time, and identify the rhythmic and melodic motives Bach uses to fill the space between the statements of the subject and the countersubject. Where does this material come from?

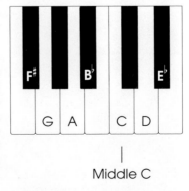

Can you find the stretto, the place where the subject enters in various voices in such quick succession that they overlap?

The March and the Rag

Repetition or recurrence is used in other musical designs as well, but not so insistently. For example, the march, familiar to most Americans through bands and parades, uses repetition in a modest and direct way. Although this is not a symmetrical A B A form, it has a definite sense of order and clarity. The march shows us that continuity and unity do not need to depend solely on repetition. Cohesiveness can be achieved with a modest amount of repetition if there is a consistent use of musical materials: rhythm, tone color, and spirit.

▼*Activity:* **Analyze a March**

How does a composer structure the sections of a march?

While you listen to a short section of "The Washington Post March" by John Philip Sousa, count and tap the basic meter (beats per measure).

This metric grouping is usually associated with the march:

left, right left, right

After you have listened to this march and heard the various sections, answer the following questions:

1. Which of the following series of letters—a, b, or c—represents the form of this march? ("I" stands for Introduction.)
   (a) I AA BB CC; (b) I AA BB AA; (c) I AA BB BB.
2. Are the sections of equal length?
3. How does Sousa create contrast?
4. How does Sousa establish the feeling of unity?

▶ The march is spirited music designed for parades and processions and is generally performed by a band. Here the New York City Marching Band performs in the Columbus Day parade. The steady and clear beat keeps the musicians in step.

Profile

John Philip Sousa
American Composer
and Bandmaster
1854–1932

JOHN PHILIP SOUSA

Did you ever make a connection between the sousaphone and John Philip Sousa? If so, you were right. The type of bass tuba that encircles the player and has a big bell over the head to project the sound was made according to Sousa's specifications in the 1890s and named after him.

Known as the March King, Sousa was born in Washington, D.C., where his father was a trombonist with the U.S. Marine Band. When he was growing up, Sousa learned trumpet, trombone, and other brass instruments, although his main instrument was the violin. He apprenticed with the marine band for seven years. After leaving the corps in 1875, he spent four years in Philadelphia playing violin in theater orchestras, teaching, composing, and conducting.

In 1880, when he was on tour with a show, he received a telegram inviting him to become the conductor of the United States Marine Corps Band. He was only 25. He directed the marine band for 12 years; during that time he composed some of his greatest marches, including "The Washington Post March."

In 1892, he formed The Sousa Band, which toured widely in North America and Europe. His brilliant showmanship kept the band a popular success for four decades. He composed many songs, a dozen operettas, and other music; but it is his marches that are remembered. Undoubtedly, the most famous of the 136 marches he wrote is "The Stars and Stripes Forever."

"The Washington Post March," "El Capitan," "The Stars and Stripes Forever," and other military marches by American bandmaster John Philip Sousa were highly popular with the American public. Scott Joplin, the great American composer of rags (1868–1917), was so impressed by Sousa's marches that he borrowed their basic form for his rags. Sousa was equally complimentary. He introduced ragtime in Europe around 1900 and always had something good to say about it to all its critics.

▼ *Activity:* **Compare Forms**

How is the form of the march similar to the form used by composers of ragtime?

You have already studied the syncopations in Scott Joplin's "Maple Leaf Rag." Now identify the distinct sections of the composition. There are four different melodies: A, B, C, and D. Can you distinguish them?

Now listen to this rag again and assign the appropriate letters to each of the nine sections. Unlike the Sousa march, this Joplin rag does not have an introduction. Are all the sections of equal length?

Unlike the Sousa march, the rag uses only one type of tone color: the piano. How does the composer create variety? unity?

Compare and contrast the form and musical characteristics of Sousa's "The Washington Post March" with Joplin's "Maple Leaf Rag."

The Rondo Form

Composers sometimes give stability to a musical work by returning to the principal theme again and again, with other themes occurring in between. It is like making a sandwich out of several thin slices of bread with something different between them. A **rondo** is *an instrumental form based on an alternation between a repeated (or recurring) section and contrasting episodes.* The result is repetition in the recurrent sections and contrast in the inner episodes. If you were to repeat one of the episodes (A B A C A B A), you would achieve repetition, contrast, and symmetry all at once!

Composers repeat musical material for effect and to build their musical forms. Repetition unifies and orders the parts. It signifies that the music is planned and not haphazard. But most important, it assures a familiarity that fixes the music in our memory.

▼*Activity:* **Determine the Form**

Analyze the form of the "Rondo all' orgarese" from Trio No. 39 by Franz Joseph Haydn.

Listen to the portion of the opening section of "Rondo all' orgarese" and show the tempo and meter of the music by clapping the accented beats and snapping the unaccented beats.

Listen again to the entire A section of the work and count the number of measures. Your teacher will indicate when the A section is completed. Listen a third time to the entire work and count the number of times you hear the A section performed. How would you label the sections between the repetitions of A?

Which of the following represents the form of the "Rondo all' orgarese"?

(a) A A A   (b) A B A   (c) A B A C A

Challenge: Count the number of measures in the returns of the A sections. Are they all of equal length? Compare the length of the contrasting sections to that of the A section.

Orders Based on Other Devices

Although most music has order, it is not governed by hard-and-fast rules or formulas. Musical structures are seldom rigid. There are no organizational traditions or systems in music that have not been violated. Music can be molded, but usually it breaks out of the mold. In other words, music is not always as ordered as we might think. Just as parallel lines, circles, and right angles are the exception in the real world, perfect order is the exception in music. Composers sometimes use pre-existing forms or designs to order their music, but they reshape them to serve their own expressive and communicative needs.

We have seen a number of ways in which repetition helps organize musical works. Composers also structure their music in ways that do not involve repetition or depend upon it solely.

The Sonata

Albums, cassettes, and compact discs by pop performing groups often have a sense of oneness about them. It may be the approach and the sound of a single group of musicians, or the style and timbre of the music that provides unity. Sometimes an album will have a general theme, which is addressed throughout the musical selections. Such albums can be viewed as lengthy musical works comprising many individual parts. In this sense, they are like suites because they are made up of a number of different pieces that are linked by a particular musical style, a central idea or subject, or a set of dances.

Classical composers often write works that have several sections or movements. One such type of composition is a **sonata** (suh-NAH-tah), *a work in several movements for one or more instruments.* By this definition, a symphony could be considered a sonata for orchestra. (By the same token, a work in several movements for three instruments is called a trio, one for four instruments is a quartet, one for five a quintet, and so forth.) A concerto, composed for one or more solo instruments and orchestra, is also a form of a sonata.

◀ The string quartet is an ensemble of two violins, a viola, and a cello. It came into existence during the Classical period and remains an important means of expression today. This ensemble of four instruments usually plays sonatas, which, like the ensemble itself, are called string quartets.

Sonatas usually have three or four movements, but they may have fewer or more. Liszt wrote a sonata in one movement; Beethoven composed sonatas in two movements; and Brahms wrote a sonata in five movements. Most of the time there are breaks between the movements, but again there are exceptions. Most sonatas for a single instrument have three movements, but this does not mean they always conform to this plan.

Regardless of the number of movements in a sonata, the first and last are usually energetic and fast. The second movement is usually slow. The three-movement form is generally marked allegro, adagio, allegro. When there are four movements, a minuet or **scherzo** (SKAYR-tzo), *a vigorous and sometimes light-hearted movement in triple meter with a middle section or trio,* is inserted between the second and the fourth movements.

Each of the movements in a sonata is organized. The first movement is most often in sonata or "sonata-allegro" form, a three-part plan in which there is an exposition, or A section, that is usually repeated; a development, or B section, in which the musical ideas introduced in A are transformed; and a recapitulation, or A section, in which the musical ideas of the exposition are repeated with some modifications. The general plan is A A B A, a more complex and lengthy version of the basic outline used in many popular songs. The movement may close with a **coda,** *usually a short concluding section.* Often, the second or slow movement is also composed in this sonata-allegro form, but it can be organized in two-part (binary) form or as a set of variations on a theme. The third movement (minuet or scherzo) is usually in three-part form. The fourth and final movement is a rondo or, again, is in sonata-allegro form. This pattern of organization applies to most works that are called sonatas, concertos (no scherzo), symphonies, and quartets. As you can see, the plan is general enough to allow composers ample leeway to be creative.

With all the various movements composed in different musical forms and contrasting tempos, what gives a sonata its overall order? Moreover, what holds these movements together so that they convey a unified expression rather than the feeling of several independent works? In a sonata, there is generally no musical repetition from movement to movement. How, then, is the overall organization achieved?

In the sonata, the design of each movement is complete within itself, yet each movement remains incomplete without the other movements. These movements might be compared to chapters in a book, each satisfying in itself but not completing the story. The tragedy that engulfs us in the first movement of Beethoven's Piano Sonata in C Minor needs the calm and solemn second movement to allow us to collect our feelings, before the third movement carries us swiftly to a tragic fate. The movements of this sonata are unified through the serious mood established at the onset of the work. Sonatas have emotional unity—the movements are held together by an expressive order.

▼*Activity:* **Find the Overall Unity**

How does a composer unify a large work made up of three separate movements?

Listen to excerpts from each of the three movements of Beethoven's Piano Sonata in C Minor (*Pathétique*) and try to determine the central organizing device.

To begin, clap the rhythmic pattern from the introduction to the first movement and chant the different durations as indicated:

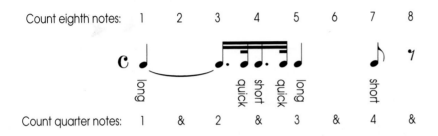

Now listen to the introduction and determine the number of times this rhythmic pattern is heard. Beethoven marked the introduction *grave*, meaning slow and serious. What other terms would describe the mood?

As you listen to the excerpts from each of the three movements, select words from the following lists that best describe the expressive qualities of each movement:

- First Movement: calm, agitated, delicate, aggressive, anxious, dreamy, turbulent, passionate, graceful, restless, soothing, tense.
- Second Movement: happy, longing, cheerful, serious, jolly, sorrowful, impulsive, meditative, pleading, light-hearted, gloomy.
- Third Movement: joyous, intense, determined, weak, agitated, hopeful, carefree, resigned, piteous, sunny, dejected, bright, hopeless.

After you listen to the excerpts, use the descriptors you have chosen to write one or two sentences that would clearly describe the mood of the movement to someone who has never heard it. Mention musical devices Beethoven used to create this mood.

Compare and contrast the emotional content of the introduction with that of the three movements. Would any of the words you used to describe the mood of one of these movements also describe mood of the other movements? How do these three movements relate to one another?

Aleatory or Chance Music

When music is performed live, a chance factor is operating. Composers cannot specify every facet in a piece exactly. Even if they could, no performer could perform a work the same way every time; there is always some slight variation. This risk factor is what makes live performance so exciting. We are never quite certain what may happen!

Aleatory music, or chance music, makes the most of this uncertainty. In **aleatory music,** *composers deliberately leave parts of the composition and performance undetermined.* They relinquish some of their control, giving those who perform the work the option to determine how the work will ultimately sound and be performed. They invite the performers to join them in the creative process.

Composers of aleatory music offer performers choices or ask them to make certain creative decisions. For example, a composer might suggest a sliding sound from low to high without specifying exact pitches or timing. Sometimes composers provide a graph of the composition that contains new signs that have to be learned, then interpreted, by the performer. In this way, the performer collaborates with the composer.

▶ Scores for aleatory or chance music may or may not use standard notation. In his work *Zyklus* or *Cycle* (1959) for solo percussionist, German composer Karlheinz Stockhausen (b. 1928) uses diagrams to guide the performer. In this work, the player is surrounded by a sequence of 16 pages of music, each the same length. (Numbers 1 and 17 are on the same sheet.) The performer chooses where to start, decides which direction to head around the circle, and sets the tempo. The circle (upper left) indicates the principal instruments in the order they enter and depart, each instrument lasting five pages (or periods). The lower circle shows the number and type of instruments used in each period and how they increase from periods 1 to 5 and from 9 to 13. In the score itself, the music moves from strictness to freedom. Period 1 uses standard notation to specifically define the rhythm, while period 17 uses approximate dots to indicate that the music is indeterminate.

The Music of Stockhausen, by Jonathan Harvey. Copyright ©1975 by Jonathan Harvey. University of California Press. Used By Permission. All Rights Reserved.

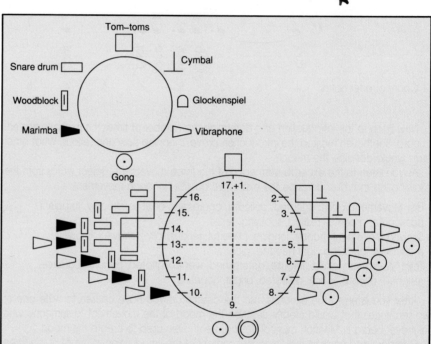

▼*Activity:* **Order and Perform**

Can performers have a role in giving order to the events in a musical composition?

Earle Brown's score for *Piece for Any Number of Anythings* on page 167 provides broad descriptions for five musical events that are to be improvised by the performers. The conductor must make the following musical choices:

- What the order of the events will be.
- How long each event will last.
- What the dynamic level of each event will be.
- Whether any of the events will be repeated.

Perform this composition for your classmates with different conductors.

Piece for Any Number of Anythings

By Earle Browne

1	2	3	4	5
long high notes	quick angular melodic lines	very legato lines	highly fragmented lines	very small noisy sounds on instruments*
slowly changing melodic lines	abrupt dynamic changes (normal sounds but vary timbre*—pizzicato, arco, etc.)	note-to-note intervals no more than a perfect fifth	note-to-note intervals always more than one octave!	* Timbral conditions may be translated into comparable or similar sounds from voices.
small intervals				
	vary durations			

Aleatory music, though left to the conductor and performers to complete, does not lack order. The composer may specify an order for the musical events or leave this to the preference of the performers. In any event, there is a plan that may or may not include some repetition. This is an open structure created by the performer from options provided by the composer. Most aleatory music is more a matter of choice than it is a matter of pure chance.

Composers today use many of the same organizational devices that you have studied in this section. Music has not gotten more complicated through the ages. The history of music is not one long, continuous development from the simple to the complex. Composers generally go just so far in one direction, then make a new beginning, often reaching for simpler, clearer, and more direct ways to express themselves.

PROJECT

Compose an Aleatory Composition

Based on three colors of your choice, compose an aleatory, or chance, composition. Select three contrasting colors as inspiration for your composition, then follow these steps:

1. Discuss the emotion that each color suggests.
2. Experiment with ways to express these emotions with sounds at hand.
3. Create a simple three-part descriptive (verbal) score similar to Earle Brown's.
4. Try performing each section with different tempos, dynamics, length, and tone colors to see the range of expressive possibilities.
5. Perform the composition with different conductors, creating the form (order) as you proceed.

Can you create a rondo? Record each composition. Decide which composition best captures the feeling and contrast of the colors.

Summary

Much of what we call order in music is what we perceive as its continuity. As performers or listeners, we sense the way a musical piece is put together, working from the smallest motive, to the parts that make up the movement, and to the movements that make up the complete work. The organization or form of the work can be perceived on many levels, starting with the musical motive, then the phrase, the section, the movement, and finally the entire multi-movement work. We can see relationships within relationships and how the details relate to the whole. We work from the smaller to the larger picture.

Today, composers are free to use the organizational devices of the past, as well as to invent new ones. What is important to remember is that they strive to bring order to their musical compositions. They apply their intellect, not just their emotions, to their work. Composers create vast and magnificent musical structures out of nothing more than vibrations, creating amazing worlds that can touch our inner beings and stir us to our depths.

Apply What You Have Learned
Chapter 9

Describe the ways music can express and evoke feeling.

Listen to an excerpt from the first movement of Rachmaninoff's Piano Concerto No. 2 (1901) and compare it with Eric Carmen's song "All by Myself" (1975) that was inspired by it.

Make notes about each piece so you can answer these questions:

1. What gives each of these works its expressive power?
2. Do the song lyrics correspond to the emotions expressed in the concerto?
3. Based on just one hearing, which do you prefer and why?
4. Using these two pieces as examples, how would you describe the ways music can express and touch our feelings?

Apply What You Have Learned
Chapter 10

Name the type of organization used in the musical examples that you will hear.

From the following list, choose the name of the musical organization that you identify as you listen to each of the six recorded examples:

march	song form (A A B A)	rondo
fugue	ostinato	rag

Artists often use a balance of repetition, imitation, and contrast to give their works a sense of order and interest. Study the painting on the facing page—a portrait of *Dr. Meyer-Hermann* by Otto Dix—and determine what device the painter used to give order to this work. Then answer the following questions:

1. What structural element does the artist use for repetition and imitation? How does this repetition and imitation give the work a sense of order? How does it suggest that the man is like his machine? How does the artist achieve contrast?
2. Compare the use of repetition in this work with Beethoven's use of a short motive in the opening of his Fifth Symphony. Explain how they function similarly as structural devices.

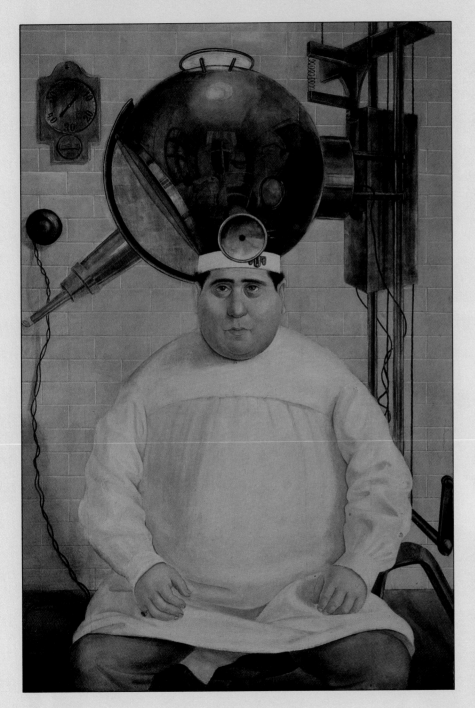

◀ In his portrait of *Dr. Meyer-Hermann* (1926), the German painter Otto Dix deliberately blended the man with the machine he operates, a commentary on the dehumanized state of humankind. The enameled surfaces and precise lines convey a rigid and over-ordered world.

Otto Dix. *Dr. Meyer-Hermann*. 1926. Collection, The Museum of Modern Art, New York, New York. Gift of Philip C. Johnson.

Music!...
To Understand
Life's Meaning

~

CHAPTER 11

Love Songs

Objectives

By completing this chapter, you will:

- Find out how universal the subject of love is in all kinds of music throughout history and around the world.
- Become familiar with the style of American popular love songs today and in the nineteenth century.
- Be introduced to typical Mexican and Egyptian love songs and see how they are similar to, yet different from, our own.
- Take a closer look at the elements of musical expression, including major and minor scales, intervals, chords, phrases, and cadences.
- Learn to create a simple keyboard accompaniment.
- Become familiar with two of the greatest love songs in opera.

Musical Terms

cadence
cakewalk
harmony
interval
oratorio
primary chords
rondeau
scale

172

*S*ong as a form of human expression is the largest and oldest category of music. People sing of work and play, of birth and death, of joy and sorrow, of faith and hope, of triumph and despair, and especially of love. Secular songs, songs that contain nonsacred subject matter, can be traced back to ancient Greece, but all we have are some of the texts. After the development of musical notation in the ninth century, it took another 300 years before secular songs were written down. Now they are a large and respected part of what music is all about.

Love Songs of Today

One of the most universal themes of music is love. People of every culture throughout the world sing love songs, and we can assume that, as soon as humans discovered singing, they must have serenaded their loved ones. Love may well have been the reason humans invented singing! The vast majority of love songs communicate just three basic messages: lost love, longing for love, and the celebration of love. The first conveys sadness, the second melancholy, the third joy.

The Major Scale

How are the three states of love expressed musically? What gives this music its special character? To answer this question, we have to look at the tonal material itself and how a composer uses it. All these works use the same basic scale, but the results are different. In music, a **scale** *is a sequence of tones arranged in rising pitches.*

The major scale has a distinctive pattern of whole (w) and half (h) steps. This is easy to see on the keyboard because the major scale can be played on the white keys, from C to C:

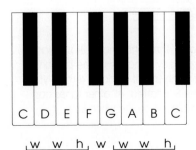

The G clef winds around the second line of the five-line staff designating it G above middle C.

Notice that the lower set of four tones (C, D, E, and F) and the upper set of four tones (G, A, B, and C) have exactly the same pattern of whole and half steps: w, w, and h; or 1 step, 1 step, and ½ step. Note that there is a whole step joining these two sets of four pitches. A whole step on the keyboard consists of two half steps. The pattern of intervals for the major scale, then, is w, w, h, w, w, w, h, or 1, 1, ½, 1, 1, 1, ½.

The major scale shown on page 173 is called the C major scale because this pattern of whole and half steps begins on C. The pattern can be transposed to any of the other 11 tones on the piano (each of the black and white keys). There are, therefore, a total of 12 major scales or keys, one on each of the 12 tones that make up the Western tonal system.

The major scale starting on G:

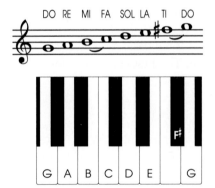

The G major key signature:

The one sharp (#) is placed in a key signature at the clef sign so it does not have to be written on every F throughout. You have to remember that all Fs are sharped when you play or sing in this key.

The major scale starting on F:

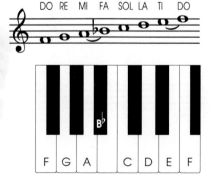

The F major key signature:

Again, the flatted note (B♭) is placed in the key signature at the beginning of each line of music to remind you that B is flatted. All other tones can be played on the white keys.

As these examples show, the black keys on the piano are named according to their adjacent white keys. The black key that lies immediately to the right of a white key and is a half-tone higher in pitch is called a sharp (#). The black key that lies immediately to the left of a white key and is a half-tone lower in pitch is called a flat (♭). The same black key can be called a sharp or a flat, depending on the key you are in. Nonetheless, whatever we call the black key, for example C# or D♭, it sounds the same on the piano or on any other keyboard instrument.

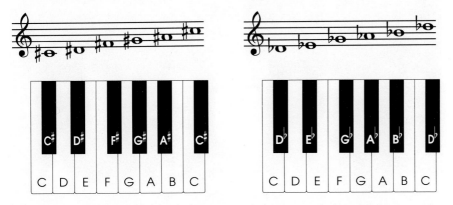

The black keys as sharps: The black keys as flats:

Intervals

Melodies are created by selecting scale tones and putting them in an order that has an expressive quality. Even with just the seven basic tones of the scale, there is considerable choice. A melody can move up by step or skip, down by step or skip, or remain the same by repeating the tone. An **interval** is *the distance in pitch between two tones.* In determining the difference in pitch between two tones, we count both tones as well as the lines and spaces between them.

unison	2nd	3rd	4th	5th	6th	7th	octave
DO/DO	DO/RE	DO/MI	DO/FA	DO/SOL	DO/LA	DO/TI	DO/DO

The smallest interval in the 12-tone Western scale is a half step or minor (meaning small) 2nd. In the major scale, as we have seen, the minor 2nd occurs between the scale degrees MI (3) and FA (4), and TI (7) and DO (8). The distance between the other adjacent tones of the scale is a major (meaning large) 2nd. A major 2nd (or whole step) is made up of two minor 2nds (or half steps). Melodies generally use whole and half steps (major and minor 2nds) and few large leaps.

▶ In most cultures, the most prevalent subject of song is love in all its moods. The French painter Jean Antoine Watteau (1684–1721) painted the theatrical character Mezzetin, the lover who sang and played the guitar but was usually rejected. This character appeared in many of the plays of that period, dressed in the same striped costume, and Watteau captured the feeling of melancholy so well that the viewer can imagine the song.

Jean-Antoine Watteau. *Mezzetin.* c. 1719. The Metropolitan Museum of Art, New York, New York. Munsey Fund, 1934.

▼*Activity:* **Discover**

How do these composers use the major scale to create different feelings?

1. Study the following two melodies from the song "You are the Sunshine of My Life" and then answer the questions.

A

You are   the   sun - shine   of __ my   life. __

B

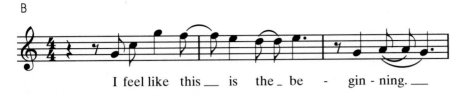

I feel like this __ is   the _ be   -   gin - ning. __

   a. In which section (A or B) does the melody move in a smooth, scalelike motion? In which section does the melody move in a series of excited leaps?

   b. What is the largest interval in section A? section B?

   c. What is the range of the melody in section A? section B?

2. Study the melodic "hook" of Hank Cochran's song "Why Can't He Be You?" and then answer the questions.

He loves   me,   too. __   His __ love is

true.   Why can't he __   be   you?

   a. How many notes of the G major scale are used in this hook? Can you hear what is basically a descending scale?

   b. How many times do you hear this hook in the song?

   c. Where is the hook somewhat different? Why?

3. Composer Harold Arlen added tones to the G major scale in order to capture a bluesy quality in his song "Stormy Weather."

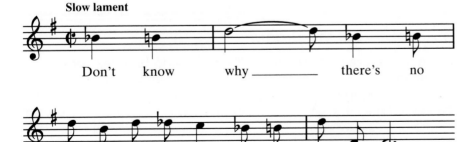

Don't   know   why _____   there's   no

sun   up   in   the   sky,   storm - y   weath - er, ___

   a. Can you tell, by studying this melody, which notes he added to the G major scale?

   b. What effect do these "blue" notes have?

   c. Point out all the places you hear and see half steps in this melody.

Mexican Love Songs

All cultures throughout history seem to have connected love with music in some form or another. In Mexico, it is common for individuals to express their emotions in a love song. Unlike traditional types of Mexican vocal music that create a rhythm for dancing, this style of singing allows the singer the opportunity to express emotion through melody and text. This romantic style was influenced by European styles of singing—especially those of Italian opera—that were popular in Mexico in the nineteenth century. Today the love song thrives in the *canción ranchera* (kahn-see-OHN rahn-CHEH-rah), or "country song," as one of the most popular types of music in the repertoire of the mariachi ensemble. Like love songs in other cultures, the *canción ranchera* speaks of love lost, sought, or found. It can speak of tragedy and betrayal, longing, or joy. In the love song "Se me olvidó otra vez" ("I forgot once again"), an abandoned woman tells of returning again and again to the same place she used to meet her lover in the hope that he will reappear. All the familiar surroundings make her forget once more that her love was unreturned and that her lover is gone forever.

Most *canciones rancheras* have a simple A A B structure. Following an instrumental introduction, the vocalist sings one or two strophes (or stanzas) of the text. Then, the singer sings an additional section that has a different character, possibly because it passes to the IV chord of the key or has a different melodic shape. Following a short instrumental interlude, the song may repeat one of the strophes and the final section (A B), and come to an end. The instrumental introduction and interlude are usually derived from the vocal melody, often the B section. The simplicity of form; the repetition of melody and words; and the echoing of the vocal melody in the instrumental introduction, interlude, and *adornos* (countermelodies in the accompaniment) all serve to highlight the message and the singer's interpretation.

▼Activity: *Feel the Drama*

Listen to the canción ranchera "Se me olvidó otra vez" and determine which emotions the singer communicates.

As you hear the music, follow the text to find out exactly what the singer is feeling. Is this a song of love lost, sought, or found? How do you know? Make a list of the emotions the singer is trying to convey.

Se me olvidó otra vez	I forgot once again
Probablemente ya	You have probably
de mí te has olvidado	forgotten me by now.
y mientras tanto yo	And in the meantime
te seguiré esperando	I continue waiting for you.
no me he querido ir	I have not wanted to leave

para ver si algún día	in order that someday
que tú quieras volver	if you were to want to come back
me encuentres todavía	you would find me here still.
Por eso aún estoy	So, I am still here
en el lugar de siempre	in the same place as always,
en la misma ciudad	in the same city,
y con la misma gente	and with the same people,
para que tú al volver	so that on your return
no encuentres nada extraño	you would find nothing different
y seas como ayer	and you would be like yesterday
y nunca más dejarnos	and we would never again part.
Probablemente estoy	Maybe I am asking
pidiendo demasiado	too much.
se me olvidaba que	I was forgetting
ya habíamos terminado	that we were finished
que nunca volverás	that you will never return
que nunca me quisiste	that you never loved me.
se me olvidó otra vez	I forgot again
que sólo yo te quise	that only I loved you.

Egyptian Love Songs

Love songs sometimes appear in quite different guises. In Arab music, for example, the Westerner might not guess on first hearing whether a song is about love or some other subject. With a bit of knowledge and study, however, he or she can begin to grasp the emotional intent and understand how various states of love are expressed in Egyptian music.

Egyptian Culture

Egyptian civilization developed in the valley of the Nile over 5,000 years ago. Most Egyptians feel great pride in this ancient civilization which reached its zenith about 1400 B.C. At that time, Thebes and Memphis were the political, commerical, and cultural centers of the world. The arts of Egypt are abundant and unique, particularly the monumental sculpture, the temples, pyramids, and the Great Sphinx. Today, Cairo, the capital city, serves as a communications center. Many of the sound recordings, radio broadcasts, films, and television programs enjoyed throughout the Middle East originate there. This explains why the Egyptian dialect and styles of music are familiar to Arabs everywhere.

Egyptian Music

To our Western ears, most Arab music may sound similar; but the various regions of the Arab world have distinct musical styles. Like Western or Chinese music or the music of India, Arab music has a long history. Its theory dates from the writings of the philosopher al-Fārābī in the tenth century. Melodic and rhythmic modes serve as the basis for musical

▶ The arts of ancient Egypt were abundant and often colossal. Some of the pharaohs that ruled Egypt built their own pyramids (left, background) in which their mummified remains would be preserved for eternity. The stone figure of the Great Sphinx (right, foreground), a mythical beast with a human head and body of a lion, symbolized the pharaoh as Horus, the god of the rising sun, who vanquishes darkness and evil. There is evidence that these ancient peoples played instruments and sang. What would their love songs have sounded like?

composition. The melodic modes often include notes that lie between the half steps of the Western scale. These may seem to be "out of tune" at first, but in fact, they are carefully tuned. Once you become accustomed to them, you will note that they are delicate and expressive, like a spice used sparingly.

The song "Ana fi intizarak" (AH-na fee in-ti-ZA-rak) ("I am waiting for you") is about a woman whose lover has left her and she does not know whether he will return. The poem describes the woman's feelings of anger and despair. It is clear that she still loves him. The phonetic spelling of the Arabic text and the English translation are as follows:

> AH-yiz AH-raf lat koon rad-BAHN
> I want to know that you're not angry,
>
> ow SHA-gil el-back in-SAN
> Or whether your heart belongs to someone else.

Although the poem deals with common, everyday personal emotions, it also expresses the pain of waiting for something good to happen. This theme appeals to many listeners in twentieth-century Egypt and the Arab world who wait for political independence, for wars to end, for families to be reunited, and for economic conditions to improve. Although the song is a love song, it expresses more general emotions. Such duality of meaning is common in songs of many cultures.

The song was recorded by Umm Kulthum (oom kool-THOOM). The composition is in a traditional style. The melody moves stepwise (conjunctly). It is based on one of the Arabic melodic modes:

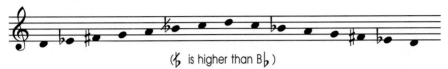

(♮ is higher than B♭)

The instrumental accompaniment is deliberately simple so as not to interfere with the singer's line. In the excerpt you will hear, the *ūd* (ood), an Arab lute, is the predominant instrument used, along with a string bass and violins.

Umm Kulthum uses the text and music to engage the listener with the mood of the song. You will be able to follow the lines easily because her pronunciation is so clear and the lines are repeated several times. Kulthum's improvisational skill is similar to that of a jazz artist, but not as spectacular. Instead, her variations of tone color are subtle, and her small melodic changes gradually engage the listener with the music and the emotion of the song. Once the listener is completely enveloped by the song, and the artist and listener become one with the music, the state of *tarab* is attained. This process requires time and attention. The ear and the imagination are captured slowly and gradually.

Umm Kulthum's performances were very long. A single song could last from half an hour to an hour. Audiences were expected to respond by requesting repetitions of phrases they especially liked, or by asking that entire sections be repeated. Together, the singer and the audience shaped the song so that each rendition was unique.

Arab music is predominantly melodic. To appreciate it, you need to focus your attention on the vocal line, listening to every note so that you are able to follow the singer's interpretation of the text.

▼Activity: *Follow the Melody*

Listen to Umm Kulthum's rendition of this excerpt from the Egyptian love song "Ana fi intizarak" and try to feel the meaning of the text.

Review the text on page 180 so that you are familiar with its meaning and the pronunciation of the Arabic. Pay particular attention to the key words "angry" (rad-BAHN) and "someone else" (in-SAN).

Listen to the excerpt several times, focusing your attention on Umm Kulthum's voice and allowing her to lead you through the lines of music and text.

Identify the important components of the performance. Judging by this excerpt, how would you describe her style?

American Love Songs of the Nineteenth Century

The history of American popular music can be told through love songs. Americans have always sung about love. During the nineteenth century, families in the bustling eastern cities gathered around the parlor piano and sang the popular songs of the day. It was customary for young, middle-class girls to take piano lessons and to be able to play for important social occasions. Since there was no radio or television, people had to invent their own entertainment.

Although a bit too formal and sentimental by today's standards, nineteenth-century parlor songs were sincere expressions. Some of these songs came from Europe; some were composed here. New music publishing houses made these songs available in sheet music. Traveling entertainers circulated the latest songs, carrying them from the eastern cities to the frontier towns. Americans everywhere were making music!

These early parlor songs use simple melodies and straightforward accompaniments. Even so, the expressive intensity of these songs can still be felt. "Annie Laurie" is a good example. This song, published in 1838, became a national hit, even though it was not an American song. The words and music are by Lady John Douglas Scott of Berwickshire, Scotland. The sentiment, however, is universal. British troops who sang the song in the Crimean War thought of Annie as the girl they left behind.

Chords

You have already heard enough **harmony**—*vertical blocks of different tones that sound simultaneously*—to know that it is one of the most expressive elements in music. These tonal blocks, or chords, consist of three or four notes that form a harmonic unit. The accompaniments of parlor songs like "Annie Laurie" rely on just a few basic chords. The combination of melody and harmony is carefully designed to create an appealing tension that teases us and then resolves. To understand how this expressive quality is achieved, it is necessary to learn how melody and harmony work together.

In any scale or key, we can build a chord above each tone or "root" by adding notes that are a 3rd and a 5th above that tone. In C major, for example, seven different chords can be formed, one above each note:

Three of these chords—*the chords built on the first (DO), fourth (FA), and fifth (SOL) degrees of the scale*—are **primary chords** or harmonies. The V chord is usually enhanced with the addition of the 7th above its root, 3rd, and 5th.

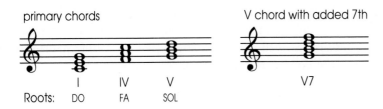

How Melodies Are Chorded

Note that collectively these three chords, even without the 7th added to the V chord, incorporate all seven tones of the scale. This means that, no matter which note of the scale appears in the melody, it can be found in one of these three chords. If the tone in the melody is in the I, IV, or V chord, that chord will probably harmonize the tone and sound all right as the accompaniment. It is a matter of compatibility.

In choosing one of the these three chords to go with the melody, be aware that each of the I, IV, and V7 chords has one tone in common with each of the other chords. For example, if we chorded each tone of the major scale with these three chords, we would have some choice of chords we might use:

These choices happen to fall on the first, fourth, and fifth tones of the scale, exactly where the three primary harmonies are formed. Therefore, you have a choice of chords on tones DO, FA, and SOL. But how do you decide which chord to pick? Simply choose the chord that sounds best. You will discover that tunes usually begin and end on the I chord (like starting and ending on home base), and that the V7 chord likes to move to the I chord.

Chording would be easy if composers just wanted to put a compatible chord under every note in the melody. But changing chords on every note stops the flow of the music. Suppose, for example, we harmonized the first line of "Annie Laurie" with chords that were compatible with each note in the melody. Using just the I, IV, and V chords, we would have the following choices:

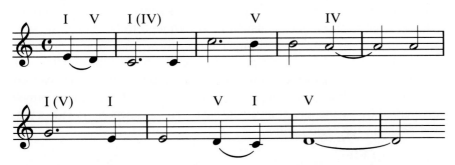

Cooperative Learning

Find the Phrases

Can you hear the musical phrases in a classic American love song? Can you distinguish the degree of tension or resolution in the resting points?

The song "Jeanie with the Light Brown Hair," by the American composer Stephen Foster was published in 1854 after Foster was reconciled with his wife Jane and their three-year-old daughter Marion. No doubt, when he wrote the song, the composer was thinking about Jane and how much he had missed her.

Listen to the arrangement of "Jeanie" and identify the musical phrases.

1. As you listen, write down the words in the text that indicate where there are pauses or breathing breaks. Discuss. Do you agree on where the pauses occur?

2. Listen to the arrangement again and see if you can gauge the degree of tension or resolution in these resting points. Next to each phrase-ending word, label the type of cadence: full cadence if there is the sound of the V7–I resolution; half-cadence if there is a hesitation on the V7 chord that wants to be resolved. (Hint: the first cadence on the word "hair" is a perfect cadence.)

We want music to have some bite—to have tones that do not quite get along, then do. We want a certain amount of dissonance as well as consonance, tension as well as relief. Now listen to "Annie Laurie" with the chords that the composer chose for an accompaniment.

▼*Activity:* **Discover**

Where is the dissonance, and where is the resolution?

Sing "Annie Laurie" while listening for the chord changes that are indicated above the melody. Note that the composer does not change chords on every note of the melody. In this way, the chord changes become important. These harmonic changes have a certain rhythm that helps to carry the melody along.

You will find the chords indicated above the melody with their individual tones spelled out in parentheses. Circle each melody tone that is not in the chord that accompanies it. These tones are dissonances that demand to be resolved.

Sing the song with the accompaniment and feel the tension that these melodic dissonances create. Draw a box around each tone of the melody that represents a resolution of the dissonance (tension). Note that the tone of resolution is always one of the chord tones.

Sing the song again with the accompaniment and accustom yourself to these clashes and their resolutions. These dissonances and consonances are what make this song, and many others, so expressive.

In bars 16–19 ("Gave me her promise true"), the accompaniment uses the chords V7, I, V, I. When the phrase is repeated in bars 20–23, different harmonies are used: V, vi, ii, III. The repetition of the melody is given variety and richness, and added expressiveness, by these different chords. The new chords are secondary harmonies that are substituted for the primary chords:

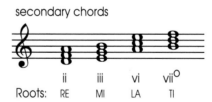

secondary chords

	ii	iii	vi	vii°
Roots:	RE	MI	LA	TI

Phrases and Cadences

A stanza of a song or a poem usually consists of four or more lines with a set meter and rhyme scheme, a pattern that is generally repeated in other stanzas. Each of these lines is usually short enough to be spoken or sung in one breath. (If humans had larger lungs, these lines would undoubtedly be longer.) As it is, poems and songs have a pause built-in after each line to give singers a chance to inhale a new supply of air so they can say or sing the next line. In music, these pauses at the end of a line or phrase are marked by a **cadence,** or *breathing break*. These cadences provide a natural pause in the melodic line.

Sometimes these cadences come at the end of a thought, where we want to convey the feeling of finality, like a period at the end of a sentence. In this case, the resting point is called a perfect or full cadence. The V or V7 chord resolves to the I (tonic) or home chord. This is often how you know the music is over. The tension has been resolved.

At other times the cadences come in the middle of an idea, indicating a temporary pause. This kind of pause corresponds to a comma and is called an imperfect or half-cadence. The music comes to rest momentarily on a V or V7 chord, which immediately conveys the feeling that the music has not ended. The half-cadence sustains the tension that has been created. The V chord needs to be resolved, so it establishes the feeling that there is more to come. It is like taking a commercial break in a television drama just at the point when the hero is about to open the box containing a poisonous snake.

Jeanie with the Light Brown Hair

Stephen Foster

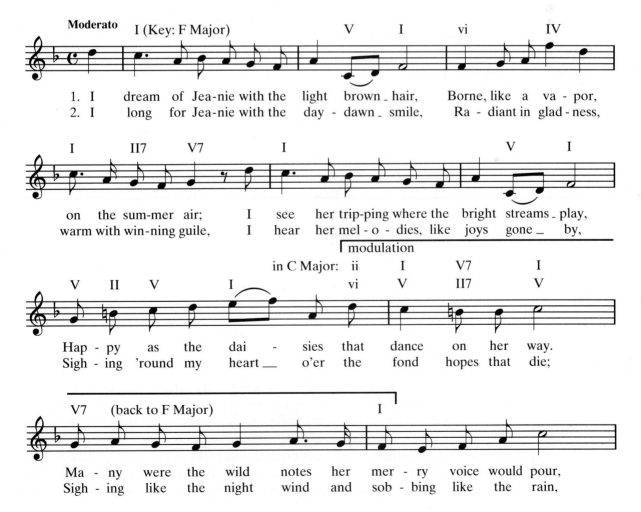

Moderato

I (Key: F Major)   V   I   vi   IV

1. I dream of Jea-nie with the light brown hair,   Borne, like a va-por,
2. I long for Jea-nie with the day-dawn smile,   Ra-diant in glad-ness,

I   II7   V7   I   V   I

on the sum-mer air;   I see her trip-ping where the bright streams play,
warm with win-ning guile,   I hear her mel-o-dies, like joys gone by,

modulation

in C Major: ii   I   V7   I

V   II   V   I   vi   V   II7   V

Hap-py as the dai-sies that dance on her way.
Sigh-ing 'round my heart o'er the fond hopes that die;

V7   (back to F Major)   I

Ma-ny were the wild notes her mer-ry voice would pour,
Sigh-ing like the night wind and sob-bing like the rain,

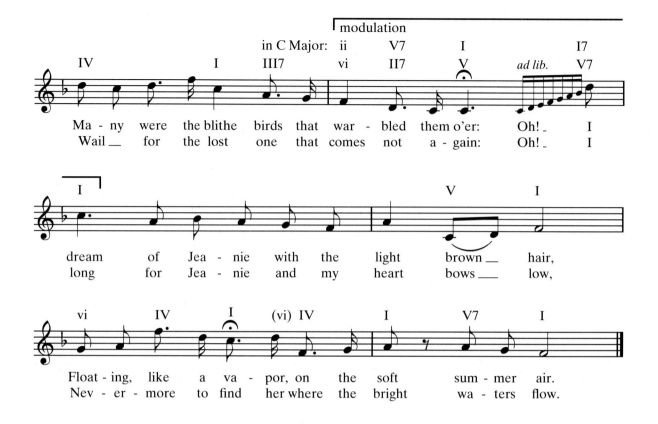

Incorporating Black Traditions

While families at home sang parlor songs like "Annie Laurie" and "Jeanie with the Light Brown Hair," a new form of public entertainment was introduced in 1828 by Thomas "Daddy" Rice who performed in blackface. At New York's Chatham Square Theater in 1843, Dan Emmett, the composer of "Dixie," transformed this form of entertainment into the first minstrel show. His Virginia Minstrels was a theatrical sensation. Soon other groups tried performing in blackface, but it was Ed Christy who gave the minstrel the unique form that made it the most popular type of entertainment in America during the second half of the century. Stephen Foster wrote many of his songs for Christy's minstrels.

As Christy developed it, the minstrel was a variety show consisting of comic songs and sentimental ballads, soft-shoe dancing and clogging, instrumental playing, comedy skits, sight gags, jokes, and amusing patter.

Minstrel shows toured widely and many of their songs became popular throughout the country. The minstrel song-and-dance routines incorporated many of the rich musical traditions that were part of the black culture at that time. After the Civil War, minstrel shows provided many black entertainers with their first opportunities to perform for white audiences.

By the last decade of the nineteenth century and the early years of the twentieth century, American popular music was not only absorbing and reflecting the black traditions, but it had also become more vital and unique because of them. One example is the song "Bill Bailey, Won't You Please Come Home?" (1902) by Hughie Cannon (1877–1912), who was one of the best of the minstrel song-and-dance men of that time. The song relates the story of how Bill Bailey's wife threw him out of the house and then begged him to come back with promises ("I'll do the cookin', darlin', I'll pay the rent"). She becomes even more distressed when she discovers he has struck it rich!

Bill Bailey, Won't You Please Come Home?

Words and Music by Hughie Cannon

▲ Seated in a semicircle on stage, the minstrel performers usually wore white gloves, colorful striped shirts, and swallowtail jackets. At center stage was Mr. Interlocutor, who served as master of ceremonies, introducing the performers and engaging them in banter. On the far left and right were the wise-cracking endmen, Mr. Tambo (right), who played the tambourine, and Mr. Bones (left), who played the bones. White performers often masqueraded in blackface, a characterization that was later denounced as racial stereotyping.

▼*Activity:* **Analyze, Create, Perform**

Use the melody from the chorus of "Bill Bailey" as the basis for creating your own love song.

Working in small groups, analyze the melody, write new lyrics for it, then perform your new love song.

1. Learn to sing the chorus. Find the basic pattern of syncopation that characterizes this piece. How many times is this rhythmic pattern repeated?

2. How many different chords are used to accompany the chorus? If the F chord is the I chord, and the B-flat chord is the IV chord, which chord is the V7? the II7? the VI7?

3. Determine the places where phrases end. Set up the number of accented (●) and unaccented (•) syllables you need in each line. The first line would look like this:

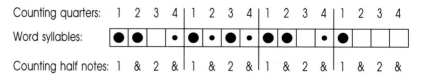

Counting quarters:	1 2 3 4	1 2 3 4	1 2 3 4	1 2 3 4
Word syllables:	● ● ·	· ● · ● ·	· ● ●	· ●
Counting half notes:	1 & 2 &	1 & 2 &	1 & 2 &	1 & 2 &

4. Select one of the major love song themes to guide your lyrical creativity (lost love, longing for love, or celebrating love). Determine what you want to say in your song. Note the rhyme scheme of the original, and develop one of your own.

5. First, write your lyrics on a sheet of paper, then hyphenate them and place them under the proper melody notes.
6. Practice performing your new version. You may choose to have someone: (a) play the melody on a keyboard instrument while you sing your lyrics; (b) accompany the song on a guitar or keyboard instrument using the six chords written above the melody; (c) improvise a rhythmic accompaniment while you sing the words; or (d) employ any combination of these performance options. Make sure your tempo and dynamics correspond to the type of love song you have written.

The delightful humor of these lyrics was not the only reason the song was an immediate smash hit and became popular from coast to coast. The song is a **cakewalk**, an *exuberant dance with syncopated rhythms that may represent an early form of jazz.* The infusion of black musical style gave American popular music a distinction that makes it recognizable anywhere in the world. In style, "Bill Bailey" is a giant leap away from earlier, European-based parlor songs like "Annie Laurie." The stilted language is gone. In its place is a directness and an honesty expressed in the vernacular—the ordinary language of the street. The rhythms, too, are fresh and catchy. The music captures the vigor and confidence of a new society discovering itself, and incorporating the best of its diverse creative resources.

Love Songs of Other Times and Places

We know that the art of communicating through original songs flourished in Europe during the twelfth, thirteenth, and fourteenth centuries. Poet-musicians called *troubadours* in southern France, *trouvères* in northern France, and *minnesingers* in Germany composed music and poetry and traveled widely, entertaining in the palaces of the feudal lords. Their songs related news and stories, and often, like today's troubadours—rap singers are one example—their songs were about love.

A Thirteenth-Century Monophonic Song

Like other trouvères of the late thirteenth century, Guillaume d'Amiens, (literally, William of Amiens [France]), sang of love. The text of one of his songs "Prendes i garde" ("Be on your guard"), tells of the secret meeting between two lovers. It is not known how trouvère melodies were originally performed. Only the melodies (not the rhythms) were notated in the manuscript.

Prendes i garde (Be on your guard)   by Guillaume d'Amiens

Take care, lest anyone see us
If someone sees us, tell me.
It's just there in that wooded grove.
Take care lest anyone see us.

The pleasant lass was looking
   after the animals,
"Charming brunette, I would
   like to meet with you"
Take care lest anyone see us,
If someone sees us, tell me.

The Minor Scale

"Prendes i garde" is in the minor mode. The minor scale has a pattern of whole (w) and half (h) steps that is different from that of the major scale. On the keyboard, the minor scale can be played on the white keys from A to A:

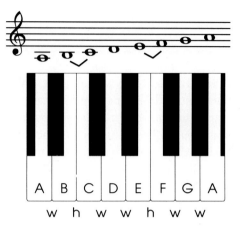

The pattern of the natural minor scale is w, h, w, w, h, w, w; or 1, ½, 1, 1, ½, 1, 1. Because this scale starts on A, it is called the A minor scale. An easier way to remember the minor scales is to relate them to their major counterpart. Play or sing any major scale from LA to LA instead of from DO to DO and you have the "relative" natural minor scale:

How can you tell whether "Prendes i garde" is in the major scale or the minor mode? One way is to take all the tones in the song and form a scale:

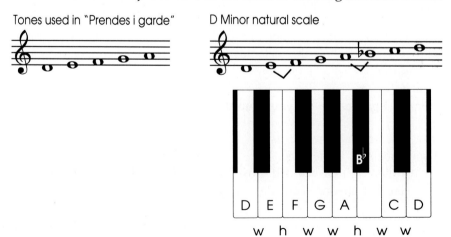

The whole- and half-step pattern reveals that the tones used in this song are the first five tones of the D minor scale. These tones suggest the minor mode. If the remaining tones of the D minor natural scale were also notated according to the pattern w, h, w, w, h, w, w, they would consist of a B♭, C, and D.

Prendes i garde

Thirteenth Century   Guillaume d'Amiens

1. Pren - des   i   gar - de ___ s'on   nous ___ re - gar - de

2. S'on   nous   re - gar - de ___ di - tes   le   moi.

3. C'est   tout   la   just   en ___ cel - [le] ___ bos - chai - ge

4. Pren - des   i   gar - de ___ s'on   nous ___ re - gar - de.

5. La   pas - tou - re - le ___ u   gar - doit   va - ches

6. "Plai - sant   bru - ne - te ___ a   vous   m'oc - troi."

7. Pren - des   i   gar - de ___ s'on   nous ___ re - gar - de

8. S'on   nous   re - gar - de ___ di - tes   le   moi.

▼*Activity:* **Determine Musical Form**

How does Guillaume d'Amiens, the thirteenth-century composer of this French *rondeau*, organize the music and the poetic form of the text?

Listen to a recording of "Prendes i garde" as you follow the music and decide which of the following patterns represents the musical form of the eight phrases of the song.

(1) A B a B a C A C   (2) A B a A a b A B   (3) A B a B a b A B   (4) A B C a D E A B

Now determine which of the above patterns represents the poetic form of the text. Assign capital letters to indicate the same music and text, lowercase letters to indicate the same music with different text. Which lines repeat the same music with different text? The poetic form you have just identified is called a **rondeau**, *a fixed poetic form of the thirteenth century.*

Learn to play "Prendes i garde" on a keyboard instrument. Decide whether the phrases are equal in length. Which phrases convey a sense of completeness or finality? How did you determine this?

You may have noticed the absence of a meter sign in the music. However, when you performed the work, you projected the presence of an underlying metric organization of triple meter. Create a rhythmic accompaniment to be played on percussion instruments while you perform the melody on a keyboard instrument.

An Eighteenth-Century Chorus

Not all expressions of love are composed as solo songs. During the Baroque period, George Frideric Handel (1685–1759) composed **oratorios**, *a sectional form for soloists, chorus, and orchestra. Solomon* (1749), like his earlier *Messiah* (1742), is a sacred work in three parts. In the third part, Handel creates an entertainment within an entertainment. King Solomon wants to show the Queen of Sheba the four human temperaments as sung by his singers with himself as the announcer. First he asks for a song evoking the melodious charms of music, and the chorus sings "Music, spread thy voice around." Then he commands his singers to create a martial mood, and they sing "Shake the dome and pierce the sky." Next there is tragedy. The chorus sings "Draw the tear from hopeless love," a vivid comparison of the anguish of lost love with death and despair. Finally, the fourth temperament is represented by the serene "Thus rolling surges rise," a balmy and carefree description of the sea.

Handel's chorus, "Draw the tear from hopeless love," depicts the emotions clearly and dramatically, as Baroque composers always tried to do. The pathos of hopeless love is exaggerated in order to arouse feelings of sympathy and compassion. The moods or affections (as they were called then) are portrayed so as to affect the listener. He achieves this intensity of emotion through the basic elements of melody, harmony, and rhythm. The melody, for example, begins with a powerful, descending octave leap immediately followed by an ascending leap of a seventh. The words "tear" and "hopeless" are set with dissonance—notes that clash harmonically:

Profile

George Frideric Handel
German Composer
1685–1759

GEORGE FRIDERIC HANDEL

Not much is known about George Frideric Handel's family life, except that he was born on February 23, 1685 in Halle, Germany. He showed musical prowess, and even though his father forbade him to study music, he smuggled a clavichord into the attic and practiced on it secretly. Reluctantly, his father finally allowed the boy to study music as well as law. After graduating from the university, he served as an organist at a local church for a year before going to Hamburg in 1703 at the age of 18. At Hamburg, a center of opera, Handel played violin and harpsichord for the operas. This experience undoubtedly contributed to his lifelong interest in composing for the theater.

In 1706, Handel went to Italy, where he honed his keyboard playing and opera composing. There, he composed concertos, sonatas, cantatas, and oratorios, but most important, he absorbed the free-flowing Italian lyricism, which was to be a hallmark of his later music. It was in England that Handel made his mark as one of the greatest composers of the Baroque era. His opera *Rinaldo* was a triumph there during his first visit in 1711. He moved there the next year, remaining in London until his death in 1759.

Handel's finest achievement was the invention of the English oratorio, a form of story-telling for soloists, chorus, and orchestra. The oratorios were dramas without scenery. Oddly, *Israel in Egypt* and *Messiah* are the only oratorios based on the Bible and the only ones without a plot. Their uniqueness and the grandeur of their choruses may account for their continued popularity.

Then there is the dotted rhythm, one of the great discoveries of the Baroque. The dotted rhythm, occurring in the minor mode at the words "wild despair," evokes tragedy and death. Appropriately, Handel sets "death" with a diminished chord.

▼*Activity:* **Figure Out**

How does Handel's music express the anguish of lost love?

Sing the opening line of "Draw the tear from hopeless love" paying attention to the dissonance on the words "tear" and "hopeless." Sing the line "full of death and wild despair" making the dotted rhythm clipped and dramatic. Now listen to the recording of this work while you follow the text:

> Draw the tear from hopeless love;
> lengthen out the solemn air,
> full of death and wild despair.

1. Which sections of the text did Handel set polyphonically?
2. Which sections of the text are set homophonically?
3. How and where does Handel use silence to good effect?

▼ The opera *Madama Butterfly* by Italian composer Giacomo Puccini is among the great tragic love stories of all time. Based on real-life incidents, the story focuses upon a young Japanese girl who falls in love with an American naval officer while he is stationed in Japan. She marries him against her father's wishes, not knowing the love is one-sided. Her rejected love is made all the more emotional by Puccini's music, the reason this opera continues to be performed throughout the world.

An Early Twentieth-Century Opera Aria

The three basic emotional states of love—lost, sought, or found—are just as common in classical music as they are in popular. As in popular music, classical songs expressing the tragedy of lost love and the search for love outnumber songs that celebrate the joys of love. We see this in the opera *Madama Butterfly* (1904) by Giacomo Puccini (1858–1924). This story-told-in-song is a very popular opera because the action is realistic and the characters are understandably human. Like most operas, this is a love story.

The story of *Madama Butterfly* recounts the tragic relationship between a young Japanese lady and an American naval officer named Pinkerton. At the age of 15, Butterfly marries the visiting lieutenant, who promptly abandons her. Despite Butterfly's responsibility as a single parent for raising their son, Butterfly remains hopeful about their marriage. She fantasizes about her husband's return and their ensuing happiness in the famous aria, "Un bel di" ("One fine day"). Unfortunately, when he does arrive, three years after leaving her, it is with Kate, his American wife. Realizing that her love has been a delusion, Butterfly blindfolds her son and then stabs herself to death.

This opera was given its world premiere at La Scala Opera House in Milan, Italy, in 1904, and its American premiere at the Metropolitan Opera in 1907. The opera continues to be one of the most popular in the world, and its essence is summed up in its most famous aria, "Un bel di."

▲ Italian composer Giacomo Puccini composed operas based upon true-to-life stories full of suspense and surprise. *La Boheme*, the story of a struggling painter and his love for the sickly Mimi, may be his masterpiece, but he composed a number of other operas, including *Tosca, La Fanciulla del West (The Girl of the Golden West), Turandot,* and *Madama Butterfly.*

▼Activity: *Discover through Analysis*

How does Puccini's music reflect the hopes and feelings of Madame Butterfly?

Listen to "Un bel di" as you follow the Italian words and their translation, and focus on the ideas that occur. Describe the dramatic action portrayed in each of the events.

1. How does Puccini organize the music to support these different dramatic actions?
2. Listen to it again and, by selecting the letter, match each of the four dramatic sections with one of the following musical descriptions.
   A. The most intense section, with the loudest dynamic level. A climactic pitch in high register is held for a long duration.
   B. Strong, powerful melody in triple meter that begins in a high register. Singing is legato (smooth and connected), with much rubato (give and take in the tempo), and a wide vocal range.
   C. Vocal phrases are short. At first the vocal range is narrow and speechlike; then it turns impassioned and full voiced, changing from duple to triple meter.
   D. The meter changes to duple. The singing is hushed, calm, and thoughtful, then more excited and expectant.

   Answer the following questions:

3. Which words mark the return of the opening melody? What is the text referring to at this point?
4. Which section employs the greatest dynamic contrasts? How do these dynamic contrasts support the text?

An American Opera Duet

Love songs are sometimes presented in the form of a duet. This can serve as the perfect medium for a lover's quarrel or to show the emotion of two people who are happily in love. One of the most famous love songs of the latter type is the duet "Bess, You Is My Woman Now" from George Gershwin's opera *Porgy and Bess* (1935), which incorporated the local dialect of the Gullah Negroes of Charleston, South Carolina, about 1912, where and when the opera takes place.

In the opera, Porgy and Bess sing their famous love duet. At first, Porgy sings alone to Bess. Then, after an expressive modulation (a change of key), Bess sings her response to Porgy. At the end of Bess's solo, Porgy echoes the "mornin' time an' evenin' time" theme before the two join in singing together. Here, both Porgy and Bess are singing different lyrics and different melodies to each other at the same time. These combined lyrics are as follows:

Bess: Porgy, I's yo' woman now, I is, I is, An' I ain' never goin' nowhere 'less you shares de fun.

Porgy: Bess, you is my woman now an' forever. Dis life is jes' begun,- Bess, we two is one now an' forever.

Bess: Dere's no wrinkle on my brow, no-how, but I ain' goin' you hear me sayin'

Porgy: Oh Bess, don' min' dose women. You got yo' Porgy, you loves yo' Porgy, I know you means it,

Bess: If you ain' goin', wid you I'm stayin'. Porgy, I's yo' woman now! I's yours forever.

Porgy: I seen it in yo' eyes, Bess. We'll go swingin' through de years a singin'

Bess: Mornin' time an' evenin' time an' summer time an' winter time.

Porgy: Hmmm————

Bess: Hmmm——

Porgy: Mornin' time an' evenin' time an' summer time an' winter time.

Bess: Oh my Porgy, my man Porgy, from dis' minute I'm tellin' you, I keep dis vow:

Porgy: My Bess, my Bess, from dis' minute I'm tellin' you, I keep dis vow:

Bess: Porgy, I's yo' woman now.

Porgy: Oh, my Bessie, we's happy now—we is one now.

▼*Activity:* **Listen Perceptively**

What makes a great love song? Listen to the duet "Bess, You Is My Woman Now" from *Porgy and Bess* and describe the musical qualities that make it so expressive.

Listen to this duet three times while you list your comments in each of the suggested areas: (a) The first time you listen to the lovers singing together on the third chorus, try to focus your attention exclusively on the melodic line sung by Bess; (b) the second time, focus your attention on Porgy's line; and (c) the third time, see if you can follow both of their lines and lyrics simultaneously.

◀ In spite of his disability, Porgy finds true love. He and Bess declare their love for each other in the song, "Bess, You Is My Woman Now." Clamma Dale and Donnie Ray Albert play the roles in the Houston Grand Opera's production of the George Gershwin opera, *Porgy and Bess.*

*S*ummary

The love song is one of the most compelling and frequent forms of musical expression. Love songs turn up in all cultures throughout history. As highly inventive and intensely expressive musical creations, they capture some of the strongest emotions we experience in our lives. Perhaps no other form of artistic expression can surpass music in representing these powerful emotions: the tragedy and anguish of lost love, the disturbingly empty and lonely search to find love, and the joy of love secured. The subject of love can reveal the best of any composer. We know it when all the elements of music come together to express these common human themes in ways that illuminate our own emotional state and let us know that we are not alone in feeling the way we do.

CHAPTER 12

Religious Music

Objectives

By completing this chapter, you will:

- Realize how music projects religious feeling, and interprets the meaning of sacred texts.
- Understand the importance of music in the practice of most of the world's religions.
- Become acquainted with music of different religions, including Hindu, Buddhist, Jewish, Christian, and Islamic faiths.
- Learn the history and style of gospel music.
- Find out how popular music has been used to express religious beliefs.

Musical Terms

cantata
chorale
chorale prelude
conjunct
disjunct
harmonics
kritis
overtones
word painting

$\mathcal{M}$usic has always had its practical uses.
Tribal music throughout the world seems to be
directly connected to, and stand at the heart of, every
aspect of tribal life. But in even more advanced societies,
much of the world's music is made to serve very real
human needs. It is precisely because it serves these
real needs that music is valued and esteemed.

Religious Music

Throughout the ages and in every part of the world, people have sought help from a divine being. As far as anthropologists can determine, every culture has believed in some type of religion or some force larger than the individual. Therefore, religions—which influence the culture and lifestyle of their people—can be used to help define many of the world's peoples. For example, The Old Testament proclaims to Western peoples their "dominion . . . over every living thing." In contrast, Native American and Eastern peoples view themselves as part of and in harmony with nature, an outlook that is manifested in their religions. Such fundamental beliefs alter the way people attend to life and live it. For many, religion becomes a central guiding hand that permeates all that they do and everything they are.

All major religions or belief systems use sound as an expression of faith and spirituality, which are difficult to understand through words alone. Like the great cathedrals, temples, holy shrines, and other religious works of art, music evokes the spiritual and helps people stay in touch with it. It expresses the mysteries of life and the search for meaning. In this sense, music joins religion to give life direction, wholeness, and purpose.

Hinduism

Hinduism is one of the oldest religions still practiced in the world. Today, some half a billion people are Hindus. Aside from the island of Bali, and the mountain kingdom of Nepal, India is the only Hindu country in the world.

Hindus worship many gods and goddesses, each with his or her own name, shape, and character. One of the most important of the many gods is Vishnu, who is thought of as the creator of life and substance. The god Shiva is the lord of the dance. Saraswati is the goddess of music and learning. Although there are many different gods and goddesses, some Hindus believe that these deities are all aspects of a single divine power.

PROJECT

Investigate Religious Music

Investigate the music used in religious services in your community. Attend a worship service and write a short paper on the role and function of music in that religious ceremony. Use the following questions as the basis for your report:

1. In what language is the music performed?
2. Who is performing the music?
3. If a choir is present, what is the vocal makeup of the group?
4. Is the music accompanied or unaccompanied?
5. Which instruments, if any, are used in the worship service?
6. Do members of the congregation participate in the music of the worship service or are they spectators?
7. What is the style of the music?
8. Describe the role of music in the worship service.

Hindus believe that all creatures are in a process of spiritual evolution; that their souls strive through successive rebirths to achieve union with Brahman, the Supreme Being and source of universal life; and that people must live righteously according to their caste, or station in life.

The Music of Hinduism

Natural connections are made between faith and the arts, which are inseparable in Hinduism. These connections are so pervasive that it is difficult to think of one without the other. **Kritis** (KRI-tees*), are Hindu religious songs that are sung in praise of a particular god or gods.* Many kritis, including "Bruhi Mukundeti," were composed in southern India during the eighteenth and nineteenth centuries by deeply religious individuals, many of whom are considered today to be Hindu saints. Kritis are usually sung by a solo artist in a concert setting.

Much of the Indian music uses the principle of theme and variations. Sometimes the variations are improvised, sometimes composed. In kritis, the variations are often both composed and improvised. The example you will hear includes only composed variations. In "Bruhi Mukundeti," the poet asks his tongue to keep repeating the different sacred names of God (Keshala, Madhava, Govinda, Krishna, Sadanand, Radha, Ram). The repeated utterance of God's names is, in itself, often seen as a religious act. "Bruhi Mukundeti," has seven lines:

1. Bruhi mukundeti rasane
   (BROO-hee mu-KOOND E-tee RA-sa-ney)
2. Keshava madhava govindeti
   (KE-sha-va MAA-dha-va go-VIND E-tee)
3. Krishna nanta sadanandeti
   (KRISH-na NAN-ta sa-DAAN-nand E-tee)
4. Bruhi mukundeti rasane
5. Radha ramana hare rameti
   (RAA-dha RAAM-a-na HA-re RAAM E-tee)
6. Raji baksha ghana shyameti
   (RAA-jee BAK-sha GHA-na SHYAAM E-tee)
7. Bruhi mukundeti rasane

The first line serves as a kind of refrain and is sung six times initially, with an additional half-line ("Bruhi mukundeti") repeated as a cadence. It recurs two more times (lines 4 and 7) and is sung two and one-half times at each appearance. This song is sung by M. S. Subbalakshmi (SOOB-ba-LAK-shmee), one of India's most famous vocalists. She sings in an ancient Indian language called Sanskrit and is accompanied by a violin and a barrel-shaped drum called a *mrdangam* (mir-DUN-gum). In the background, you will also hear a drone instrument called a *tambura*. By repeating the tonal center over and over, this four-stringed instrument establishes a firm foundation for the melodic activities occurring above it.

▲ Above is a statue of Saraswati, the Hindu goddess of music and wisdom. The arts are such an integral part of Hinduism that it is difficult to separate the two. Religion and art, music, and drama merge in Hindu life.

Saraswati. Pallu, Bikaner, Rajasthan, India. New Delhi National Museum, India. 1–6/278.

▼*Activity:* **Explore Repetition and Contrast**

Listen to the kriti "Bruhi Mukundeti" and note the balance between repetition and contrast.

Read the words to this kriti aloud. Line 1 (see page 200) is sung six and one-half times, and lines 4 and 7 are performed two and one-half times.

Listen to the performance and answer the questions below. After the singer introduces each line, she repeats it a number of times. The composer has added subtle (and not so subtle) musical variations to these repeated lines:

1. How many times are the other four lines heard?
2. Why is this repetition important?
3. What musical elements provide contrast in this performance? (Possibilities include altering the melodic contour, melodic rhythm, dynamics, and adding ornamentation.)

Buddhism

Through meditations on his 35th birthday, Siddhartha Gautama (c. 563–483 B.C.) received revelations that made him Buddha (meaning "awakened"), the Enlightened One. He then set a mission for himself to show others how to attain this enlightenment, and the faith known as Buddhism was born. After 2,500 years, this faith still guides more than 200 million people, mostly in southeastern Asian countries such as Myanmar (formerly Burma), Thailand, Cambodia, and Vietnam.

Buddhists believe that in order to attain enlightenment the individual must look inwardly, not to any gods. They believe that God does not intercede on earth. The ideal is to shed earthly desires to reach the state of *nirvana*, a peace of mind devoid of any desires or thoughts of pleasure. It is also believed that a life well lived brings rewards in the next life.

The basic teachings of Buddhism are contained in the Four Noble Truths. These describe life as suffering, sorrow as arising from craving, the elimination of suffering, and the path of actions by which one can escape from suffering. After Buddha's death, Buddhism separated into two schools: Therevada (TEH-ra-VAH-da) and Mahayana (MAH-ha-YAH-na). Both schools follow Buddha's basic teachings but differ in interpretation and practice.

Therevada Buddhism, the more orthodox school, moved south from India to Sri Lanka, Cambodia, Thailand, Laos, and Myanmar. In these countries, animism (spirit worship) and Hinduism, which predate Buddhism, still play a part in the religious life. Therevada Buddhism maintains the original teachings and focuses on monks achieving enlightenment through the disciplined practice of individual meditation in a monastery. Ceremonies and rituals are not integral parts of worship. A strong relationship exists between the monks and the rest of society, to whom the monks provide education and counsel. By donating food and other supplies to the monks for subsistence, people accumulate merit that contributes to their rebirth into a higher order.

▶ A Buddhist monk plays a temple drum. Music is an important part of Buddhist ceremonies. Buddhism is a major religion or belief system in spite of the fact that Buddha made no claim to divinity, nor did he offer reliance on any gods. He taught that we must look for salvation within ourselves.

Mahayana Buddhism is found in Tibet, China, North and South Korea, and Japan. In this form of Buddhism, worship is ceremonial and ritualistic. Mahayana Buddhism relies on the *Bodhisattvas* (boh-di-SAHT-vahs), or human embodiments of the Buddha, to work actively for the good of suffering beings. Unlike Therevada monks, Mahayana monks promote Buddha's teachings through ceremonies and rituals, thereby reaching a greater number of people. Here, too, other religious traditions such as shamanism, Taoism, and Confucianism have blended with Buddhism.

Music in Therevada Buddhism

Religious ceremonies in Therevada Buddhism, as practiced in Southeast Asia, include chants, drums, and gongs. Since instrumental and vocal music are viewed as the cause of deviation and distraction from the solemn meditation that leads to enlightenment, this type of music is prohibited as part of religious worship inside the Buddhist temple.

Outside the temple, music is an integral part of Buddhist ceremonies and rituals. It is heard at weddings, funerals, and religious festivals and celebrations, where its function is to establish atmosphere and entertain. The music may invoke spirits and gods that are considered animist or Hindu but still fit within Southeast Asian Buddhist tradition.

educated its people through magnificent pageants and passion plays (that told the Christmas and Easter stories), and splendid celebrations on feast days—all with glorious music.

For almost 1,500 years, Rome was the center of Christianity. The early history of music, therefore, is largely a history of Catholic church music—from Gregorian chants, motets, cantatas, and organ works to compositions for chorus and orchestra.

The Mass

The principal form of the Catholic liturgical service is the mass. Through the ages, composers have written music for the sung portions of the mass, and the tradition has continued into our own time. One of the functions of religious music is to interpret the text of the mass and express its ultimate meaning. Music forces us to linger over the words and ponder them.

Ludwig van Beethoven was a master at **word painting,** *the technique of making the music portray the meaning of the words.* This technique was developed by Renaissance composers. Beethoven's *Missa Solemnis* ("Solemn Mass") provides some excellent examples of word painting and the meaning it can impart.

This work is unusually long, and it requires a great number of performers—soloists, chorus, and a large orchestra. It seems more suited to the concert hall than to a liturgical service, and that is generally where it is performed today. (Beethoven originally conceived his *Missa Solemnis* as a liturgical work, although one for an event of exceptional magnificence. His good friend and patron, the Royal Archduke Rudolph, was to be installed as archbishop of Olmutz, and this was to be the music for the grand service. Unfortunately, Beethoven did not complete the work until two years after the occasion had taken place!)

The *Missa Solemnis,* like most other masses, is organized in five poetic sections: Kyrie, Gloria, Credo, Sanctus, and Agnus Dei. Beethoven uses his large performing forces to dramatize and enhance the many different meanings within this vast liturgical text. An excerpt from the Gloria, the second section of the mass, illustrates how he uses sound to interpret the words. If we were merely to speak these words, we might find it difficult to decide which lines exalt and praise God and which are more prayerlike:

Gloria in excelsis Deo,	Glory to God in the highest,

Et in terra pax hominibus
    bonae voluntatis.
	And on earth peace to men of
	    good will.

Laudamus te,	We praise Thee,
Benedicimus te,	We bless Thee,
Adoramus te,	We adore Thee,
Glorificamus te.	We glorify Thee.

Beethoven's musical setting of the text makes clear his sense of divine glory as well as his humility as a man in the face of it.

▼Activity: *Discover Word Painting*

How does Beethoven paint different musical pictures to convey the meanings of the text in the Gloria of his *Missa Solemnis*?

Listen to the opening of the Gloria, and describe how Beethoven's theme paints the meaning of the words "Gloria in excelsis Deo." Show the melodic contour with your hand.

Allegro vivace

Glo - ri - a   in ex-cel - sis   De - o,

How do the orchestra and voices treat this theme? Describe the tempo and rhythm. Is the setting polyphonic or homophonic?

Listen again to the opening Gloria, focusing on the second line of text, "Et in terra pax hominibus bonae voluntatis." How does Beethoven paint the meaning of these words? Describe the musical elements that amplify the meaning.

How is such a musical contrast between these two lines of text justified?

Describe Beethoven's musical treatment of the next lines of text. How does he interpret these words?

How did Beethoven create a sense of musical unity and variety through word painting in this opening section of the Gloria?

The Hymn

On October 31, 1517, when Martin Luther posted his "Ninety-five Theses Upon Indulgences" on the door of the Wittenberg Castle Church in Germany, he ended the preeminent role of the Catholic church in Western Europe. At the time, Luther, himself a Catholic priest, took issue with the right of his churchmen to extract monies for certain favors they bestowed. He created an uproar that finally split the church. In 1529, when Luther was prohibited from teaching by the Catholic rulers in Germany, his supporters protested, and the Protestant movement was born. Protestantism extolled the authority of the Bible and each person's direct relationship with God. Since that time, Protestantism has grown in many different forms and has deeply affected Western thought and civilization.

Luther's idea that people should have a direct relationship with God can be seen in his music. He translated the Bible into German so that people could read it themselves. (At the time, the official language of the Catholic church was Latin.) He composed simple, yet powerful, hymns in the people's own language. "A Mighty Fortress Is Our God" is a good example.

Later composers used the **chorale**, or *hymn tune*, as the basis for various kinds of musical works. For example, Felix Mendelssohn used the chorale "A Mighty Fortress" as the first theme in the fourth movement of his Symphony No. 5 in D Major (*Reformation*). Mendelssohn composed

Cooperative Learning

Determine

How does the melodic contour affect the expressiveness of a melody?

Listen to Martin Luther's hymn tune "A Mighty Fortress Is Our God" and try to hear the logic and power of the form. Facing a partner, create a mirror image of the phrases by moving your hand in an arc. Which phrases convey a sense of completeness or finality? What is the basis for your determination? Why is this tune so powerful? (Hint: Study the use of DO (tonic) and SOL (dominant), the two most important tones in the scale, throughout the tune.)

the work in celebration of the 300th anniversary of the Augsburg Confession, the document that set forth the principles of Protestantism in 1530. In this orchestral work, he used the chorale theme in a dramatic rather than religious way.

A Mighty Fortress Is Our God

Words and music by Martin Luther, 1529

A might-y for-tress is — our God, A bul-wark nev-er fail - ing, Pro-tect-ing us — with staff and rod, His pow-er all pre - vail - ing. What if — the na - tions — rage, And surg-ing seas ram - page; What though the moun-tains fall, The Lord is God of all; On earth is not His e - qual.

▼*Activity:* **Track the Musical Events**

Listen to the fourth movement of Felix Mendelssohn's Symphony No. 5 in D Minor and hear how he builds the movement around the chorale theme.

Try to identify each of the following successive musical events.
All nine phrases of the chorale "A Mighty Fortress" (first theme) are presented:

1. Phrase 1, solo flute, piano (*p*);
2. Phrase 2, woodwinds added, still *p*;
3. Phrases 3 and 4, woodwind choir, mezzo forte (*mf*);
4. Phrases 5 and 6, strings and brass added, still *mf*;
5. Phrases 7 and 8, full orchestra, forte (*f*);
6. Phrase 9, brass choir, fortissimo (*ff*).
7. Transition: The first three phrases of the hymn tune are presented as a transition to the second theme.
8. Second theme: Mendelssohn adds his own original theme, the first part of which is a rocket-style ascending melody that is very active and dramatic:

9. Second theme: The second part of the theme is based on this rhythmic pattern:

10. Fugato (small fugue), based on fragments of the second theme.
11. Closing theme, martial in character, with repetition of this rhythmic pattern:

12. Development: Based on the first part of the second theme (number 8 above).
13. Transition to the chorale melody played on cello, then clarinet.
14. Recapitulation: Second theme is used as the subject of a fugue.
15. Chorale melody is heard in long notes above the fugue.
16. Closing theme (number 11) is heard again:

17. Coda: An ending that concludes with a dramatic and compelling statement of the entire chorale for full orchestra (*allegro maestoso*).

Cooperative Learning

Explore and Experience

Experience how Bach added counterpoint to a chorale to give it new interest.

Learn to sing or play the chorale tune "Sleepers Awake." Analyze and compare the melody of this chorale to "A Mighty Fortress." Is the melodic contour similar or dissimilar?

Learn to sing the chorale melody or play it on a keyboard instrument or on bells. How did Bach change this tune?

Have someone who can read music play the counter melody. Why do the chorale and counter melody contrast so starkly with each other? Now perform the chorale melody with the counter melody. This is a good example of two-part non-imitative counterpoint.

Listen to the recording of this movement from Cantata 140 and make a listening map of the texture by indicating an "R" for the instrumental melody or "ritornello" sections and a "C" for the chorale melody with the counter melody.

Challenge: Learn to play the bass line on a keyboard instrument or a synthesizer. Perform all three parts together in counterpoint.

Johann Sebastian Bach also borrowed chorale melodies and used them as the basis for constructing new works. He often improvised on the organ, using a familiar chorale melody as the basis. These became known as **chorale preludes,** *compositions that served as introductions to the singing by the congregation.* Today these works are often used as preludes or postludes to the religious service.

Many of Bach's cantatas rely on hymn tunes as sources of their inspiration. As developed in the seventeenth century, a **cantata** is *an accompanied vocal work in a number of movements with a sacred or a secular text.* Bach incorporated the sacred cantata into the Protestant church service. These works have a magnificence because of Bach's skills as a composer in expressing his unflagging faith. Normally, these cantatas end with a simple harmonized chorale or hymn that was sung by the congregation. In this sense, cantatas were participatory. Sometimes the chorale served as the basis for other movements of the cantata. The use of recognizable hymn tunes made these works readily familiar and gave them a kind of popular appeal. Cantatas were the Protestant equivalent of the mass. They became increasingly elaborate, with movements for soloists interspersed with choruses, all accompanied by a small orchestra. The chorale, however, remained the essential ingredient.

Profile

Felix Mendelssohn
German Composer
1809–1847

FELIX MENDELSSOHN

Felix Mendelssohn was born in Hamburg, Germany in 1809. His father, a banker, provided him with all the advantages that accompany money and community standing. Felix and his sister, Fanny, who was also an accomplished musician, received their early musical education from their mother, Leah. In 1817, at the age of eight, Felix Mendelssohn began studying with Karl Friederich Zelter, and one year later made his musical debut. In 1819, the Berlin Singakademie performed his setting of Psalm 19, and when he was 17, Mendelssohn composed his most popular work, the overture to *A Midsummer Night's Dream*. After attending the university in Berlin for three years, he finally settled on music as his profession.

After leaving the university, he made his first of ten visits to England, where audiences adored him. Inspired by the scenery while touring Wales and Scotland, Mendelssohn composed the *Hebrides* Overture and later his Symphony No. 3 ("Scottish"). His works include music for piano and voice as well as his famous *Violin Concerto* (1844) and his great oratorio, *Elijah* (1846). Throughout his life, he continued to tour, compose, and campaign to raise the standards of the public's musical taste. He also founded and administrated the Leipzig Conservatory. He is credited with popularizing the music of J. S. Bach after almost a century of neglect.

Sleepers Awake!

J. S. Bach

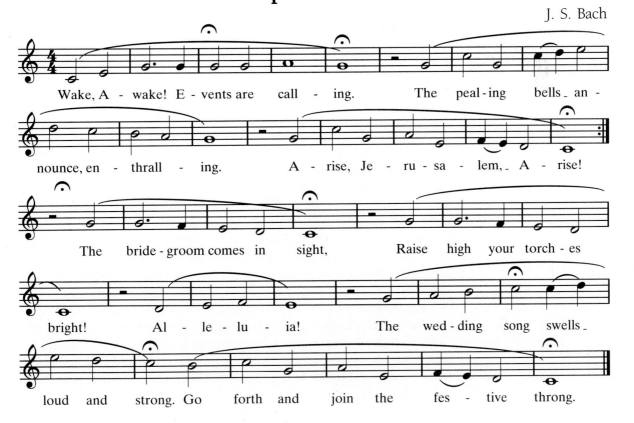

Wake, A - wake! E - vents are call - ing. The peal - ing bells an -
nounce, en - thrall - ing. A - rise, Je - ru - sa - lem, A - rise!
The bride - groom comes in sight, Raise high your torch - es
bright! Al - le - lu - ia! The wed - ding song swells
loud and strong. Go forth and join the fes - tive throng.

▲ Church singers in New Orleans sing gospel music, a lively and fervent form of Christian musical expression. Originally a style of vocal music associated with evangelistic revival meetings, gospel music is an American creation that is now sung widely throughout the United States and admired around the world.

Gospel Music

After the Civil War in the United States, Negro churches emerged with their own kind of Protestantism. The Negro spiritual, which had its roots in slavery, was the predominant style of black sacred music in the latter part of the nineteenth century. Between 1871 and 1879, the Fisk University Jubilee Singers toured this country and Europe, popularizing concert versions of the spiritual. These spirituals were sung without instrumental accompaniment, and singers were not permitted to improvise or interject their own personal emotions.

Around 1895 in Lexington, Mississippi, a group of Baptist clergymen led by Charles Henry Mason left the Black Baptist church because of doctrinal and liturgical differences. By 1906 this splinter group had evolved into the fundamentalist Church of God, centered in Memphis, Tennessee. Members believed in the literal meaning of the Bible and sang spirited songs accompanied by tambourines, drums, and piano. Although these were not called by any particular name, they were early black gospel songs.

Later, members established the Church of God in Christ in other major cities across the United States. They spread these musical traditions and influenced the development of black gospel music. The gospel song borrowed three basic song types from the spiritual: (1) call-and-response chant, (2) the slow, syncopated, long-phrased melody, and (3) the fast, syncopated motivic melody.

▼Activity: *Hear the Musical Events*

Listen to a typical black gospel song, "Perfect Praise," and distinguish what is going on musically.

Using the following list of the successive musical events, try to hear each event described as it occurs. Note: the events are not all of the same length. On a separate piece of paper, answer the questions by using your musical ears.

1. An introduction is performed by a solo piano, highly ornamented with fill-in notes and chords, blues chords, heavy accents, played in a percussive style mixed with legato.

2. Entrance of instrumental accompaniment. Can you name the instruments?

3. Vocal solo enters. What type of voice does the soloist have?

4. Choir enters with repeat of the melody sung in event number 3. What does the soloist do?

5. Repeat of event number 4. Soloist improvises.

6. Second verse of song. Choir sings contrasting dynamic level while the soloist sings various words (vocables) and improvises.

7. What happens here?

8. Tenors enter with the final section of the piece. Choir sings refrain, "Jesus excellent."

9. Tenors repeat event number 8. What section of the choir enters with a counter melody? Choir again sings the refrain, "Jesus excellent."

10. Tenors repeat event number 9 and are joined by the soprano section singing a counter melody.

11. Event number 10 is repeated *a cappella* with hand claps. Choir sings refrain and fades out.

Other styles of music in the early 1900s also influenced the development of gospel music. While many spirituals tended to be somber, the jubilee was primarily happy and lively. The spirit of the jubilee became the spirit of gospel music. Then, too, the white revival hymns or white gospel songs that were sung at large religious crusades and camp meetings contained lively rhythms as well as call-and-response chants. The antiphonal style used in performing these hymns in which part-singing was answered by part-singing was also borrowed, along with the term gospel.

The Negro spiritual, jubilee, and white gospel song influenced the first major black gospel hymn composer, the Rev. Charles Albert Tindley (c. 1851–1933), who was born in Berlin, Maryland. Tindley wrote over 50 hymns for his East Calvary Methodist Church in Philadelphia. Itinerant preachers carried them everywhere.

Black gospel music gained national recognition during the 1940s and 1950s. Through recordings and tours, Sister Rosetta Tharpe was one of the first gospel singers to achieve a national following. Today, gospel music

Profile

Thomas Andrew Dorsey
American Composer, Performer,
and Band Leader
1899–1993

THOMAS ANDREW DORSEY

Known as the Father of Black Gospel Music, Thomas Andrew Dorsey was a former blues pianist, composer, and band leader for blues singer Gertrude "Ma" Rainey. Dorsey set religious texts to tuneful melodies, adding blues notes, lively rhythms, and syncopated piano accompaniments. He credits the Rev. Charles Tindley's hymns as a model for his own gospel songs.

Dorsey needed perseverance and courage in the face of many disappointments to become accepted as a legitimate gospel composer. In the 1930s, many of the large orthodox Black Baptist churches would not allow gospel music in their worship services because of its similarity to the popular music of the day. They called gospel music "the devil's music."

Traveling from church to church, Dorsey sang his music and taught it whenever ministers gave him the chance. He published over 400 gospel songs, and he brought his five-cent copies with him. Eventually, the spirit and the sincerity of his music won acceptance. Renowned gospel performers Mahalia Jackson, Clara Ward, Roberta Martin, and the Rev. James Cleveland are indebted to Dorsey's efforts on their behalf. His most famous song, "Take My Hand, Precious Lord," was written after the sudden death of his first wife and son during childbirth. It has been sung in over 40 languages.

permeates the fabric of music in America. The fervent religious feeling, personal expression of the singers, the infectious harmonies and syncopated rhythms, and the strong rhythmic drive of the instrumental accompaniment continue to evolve and change.

The word gospel literally means good news. It expresses in song the message of Jesus Christ's birth, mission, and gift to mankind. Gospel music can now be heard in religious services of every type, Protestant and Catholic. No other style of sacred music incorporates the free interpretation of the vocal and instrumental parts by the performers, or invites the kind of audience participation, that gospel music does. This is an original American creation that is recognized and admired throughout the world.

▼Activity: **Participate**

Sing your own version of the gospel song, "Ordinary People" by Danniebelle Hall.

Listen to the recording of this song while you follow the music. Repeat several times until you know the melody and rhythms and can sing along.

Using the recorded accompaniment, sing your own version of this song, being free about your expression. Try creating a solo and response by having a group repeat the phrase "ordinary people" where you feel it is appropriate.

This piece is in slow 4/4 time. Does it lend itself to clapping on the offbeats—2 and 4? Why or why not?

Ordinary People

Danniebelle Hall

like that lit-tle lad who gave Je-sus all he had; how the

mul-ti-tude was fed with a fish and loaves of bread! What you

have may not seem much, but when you yield it to the touch of the

Mas-ter's lov-ing hand then you will un-der-stand how your

life could nev - er be the same. Just or - di - nar - y

⊕ CODA

place it in the Mas - ter's hand. _ Yeah. _ Oh, your

rit.

lit - tle be - comes much as you place it in the Mas - ter's hand. _____

Popular Religious Music

As churches continue to relate to the contemporary world, they tend to embrace today's music and appeal to people by using vernacular forms: pop, gospel, rock, and country. Throughout history, churches have periodically embraced the musical forms and styles of the day. Christianity dressed in the garb of popular music should not be shocking; but when Andrew Lloyd Webber's rock musical *Jesus Christ Superstar* opened on Broadway in 1971, it caused a stir. Webber set well-known biblical stories to the wild, commercial, popular music of the day.

▼*Activity:* **Discover**

How does Andrew Lloyd Webber's music reflect the feelings Judas expresses in the song "Heaven On Their Minds"?

Listen to "Heaven On Their Minds" from the musical *Jesus Christ Superstar* as you follow the text. Describe Judas's state of mind.

Clap the basic beat while you chant these rhythmic patterns on "doo":

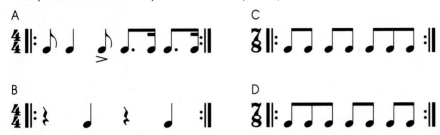

Listen to Judas's song again and determine which of these patterns is heard in each of the six sections of text and three musical interludes. Make a list. Then answer these questions:

1. Which rhythmic pattern creates the greatest tension? Why?
2. Which pattern creates the least tension? Why?
3. Which pattern follows the rhythm of the words?
4. Which sections of text are set with the most intense changes of dynamics?
5. In which sections does the composer use a wide vocal range?
6. Based on their musical characteristics, which sections of text reflect the greatest amount of tension? the least? Justify your answers.
7. How does the music evoke the text?

Islam

Islam, the youngest of the great religions, is second only to Christianity in numbers of believers. The term Islam refers to the "peace that comes when one's life is surrendered to God." A follower of Islam is called a Muslim, meaning "one who submits." The Prophet Mohammed (A.D. 570–632), founder of the religion, is considered to be the last of God's prophets, along with Adam, Noah, Abraham, Moses, and Jesus. After Mohammed's death, his followers carried this new religion westward to Spain and West Africa, and eastward as far as Indonesia and China. It is now the dominant religion of North Africa, the Middle East, Pakistan, Malaysia, and Indonesia.

Muslims believe in only one God, Allah. The Koran, the sacred text written in Arabic, is believed to be God's revelations to Mohammed. It provides guidelines to help people cope with human situations.

The Culture of Pakistan

Pakistan is a small country in comparison with India, its giant neighbor. It encompasses low coastal areas on the Arabian Sea as well as some of

▶ Muslims come to worship at the mosque in Bander Seri Begawan, capital of Brunei on the northwest coast of Borneo, near Malaysia and Indonesia (southwest of the Philippines). Islam, the religion of these people, spread from the birthplace of Mohammed in Mecca, Saudi Arabia, both westward and eastward.

the world's most remote regions in the high Karakoram Mountains, an extension of the Himalayas. The separate nations of Pakistan and India were created in 1947 when the British gave up their control over most of these regions.

Most of the people in Pakistan are Muslim and speak a language called *Urdu*. Their lives reflect their geographic location halfway between the Middle East and India.

The Music of Pakistan

Because some orthodox Muslims do not approve of music, a number of fundamentalist Muslim rulers have tried to suppress the practice of music in their countries. Even so, most Muslims and Muslim cultures enjoy a wide variety of musical activities. Some even use music in the practice of their religion. Pakistan is such a country.

One of the most popular forms of religious music in Pakistan (and parts of India) is called *qawwali* (kha-WAA-lee). This rhythmic, fast-paced music is used especially by groups of devout Muslims called *Sufis* (SOO-fees). During religious celebrations, these men dance to qawwali. Through drumming, hand-clapping, and repetitive religious lyrics, the dancers are induced into a religious trance. The rhythms help create the sense of religious ecstasy the dancers seek. By this means, Sufis believe that they may better experience the blessings of God. During a performance, everyone may clap—the singers in the chorus, the dancers, and the members of the audience.

Another important stylistic feature of qawwali is the use of both solo singers and chorus. The text is sung by soloists and chorus, whose parts alternate and sometimes overlap. In the qawwali excerpt from "The Strings of God's Lute Are in My Body," performed by the Sabri Brothers and their ensemble, the words are as follows:

Even those who think that they know you
Have not reached the depth of you;
Only you know the extent of your divinity.

Oh, my God, my God, God of all creation
You can capture a river in a cup.
I pray to you to grant peace to the whole world.

▼ *Activity:* **Discover**

Listen to this excerpt from a performance of qawwali, an Islamic religious dance. Can you figure out the rhythmic movement and interrelationship between soloists and chorus?

One of the drums is the tabla; the other is a barrel-shaped instrument called a *dholak*.
Clap along with these qawwali musicians and try to answer the following questions:
1. Is this music moving in groups of threes or groups of fours?
2. Are there sounds that are moving steadily faster than your hand claps? steadily slower?
3. Are there sounds that seem to move consistently in contrast to your hand claps?
4. Are there many places where the singing of these two groups overlap?
5. Can you decide which is more important, the soloists or the chorus?

Summary

All of the world's great religions are practiced in North America and all the music of these faiths is also performed here. The United States is as pluralistic in its religions as it is in its cultures and ethnicities. No one religion is dominant. Today, rock, jazz, country and western, and soul music have entered the sanctuary, as churches and synagogues have become involved in the concerns of our contemporary world: discrimination, hunger, injustice, drugs, poverty, illness, and homelessness. These common concerns, like the music that expresses them, blur the distinction between the sacred and secular worlds. Sacred and secular musical styles, too, share common features.

Many of the great musical traditions of the world grew directly from religious traditions. Gregorian chant, the mass, the hymn or chorale, the cantata, and gospel music are examples of musical forms that have sprung directly from the Christian religion. Other religions have also spawned distinctive music: Hinduism in India has produced kritis; Buddhism in Tibet has created Mahayana chant; and Islam in Pakistan has produced qawwali.

Music is part of most religions. It evokes the spirit and the mystery of life better than any other form of human expression. By interpreting the meaning of sacred texts, music clarifies and intensifies their implications. Through music, the words are lifted to a higher power. By this means, music transports us into the spiritual world so that we can connect with our own spirituality and our quest for salvation.

CHAPTER 13

The Music of Celebration

Objectives

By completing this chapter, you will:

- Find out how music is used as an essential part of celebration in all cultures.
- Realize how Irving Berlin's music celebrates the human spirit.
- Become familiar with the music of Native American festivals.
- Learn the characteristics of national anthems.
- Investigate the role of the band in celebration.
- Become acquainted with some of the music of Charles Ives, Sir Edward Elgar, Peter Ilyich Tchaikovsky, and Modest Mussorgsky.
- Discover how music is used in celebrations in Nicaragua and Japan.

Musical Terms

band
bugaku
concert band
gagaku
marimba
national anthem

*A*ll humans celebrate. The expression of joy, pride, solidarity, triumph, and other emotions that make our spirits soar is universal. Music often constitutes one of the most important ways humans express these feelings. Usually national celebrations commemorate the life of a great leader or a pivotal event in the nation's history. They might also be solemn and dignified in the case of a hero's death or recognition of those who have died in service to the nation. Invariably these are public events that bring the community together and demonstrate its unity. The music for such events allows the group to share its social values and unite in spirit. In a very real sense, music is often the means by which the feelings of community are coalesced.

Pomp and Circumstance—American Style

In American society, celebration is expressed with symbols such as flags and turkeys, and through events such as parades, parties and fireworks exhibitions. Some celebrations such as the Fourth of July and Thanksgiving happen on a regular basis. Others such as inaugurations, weddings, anniversaries, homecomings, graduations, and championships occur less regularly and more spontaneously. Almost always there is music.

Irving Berlin—Celebrating Life

One American who was a genius for tapping into the American spirit was Irving Berlin. He wrote the melodies and lyrics for songs that celebrate special occasions: "Easter Parade" (1933) and "White Christmas" (1942). He celebrated America through songs such as "God Bless America" (1938) and "Oh, How I Hate to Get Up in the Morning" (1942), the latter a spoof on being a private in the army. But many of Berlin's songs simply celebrate the joy of being alive, for example, tunes such as "There's No Business Like Show Business" (1946) and "Top Hat, White Tie, and Tails" (1935). Berlin was a master at grasping and expressing the subtle, internal aspects of human experience.

One of Berlin's most celebratory songs is "Puttin' on the Ritz" (1930). In it he captures the rhythm of ragtime, contrasting a syncopated melody played with the right hand against a steady beat in the left-hand accompaniment. Now, however, the melody was to be sung rather than just played on the piano. This meant that he had to invent lyrics that ragged—words that have verbal accents and rhymes that deliberately go against the steady beat—no easy feat! The result is vocal ragtime:

DIFF-'rent TYPES
who WEAR a DAY coat
PANTS with STRIPES
and CUT-a-WAY-coat,
PER-fect FITS,
PUT-tin' on the RITZ!

COME let's MIX
where ROCK-e-FELL-ers
WALK with STICKS
or UM-ber-EL-las
IN their MITTS,
PUT-tin' on the RITZ!

▼*Activity:* **Challenge**

As you listen to Irving Berlin's song "Puttin' on the Ritz," tap the steady beat and the rhythm of the melody at the same time!

First, listen to "Puttin' on the Ritz" and tap the steady beat. Identify the meter and tempo of the song. What is the song about?

Listen to the song again and concentrate on the rhythm of the melody. The unique character of this rhythm is based on this syncopated pattern:

Tap this rhythm. Recite the words (above) to it.

Now try tapping both the steady beat and the rhythm of the syncopated melody at the same time.

American Indian Festivals

One of the most prevalent contemporary Native American cultural events is the powwow. For participants, it is an opportunity to proudly express, share, and celebrate a heritage. The gathering, which may last from one to several days, is always a time for music, dancing, socializing, feasting, and selling crafts. It sometimes includes such activities as parades, horse races, and rodeos. Several varieties of contest dancing occur at most powwows, and they provide excellent examples of Native American music.

Men's Traditional Dance. Dating from older tribal styles, the Traditional Dance is a favorite among today's Indian men and boys. The movements of the traditional dancer are stately and not as rigorous as in other dances.

Men's Fancy Dance. As it has evolved from earlier forms, this is one of the most exciting, colorful, and physically demanding of Indian contest dances. The movements must be innovative, polished, fast, and natural-looking, and they must be precisely in step with the fast and tricky rhythms

Profile

Irving Berlin
American Composer
1888–1989

IRVING BERLIN

The story of Irving Berlin is almost a Horatio Alger tale. In 1892 when he was four years old, he and his parents fled a pogrom—the organized persecution of a minority group—in the Siberian village of Temun and immigrated to America. His real name was Israel ("Izzy") Baline.

Berlin spent an impoverished boyhood in the Russian-Jewish ghetto of the Lower East Side of New York City where he apprenticed as a singing waiter. His interest in music and his gift of playing the piano by ear drew him to Tin Pan Alley, the collection of brownstone houses on West 28th Street where music publishers had their offices. Here he pounded out the new tunes to sell the popular sheet music of the day. He was soon writing his own tunes.

In 1911, Berlin wrote his first big hit, "Alexander's Ragtime Band." It made him famous. Like most of the thousand or so songs he composed during his lifetime, he wrote both the words and the music. What he lacked in formal education, he compensated for in other ways. He couldn't read music, so a music secretary wrote down his melodies and harmonized them.

Berlin was an ardent patriot, grateful for the riches his adopted country had heaped upon him. Perhaps more than any other songwriter, he had the gift of expressing the universal sentiments of the American people. He wrote the scores for a number of successful musicals starring Fred Astaire. Among his many Broadway musicals are *Annie Get Your Gun* and *Call Me Madam*, two shows that are still widely performed in the United States and Canada.

In spite of all his success, Berlin's career was marked by a number of ups and downs. He suffered enormous self-doubt, and as he grew older, he mistrusted others, particularly in business matters. He was so obsessed with preserving his musical legacy that he tightly held the reigns on his music. Berlin died in 1989 at the age of 101, a lonely and isolated man, but hardly a forgotten one.

---

of the Contest Songs performed by the singers. At these events, the competition is keen, generating enormous excitement among the observers. As with any art form, it takes years of hard work, practice, and contest experience to become the kind of accomplished dancers that these champions represent.

The Grass Dance. Another popular style of dance for men at powwows throughout North America is the Grass Dance. For this competition dance, the dancers wear a special type of regalia.

Women's Traditional Dance. The movements are subtle and delicate in the women's Traditional Dance. The faces of the dancers are quietly proud and strong. Their tanned buckskin dresses, decorated with elk's teeth, sea shells, intricate bead work, and other items, evoke the past.

Women's Fancy Dance. Young Native American women demonstrate their creativity and athleticism through the individualized and energetic movements of the Women's Fancy Dance, which is sometimes called the Shawl Dance. This is a relatively new style for Native American women, requiring hard work, that exhibits pride in cultural and artistic expression.

▲ Dressed in the regalia of his ancestors, a Native American celebrates his cultural heritage at a traditional powwow. Although the powwow grew out of social gatherings held by the Plains Indians, today it attracts participants from many different tribes.

▼*Activity:* ***Observe American Indian Traditions***

Watch the video of Native American dancers and try to grasp the role of music and dance in Native American culture.

You will see the following dances as performed at the Winnebago Annual Powwow: (a) Men's Traditional Dance; (b) Men's Fancy Dance contest; and (c) The Grass Dance competition. The following dances were performed at the Rosebud Reservation in South Dakota by women of the Lakota tribe: (d) Women's Traditional Dance; and (e) Women's Fancy Dance (performed by a young Lakota woman by the name of "Grace Her Many Horses"). Answer the following questions:

1. What is there about the Grass Dancers that suggests the tall grasses of the prairie?
2. How would you compare the Women's Traditional and Fancy Dance styles?
3. Why do you think Native American dancers prefer the words regalia or outfit instead of costume to describe what they wear when dancing?
4. In the song performed for the Women's Traditional Dance, is the men's vocal range high or low? Is the vocal quality relaxed or tense? Are the rhythmic accents on the beat or off the beat?
5. What is the most obvious musical difference between the songs sung for the Men's Fancy Dance and the Men's Grass Dance?

National Anthems

Nearly every country has its own officially designated **national anthem**, *a song of praise or devotion.* These anthems are the musical equivalent of the country's motto or flag and are meant to stir up pride and evoke patriotism. They are often performed on ceremonial occasions, particularly to honor the head of state. On international occasions, they are useful as a salute to participating nations. At the Olympic Games, for example, winners are honored by the performance of their country's anthem.

Most national anthems have a marchlike character. The first such anthem was Spain's "Marcha real" (1770). The model for this type of anthem, however, is the French anthem, "La Marseillaise" (Chant de guerre pour l'armée du Rhin, "the war song for the army of the Rhine") (1792). Many national anthems were written during wartime and reflect martial themes of sovereignty, conquest, freedom, and other national sentiments. Although "The Star Spangled Banner" celebrates a victory, its meter is in three, not four, making it less martial in feeling.

Some anthems are stately hymns. The primary model for this type of anthem is Great Britain's "God Save the King/Queen." Many of the countries that use this type of anthem are former British colonies. Fanfares constitute anthems for some Middle Eastern countries such as Kuwait and the United Arab Emirates. The operatic anthems popular among South American countries were undoubtedly influenced by nineteenth-century Italian opera. In contrast, Asian countries tend not to rely on European models but use their own folk music traditions. Good examples are the national anthems of Japan and Tibet.

PROJECT

Adopt a Different National Anthem?

Should the United States adopt a different national anthem? Put your research skills to work to answer the question.

The issue: Many people believe that "The Star-Spangled Banner" is too difficult to sing. Others believe that it is too militaristic and does not reflect peaceful democratic ideals. Should Congress maintain the present anthem or adopt a new one? To study the issue, choose either A or B:

A. Read the news articles about the suitability of our national anthem. Then study the words and melodies of the leading contenders for the new national anthem. Are there other choices that should be considered? Which one do you think best suits this nation and why? Write your own "letter to the editor" that describes your personal point of view in this debate.

B. Take a public opinion poll. Organize a team of three to five researchers. Each member of the team should interview at least 10 people, five from your school and five from the community. Simply ask all respondents two questions:

1. Do they recommend keeping the present national anthem or choosing a different composition?
2. What song would they suggest as a substitute and why?

When all interviews are complete, compile your research data. Report to the class the percentages of those favoring the current anthem and those favoring a new song. Make a list and tally the suggestions for the substitute anthems.

National anthems function with varying degrees of success. Neither the words nor the music of many of these anthems are the finest examples of the poetry or music of their countries. Still, the words and the melodies are generally stirring and often memorable. The national anthems of the United States and France, both revolutionary, marchlike tunes, are among the most stirring and memorable.

"The Star-Spangled Banner" was adopted as the official national anthem only in 1931. The melody already existed when Francis Scott Key wrote his verses to it in September 1814 while being held on board a British ship in Baltimore Harbor. The British had bombarded Fort McHenry during the night, but when morning broke, the American flag was still flying. The melody by the English composer John Stafford Smith was based on "To Anacreon in Heaven" a well-known song of the era.

▼Activity: *Compare National Anthems*

Can you determine what makes the national anthems of the United States and France difficult to sing?

Listen to the national anthems of the United States and France and try to discover what makes them sound patriotic.

Once you are familiar with the sound of both anthems, look at the notation and audiate their melodies. Compare the anthems and try to find the elements they share in common. On a sheet of paper, make a column for each anthem and answer these questions:

1. What is the range of each piece?
2. What is the length (total number of measures) of each anthem?
3. What is the meter of each?
4. How would you describe the form?
5. What melodic similarities do you hear?
6. What rhythmic similarities do you hear?
7. What messages do the texts convey?

Many people have complained that both of these anthems are difficult to sing. Based on your analysis, what are the difficulties in each piece?

Music for Special Occasions

Americans celebrate in many different ways, and music is usually there to give the occasion just the right spirit. Even though we are not big on pomp, we have invented our own kinds of celebrations. About as close as we come to real pomp is in the playing of "Hail to the Chief" whenever the president of the United States appears in person. On the Fourth of July, our most important national holiday, we get out the flags, parade down main street, and have a fireworks display. Otherwise, our celebrating is more modest and homespun. We commemorate important stepping stones in our lives—graduations, weddings, and anniversaries of various kinds—by joining together in a public ceremony with appropriate music.

La Marseillaise

Translation by Charles Fowler

Music and Words by
Claude-Joseph Rouget de Lisle, 1792

The Star-Spangled Banner

Lyrics by Francis Scott Key, 1814

Music by John Stafford Smith

2. On the shore dimly seen through the mists of the deep,
   Where the foe's haughty host in dread silence reposes,
   What is that which the breeze, o'er the towering steep,
   As it fitfully blows, half conceals, half discloses?
   Now it catches the gleam of the morning's first beam,
   In full glory reflected now shines on the stream.
   'Tis the Star-Spangled Banner, O long may it wave
   O'er the land of the free and the home of the brave!

3. Oh thus be it ever when free men shall stand
   Between their loved home and the war's desolation!
   Blest with vict'ry and peace, may the heaven-rescued land
   Praise the power that hath made and preserved us a nation!
   Then conquer we must, when our cause it is just,
   And this be our motto: "In God is our trust."
   And the Star-Spangled Banner in triumph shall wave
   O'er the land of the free and the home of the brave!

Parades

What would a parade be without a band? In many parts of the world, but above all in the United States, the band has a revered place as a celebratory musical ensemble. Almost without exception, high schools, colleges, and universities have bands that perform for sporting events, community celebrations, and patriotic holidays. A **band** is *a large instrumental ensemble consisting primarily or solely of wind and percussion instruments.* There are military bands, marching bands, and symphonic or concert bands. The word band has also been applied to jazz and dance ensembles, although the term "combo" is more often used to designate small groups, and "big bands," groups of 15 or more.

Bands have always had, and still have, a role in the military. In the United States, each of the services—army, navy, marines, and air force—has its own bands. Military bands rallied the troops during the Revolutionary War, so they predate the founding of the nation. Bands buoyed up the spirits of men enduring hardships, and the familiar tunes provided a link with home. One Civil War soldier recalled: "How we boys used to yell at the band for music to cheer us up when we were tramping along so tired that we could hardly drag one foot after the other. . . . That good old tune we called 'Hell on the Rappahannock' had enough music in it to make a man who was just about dead brace up, throw his chest out, and take the step as if he had received a new lease of life." Patrick Gilmore, a conductor of a Union army band, composed a number of marches and wrote the words to "When Johnny Comes Marching Home."

The **concert band** is *basically an expanded version of the wind and percussion sections of the orchestra.* Unlike orchestral music, however, band music is not written for stringed instruments. Concert bands usually include saxophones (invented by Adolphe Sax in 1840), instruments rarely heard

Cooperative Learning

Identify the Instruments
Can you name the instruments you hear in an American concert band?

To test your knowledge of the instrumentation in the concert band, review John Philip Sousa's "The Washington Post March." Working in small groups, write down the names of all the instruments you hear.

Just as Sousa's march conveys a feeling of celebration, so too does "American Salute" by Morton Gould. Even the title suggests a patriotic type of celebration: Gould based his band composition on the familiar folk song, "When Johnny Comes Marching Home." This 16-measure song had become one of the most popular pieces in America by the end of the Civil War. Gould's band version is written as a type of theme and variations in which different instruments play successive statements, each in a new key.

Listen to a performance of this piece and see if you can identify the instruments that are featured in each variation.

▶ The year that the United States entered into World War I, American painter Childe Hassam (1859–1935) created a series of flag paintings to celebrate Anglo-French-American cooperation, America's patriotism, and the power of modern technology, symbolized by New York's skyscrapers. He dedicated this painting—*Allies Day, May 1917*—to "the coming together of the three peoples in the fight for democracy."

Childe Hassam. *Allies Day, May 1917*. 1917. National Gallery of Art, Washington, D.C. Gift of Ethelyn McKinney in memory of her brother, Glenn Ford McKinney.

in orchestral music. This basic difference in instrumentation tells the listener whether an ensemble is a band or an orchestra. There is a reason why stringed instruments are not included. Bands frequently perform outdoors and while marching. The sound of stringed instruments outdoors does not have much carrying power, nor do cellos and basses lend themselves to being carried down the street! The band, by its very nature, is a noisy ensemble. That is why it can be so exciting.

Holidays

Americans like their national holidays, which are always a cause for celebration. Charles Ives (1874–1954), a remarkable composer from Danbury, Connecticut, wrote *A Symphony: Holidays* in four movements: "Washington's Birthday," "Decoration Day," "Fourth of July," and "Thanksgiving and/or Forefathers' Day." He composed these movements between 1904 and 1913.

Ives had often heard the bands marching down Main Street on the Fourth of July, their sounds overlapping so that the various tunes—always very American—were like counterpoint fading one into the next. This is the effect he tried to capture. Ives was so inspired by our American tunes and our national holidays that he based this symphony on them.

▼Activity: *Experiment with American Tunes*

What is the musical and expressive effect when several familiar American tunes are performed at the same time?

Learn to perform a phrase from each of the following American songs on keyboard instruments or bells. Members of your class who play band or orchestral instruments can also perform any of these songs.

Columbia, the Gem of the Ocean

The Battle Hymn of the Republic

The Battle Cry of Freedom

Reveille

Perform the four melodies at the same time. Change the tempo, meter, and dynamics. Describe the musical and expressive effect.

Now listen to how Charles Ives used this same musical device in his composition "Fourth of July." Make a list of the tunes you recognize.

After you have listened to "Fourth of July" a second time, write a short paragraph describing how Ives created a sense of celebration in this work. How did he paint a musical picture of this holiday?

Graduations

One of the principal events in the lives of Americans is high school graduation. More than any other event, it marks the division between adolescence and adulthood. This, surely, is a time for rejoicing. There is the ceremony, serious and formal, when diplomas and awards are conferred on the graduates. Later, there is usually a certain amount of hoopla. Music plays a role in each. College graduation is also a time of celebration.

▼*Activity:* **Analyze and Decide**

What musical characteristics make a composition appropriate for pomp and celebration?

Listen to the musical selection and decide the type of event at which you might hear it. List the musical characteristics you used to make your decision.

Analyze *Pomp and Circumstance, March No.1* by Sir Edward Elgar (1857–1934). How does the composer capture a sense of celebration and pomp in this composition? How is contrast achieved? Which musical characteristics have made this famous melody one of the hit tunes in all of Western music?

Celebrations in Other Countries

Celebrations can take many forms, from simple, heartfelt occasions with dancing in the streets to elaborate and formal ceremonies of great splendor. In other countries, celebrations reveal an amazing breadth of expression. Without exception, music is a central element in these celebrations, evoking both the culture and the particular occasion. Quite often, music is tailor-made for these celebrations. In some cultures, however, there is a whole array of music ready-made for festive occasions with its own style and even its own particular instrumentation.

Festivals in Central America

Much of the music heard at festival celebrations in Central America is played on the marimba (mah-REEM-bah). Marimbas throughout the region are similar to one another, but their exact shape, sound, and way of being played varies from country to country. The Central American **marimba** is *a wooden xylophone played by one to as many as eight musicians,* depending on the size of the instrument and local custom. Each player strikes the keys with two to four sticks with rubber knobs at the ends. Some marimbas have wooden keys arranged and tuned to the white keys on a piano (diatonic scale). Others have keys arranged to correspond to both the white and black keys (chromatic scale). Below each key is a resonator tube with a small membrane stretched across a hole, which makes a buzzing sound when the marimba is played.

The model for these marimbas was probably brought to Central America by African slaves during colonial times (from approximately the sixteenth through eighteenth centuries). Although slaves were not permitted to bring musical instruments with them on their journey to the New World, they could have easily fashioned new instruments from the abundant hardwoods in Central America. While the instrument derives from African prototypes, most of the older music played on the marimba is Hispanic in character. It has a 6/8 meter and generally involves only three chords— I, IV, and V7. Many pieces that accompany dancing consist of only two or three melodic sections that are repeated many times.

 In Nicaragua and Guatemala, the marimba is played in the streets on festive occasions. Depending on the size of the instrument, several musicians often join together to perform, creating melody and harmony parts by improvising on the low, middle, or high tones.

The Masaya province of Nicaragua features a type of marimba that is tuned to the diatonic scale. Generally it is accompanied by two guitars. Music performed on the Nicaraguan marimba is public music, especially suited for festive occasions and dancing. Popular occasions for marimba playing are birthdays, festivals for the patron saints of villages, and Sunday afternoons in town plazas. "El Sapo" (ehl SAH-poh, "The Frog") is a well-known folk dance of Masaya.

El Sapo

Traditional Nicaraguan

▼*Activity:* **Perform "El Sapo"**

**See if you can capture the lively and spirited rhythm of
"El Sapo" in your own performance.**

Listen to the recording of "El Sapo" and tap along on the rapid eighth notes while you count the six beats.

Starting with a comfortable tempo, practice tapping and counting the following rhythms, keeping the eighth note steady. Feel the accents switch from two to three in a measure. This is the playful ambiguity that you have heard before in Hispanic music.

Using the simplified melodic excerpt of "El Sapo" with the chords indicated, practice playing the melody and chords using guitar, piano, or marimba.

Chords:

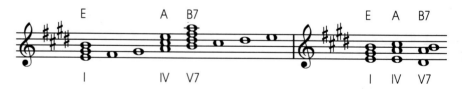

Guitar strokes: up with thumb (↑) and down with fingers (↓):

Celebrations in the Music of Japan

The music of celebration is not always as relaxed as the folk music of Nicaragua. Some ceremonies are more formal and demand a different kind of music. Japan is a nation steeped in ancient traditions. Celebrations there treat rulers with deference and dignity, and the music reflects this attitude.

Japanese Culture

Japan is a mountainous nation of many islands on the northeastern rim of Asia. As an isolated island nation, Japan was able, until relatively recently, to decide whether to bring in outside cultural influences. The country has alternately gone through periods of isolation and of intense borrowing. From the sixth to the ninth centuries, for example, Japan eagerly absorbed the flourishing culture of China. Then, it largely suspended contact and concentrated on developing its own distinct culture. With the rise of the shōgun or military rulers in the twelfth century, outside influences gradually began to be felt once more. Then for 200 years, beginning in the early seventeenth century, a series of Tokugawa (toh-kuh-gah-wah) shōguns practically closed the country to the outside world.

In the 1850s, the United States succeeded in opening Japan to foreign trade. The Tokugawa rule collapsed and was replaced by a renewed imperial system that embraced modernization and westernization.

Japanese Music

Along with many other aspects of Western life and society, Japan has absorbed the musical culture of the Western world. Typical Japanese today are more likely to listen to Beethoven or Miles Davis than to their own traditional music. In the march toward westernization, some forms of traditional music have been lost. Yet Japanese traditional music is still very much alive, existing alongside westernized popular songs and symphonic music. Many types of highly developed traditional Japanese instrumental music, accompanied song, and sophisticated music-dramas, as well as vibrant folk and festival music, are maintained by a core of professional and amateur musicians.

Festivals in all parts of Japan provide many occasions for celebration. Music for these occasions is generally a type of folk music that uses drums and flutes. You will hear one form of traditional Japanese music that expresses celebration: music that is part of the ceremonies of the imperial court, and therefore of an old and stately tradition.

Traditional Japanese music is often constructed from stock melodic and rhythmic patterns. This mosaic technique extends back to the oldest surviving music, **gagaku** (gah-gah-kuh), which means "elegant music," *an orchestral music (sometimes with singing) that is used at imperial court ceremonies and at temples and shrines.* For example, it was performed at the coronation of Emperor Akihito in 1990, continuing a musical tradition that is more than 1,200 years old. Much gagaku was originally imported from the Asian mainland, particularly China. Typically, it was absorbed and heavily adapted to conform to Japanese tastes and needs. It reached its full development in the years A.D. 750 to 950. The term gagaku refers both to purely instrumental music and to music for dance or **bugaku** (buh-gah-kuh), *which consists of a wide variety of costumed dances, many using striking masks.* One example of bugaku is "Batoo" (ba-toh).

The "Batoo" is a dance believed to have originated long ago in Southeast Asia. It is thought to have been brought to Japan around A.D. 740 by a Buddhist priest. Over the centuries, it has remained a relatively popular,

▲ One example of bugaku is "Batoo," which is an ancient Japanese dance that is still performed frequently, usually at temples and shrines on ceremonial occasions. The movements are highly stylized, and the music is played on traditional Japanese instruments.

Bugaku Dancers. Handscroll. 1408. Asian Art Museum of San Francisco, San Francisco, California.

frequently performed composition. The title "Batoo" seems to refer to the downward pull of the hand over the dancer's head. It may also describe the prominent forehead on the mask. The dance has two possible interpretations. The solo dancer may be celebrating the slaying of a tiger that killed his father, or he may be pulling at his hair in sorrow over the slaying of his father.

The danced version of "Batoo" uses the following six instruments—three wind and three percussion:

- *ryuuteki* (ree-yoo-teh-kee)—a lacquered bamboo transverse flute;
- *hichiriki* (hee-chee-ree-kee)—a lacquered bamboo double reed pipe;
- *shoo* (show)—a free reed multi-pipe mouth organ;
- *san-no-tsuzumi* (sahn-noh-tsoo-zoo-mee)—a small double-headed drum played with one stick;
- *taiko* (tie-koh)—a large suspended drum played with knobbed sticks; and
- *shooko* (show-koh)—a small suspended gong played with hard sticks.

The melody of the prelude, played on the ryuuteki and hichiriki, is in free rhythm (no definite meter) and is heterophonic, meaning that it is played simultaneously on both instruments but with variants appropriate to the traditional way these instruments are played. Free rhythm is common in Japanese traditional music. Free rhythm does not mean improvisation. On the contrary, each detail of this music, including the relationship between the instruments, is precisely determined and is played the same way each time.

▼Activity: *Follow the Musical Events*

As you listen to the Japanese "Batoo" dance music, try to follow the events that are described.

Prelude, *Netori* (neh-toh-ree), in free rhythm:

1. Chords of the shoo;
2. Melody on the ryuuteki and hichiriki is played in heterophony;
3. San-no-tsuzumi drum beats four times;
4. The introduction ends with a sustained fundamental pitch (like DO), then pauses.

The dance in a 5-beat pattern (2 + 3):

5. Starts with flute solo; other instruments join in shortly;
6. Hear the steady, rather slow beat;
7. Try to hear recurring patterns of a few notes.
8. Can you detect that a large section is repeated exactly?
9. The piece ends with a short pattern in free rhythm, again emphasizing the fundamental pitch.

What do you think is the nature of this dance ceremony?

Cooperative Learning

Answer with Your Ears

How does Mussorgsky's setting of this simple, folk-like melody create a sense of pomp, celebration, and festivity?

Working in small groups, learn to play this hymn of praise on a keyboard instrument or bells. This theme, based on a Russian folk hymn, is used in the dazzling "Coronation Scene" from the opera *Boris Godunov* by Modest Mussorgsky.

Is the melody primarily conjunct or disjunct? Does it have a wide or a narrow range? Is the melody easily sung? Is the rhythm of the melody simple or complex?

Listen to the music of the "Coronation Scene" from the opera. Describe the change of mood when Boris appears. How is the musical treatment of the text he sings different from that of the opening statement of celebration?

What mood is portrayed by the music and the text at the end of the scene? Summarize the way in which Mussorgsky organized the music to support the contrasts of mood in the text.

Coronations

For sheer majesty and stately grandeur, the ceremonies of the courts of Europe and Russia have been difficult to surpass. Coronations, the crowning of a new monarch or sovereign, are particularly ostentatious occasions in which "all the stops (referring to the organ) are pulled out." Coronations are lavish events that demand opulence and extravagance. Music for such events is equally as impressive.

Coronation in Russia

One way to experience a coronation is to see it enacted on stage. The opera *Boris Godunov* by the Russian composer Modest Mussorgsky (1839–1881) provides just such an opportunity. This opera is based on historic events as related in a play by Alexander Pushkin. Boris Godunov (c. 1551–1605) was one of the early czars or rulers of Russia.

▶ In the courtyard of the Kremlin in Moscow, the bells of two great cathedrals toll as the people gather to proclaim Boris Godunov the new czar. In the photo at right, Nicolai Ghiaurov portrays Godunov, wearing jewel-encrusted coronation vestments in the Metropolitan Opera's production of Modest Mussorgsky's *Boris Godunov*, an opera based on events in Russian history.

Profile

Modest Mussorgsky
Russian Composer
1839–1881

MODEST MUSSORGSKY

In 1863, Modest Mussorgsky moved in with five other young men in a flat in St. Petersburg where they exchanged ideas on art, philosophy, religion, and politics. It was here that Mussorgsky absorbed the belief that art must relate to life and communicate with people, an idea that consumed him the rest of his life. This group, often referred to as the Mighty Handful, espoused aesthetics that revered Russian folk songs, stories, and ideals. They rejected German, French, and other European influences, citing the importance of music as a national art that must be used to properly educate and inspire audiences.

Born to a wealthy family in 1839, Mussorgsky was taught by his mother how to play the piano. Even though he showed great musical talent at a young age, he entered the Cadet School of the Guards in St. Petersburg in 1852. Mussorgsky dabbled in music at school, even composing a bit, but in 1856 he began a short stint in the Regiment of Guards. He soon met the talented young composer, Mily Balakirev, who agreed to give him lessons in musical form. In spite of such efforts, Mussorgsky's work suffered from insufficient training and a lack of self-discipline. Many of his works were left unfinished. The few works that Mussorgsky did complete are generally unpolished, but genuine in intent, and stirring.

Despite his lack of a rigorous formal training, Mussorgsky's compositions are special because they celebrate the common individual and the Russian character. The opera, *Boris Godunov* (1868–1869), recounts the life of a czar, but treats him irreverently. *Pictures at an Exhibition* (1874) is one of Mussorgsky's best-loved works, juxtaposing lyric and comic elements. Unfortunately, Mussorgsky's career was hampered by alcoholism, which caused his death in 1881 at the age of only 42.

The story of the opera is, in fact, the history of the period. Besides Boris, one of the other principal characters is the Russian people, who form a great chorus in some of the scenes, the "Coronation Scene" being an excellent example. Scene 1 of the Prologue provides the background of the action. The heirs of Ivan IV ("the Terrible") have died, and the nobility and the people want Boris to become czar. He is reluctant—but not for long. It seems that Boris has been plotting to be czar, even going to the extent of causing the murder of Dmitri, the young heir to the throne. Scene 2 of the Prologue recreates his coronation before our eyes. The place is Moscow in the courtyard of the Kremlin between the two great cathedrals. The people cry, "Long live the czar!" Boris appears before the people. He is in a somber mood, suffering a guilty conscience. The great bells toll, and the people join in a magnificent chorus based on a simple folk-like tune:

Like the sun in all   splen-dor ris-en in glo-ry, Bor - is!

Profile

Peter Ilyich Tchaikovsky
Russian Composer
1840–1893

PETER ILYICH TCHAIKOVSKY

Tchaikovsky personified the melancholic spirit of Romanticism. He had a difficult time understanding who he was or accepting himself. Although he took piano lessons as a child and music made a strong and lasting impression on him, even helping him endure the loss of his mother when he was 14, he studied for the legal profession and served as a clerk for several years. When he was 23, he resigned and dedicated himself to music.

Tchaikovsky enrolled full time in the St. Petersburg Conservatory in 1863. There, he achieved his first modest success as a composer and conductor. He then reluctantly accepted a position in Moscow where he composed his first symphony, his first opera, and in 1869, his first masterpiece—the orchestral overture fantasy, *Romeo and Juliet.*

His gift for rich and impassioned melody and full-blooded drama made his music suitable for ballet, and he composed three fine works: *Swan Lake* (1877), *The Sleeping Beauty* (1889), and *The Nutcracker* (1892). Among his operas is *Eugene Onegin* (1879). He also composed concertos for violin and for piano that are frequently performed today. His theatrics can be heard in his well-known *1812 Overture*, which calls for salvos of artillery at its end. In combining his classical sensibilities with his Russian passions, Tchaikovsky's reputation increased. He conquered his fear of audiences and successfully toured Europe and America. In 1893, he finished the magnificent and melancholy Symphony No. 6 in B minor, the *Pathétique*. His success was cut short when, nine days after its premiere, he died.

The opera tells the story of Boris's reign and of the threats to unseat him as czar by a pretender masquerading as the Czarevitch Dmitri whom Boris had murdered years earlier. Now Boris has doubts and guilt. The story focuses on the fall of this once mighty czar whose inner demons turn him into a madman and finally cause him to die. Although the opera ends with Boris's death, history bears out that this false Dmitri raised a large army and, after Boris's death, killed his heirs and had himself crowned czar. He was czar for only a year before he too was assassinated in a plot by another ambitious pretender to the crown.

Other Celebrations

The well-known *1812 Overture* by the Russian composer Peter Ilyich Tchaikovsky (1840–1893) does not celebrate the War of 1812 as the title suggests. The Russians had nothing to do with that particular war. Instead, this overture was written because Tchaikovsky was asked to compose an orchestral work as part of a Russian art and industry exhibition to be held in Moscow. He knew that a new cathedral would be completed and was to be opened during the exhibition. The *1812 Overture* was written to commemorate the events of that year in Moscow.

The overture is distinguished by its gigantic proportions: the composer used cannons, bells, and an unusual collection of percussion instruments to achieve his bombastic effects. It contains some recognizable Russian folk tunes, as well as the stirring melody of *La Marseillaise.*

This overture is either the greatest musical expression of celebration ever created or the all-time potboiler of pomp. In many ways, it typifies the romantic and expressive ideals of music written during the late nineteenth century. Although it is often played at festive events such as fireworks exhibitions on the Fourth of July, it has also been criticized as being shallow and tasteless. In 1946, music historian Gerald Abraham called the work "one of the most dreary and most repulsive works in the whole of music," labeling it "noisy, vulgar, and empty." Still, this work is played frequently and is a smashing success with the public.

▼Activity: *Judge*

How would you rate the quality of the *1812 Overture*?

Many people consider Tchaikovsky's *1812 Overture* to be one of the best examples of musical celebration ever created. But, is it good music? Opinion is divided on this question. Some critics rate it highly while others condemn it. Where do you stand?

Listen to the overture and rate it according to:

1. Quality of the overture as music for celebration; and
2. Quality of the overture as a musical masterpiece.

Write a paragraph that supports your critical judgment. How does your opinion compare with Gerald Abraham's (above)? Who is right?

Summary

Whenever and however people celebrate, music is usually there proclaiming, reinforcing, and dramatizing the occasion. In fact, music is such a natural part of human festivity in all cultures that it is difficult to think of celebrating without it. In the United States, we regularly salute our nation and commemorate our national holidays with music. In other nations, people dance and observe ancient rituals using their own native instruments and forms of music. Ceremonial events such as royal weddings and coronations are cause to call forth the heralding trumpets, massed choirs, bands, and orchestras.

But why music? Why are great orations and fantastic fireworks displays not enough? The answer bores deeply into what music is and what it does for us. Music, perhaps better than any other means, permits us to express the particular spirit of human celebration. It can proclaim dignity and stateliness, solemnity and honor, heartfelt devotion and belief, jubilation and triumph, and the simple, joyous fun of human camaraderie. Periodically, as humans, we have to parade our feelings and know that we all feel the same way. That is how we bond into communities and care about each other. Music allows us to share our humanity in the common experience of elation. Without it, life would be diminished.

CHAPTER 14

Condolences in Death

Objectives

By completing this chapter, you will:

- Learn how all kinds of music—jazz, classical, folk, and popular— are used to express emotions connected with death.
- Find out how music is used in the funeral ceremonies in Bali and in West Africa.
- Discover the relationship between New Orleans jazz and West African music.
- Become familiar with the "F" or bass clef and the Grand Staff.
- Experience how music is used to express death in the musical *Les Misérables* and the opera *Wozzeck*.

Musical Terms

atonal
bass clef
book
Grand Staff
ground bass
lieder
opus
through-composed
tonality
treble clef

*A*ll human beings have a natural instinct to
survive, to live, and to create more life. Death is the
antithesis of life, yet it is part of life's process. All living
things wither and die. For young people, understanding
and coping with death is particularly difficult. From the
beginning of our lives, we fill our minds and our days
with learning how to live. We spend our time finding
out what life is and can be. Death seems remote.
It appears to be something that only the elderly need
to think about. That is why, perhaps, when an
accident suddenly claims a young person's life,
there is a tragic sense of shock and loss.

Expressions of Death

Death—the loss of a loved one, an admired leader, a cherished friend—
is a reality in our lives. It is one of our most difficult emotional experiences. Religion is one place we look for help in understanding and coping
with death. All religions give hope and consolation despite the inevitability of death. In almost all the rituals humans have developed to memorialize and commemorate a life that has been stilled, and to console those
who mourn, music plays an essential and compelling role. The requiem,
introduced in Chapter 9, is one way music addresses the subject of death.
There are many others, representing just about every type of music.

"Taps"

One of the most haunting musical expressions of closure, or ending, is
the deceptively simple "Taps," a melody attributed to General Butterfield
at the Battle of Richmond (1862). This short instrumental piece is usually
performed by a single trumpet or bugle to signal the end of the day at
military bases. It is also used as a final farewell at most military funerals.
The melody is based on the "open" natural tones of the trumpet or bugle,
those pitches that result naturally by blowing air through one length of
the pipe. To play these different tones, the player has to increase or decrease
the air pressure and change the formation of the lips on the trumpet. These
tones are played without the use of the valves, which allow the performer
to vary the length of the pipe. In contrast to the trumpet, the bugle does
not have any valves and is, therefore, more limited in the tones that it can
produce.

P R O J E C T

Analyze Expressions of Death

To aid in understanding how
people view music in expressing
their deepest feelings regarding
death, ask five adults that you
know what specific piece or
pieces of music they would like
played at their funeral or memorial service. Ask them what it is
about the particular selection(s)
they mention that makes them
important and meaningful to
them. Bring a recording (or the
sheet music) of one of these
pieces of music to class.

▼Activity: **Analyze**

What musical characteristics give "Taps" (above) its farewell quality?

Listen to a performance of "Taps" and make a list of the musical and emotional qualities that create the haunting mood. Try to comment on each of the elements listed. Is the piece in major or minor tonality?

Try to sing or play "Taps," attempting to reproduce the same type of mood.

The New Orleans Funeral Parade

People deal with death in many different ways, and music reflects these differences. "Taps" seems to speak of our vulnerability and mortality. It evokes the silence and emptiness that results when someone dies. Other expressions of death celebrate the life of the deceased and the entry of the soul into a better world. Surprisingly, perhaps, these are basically happy expressions. Like "Taps," the New Orleans funeral parade is also a send-off, but its message and feeling are different.

From the earliest times, New Orleans was a mixture of cultures. The population consisted largely of whites from various backgrounds, Africans, and Creoles—people of mixed parentage. By the 1860s, Creoles and blacks began to form their own marching bands. These bands, which usually numbered no more than a dozen performers, were connected with lodges and social clubs. The organizations paid their bands to accompany dead members to their graves. Marching to and from the gravesite was a practice peculiar to New Orleans, documented as early as 1820. Notices of these parades were published in the newspaper.

▼Activity: **Experience a New Orleans Funeral Parade**

Watch the video of the New Orleans funeral parade, then discuss the following questions:

1. Is there anything about the parade that would tell you it is connected with a funeral?
2. What tells you that this music is jazz?
3. What instruments are used?
4. What justification is there for the "up" mood?
5. How does this music help people to cope with the loss of a loved one?

▲ In New Orleans, the funeral procession, led by a jazz band, is a part of the ritual that accompanies death. Here music is used, not to mourn, but to celebrate the life of the deceased.

The black bands had a freer and more rhythmic way of playing than the creole bands, and there was intense competition between them. There were contests between the uptown black bands and the downtown creole bands; but by the late 1870s and 1880s, musicians from both backgrounds joined to play jazz. Typically, the bands were composed of trumpets or cornets, trombones, horns, clarinets, and drums, but other instruments such as tubas and flutes were added if they were available. Usually the march to the gravesite was accompanied by a slow hymn or mournful dirge, but the march back had a definite "up" mood. On its return, the band might strike up a lively spiritual such as "When the Saints Go Marching In."

Young people followed these street bands. The bandsmen became their heroes, and many of these youths were inspired to learn to play instruments at an early age. They emulated their idols, playing and dancing along the line of march. Often they would run to the cemetery to be ready for the trip back. These boys and young men—called the "second line"—followed the funeral band parade on the way home from burials, when the music was lively, and they could join in the happy celebration of the life of the departed. Funeral parades are still part of life in New Orleans.

▲ If people did not die, there might not be as much great art as there is. People, often unconsciously, try to leave something of themselves behind. The tomb of Tutankhamen, which contained the Egyptian king who lived about 1350 B.C., was discovered in 1922 and contained great art treasures befitting his status. These tombs are decorated with scenes of everyday life—domestic, ceremonial, and military—so that the dead are assured the comfortable continuance of their previous lives.

Non-Western Expressions of Death

Music has been used in all cultures as a way to express grief, to give tribute, and to console the survivors. Death has a haunting mystery that music somehow embodies. But music does something more. It makes our grief universal. It reaches into the soul of humankind to make the lament larger than our own personal sorrow and, therefore, more tolerable.

The arts play an important role in marking the rites of passage—from birth and infancy, through childhood, adolescence, and early adulthood, to middle age, old age, and death. The extent to which various cultures celebrate these passages differs widely. Some societies, for example, have elaborate marriage ceremonies and funerary rites but pay little attention to birth. In the United States, graduation exercises are a form of passage from adolescence into early adulthood. Societies often celebrate such passages in elaborate public rituals.

Cremation Music of Bali

Some cultures use music as an essential part of the ceremonies connected with death. One of those countries is Bali, a small tropical island (about the size of Delaware) that is known for its artistic traditions. The climate and the landscape are so beautiful, and the people so friendly and peaceful, that Bali has frequently been compared to paradise.

Cremation (*nagaben*) is considered to be one of the most sacred duties of the Balinese. After a period of interment, the bones of the dead are gathered and placed inside elaborate, brightly colored coffins fashioned in the form of bulls, cows, and other animals, and decorated with golden streamers. Usually many families join together to cremate their dead at the same time. An important part of the day-long ritual is the procession, accompanied by bright music played on gongs, drums, and cymbals, that takes the coffins to the cremation site. As the remains are burned, the souls of the dead are liberated. Later, another procession takes the ashes down to the sea in tall white spires decorated with gold foil and thousands of mirrors that flash in the sunlight. While they sing, relatives wade out into the water and cast away the ashes, finally releasing the soul. The cremation ceremony in Bali is an occasion for celebration, not for mourning.

On the eve of the cremation day, a great procession is held to take the effigies to the house of the high priest for a final blessing. All the relatives of the dead parade in their finest clothes, accompanied by a gamelan orchestra, dancers, banner- and flag-bearers, and files of women bearing offerings. The processional music is an essential part of the ceremony. The gamelan orchestra consists of metal gongs of various sizes and wooden and metal xylophone-like instruments that are struck. The precisely coordinated five- or seven-tone music combines rapid cross rhythms and intricate syncopated melodies to create an intoxicating music of dramatic and mystical moods.

In 1947, Colin McPhee, an American composer then living in Bali, wrote this account of the gamelan gambang music that is played only for the rites of death, prior to the great procession:

> Above the dry, wooden sound of ancient xylophones that rattled a hollow accompaniment there range the hard metallic tones of *gangsas* [metal instruments that play the melody] in a strange, anvil-like chorale, irresolute, uncertain, as though the players could barely recall the melody. On and on the music played, passionless, colorless, filling the air with mournful sound that seemed curiously at variance with all the excitement and confusion. There were many guests, and the rich aroma of festive cooking floated over the walls from the kitchens, the smell of spice and freshly grated coconut, of roasting turtle and pig.

The gamelan gambang, or sacred ensemble, consists of four *gambangs* (wooden xylophones) and two *sarons* (metallic xylophones or *gangsas*). The 14 keys of the *gambang* are arranged to permit octaves to be played with special forked hammers. These hammers are used chiefly to play rhythmic figures. The rhythms, played in interlocking style, dovetail in a complicated manner to create a rapid and unbroken continuity. The melody, which is in a syncopated rhythm, is sounded in octaves on a pair of seven-keyed *sarons*. The melody is played in what seems to be a casual, almost faltering way, as though deliberately independent of the basic beat. Actually, this music uses a complex form of polyrhythm.

▲ In the Indonesian province of Bali, the people perform the ceremony of cremation according to their Hindu religious beliefs. Music and other arts are an integral part of this festive ritual.

▼Activity: *Describe*

Listen to the Balinese gambang music and try to describe it.

Identify the means, expression, order, origin, and use of this music. Watch the video of the cremation ceremony and determine the mood or moods the music conveys.

Honoring the Dead in West Africa

Throughout Africa, music functions as an integral part of social life. Ceremonies and rituals that reflect life's passages—birth, adolescence, marriage, and death—typically include music. To most sub-Saharan Africans, death is believed to be a transformation from one state of being to another. The person enters another form of existence, joining the company of others who have died. There is a sense of going home.

Through the many elaborate rituals connected with death, the living maintain contact with those who have died. Great importance is placed on remembering and paying respect to ancestors who have made possible the lives of those who have followed, as well as those who have made important contributions to the well-being of the group. The music performed in funeral processions and at festivals often commemorates ancestral figures.

West African Culture

The Hausa (HOW-sah) people use music to honor their dead. This African ethnic group, which numbers about ten million people in northern Nigeria and southern Niger, is almost exclusively Muslim. Although the Hausa practice agriculture, they also have a reputation as merchants, which is understandable in view of their location near the ancient trade routes that cross the Sahara Desert. Theirs is the prevailing trade language along the southern edge of the Sahara, and their adaptation of the Arabic alphabet has long been used in business in the area.

The Music of West Africa

The Hausa believe in the power of music to make things happen. They value music for its usefulness. They also see a close relationship between music and movement. The two go hand in hand. Body motion is an integral part of their music-making. They venerate their ancestors in burial rites that include funeral processions. The music frequently uses repetition—often including ostinatos (melodic and rhythmic)—as a background for continuous variation. The timbres tend to be complex. For example, percussion sounds are combined with a wide variety of instruments and often with voices. There are complex cross rhythms between the instruments. This combination of sounds gives the music a multilayered texture.

One example of this music is "Sara" (SAH-ra), which is performed in honor of the dead Hausa kings. "Sara" is performed on official occasions, including feast days. It retraces the history of the Hausa kings in the Kantche area of Niger. It might be heard on Islamic holy days when the emirs or rulers ride in procession to and from the mosque.

▼Activity: *Compare and Contrast*

What are the similarities and differences between "Sara," a West African musical salute to the dead Hausa kings, and the processional music of a New Orleans funeral parade?

Listen to "Sara" and try to identify the drums, double-reed instrument, trumpets (with just two tones), and the bell. Think of the meter as if it were in 12. Can you count it? Is there any repetition? What is the tempo?

Watch the video of the New Orleans funeral procession you saw earlier. Concentrate on the music that is played on the return from the cemetery. What is the meter? Is there any repetition? What is the tempo?

Compare the African and American funeral music according to the following: (1) The relationship of music and movement; (2) the spirit of the music (remember, both examples are associated with death); (3) the variety of timbres that are used; (4) the tempo; (5) the texture—simple or complex; and (6) rhythmic repetition and variety.

Are there similarities between the two examples, and if so, how do you account for them?

This excerpt from "Sara" uses seven *ganga* (GAH-ngah) drums, somewhat shorter than conga drums, that are hung by straps from the shoulders of the musicians and played with curved sticks. These ganga drums are double-headed and have attached snares—lengths of spiraled wire or gut strung across the bottom for added vibration. The ensemble includes a conical double-reed instrument, the *algaita* (al-GAH-ee-tah), and two long trumpets called *kakaki* (kah-kah-kee). The latter add a proud and grandiose sound befitting Hausa dignitaries. These horns have two pitches that are sounded at the interval of a fifth. A bell or *kougue* (koh-oo-goo-eh) completes the ensemble.

Death Expressed in Classical Music

Throughout the ages, Western classical musicians have dealt with the emotions of death. One of the most moving expressions of death was composed by J. S. Bach during the first half of the eighteenth century. For his *Mass in B Minor*, Bach composed a short chorus on the subject of the crucifixion of Jesus. Actually, he adapted the music from one of his cantatas, taking great care to refine and improve it. This work may be the most profound statement ever made of human pity, divine suffering, and the mysterious silence of death. The text derives from the Credo of the Latin Mass:

Crucifixus etiam pro nobis   And He was crucified also for us
sub Pontio Pilato,   under Pontius Pilate.
passus et sepultus est.   He suffered and was buried.

Bach set the whole work over a four-measure bass ostinato figure:

This underlying or **ground bass** is *a four- or eight-measure bass line that repeats constantly under one or more changing upper parts.* In this case, it produces an emotional throb. The chromatic descent of this melodic ostinato expresses the weightiness of grief.

The bass pattern is notated using the *F clef,* or **bass clef,** which points out the note F that is a fifth lower than middle C:

As discussed in Chapter 11, the *G clef*, or **treble clef**, designates the note G, which is a fifth higher than middle C. Together, they form the **Grand Staff**:

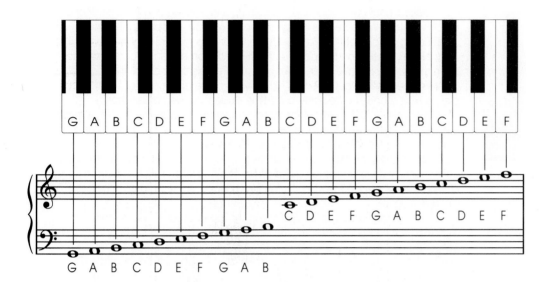

The Funeral March in Classical Music

Although Ludwig van Beethoven wrote a funeral march as the third movement of his Piano Sonata in A-flat Major, Op. 26, the most famous funeral march is probably Frédéric Chopin's *Marche funèbre*, from his Piano Sonata in B-flat Minor, Op. 35. **Opus** *refers to a single piece or set of pieces, usually numbered in the order in which they were composed.* It was this music that was used to accompany the horse-drawn caisson holding the coffin of President John F. Kennedy as the funeral procession moved from the United States Capitol down Pennsylvania Avenue on its way to Arlington Cemetery. The president had been assassinated on November 22, 1963, in Dallas, and the entire world mourned his death.

Chopin's march is in minor tonality (B-flat minor). He uses a heavy plodding bass with a somber melody in dotted rhythm that evokes tragedy. The slow (*lento*) tempo and dramatic dynamics create a powerful expression of reverence and sorrow.

Cooperative Learning

Look, Listen, and Discuss

Why was Frédéric Chopin's *Funeral March (Marche funèbre)*, Op. 35, an appropriate choice for the funeral procession of President John F. Kennedy on November 25, 1963?

Look at the photo of the funeral procession on page 254 while you listen to the funeral march as originally composed for the piano. What kind of an arrangement would be appropriate for this outdoor procession?

What musical characteristics make this music so gripping in its effect?

Profile

Frédéric Chopin
Polish Composer
1810–1849

FRÉDÉRIC CHOPIN

Frédéric Chopin was born and raised in Poland, the son of a French father and a Polish mother. While he was in high school in Warsaw, Chopin studied music with Jozef Elsner, director of the Warsaw Conservatory. His musical genius asserted itself early. He improvised on the piano brilliantly and soon began to compose and to perform publicly. His love for the piano dominated his life and was the focus of his creative energies. He published his first work for piano at the age of 15. After completing high school, he became a full-time student at the conservatory.

At the age of 20, he set out for Vienna to explore a larger world. He settled in Paris in 1831. There he established himself as the leading teacher of piano and one of the greatest pianists of his time, although he seldom performed in public, savoring his privacy and preferring to devote his time to composition. His works impressed contemporary composers such as Franz Liszt, Hector Berlioz, Felix Mendelssohn, and Robert Schumann, and had a profound influence on such later composers as Richard Wagner.

In 1837 during a period of depression, he composed his well-known *Funeral March*, which he later inserted as the slow movement of his *Piano Sonata in B-flat Minor*. The next year, he fell in love with George Sand (Aurore Dudevant), a novelist known for her unconventional ideas and well-publicized love affairs. During their ten-year relationship, Chopin wrote some of his most impressive works, many of which are imbued with a Polish flavor, particularly his dances—mazurkas, polonaises, and waltzes. He composed nocturnes, etudes, ballads, scherzos, preludes, sonatas, and concertos—all for piano. His melodies draw their expressiveness from his harmonically inventive, technically brilliant accompaniments. Tuberculosis cut short his life at the age of only 39.

▶ In November of 1963, the coffin of President John F. Kennedy was carried in a horse-drawn caisson from the U.S. Capitol, down Pennsylvania Avenue past the White House and on to its final resting place in Arlington National Cemetery. The music that accompanied the procession was Frédéric Chopin's *Funeral March*.

Death Expressed in the "Art" Song

The Erlking is a narrative ballad composed in 1815 by Franz Schubert (1797–1828), one of the masterful German composers of the nineteenth century. The poem is by Johann Goethe (1749–1832), a German poet of Schubert's time. Goethe's poem describes a father bearing his dying son, who is delirious with fever, on horseback through a storm. Four characters tell the story: a narrator, the father, his son, and the Erlking, who symbolizes death. In the central part of the poem, the father and the Erlking, a phantom figure, vie for possession of the child in a dialogue that mounts in tension and anguish. From the beginning, the rapid triplet pattern of repeated notes of the piano accompaniment portray the galloping horse, the storm, and the father's frantic ride to save his child.

▼ Activity: *Perform and Figure Out*

Learn to play the triplet pattern of repeated notes that Schubert uses in the piano accompaniment of *The Erlking* to suggest the fleeting horse:

Read the translation of the poem and bracket the lines and label them according to who speaks them: N for Narrator; F for Father; S for Son; and E for Erlking.

Now listen to the performance in German while you follow the English text. (In order to follow the text, it will help to know that there are the same number of syllables in both the German and the English. Unlike the English translation, the German text rhymes at the end of each line.) How does the singer help you to know when the speaker changes? How does Schubert use dynamics to help you tell who is speaking?

How many times does Schubert interrupt the repeated triplets in the piano accompaniment? Which one of the people in the story speaks without the triplet figure?

Extra Credit: Compare two performances of *The Erlking*.

Schubert treated each character differently, and the baritone who sings this song usually varies his voice quality to distinguish between them. Schubert set the father's part in the lowest register and gave his melodies a firmness and strength. In contrast, the Erlking's part lies in the middle-voice register, and Schubert has him speak in hushed tones, as if from another world. He beckons his prey with sinister seductiveness, singing in major while the rest of the work is in minor. In further contrast, Schubert set the boy's part in the upper register where each of his abrupt and desperate appeals is sung at a higher pitch and announced with a shrill dissonance.

This poem does not have a series of verses and a recurring chorus like many of our folk and popular songs. Here, each of the stanzas varies in number of syllables and accents. For this reason the poem demands a **through-composed** setting, which means *a setting of text in which different music is provided for each stanza of the poem* rather than one in which musical themes repeat in a consistent pattern. In this through-composed form, each part of the text is given a distinctive musical setting befitting the sentiment of the words. Schubert sets each stanza to different music that evokes the emotional meaning of that particular text. His melodies are not created out of short motifs or hooks like the melodies of most folk and popular songs. Instead, they usually unfold for as long as the stanza of poetry.

▼Activity: **Analyze**

How does Schubert achieve a sense of unity?

Schubert's accompaniment contains a violent rising and falling figure in the bass that begins with a triplet figure:

Using the Listening and Performance Grid, count the measures from the beginning of the piece and place an "X" in the first row of boxes in the bars in which you hear this rhythmic figure recur. Is there a consistent pattern? What feeling is conveyed?

Listen to the piece again. In the second row of boxes, mark an "X" on the correct beat and in the bars where Schubert changes from one narrative voice to another.

What, then, holds the music together? In *The Erlking*, it is the triplet rhythm in the accompaniment that binds the words and melody into one unified statement. In addition, there is a consistent style and tempo throughout. The musical ideas serve the drama and logic of the text, and the compelling developments of the story help to hold the work together. The final line is almost spoken. There is a pause before the final two words "is dead," followed by two chords, making a very dramatic ending. The somber mood of this ballad is typical of many Romantic songs.

Like all good songwriters, Schubert tried to capture and convey the meaning of the text in every element of the music—the melody, rhythm, harmony, and the character of the accompaniment. As a composer of more than 600 "art" songs, or **lieder** (LEE-der) *the German word for songs,* Schubert's achievement is unique and outstanding. He had a profound ability to capture the emotional essence of a poem in his music. The ideal of any song composer is to interrelate the words and music so completely that they become one message. That was Schubert's genius.

Profile

Franz Schubert
Austrian Composer
1797–1828

FRANZ SCHUBERT

Although he only lived to be 31 years old, Franz Schubert was the supreme creator of the German art song. His genius was in applying his keen musical sense and his seemingly inexhaustible source of melody to fit his music perfectly to the poem. Before him, other composers had put their best efforts into composing long musical forms. Schubert took the simple, short popular song and raised it to a highly expressive art form. He gave songs his utmost effort.

Schubert composed *The Erlking* (The Elf king) when he was 17. That same year he composed 144 songs, creating as many as eight songs in one day. He had to wait six years for the first public performance of *The Erlking* and was finally able to publish it in 1821 as his Opus 1. In spite of his genius, Schubert had a difficult time making a living as a composer and teacher.

Schubert spent his entire life in Vienna. His giftedness showed early. As a young boy, he studied violin, piano, organ, singing, and theory. At the age of 11, he was admitted to the Vienna court choir as a singer, and he played violin in his school orchestra.

In his brief life, Schubert composed prolifically. He wrote several operas, six masses, nine symphonies, including the famous *Unfinished*, a number of works for piano, and many chamber works for a variety of different instrumental combinations. The latter, along with his songs, are among his most performed works today.

The Death Scene from the Opera *Wozzeck*

If you think about it, there is probably nothing more dramatic than death. Almost all great stories have scenes of dying. This is also true of opera. There are great "death scenes" in many operas, but one of the most dramatic is in the opera *Wozzeck* (VOT-zehk) by the Austrian composer Alban Berg (1885–1935). This opera, completed in 1922, uses dissonance with powerful effect. The work uses a melodic and harmonic vocabulary that breaks out of the major-minor tonal system. It is **atonal**, meaning *there are so many chromatic pitches that the sense of a tonal center is obliterated.* Once you are absorbed in the story, however, you probably will not miss the feeling of the traditional tonality. **Tonality** *refers to the major-minor system of pitches.*

Berg's imagination was sparked in 1914 when he saw the play *Woyzeck* by the German dramatist Georg Büchner (1813–1837). During the First World War, while he was serving in the Austrian army, Berg adapted the play as an opera. No doubt the traumatic experience of the war helped Berg relate to the tragic figure of Wozzeck, a soldier who is driven to murder and madness by a hostile society.

The opera is in three acts, each with five scenes that are connected with short orchestral interludes. Through the music, we are drawn into Wozzeck's world to experience his hallucinations and grotesque visions. The music projects his disturbed and abnormal mental state. In this nightmarish world, Wozzeck is tormented by his sadistic captain, used as a guinea pig by a half-crazed doctor, and betrayed by his mistress Marie. When his relationship with Marie is destroyed, his mind shatters completely, and he plunges into oblivion. Berg's music actually allows us to experience these distressing areas of human experience.

Is the music as chaotic as the mind it portrays? Surprisingly, it is highly structured even though it may not sound at all ordered. Berg based the work on recurring motives and sections that gather emotional meaning through their prior associations in the plot. His music is appropriate to the action—a waltz, for example, for the tavern scene. Throughout the murder scene in Act III (Scene 2), a single note B is sounded, as if it were the idea of murder itself rising and submerging and rising again in Wozzeck's thoughts, finally exploding in the horrifying act itself.

The music for this scene is an invention on a single pitch!

▶ The subject of death has fascinated artists throughout the ages. German graphic artist Käthe Kollwitz (1867–1945) spent her life recording the grimmer aspects of the human condition. Her stark and moving images express the plight of the downtrodden and the horrors of war. Here, with masterful sympathy, she portrays the *Call of Death* (1934), depicting herself with the hand of Death on her shoulder.

Käthe Kollwitz. *Call of Death.* 1934. Private collection.

▼*Activity:* **Decide**

Does the repetition of a single pitch function as a structural or an expressive device?

Isolate the single pitch B on any melodic instrument. Using only the pitch B, create a musical idea that expresses the mood of the following words: calm, delicate, dreamy, and soothing.

Again, using only the pitch B, create the mood of the following words: turbulent, agitated, passionate, and tense.

What musical elements did you use to create the two contrasting moods?

In Alban Berg's opera *Wozzeck*, the uncontrolled obsession of Wozzeck to murder Marie is symbolized by the use of the insistent pitch B. This pitch appears throughout the scene in various instruments, registers, rhythm patterns, and dynamic levels.

Follow the German words and their translation as you hear them. How do Berg's treatment of the pitch B as well as other musical devices reflect the feelings embodied in the text?

Death Expressed in Spirituals

Because death is something all humans must face, it is a subject that has been explored in all kinds of music—classical, folk, jazz, and popular. We try to give expression to it because we need to understand and cope with it. Many Negro spirituals, for example, speak of the promised land:

> I'll meet you in de mornin',
>   When you reach de promised land;
> On de oder side of Jordan,
>   For I'm boun' for de promised land.

For many slaves, such songs had powerful double meanings. True, they spoke of the hope of reaching heaven, but heaven also referred to reaching the north and freedom. In the spiritual "Swing Low, Sweet Chariot," the line "I looked over Jordan and what did I see, Coming for to carry me home" might refer to the Ohio River. The "band of angels" could be a group of friends, and "home" might refer to the free states.

▼*Activity:* **Describe**

What musical characteristics illuminate the emotions inherent in the words of the spiritual "Hush, Hush, Somebody's Callin' Mah Name"?

Read the text of the spiritual. What is the text describing? What specific words tell you this?

Now listen to the recording or sing the spiritual and decide how the music conveys what the text is describing.

Identify the measures of music that could be described as spiritual moaning. Is the spiritual moaning just as effective as the words or more so? How is the natural rhythm of the words (as you would speak them) captured and embodied in the music?

Hush, Hush, Sombody's Callin' Mah Name

Arrangement by J. Jefferson Cleveland
and Verolga Nix

2.   Sounds like Jesus. Somebody's callin' mah name, . . .

3.   Soon one mornin', death'll come creepin' in mah room, . . .

4.   I'm so glad. Ah got mah religion in time, . . .

5.   I'm so glad. I'm on mah journey home, . . .

* The B♭ indicates the note of the E♭ chord that is in the bass.

Death Expressed in Jazz

Even though its tunes are usually thought of as "up," jazz has been tinged with the blues. This tint can sometimes assert itself to shade the whole. This is usually the instance on those rare occasions when jazz musicians turn their attention to the subject of death. The New Orleans funeral parade is one way that death is expressed through the jazz medium, but there are others.

Music and Controversy

John Ruskin, nineteenth-century art critic, wrote that "Great nations write their autobiographies in three manuscripts—the book of their deeds, the book of their words, and the book of their arts. Not one of these books can be understood unless we read the other two, but of the three, the only trustworthy one is the last." In Ruskin's view, the arts present a more honest overall picture because they sometimes probe the meaning of life and events, and raise troublesome questions about them. They dig at the truth.

It is this quality of probing for the truth that has sometimes caused the arts to be considered controversial. Some people become irritated when their beliefs and practices are questioned. When the arts express alternative views that challenge the way people think and act, people sometimes react against them. They view them as subversive and dangerous, even immoral. Often such people prefer to impose their own viewpoints on others. Those who would limit viewpoints to their own are not supporters of American freedom and democratic ideals as guaranteed by the First Amendment to the Constitution of the United States.

The arts are often outspoken. They can console us. They can also disturb and rile us up when they present different and unexpected visions of the world. The arts often confront us with more than the comfortable aspects of life. Music expresses love, joy, spirituality, celebration, and hope, but it also explores life's darker aspects: distress, anxiety, loss, sorrow, and death. Like the other arts, music expresses the highest human aspirations. It also awakens us to our failings and to truths about life that may be disturbing. In this way, music helps us better our human ways.

Profile

Billie Holiday
American Jazz Singer
1915–1959

BILLIE HOLIDAY

Born in Baltimore in 1915, Eleanora Holiday suffered through an undeserved stint in a reform school and several unsavory jobs during her impoverished youth. Choosing the nickname "Billie" from her favorite movie star, Miss Billie Dove, Holiday moved to New York in 1929, where she sang in small clubs before being discovered by John Hammond in 1933. Hammond, impressed by a performance in Harlem, set up Holiday's first recording sessions with Benny Goodman's studio band, but it was her appearance at the Apollo Theater and the invention of the jukebox in 1935 that really boosted her career.

Like other black artists of the Jazz Era, Billie Holiday's talent was at the mercy of club owners and record industry moguls who were predominantly white. Club owners prevented her from mingling with customers, forcing her to use service entrances and to stay in dressing rooms or by washrooms in between her songs. More than once, these conditions got the best of her, and she left without her salary or prospects of another job. At recording studios, publishers most often chose the music to be performed, based on what would sell. Fortunately, Billie added her own heartfelt warmth to every song she sang.

Although Holiday worked with several big bands from 1933 to 1938, she returned to singing at clubs where she did not have to compromise her unique jazz style. In songs such as "Fine and Mellow," "T'ain't Nobody's Business," "Strange Fruit," and countless others, she sang about real aspects of life, including racism. As a songwriter, she dealt with the subject of abusive husbands in "Don't Explain" and with the failure of people to heed God in "God Bless the Child." Singlehandedly, she brought the "real" world to popular singing, an innovation that changed popular music fundamentally. Her addiction to drugs and alcohol led to her death at the age of 44 in 1959.

Cooperative Learning

Discuss "Strange Fruit"

Why would the song "Strange Fruit" have been controversial in 1939?

Why might some people not have wanted to hear this song or allow it to be sung?

Why did it take courage for Billie Holiday to perform this song?

One example of how music can be controversial is the song "Strange Fruit," which Billie Holiday recorded in 1939. The poem and the music, both by Lewis Allan, dared to express in metaphor the subject of lynching in the South. Holiday's performance of the song is pained but never self-pitying. She tells it "like it is." A muted trumpet sets the mood. Then the piano states the melody. The singing is dramatic but controlled. The accompaniment has a funereal beat.

Death Expressed in Popular Music

Like many works for the stage, the enormously popular musical *Les Misérables* is based upon a preexistent work, in this instance, the nineteenth-century epic novel by the great French writer Victor Hugo. The musical was adapted by a team of artists from England and France. The **book**—*the story and the dialogue of a musical*—for the show is by Alain Boublíl and Claude-Michel Schönberg. The lyrics are by Herbert Kretzmer and Alain Boublíl, and the music is by Claude-Michel Schönberg.

Following the novel, the musical presents a panorama of love and death during a time of political and social revolution in France. The story is complex and covers most of the long life of Jean Valjean (jon val-JON). But the story is also, at moments, exciting, heartbreaking, stirring, and triumphant. The brilliant and memorable musical score guarantees the audience an emotional wallop. The tunes are unforgettable. This work is not simply a collection of beautiful melodies, however. It is a musical with a strong message: the importance of people loving and caring for each other and the need to rid society of social injustice.

Act II takes place during the turmoil following the French Revolution. The students have built a barricade and are manning it against impossible odds. The army warns the students to "Give up your guns—or die!" The next day, the army attacks the barricade and kills most of the young rebels. Valjean escapes into the Paris sewers carrying the unconscious and seriously wounded Marius on his back. A few months later, Marius, unaware of the identity of his rescuer, has recovered. Sadly, he returns to the café where his young revolutionary friends used to gather. There, in the midst of all the empty tables, he recalls the days of the barricade when all his friends lost their lives.

Like other well-constructed compositions, "Empty Chairs at Empty Tables" is based on a musical motive that recurs throughout the piece, sometimes with slight variation:

This song expresses the loss Marius feels, as well as his own guilt, for being the only one among his young rebel friends who survived.

Summary

Humans express death in a variety of ways in all kinds of music. We honor the deceased by celebrating the life of the individual with a jazz parade or a solemn funeral march. We memorialize people through jazz and classical music, by a lone trumpet, by a voice raised in song, and by instruments that give expression to our sorrow and loss. Through music we can begin to understand the terror and violence that sometime accompany death, and learn to be compassionate.

Death is part of the unfolding drama of life. It is music that so often permits us to express what is otherwise inexpressible—those quiet, unexpected, or powerful events that sweep a human life away. Music helps us deal with this perplexing inevitability that hovers over us like an assured promise. It lets us know that the hurt we feel is shared by others and that it is natural and human. It permits us to pause and remember, to console and to cherish, to weep and to mourn, in other words, to get in direct touch with our deepest feelings, distill them, release them, and put them outside of ourselves where we can understand them better.

Cooperative Learning

Detect

Listen to the song "Empty Chairs at Empty Tables" from the musical *Les Misérables*, and try to determine the musical qualities that make it expressive.

Working in small groups, answer the following questions:

1. How many times is the motive (left) either repeated or imitated (sung at a lower or higher pitch)?
2. Is the piece in major or minor tonality?
3. What is the overall form of the song?
4. Does the piece stay in the same key? If not, at what point does it change?
5. Is the melody primarily disjunct or conjunct? Does the composer vary this? When? Why?
6. What specific qualities in the performance and the orchestration contribute to an understanding of the message the composer is trying to convey?

Apply What You Have Learned
Chapter 11

What are the differences and similarities between two love songs?

Listen to Harold Arlen's song "Stormy Weather" and Giacomo Puccini's song "Un bel di" (One fine day) and make a list of the differences and similarities between the two. Comment about as many musical characteristics as you can, including the basic style, message, mood and intended audience, and such musical characteristics as the sources of sound, and the rhythm, melody, and dynamics.

Apply What You Have Learned
Chapter 12

What characteristics determine whether a musical composition is religious (sacred) or nonreligious (secular)?

Listen to "African Sanctus" by David Fanshawe, then answer these questions:

1. Which aspects of the piece might be considered religious?
2. Which aspects sound secular?
3. Which styles of religious music that you have studied in this unit are represented in this composition?
4. Would you consider this composition a sacred work? Why or why not?

Apply What You Have Learned
Chapter 13

What musical characteristics support and embody the sense of celebration in Dmitri Shostakovich's *Festive Overture* (1954)?

In spite of the controversy his orchestral works aroused among the ruling communist party and the constant censorship he endured, Shostakovich produced remarkable works—sturdy, highly emotional, lyrical, and dramatic. His *Festive Overture* is triumphal, expressing his indomitable spirit.

As you listen, create a map of the musical events in this composition. Focus your attention on the musical qualities that make this work festive. In creating your map, try to include musical descriptors of the following:
- How the composition begins and ends.
- The ebb and flow, including crescendos and decrescendos.
- Orchestral tone color and the use of the four families of tone color (brass, woodwind, strings, and percussion).
- Tempo designations.
- Texture—the contrast of homophonic and polyphonic sections.
- Melodic rhythm (use of long and short durations).
- The use of dancelike rhythms.
- The expressive use of percussion.
- The extensive use of syncopation.

Use your map of the *Festive Overture* as the basis for a written composition describing how Shostakovich ordered the musical events as a statement of celebration.

Apply What You Have Learned
Chapter 14

Determine what musical devices make a song express death.

The poignancy of a song such as "Danny Boy" (page 114) comes from the thought that a lover who is called to war might return after the lover at home has gone to the grave. The folk song "Johnny Has Gone for a Soldier" alludes to death in a less direct way, but nevertheless evokes the sorrow surrounding the loss of a lover during the Revolutionary War.

Johnny Has Gone for a Soldier

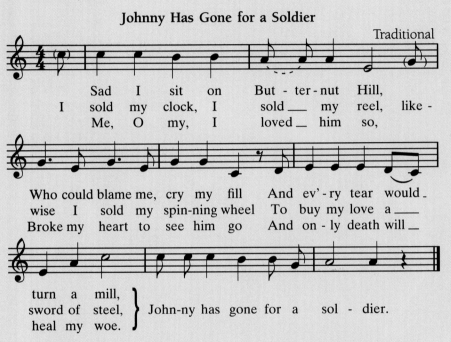

Traditional

Sad I sit on But-ter-nut Hill,
I sold my clock, I sold __ my reel, like-
Me, O my, I loved __ him so,

Who could blame me, cry my fill And ev'-ry tear would __
wise I sold my spin-ning wheel To buy my love a __
Broke my heart to see him go And on-ly death will __

turn a mill,
sword of steel, } John-ny has gone for a sol - dier.
heal my woe.

The melody of "Johnny Has Gone for a Soldier" is based on the A minor scale; and it can be harmonized with just two chords:

A minor scale   A minor   E minor
                      i or i   v

Create a performance of "Johnny Has Gone for a Soldier." Decide if the performance would be more effective as a solo or as an ensemble. What instruments would provide an appropriate accompaniment? Include your suggestions for tempo, dynamics, harmony, and tone color.

Name the pitches that make up the I and v chords in A minor. Harmonize "Johnny" using these two minor chords by following this procedure: Examine each melody tone and find the chord to which it belongs, then place the root of the chord in the bass (left hand), and play the chord with your right hand.

Music!...
To Let Us
Create

~

CHAPTER 15

Communicating with Sound

Objectives

By completing this chapter, you will:

- Understand how musical communication depends on the combination of musical elements.
- Learn the important role of texture in musical expression.
- Become acquainted with Arabic rhythm and how it is combined with melody to create Syrian music.
- Discover the uniqueness of Balkan vocal textures.
- Learn about expressive tools such as harmonizing, modulation, and arranging.
- Discover the important role of the music arranger.
- Be able to distinguish an arrangement from a transcription.

Musical Terms

arranger
harmonizing
idée fixe
modulation
obbligato
program symphony
transcription

*S*ound is the basic raw material of all musical communication. It might consist of the distinct pitches of a particular scale, a set of noises of indeterminate pitch, or a combination of both. During the creative process, sound is manipulated in a number of ways to give it character and dimension. Musical creators shape sound by giving it a particular melody, rhythm, dynamics, form, timbre, and texture. These elements are the tools a composer or arranger uses to shape sound into an expressive statement.

The Integration of Musical Elements

We have already investigated many of the musical elements the composer uses. Up to this point, we have looked at and listened to these various elements as separate and distinct entities. Now we will begin to see and hear them in a more comprehensive way. We shall ask you to hear more than one of the elements at the same time, to recognize that they work together, not separately. We are now going to blur the divisions deliberately in order to see music for what it is—an integration of all these elements.

There is no melody without rhythm, and, most often, rhythm is expressed in combination with the melodic movement of tones. Dynamics are not heard in isolation but as they affect the melody and rhythm in all parts. Form, timbre, and texture are applied across the board, affecting the other elements, and emerging from them. Music is not a juxtaposition of isolated elements, but rather a cohesive consolidation of related events.

Texture

One of the most expressive aspects of music is its texture: the arrangement of the horizontal and vertical sounds. It is this element that gives music much of its character and, therefore, its individuality and mood. Texture describes how different musical sounds occurring at the same time relate to one another. You have heard various musical textures: monophonic, heterophonic, homophonic, and polyphonic. Texture refers to the density of the sounds—the degree to which they are active or inactive, thick or thin. Texture can indicate how the melodic element of the music connects with the tones that sound simultaneously with it—a series of chords, a rhythmic line, another melody, several other melodies, or even a repetition of the same melody.

Texture, then, describes the integration of musical elements. It is often reinforced by the choice of timbres so that the combination of elements may be smoothly blended (like a fabric in one color) or deliberately contrasted (like a pattern or plaid). This interplay of elements gives music its emotional and communicative charge.

Our Western music is highly developed in timbre, harmony, and form. Music from other parts of the world is sometimes more highly developed in other ways. As you have seen and heard, rhythm in the music of India and Africa can be sophisticated and complex. It can go far beyond our steady two- and three-beat patterns. Highly developed rhythm is also characteristic of some of the music from the Arab world, the music of Syria being a good example.

The Culture of Syria

Syria has a long history as an important Middle Eastern province because its trade routes connect Mediterranean countries with those to the east. One of Syria's great river systems, the Euphrates, is interrupted by several hydroelectric dams that drive the industrial development of the major cities, Damascus, Aleppo, and Homs. For centuries these cities have served as inland "ports" to a desert "sea," welcoming caravans to and from Europe, Asia, and Africa.

Syrians view their culture as deriving from ancient civilizations such as Mesopotamia and from the Arabs who conquered the region in the seventh century. Most Syrians are Arab-speaking Muslims. The way of life in Syria is similar to that in neighboring Lebanon, Jordan, and, to some extent, Turkey. This larger Arab cultural area, which reflects the similarities that exist among the Arab people of the region, is sometimes referred to as Greater Syria. The music throughout this area also has many similarities.

Classical Music from Syria

The Arabic music of Syria draws upon the same classical system of melodic and rhythmic modes and compositional practices used in Egyptian music, but incorporates regional variations in tuning and style. Although Syrian music is recognizably Arabic in a general sense, folk songs and dances differ within Syria as they do throughout the Middle East. In the city of Aleppo, for example, there has been a revival of performances of old classical pieces believed to have originated in the rich Arab courts of the Middle East and Spain during the time of the Arab Empire. This repertory includes songs called *muwashshahat* (moo-wah-shah-HAT) that are in very complicated meters. Some have the equivalent of 24 or 48 beats per measure!

Another example of this classical music is *samai* (sah-MAH-ee), an instrumental genre with ties to Turkish music. One of the most popular and accomplished performers of this music is Sabah Fakhri (sah-BAH FAKH-ree), a Syrian from Aleppo who plays the ūd and sings. He and his ensemble perform in concert and on television, and they have made recordings.

The rhythmic pattern (or rhythmic mode) is an important defining feature of both the *muwashshahat* and *samai*. To understand how the rhythmic system of Arabic music works, you must observe the following:

1. A single pattern may have from 2 to 48 beats, rarely more.
2. A pattern consists of hard or stressed beats, called *dum* (doom), and soft or unstressed beats, called *tak*, as well as rests or silences. (You may recall that in the music of India these stressed and unstressed sounds were called *dum* and *te*. See page 43.)
3. Unlike their Western counterparts, Arabic rhythmic patterns often include more than one stressed beat per pattern.
4. The skilled drummer plays the rhythmic pattern clearly, making certain the *dums* are heard. At the same time, the drummer also improvises by adding flourishes that take advantage of the various tone colors that can be coaxed from the drum. This is similar to the way good jazz or rock drummers improvise while they maintain the basic beat. In Arabic music, the basic rhythmic pattern is a complex combination of stressed and unstressed beats and silences.
5. The percussion part (played on the *riqq* [rick] or tambourine in the following example) is often very elaborate and always clearly heard, even though it is never overwhelmingly loud. Other instruments often used in Arabic music include the *qānūn* (kah-NOON) or plucked zither, the *ūd* or lute, and the *tabla* or hourglass drum.

▼Activity: *Perform*

Learn to play a well-known Arabic rhythmic mode.

Listen to the excerpt of a samai and try to hear the following often-used Arabic rhythmic mode called *samai thaqil* (sah-MAH-ee thah-KEEL):

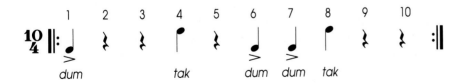

Practice tapping the steady beat while you say *dum* and *tak*. Use a comfortable tempo of about 104 beats to the minute (the speed of the performance). Repeat until the rhythmic flow becomes automatic. Then listen to the performance again and try to tap and speak the rhythmic mode along with it.

Does one instrument play the melody, or are there several? Can you distinguish all the instruments described above?

Which is most important in this music—(1) rhythm, (2) melody, or (3) a combination of both?

▶ The Bulgarian State Radio and Television Female Vocal Choir regularly tours and performs within the United States, portraying the long Bulgarian history of women's choral groups. They wear their traditional attire during performances, adding visual impact to their remarkable vocal textures and haunting timbres.

Cooperative Learning

Discover the Secret

As you listen to the folk song "Bajo le Ivane," see if you can discover one of the secrets of Bulgarian singing.

Working in small groups, consider the following questions:

1. Are the singers all singing the same rhythm? Asked another way: are they singing the words at the same time?
2. Are the singers all singing the same melody throughout the song?
3. How are the singers creating musical variety in their song?
4. What makes this Balkan homophonic sound different from that of a church hymn?
5. What is different about the sound of these voices? What does this tone quality add to the musical expression?

The Culture of Bulgaria

The Balkan peninsula includes the countries of Albania, Romania, Bulgaria, Greece, and former Yugoslavia. The position of the Balkans between Europe and Asia has affected their history as well as the ways these people live, work, dress, and make music. At one time or another they have been dominated by their large and aggressive neighbors—the Mongol Empire, the Byzantine Empire, the Ottoman Empire, the Austro-Hungarian Empire, and the Soviet Union. These dominations and many other influences have enriched the Balkan culture.

Bulgaria is slightly larger than the state of Ohio, and although somewhat industrialized, it is a predominantly agricultural country. Until 1918, Bulgaria was part of the Ottoman Empire; so it has absorbed some Middle Eastern customs. The culture is still tied closely to village life.

Balkan Vocal Textures

Much of the musical life of Bulgaria is connected to the daily or seasonal customs and tasks of country village life. The people use their abundant folk songs to celebrate weddings, births, and religious holidays. The same songs, sung and/or played on a variety of instruments, provide music for dancing, which is one of the main forms of entertainment at all festive occasions. The people use songs to help pass the time while working in the fields or to coordinate their movements during certain kinds of tasks such as harvesting crops, sorting vegetables, or weaving and spinning. Even today, when technology has eliminated many of these jobs, the songs are remembered and performed.

There is a long tradition of women singing in Bulgaria. Over the centuries, they have developed remarkable vocal textures and haunting timbres. Singing distracted them from the tedium of their work. As with all folk music, these unusual vocal practices were created communally by the village people doing the singing. One of the most prevalent textures in Bulgarian singing is homophony, two or more different pitches sounding simultaneously, all with the same melodic rhythm.

The folk song "Bajo le Ivane" (BOTCH-oh lay ee-VAHN-ay) ("Brother Ivan") is a typical example of homophonic texture. The song was sung by women as they worked in the fields harvesting crops such as wheat, rye, and barley. In it, an older sister gives her brother advice about how to choose a hard-working wife. In the field, the hardest workers are at the front of the line! Here is a translation of the lyrics: "Brother Ivan, don't look at the girls in the winter at the dance, when they're fair and rosy. Look at them, brother, in the summer fields. Who leads the line? Who works in the middle? Who picks up around the edges? Who sits in the shade rocking a baby boy and singing him a song?"

Homophonic texture is given additional interest when a more complex meter and a rapid (and challenging) tempo are used. The song "Mome odi" (MO-may oh-DEE) ("A Girl Walks") is from the region known as Macedonia, a cultural area now situated in the three nations of Bulgaria, Greece, and former Yugoslavia. It uses a combined meter of 3+2+2, or seven beats per measure. Like many of the songs from this region, the beats go by quickly (the tempo is fast)! The two parts begin together, separate, and finally merge again at the cadences, alternating between monophonic and homophonic texture. Translated, the text says: "A girl walks through the grassy fields, through the wide sunny fields."

▼Activity: **Test Your Voice and Ears**

Listen to the homophonic song, "Mome odi" and learn to clap the rhythm and sing the words.

Perform the 7/8 meter by clapping the first beat of each group of 3 or 2 beats while you count to seven quietly:

beats:	1	2	3	1	2	1	2
claps:	●			●		●	

Your clapping should produce a long-short-short pattern.

When you are comfortable with this rhythmic pattern, try singing the song. Much of the melodic rhythm of this song uses the same long-short-short rhythmic pattern.

Mome odi ("A Girl Walks")

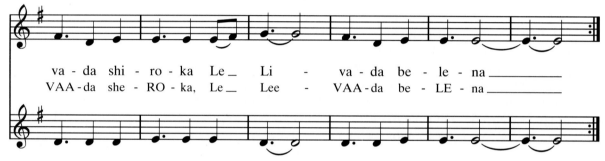

First line is in Bulgarian dialect. Second line indicates the phonetic pronunciation.

Harmonizing

As we have heard in the previous two musical examples, making up a harmony part is an art that can be accomplished in a variety of ways. We can assume that the women who sang these songs knew the tune but made up the second part as they went along. They did not learn the second part from notation, but created it "by ear" according to their folk song tradition.

Harmonizing is one of the tools of music making. **Harmonizing** is *the ability to invent on the spot a vocal line that will complement a melody*. "On the spot" means that the harmonization is being created spontaneously, as the melody is sung. Harmonizing literally means to sing or play "in harmony." It is usually done by ear without the benefit of printed notation.

You know from your experience with Mexican music that the singers often prefer to harmonize at an interval of a third, creating a second part that is parallel to the melody. Much of this kind of vocal harmonization is in just two parts. Gospel choirs also create harmony by ear, but in this instance, there may be several parts, each corresponding to the general range of the singers' voices. Altos, tenors, and basses may create individual parts to form chords that support the soprano melody, while a solo voice adds still another **obbligato**, *or subordinate melody above*. The texture here becomes dense and complex.

▼*Activity:* **Harmonize**

Try to harmonize "The Golden Vanity" by singing (and inventing) a new part that stays within the three chords of the song.

Use the following steps:

1. *Find and Mark the Chord Changes.* Follow the music for "The Golden Vanity" as you listen to the recording of the song. As you listen, put an "X" above each measure where you hear the harmony (or chords) change. The first four are done for you on the music. Your job is to find the remaining five chord changes.

2. *Write in the Chord Names.* "The Golden Vanity" uses the three basic chords in the key of A major: I or A, IV or D, and V7 or E7. Next to the "X" where you have marked chord changes, write in the proper name and symbol of the chord.

3. *Sing the Chord Roots as a Harmonization.* Use your chord symbols as a guide to select the pitches for your harmonization. Use solfège syllables to sing the chord roots: sing DO every time you hear the I or A chord; sing FA (up a 4th) every time you hear the IV or D chord; and sing sol (up a 5th) every time you hear the V7 or E7 chord. Sustain each pitch until the song moves to the next chord. Put the two parts together, maintaining the same rhythm as the melody. This gives you a basic harmonization.

4. Now that you are beginning to hear the chord changes, try moving beyond the basics. Remember, harmonizing requires some risk-taking! Try starting your second part above the melody, choosing another pitch in the A chord—C# or E. Feel your way along through the tune, sliding around until you find a tone that goes with the harmony.

5. Play the chords on any chording instrument (guitar, keyboard, autoharp, or accordion) while other students harmonize the song.

◀ Artists use different textures for expressive purposes. In his painting, *Grainstack (Thaw, Sunset)*, the French Impressionist painter Claude Monet (1840–1926) captured the look of a haystack on an overcast day. The coarse texture of the hay contrasts with the smooth, snowy blur of the field and sky.

Claude Monet, French, 1840–1926. *Grainstack (Thaw, Sunset)* 1891. Oil on canvas. 64.9 x 92.3 cm. Copyright 1990, The Art Institute of Chicago, Chicago, Illinois. All Rights Reserved. Gift of Mr. and Mrs. Daniel C. Searle, 1983.166.

In much of this folk music, instrumentalists also add parts by ear, following the appropriate chord patterns. These parts complement the melody and enrich its overall effect. This is the essence of improvisation in jazz. The instrumentalists know the chord changes, and they invent a part for their own instrument that weaves through that pattern of chords. We usually call harmonization on instruments "improvisation" and improvisation with voices "harmonization."

Modulation

Another device often used for expressive purposes is **modulation**, *the changing from one key to another.* This effect can be compared to the sun coming out after a rain. A new key can give a feeling of refreshing brightness. It can also create the reverse—a darkening or dampening of the spirit. Then, too, modulation is often used as a device for marking the divisions in a musical form, setting them off in a related tonality.

Modulation is fairly common in longer musical works. One simple way of modulating is to use a chord that is common to both keys. This pivot chord is used to go from the old key to a full cadence in the new key:

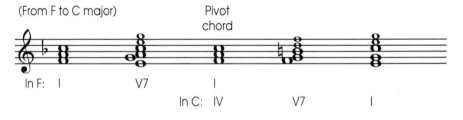

▼Activity: *Listen and Decide*

How does the composer of this gospel song use modulation to reflect the meaning of the words?

Follow the different ways the same melody is presented as you listen to "One More Valley." Determine how many times the melody is repeated. Does the melody sound higher or lower each time it is repeated?

What does the text of "One More Valley" describe?

What musical characteristics help support the words of the text?

Why do you think the composer chose modulation to illuminate the meaning of the text of this song?

Musical Creation

As you have heard in these examples, music is the result of a combination of various musical elements working together. For anyone who would choose to create music, then, the task is to plan how all the elements can be used to reinforce each other in one cohesive design. It is not much different than a painter who has to consider how line, shape, form, space, color, and texture can be brought together to realize a visual idea or concept. If you were creating a teleplay, you would have to be concerned with such matters as plot (conflict, climax, and resolution), setting, characterization, dialogue, and tempo. The creator has to think in several dimensions simultaneously. This is certainly true of the composer and musical arranger.

The Composer

Composers decide what they want to express and then assemble the combination of sounds that will communicate their intent. A composer, for example, might choose to convey the emotion of real or imagined events and use an array of orchestral timbres as the medium. Such is the case with Hector Berlioz's *Symphonie Fantastique,* originally titled "Episode for the Life of an Artist" (1830). Here, the composer deliberately sets out to express a fantasy based upon an event in his own life.

He composed a **program symphony**, *a pictorial or descriptive orchestral work in several movements.* The composer may or may not supply listeners with a verbal description of the music's content. It is important to remember that music does not have to be inspired by specific events; it can simply express an abstract thought or emotion. The *Symphonie Fantastique* can be listened to on two levels—as a musical description and as pure musical expression.

Berlioz believed strongly that listeners would benefit by knowing the details of the story. He wrote the following recommendation about knowing the extra-musical program before hearing the music: "The distribution of the programme to the audience at concerts where the symphony is to be performed is indispensable for a complete understanding of the dramatic outline of the work."

This program symphony is in five movements, and its story sounds much like a contemporary soap opera. It is about a young musician who has a very sensitive personality, a wild imagination, and an uncontrollable romantic interest in a woman who simply does not love him. This is how Berlioz outlined the story in his preface to the work:

> A young, morbid, ardent musician in a state of amorous despair poisons himself with opium. The dose, insufficient to kill him, plunges him into a delirious sleep during which his sensations take the form of musical ideas in his sick brain. His beloved becomes a melody, an *idée fixe* (fixed idea) which he hears everywhere.

The musician's dreams are transformed into musical imagery. The five movements tell the progression of the story: "Dreams and Passions," "A Ball," "Scene in the Country," "March to the Scaffold," and "Dream of Witches' Sabbath." The love theme or **idée fixe** (ee-day FEEKS), *a fixed melodic idea that recurs throughout all five movements of the symphony,* is a device Berlioz created to give the composition unity. Here is how Berlioz describes the fourth movement, "The March to the Scaffold":

> [The young musician] dreams he has killed his beloved, that he has been condemned to death and is being led to the scaffold. The procession advances to the sound of a march now somber, now wild, now brilliant, now solemn. Loud outbursts are followed without pause by the plodding sounds of marching feet. The idée fixe appears for a moment like a last thought of love cut short by the fatal blow of the guillotine.

As a Romantic composer, Berlioz had the enriched harmonic resources, the colorful orchestration, and the free creative sense of expression that enabled him to communicate his ideas in graphic detail. This work shows what an imaginative and brilliant composer can do with the resources of a symphony orchestra.

▼Activity:　***Discover***

By comparing the two themes below from "March to the Scaffold," can you determine which is the love theme (idée fixe) and which is the march theme? How do you know?

Study the score as you listen to the final moments in this movement. Try to hear the love theme (idée fixe). The clarinet plays the idée fixe love theme one final time, suggesting that the man's last thought is of his beloved. Then hear the blow of the guillotine, and the man's head rolling into the basket on the scaffold. Can you detect where these events take place in the score?

Orchestra Score

Fantastic Symphony

Hector Berlioz

Excerpt, Movement IV, "March to the Scaffold"

Profile

Hector Berlioz
French Composer
1803–1869

HECTOR BERLIOZ

Hector Berlioz exemplified the struggling artist. The real recognition of his genius came long after his death. His early experiences with music were minimal but evidently made a strong impression. At the age of 17, in spite of Berlioz's preference for a career in music, his father persuaded him to go to Paris to study medicine, following in his father's footsteps. Inspired by the rich musical life in the city, Berlioz abandoned medicine even though it alienated his parents for years. After studying in Italy, he settled permanently in Paris. Because his compositions provided little income, he was forced to earn a living as a critic, a job he did well but hated.

In the late 1820s, Berlioz, as a young man, went to the theater to see Shakespeare's *Hamlet.* The role of Ophelia was played by a beautiful Irish actress named Harriet Smithson. Although Berlioz had never actually met this actress, he fell madly in love with her. Early in 1830 as he was trying to compose his *Symphonie Fantastique,* he wrote a letter to a friend describing his real but irrational passion for this actress. His letter reveals the very heart of Romanticism: "I am again plunged in the anguish of an interminable and inextinguishable passion, without motive, without cause. She is always at London, and yet, I think I feel her near me; all my remembrances awake and unite to wound me. . . . 'Tis terrible! O unhappy one! If she could for one moment conceive all the poetry, all the infinity of a like love, she would fly to my arms. . . ." In 1833 Miss Smithson accepted his proposal of marriage. Later, his ideal of love was shattered by the realities of their marriage and they divorced.

Berlioz poured his emotions into his scores, translating his life into his music. Literary works inspired many of his compositions, among them the symphonies *Harold in Italy* (based on Byron's *Childe Harold*) and *Romeo and Juliet* (based on Shakespeare's play). His choral works include *The Damnation of Faust* (based on Goethe's *Faust*), the monumental *Te Deum,* the *Requiem,* and the oratorio *L'enfance du Christ.* He composed a number of works for solo voice and orchestra, as well as works for the stage, including the opera *Les Troyens.*

The Musical Arranger

In the broadest sense, composers arrange all the elements of music when creating a work. But the term **arranger** is *usually applied in a more limited way to designate someone who reworks preexistent musical material.* The arranger adapts a composition written for one performing medium to another or recomposes a work to suit different circumstances.

The composer and the arranger manipulate sound in all its dimensions, but their roles are different. The composer often starts with a blank canvas and creates a totally new musical work. Occasionally, the composer will base his or her ideas on an existing theme or work, but what emerges is essentially a new piece of music. In contrast, an arranger takes a composition and adapts it, or otherwise alters it, to make it suitable for a performing medium, occasion, or purpose different from the one for which the composer originally created it. For example, in celebrating the inauguration of a new president, a composer may be commissioned to write a

◄ Among the performing groups at the U.S. Naval Academy in Annapolis, Maryland, is the Drum and Bugle Corps, a brigade of 120 midshipmen. The bugle line consists of soprano, mellophone, flugelhorn, baritone, and contrabass sections. The drum line consists of snare, bass, and cymbal sections as well as tom-toms and marching timpani. Here they perform at the Navy versus Penn State football game.

new work, whereas an arranger may be hired to create an updated version of "The Battle Hymn" scored for heralding trumpets, brass bands, and mixed chorus.

Sometimes arrangements are made to augment the limited repertory of music available for a particular instrument or voice. A work for cello, for example, may be rescored for string bass. An arranger may also simplify a virtuoso work so that it is less difficult and can therefore be performed by an amateur or by a student with limited ability.

Musical arrangements exist from all periods of music history. Arrangers often update a musical work, giving it a contemporary sound and feeling. They will arrange a popular work such as Rimsky-Korsakov's "Flight of the Bumblebee" so that it can be performed by every conceivable combination of instruments—even including voices. They might even attempt to popularize this musical masterpiece by jazzing it up for use in a television advertisement! Not all arrangements serve the best interests of the original composer. On the other hand, arrangements of Bach's instrumental music for synthesizer, or for voices (for example, the Swingle Singers) have brought Bach's work to the attention and admiration of new and younger audiences.

Like the ingredients that go into a recipe, each of the elements of music—the composer and arranger's tools—have to be figured out. Each

P R O J E C T

Create Your Own Arrangement

Working in small groups, arrange the folk song, "Trampin'" for vocal or instrumental performance or a combination of both. Choose one of the following:

A. Make a folk song arrangement with a natural vocal line and simple accompaniment on guitar or keyboard instrument.

B. Make a free-wheeling arrangement in any style you choose. Alter as many musical elements as you wish. Tinge it with the style of jazz, rock, rap, or classical music. Be prepared to perform your arrangement for the class.

Cooperative Learning

Determine

How does the arranger manage to hold a medley of songs together?

Listen to the medley arranged for marching band by Ted Mc-Daniel. Working in small groups, listen to the medley and answer the following questions:

1. Which of the songs can you identify?
2. What musical tools hold the medley together and create a unified work?
3. Since this arrangement was done for the football field, why is it more appropriate than the original songs might have been?

ingredient of the musical pie has to work with the other ingredients to create the desired overall result. Change one of these elements and you change the effect. That is what is so fascinating—and challenging! Arranging and composing are exacting arts involving many choices. The person creating the music has to be able to hear all the musical elements and their combinations in order to achieve the intended effect.

Transcribing Music

George Frideric Handel (1685–1759) frequently used the works of other composers or earlier works of his own in his compositions. Nearly half the choruses in his oratorio *Israel in Egypt* were based on the works of other composers! Likewise, J. S. Bach (1685–1750) arranged numerous pieces as new compositions. Most of his 13 harpsichord concertos are arrangements of compositions he originally wrote for the violin. The practice of reusing musical material was common during the eighteenth century. Composers clearly felt that a good musical idea was worth reusing.

The artistic involvement of the arranger can vary greatly. An arranger can simply take the exact notes of the composer and score them for any combination of instruments or voices. This is largely a mechanical process involving few if any musical decisions. Usually, such arrangements are called transcriptions, because they adhere so closely to the original. **Transcriptions** *simply transfer music from one medium to another.* For example, composers often transcribe vocal music for instruments. This allows a band to play what is essentially a vocal composition.

Transcriptions take many forms. In Europe during the Baroque era, (c. 1600–1750), composers borrowed freely from themselves and from one another by transcribing or arranging preexistent compositions, as well as by transcribing music from one medium to another. Today, of course, borrowing the music of another composer is a violation of copyright, unless the arranger acquired permission or the rights to use the material.

▼ *Activity:* **Evaluate and Perform**

Which version do you find more moving—the original or the transcription?

Thousands of vocal works have been arranged for instrumental ensembles. One example is the famous navy hymn "Eternal Father, Strong to Save." While you follow the score, listen to two different versions of the hymn: first, a choral version; second, the hymn (without words) played by a concert band. After you have listened to both examples, answer the following questions:

1. How does the arrangement for band differ from the choral original?
2. Which do you find more moving? Why?

Listen again to the arrangement for band and try to sing the words along with the band.

Eternal Father, Strong to Save

William Whiting, 1825–1878

John B. Dykes

Telling the Difference

An arranger can be enormously innovative with the original work, filtering it through his or her imagination to create a work of wholly new merit and expressiveness. Gioachino Rossini's *William Tell* Overture (1829) has been transcribed and arranged for various performing media. Most transcriptions remain fairly close to the original. They usually do not alter substantially the melody, rhythm, or harmony. Arrangements, on the other hand, are often very different from the original in musical treatment and effect.

▼ *Activity:* **Distinguish and Judge**

Can you tell the difference between a transcription and an arrangement?

The notes below represent one of the most famous musical themes of all time. You may recognize it as a cartoon theme or as the music from old western films that featured the Lone Ranger. The music was originally composed by the composer Gioachino Rossini as an overture to his opera *William Tell.* Try to read and tap the rhythm of the melody with your index fingers until you recognize it.

Listen to the original version of the overture so you can familiarize yourself with what Rossini intended.

Now listen to the other versions of this melody and see if you can tell which are transcriptions and which are arrangements. Mark your answers on a sheet of paper. Identify the performing medium in each of the examples. Then answer these questions:

1. Which excerpt is the closest to Rossini's original overture?
2. Which excerpt is the furthest from Rossini's original?
3. Which one might be most likely to make Rossini "roll over in his grave"? Why?
4. Which of the examples (original, arrangements, or transcriptions) do you find most creative? Why?

Through arrangements and transcriptions, one piece of music can be used in many different ways and for many different purposes. Arrangements may modify the work slightly or radically. The arranger uses his or her creativity to rework the piece, and perhaps even to add to it. In the process of arranging, all the musical elements may be reworked so that a new musical creation results. As musical styles and tastes change, arranging permits music to be updated. This is an important way that music is kept vibrant and alive.

Profile

Gioachino Rossini
Italian Composer
1792–1868

GIOACHINO ROSSINI

Gioachino Rossini was a successful opera composer who was unrivaled in prestige and influence during the first half of the nineteenth century. As a youth, he composed music for the viola, violin, and piano, but did not train formally until enrolling in the Liceo Musicale in Bologna, Italy, at the age of 14. He graduated in 1808 and received his first commission in 1810. He achieved immediate success with his opera *La Cambiale di Matrimonio* (Marriage by Promissory Note). Rossini secured his position in the operatic limelight by composing well-received scores at a rapid pace, earning a worldwide audience by the time he was 21.

Rossini's music is characterized by rhythmic verve and melodic lyricism. Catering to the popular tastes of opera fans in Italy, Rossini composed in the *bel canto* style, allowing singers to show off their range and endurance. His opera orchestrations could be opulent, and his overtures were often masterpieces in their own right. He satisfied audiences by turning out at least one new opera every year. These include the popular *Barber of Seville*, a comic opera, and *William Tell*, a dramatic opera.

Rossini stopped publishing music in 1829, at the height of his popularity. His disagreement with operatic trends and his declining health may have been factors contributing to his retirement. Content with providing commentary and criticism on musical works and trends, Rossini lived comfortably in Bologna and Paris until his death in 1868.

Summary

Composers and arrangers use every possible musical device—rhythm, melody, harmony, dynamics, texture, timbre, and form—to create musical works. Folk, popular, and classical music are created from these same musical elements and processes. So is most of the music of the world. Although we sometimes single out one or more of these elements to listen to individually, it is the coordination of all these elements that gives the music its overall effect. That is why it is important to pay attention to the musical texture—how all the elements are combined.

Composers and arrangers fulfill different roles in the creation of music. Both manipulate and integrate the musical elements to create an original work, but the arranger generally starts with an existing work, whereas the composer most often invents totally. Arrangers recast music for new roles and uses. In any case, whether the music is composed or arranged, it is a synthesis of elements that speak together as one force. That is the challenge of the creative process in music—to devise a unified and communicative statement out of a combination of many elements. That is the challenge to the listener as well—to hear the larger overall musical effect that emerges from the details.

CHAPTER 16

Making Musical Decisions

Objectives

By completing this chapter, you will:

- Explore the creative process in music.
- Discover the organizing device that underlies the 12-bar blues.
- Learn how the Balinese use interlocking rhythms expressively.
- Find out how composers achieve unity and variety in the musical form called "theme and variations."
- Be introduced to the tone-row system and the work of Arnold Schoenberg.
- Acquire some perspective about your own creativity.

Musical Terms

"blue" notes
blues
interlocking rhythms
Kecak
retrograde
theme and variations
tone row

*C*omposers are people who speak their
mind primarily through music. Every human
being needs to communicate, and we all do so in a
variety of ways—through the medium of words
(written or spoken), through scientific or mathematical
symbols, through gestures and movements
(including acting and dancing), through pictures
(drawings, photographs, paintings, film, and video),
and through sound. Music is one of the major ways
humans convey certain kinds of thoughts and feelings.

Conveying Reality

Some messages are better told through one medium than another. For example, to give someone a general idea of the Grand Canyon, you could use a verbal description: "The Grand Canyon, the world's largest gorge, is a spectacle of multi-colored layers of rock." If we want to convey its vastness, we might use mathematics: "The Grand Canyon is over one mile deep, four to eighteen miles wide, and more than 200 miles long." If we want to depict the Grand Canyon in visual terms, we might choose to photograph or paint it. If we want to convey the emotional impact of the Grand Canyon, we might write a poem or depict it in music, as did Ferde Grofé when he wrote the *Grand Canyon Suite.*

Each of these media conveys a different aspect of reality. When we want to communicate, we select an appropriate medium of expression. If we want to tell people the size of the canyon, we would not choose music as our medium. But if we want to convey the emotional meaning, music might be a better choice than words or mathematical symbols. Each medium is important because it conveys something unique, something that cannot be "said" as well any other way.

Whatever medium we choose to use to communicate our insights about, feelings toward, and reactions to the world around us, we have to create our own message. If we choose to communicate in spoken words, we have to know a language and how to speak or write effectively. If we choose to communicate through music, we have to know musical language and how to use it expressively. When we set out to represent aspects of the world through an art form—whether in dance, poetry or prose, theater, visual art (including painting, drawing, and sculpture), or music—we must learn how to manipulate the elements of that art so that they communicate what we want to convey. In this chapter we will explore how we can use the medium of music for expressive purposes.

The Creative Process

In describing the composing process, French composer Arthur Honegger (1892–1955) said, "Imagine the gold miner—from early morning on, he digs with his pick, he perspires, he is exhausted, he will never find anything, and suddenly there is a nugget; he cannot believe his eyes . . ."

We know from the appearance of Beethoven's sketchbooks that his tonal ideas went through many revisions, but he discovered many gems. Musical creation did not come to him easily or in finished form. In contrast, music seemed to sing in Chopin's head or flow out of his piano. Only rarely did he have to agonize over a passage in order to get it to please him.

Inspiration

Composing can be a struggle or a spontaneous act. The difference is often attributed to inspiration—a mysterious force not easily explained. The original idea for a creative work may seem to be inspired because it appears to come from nowhere and seize the imagination. In spite of the romantic notion of inspiration, creativity is essentially a mental process. Even the excitement and emotion that may accompany the initial idea originates in the mind. Creativity is probably the most demanding of all the thought processes because it produces something where there was previously nothing.

Purpose

As you learned in Chapter 15, composers use melody, rhythm, harmony, dynamics, timbre, form, and texture to create musical expression. One of the mysteries of the art is how one composer can use all these devices to little or no effect, while another can use the same devices to achieve electrifying impact. In music, as in any other art, the composer has to have a mission—a need to say something.

Making Decisions

Composing, like painting, sculpting, writing, designing, and choreographing, involves making decisions. The composer has to decide what he or she wants to say and what is the best musical means to express it.

It takes considerable thought and planning to combine the materials of music into a statement that is cohesive and balanced, yet varied enough to be interesting. Musical creators cannot be careless about anything, lest the result sound hasty and slipshod. Many factors have to be brought together in musical expression. All the musical elements must merge together to create a cumulative, unified effect.

In the creative process, composers make decisions about each of the musical elements. The rhythm can be simple or complex, plodding or upbeat, subtle or driven. The melody might be conjunct or disjunct, flowing or angular, narrow or wide-ranging, short or long. The dynamics can remain constant at one level of loudness, contrast several levels, or change

---

Cooperative Learning

Create

Try your hand (and ear) at creating your own great love theme.

Listen to the love theme from Tchaikovsky's Overture to *Romeo and Juliet* (1869, final version 1880).

Working alone or in small groups, compose a love theme for one instrument and be prepared to share it with your classmates.

gradually or abruptly. The elements can be ordered through repetition and contrast, by the use of motives, imitation, and emotional unity, or by turning some of their decisions about order over to the performer.

Composers give their music texture by using a single line or melody (monophony), or by combining many lines or melodies in a dense blend of sound. They can combine sounds in a number of ways by using polyphony, homophony, or heterophony. Like visual artists, composers select a color palette—one consisting of a particular selection of tone colors or timbres that will best realize their musical idea. The sounds they choose may be produced by conventional instruments or voices, or electronically. They may use a single instrument, a symphony orchestra, a band, a chorus, a synthesizer, or a combination of these. In all these ways, composers shape sound into expressive statements. The number and range of musical decisions the composer makes are astounding.

Getting Started

How does the creative process in music begin? Andrew Lloyd Webber (contemporary composer of the musicals *Jesus Christ Superstar, Evita, Cats,* and *The Phantom of the Opera,* among others) says he really does not know

◀ Music-making is a popular pastime for many Americans. They not only learn how to play instruments and sing, but also to improvise and compose their own music. They learn how music can be used as a means of communication between people.

how he composes. He doodles on the piano, and when he finds something he likes, he writes it down. "If I remember it," he says, "it must be all right." Sometimes he starts with the lyrics; at other times, the music.

Sometimes composers start with a musical form. Form in music is like a plot in literature. It is the outline, the skeleton. This structure provides only the format, leaving ample leeway for many different expressions. Form does not control thinking, feeling, or message; it provides a blueprint for releasing them.

Certain musical devices, such as interlocking rhythms or the twelve-tone technique, can also provide the creative impetus. In this chapter, you will be invited to create by composing a blues, or a theme and variations; or by using interlocking rhythms or twelve-tone technique.

The 12-Bar Blues

Many of the songs you hear daily are based on the **blues**, *songs of frustration, ordeal, or longing* that are expressed very personally. Usually blues are based on a 12-bar (sometimes an 8- or 16-bar) harmonic pattern that is repeated over and over. This simple yet elegantly ordered framework gives musicians a means of expression that is limited only by their imagination. To recognize a 12-bar blues tune, you must be able to recognize the pattern of repeated harmonies. The blues form is usually based on just three chords:

The tonic or I chord is built on the first degree of the scale. The dominant or V chord is built on the fifth degree of the scale. The subdominant or IV chord is built on the fourth degree of the scale (that is, on the fifth scale degree *below* the tonic, hence the name *sub*dominant). These chords are often made into dominant-seventh chords by the addition of the seventh above the root tone:

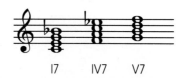

By knowing the harmonic pattern, and repeating it over and over, musicians can improvise vocally and instrumentally by creating melodies that are compatible with these chords. In the blues, harmony serves as the basis for musical organization. This continuously repeating, sequential pattern of chordal changes provides the foundation upon which each blues tune is built. A repeated harmonic pattern, then, is another fundamental way that music is given order. You, too, can use this pattern to create blues.

◀ Born in Mississippi in 1915, Muddy Waters (McKinley Morganfield) became the most important electric blues performer in post World War II Chicago. Known all his life by his childhood nickname, Muddy Waters accompanied his amplified blues singing on guitar, backed by harmonica, piano, drums, bass, and rhythm guitar—a combination that influenced the development of popular music in the 1950s and 1960s. He died in 1983.

▼Activity: *Find the Roots*

Can you play and sing the roots of the blues chords?

Look at the notation on page 290 and try to play on a keyboard or mallet percussion instrument the roots of the three chords printed here: C, F, and G. Try to sing these roots using the proper solfège syllables: DO, FA, and SOL.

As an extra challenge, try to play all three chords. One way to do this would be to play each one using the right hand in the following manner:

1. Locate and play each note separately;
2. Arpeggiate the chord by playing each note separately in rhythm; and
3. Sound the entire chord by playing all four notes simultaneously.

▼*Activity:* **Discover**

Can you hear and hum the 12-bar blues pattern?

The key to recognizing a 12-bar blues is to be able to recognize the pattern of repeated harmonies. Listen to Buddy Guy's "There Is Something On Your Mind" and try to follow the harmonic movement to detect when you hear the chord changes.

Follow these steps:

1. Use the 12-bar grid supplied by your teacher to help keep your place in the music. As you listen to the music, count the measures like a musician and mark an X in each blank "measure box" (top row) where you hear a chord change. Listen to the music again and check your changes.
2. As you listen to the music once more, hum the root of each chord: I or DO, IV or FA, V or SOL. See if you can discover which chord (I, IV, or V7) is played on each change. (Hint: The first chord change is in measure 5; after that there are four more changes in the sequence.)
3. Listen again and label each measure (bottom row of boxes) with the syllable (DO, FA, or SOL) of the chord root. (Hint: You will begin in measure 1 on DO and continue this harmony for four measures until it changes in measure 5.) Use your voice and audiation skill to tell you the scale degree (FA or SOL) that is the root of the new chord in measure 5. Continue this labeling through measure 12.
4. Now relabel your syllables with their chord numbers: DO = I; FA = IV; and SOL = V7. Once you have completed this step, you will have written out the complete harmonic sequence for the 12-bar blues!
5. Listen to Buddy Guy one more time to check your chord pattern. Hum the roots of the chords or quietly sing the chord numbers as you listen.

The Words

The lyrics of the blues are simple and direct. They usually express painful experiences that reveal the darker side of life. The poverty-stricken area known as the Mississippi Delta, which lies on the east bank of the Mississippi River south of Memphis, is generally thought to be the birthplace of the blues. In the years following the Civil War, black Americans invented this form of music to express their feelings of misery and desperation. They used the blues to vent their personal anguish.

These very honest, personal expressions dealt with basic concerns that flooded the lives of the poor and downtrodden. But the blues lyrics do not just complain. They express both the grief and the reason for it. In this way, the blues lyrics gave hope. They put people in charge of their own problems. In the blues, each 12-bar section represents a verse that consists of three lines. The first states the situation, and the second usually repeats it exactly, assuring clarity and building tension. Then the third or rhyming line resolves the situation:

> Gonna lay my head right on the railroad track,
> Gonna lay my head right on the railroad track,
> If the train come 'long, I'm gonna snatch it back.

If you see humor in the third line, you are correct. The third line often dashes the self-pity that was built up in the other two.

Blues typically have many verses. As you might guess, the problems of love were also a favorite subject. The great blues composer William Christopher (or W. C.) Handy (1873–1958), called the "father of the blues," published his "St. Louis Blues" in 1914. Here is the first verse:

> I hate to see de ev'nin sun go down,
> Hate to see de ev'nin' sun go down,
> Cause my baby, (s)he done lef' dis town.

Many blues songs like this one became classics that jazz artists used for their improvisations, a practice that has led to confusion about the blues as a form distinct from jazz and other types of music. Whether it is rendered in a jazz, rock, or pop version, the 12-bar blues chord pattern is a highly individualistic musical form and expression. Even its deliberately plain, everyday street language is part of its down-home attraction. What may confuse some people are all the songs (like "Stormy Weather") composed in the style of the blues, but not necessarily in the classic 12-bar blues pattern.

The blues serve as the basis for much of the rhythm and blues ("R & B"), jazz, and popular music that we hear today, including the music of B. B. King. Therefore, the ability to distinguish this form is important.

The themes of human frailty and triumph expressed in the blues probably account for the fact that this original, rural black American musical form became the most extensively recorded of all folk music. The blues have been the single most important influence on the development of Western popular music in the past several decades.

Blue Notes

The blues vocalist typically "bends" or flattens certain tones of the diatonic major scale, imitating the sliding of the jazz trumpet or clarinet that gives the effect of wailing or sighing. What makes a blues melody really distinctive, however, is the use of the blues scale with its flattened **blue notes**, *the lowered third and seventh scale degrees*. The flatted fifth degree is a more recent addition.

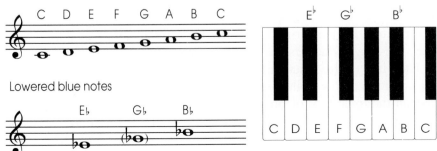

Profile

W. C. Handy
American Blues and
Jazz Composer
1873–1958

W. C. HANDY

W. C. Handy was one of the first artists to popularize the blues musical style. Born to former slaves in Florence, Alabama in 1873, William Christopher Handy grew up listening to folk and country music. In his youth, he played the cornet in a band and sang tenor in a quartet. He tried to keep this secret from his father, a Methodist preacher who did not approve of secular music. However, Handy just had to play music!

After a slow start, Handy became an accomplished professional musician, performing with a minstrel show throughout the country. One night after seeing the popular response to an untrained trio playing black folk music, Handy began to arrange these songs for his own band. People loved them, and Handy's band became so popular, he split it into three bands, a total of 67 people. Unable to find a publisher for his music, Handy decided to publish it himself.

In 1912, Handy published the popular "Memphis Blues," gaining mass exposure for the blues medium and starting a blues craze. His success grew with compositions such as "Beale Street Blues," "St. Louis Blues," and "Joe Turner Blues." These pieces were a break from the prevailing ragtime style and led to a wide public appreciation for Negro folk blues, the secular counterpart of Negro spirituals. Handy died in 1958, leaving behind a wealth of material that contributed something new and unique to American and world music.

The Melody

Like most good melodies, the blues melody breathes. It takes up only two-and-a-half bars of each four-bar phrase. This resting time allows the singer time to make up new verses. During this break, the accompanying instrument(s) improvise, or if the vocalist is certain of the lyric, he or she can improvise as well. In the first version of "Joe Turner Blues," this break is filled in with the improvised "Oh Lawdy." Because few, if any, of the musicians who created the blues could read music, they relied on verbal and musical improvisation.

The name Joe Turner struck terror in some people's hearts. Joe was the brother of Pete Turney, who was governor of Tennessee from 1892 to 1896. ("Turner" is a mispronunciation of "Turney.") It was Joe's job to take the convicts from Memphis to the Nashville penitentiary. W. C. Handy created his own version of "Joe Turner Blues" (see Version 2). Handy's rendition shows how much liberty could be taken with these familiar tunes. There were many versions and sets of words. By the time Handy published his version in 1915, Joe Turner had evolved into the unappreciated lover who sings the song. What remains fairly consistent is the 12-bar chord pattern.

Each line of the lyrics in a blues represents a complete thought. The melody reflects this finality. At the end of each line, the melody comes to rest on the tonic (DO) or on one of the tones of the tonic chord (DO, MI, or SOL). This frequent return to the tonic produces an almost hypnotic effect.

Joe Turner Blues
(Version 1)

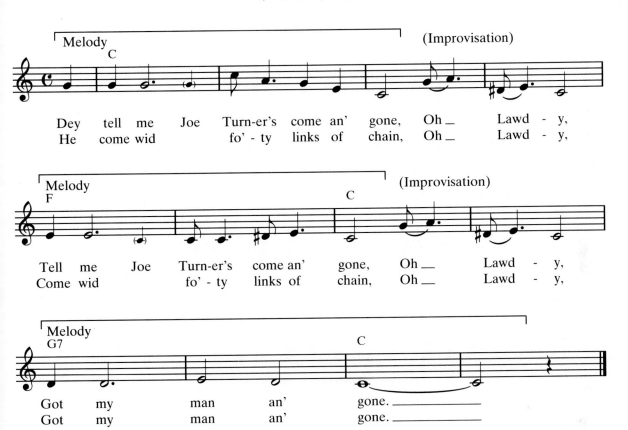

Melody   (Improvisation)

Dey tell me Joe Turn-er's come an' gone, Oh — Lawd - y,
He come wid fo' - ty links of chain, Oh — Lawd - y,

Melody   (Improvisation)

Tell me Joe Turn-er's come an' gone, Oh — Lawd - y,
Come wid fo' - ty links of chain, Oh — Lawd - y,

Melody

Got my man an' gone. _____
Got my man an' gone. _____

Joe Turner Blues
(Version 2)

W. C. Handy

you and _ I must _ part. _____ And ev - 'ry

day you _ lost your _ Joe. _____

Balinese Interlocking Rhythms

Musical creation can take many forms, and the impetus to create can come from many sources. Borrowing ideas from other cultures is one way to initiate the creative process. For example, the music of Bali provides a good illustration of how borrowing can serve as the stimulus to our own creativity.

The Balinese combine different sounds in a highly complex and coordinated way. Music is fundamentally a social art, and the Balinese make the most of it. Balinese music illustrates the expressive possibilities afforded by an ensemble. In Balinese music, rhythmic precision between performers is carried to its ultimate. One particularly interesting example can be heard in the *Kecak* (Keh-CHAK), sometimes called the "Monkey Dance." This theater spectacle, which was derived from trance rituals, is now performed outdoors for tourists after sunset.

Based on the Hindu epic, the *Ramayana* (Rah-MI-yah-nah), the ***Kecak tells the story of the great battle between Prince Rama and the evil ruler Rawana (Rah-VAHN-nah), who has abducted Rama's wife Sita.*** After a long struggle, Rama and his friends, Sugriva, the king of the Monkeys, and Hanuman, the white monkey general, overcome Rawana and rescue Sita. The story is told by a chorus, narrators, and dancers who portray different characters. The chief narrator sometimes comments upon the action but more often translates the words of the second narrator who speaks in *Kawi*. Kawi is the formal language of these old sacred texts that is no longer understood by most Balinese. But it is the men's chorus that steals the show.

Prince Rama is aided by the monkey king and his monkey army, portrayed by 100 to 150 men seated in five or six tight concentric circles, their backs to the audience. The shirtless men, including many teenagers, wear checkered black and white loincloths symbolizing good and evil in equal measure. (In Hindu epics, good does not necessarily triumph over evil, but exists in an eternal struggle.) The leaders of the chorus sit on one side of the inner circle; the narrators sit on the other. In the middle, where much of the action takes place, the army faces a large branching wooden torch with a flickering flame. With their voices and bodies, the men express their reactions to the events. They sway, circle, and bend, thrusting up and stretching out their hands as they chant *chak-a-chak,* with almost threatening energy. They may sway like the trees in the forest, or act the role of a serpent, the wind, or other elements in the story. Throughout the drama, they imitate the sound of monkeys in intricate, **interlocking rhythms** called *kotekan* (ko-TEH-kahn)—*syncopated rhythms, executed at high speed, that give the drama a unified urgency.*

▶ Outdoors at night under a flickering torch, the Balinese music drama *Kecak* tells the great hindu epic *Ramayana.* Often more than 150 men sit in concentric circles and rise, sway, fall backwards, and extend their arms, chanting with explosive, precisely executed rhythms. Their music expresses the many emotions of the unfolding drama.

In one of the dramatic high points, Prince Rama's wife is abducted by Rawana, the evil king of Langka (Sri Lanka) and is carried off. Rama, Sita's husband, is in trouble, and his brother, Laksmana, has gone off to help him. Before leaving Sita, Laksmana has drawn a protective circle around her on the ground in the forest. As the scene starts, we see Rawana disguised as Pedanda, a priest, reciting a religious passage as a pretext for talking to Sita. The *Chak* chorus, heads bowed, sings and sways slowly. Pedanda addresses Sita using the guttural Low Balinese as would a high priest in talking to an inferior. He tells her that he has been meditating for seven days and has not eaten or had anything to drink. He asks her to give him one swallow of water.

Sita offers Pedanda her food, but when she leaves her protective circle and gets close to him, he grabs her and changes into Rawana. Now the Chaks chant excitedly, bobbing their heads up and down. Sita calls to Laksmana for help, but Rawana asks her not to call out but to go with him to his kingdom. The Chaks seem possessed by Rawana's power. At his gesture, they rise to a crouch and wave their arms. As Rawana dances to tell the world he has captured Sita, they clap their hands in celebration. At the end of the scene, the men form a mountain of frenzied energy around Rawana. As they raise their arms and shake them intensely, Rawana vanishes, and they fall backwards.

P R O J E C T

2: Create a Dramatic Scene Using Interlocking (Kotekan) Rhythms

Working individually or in teams of two or three students, use the example of the Balinese *Kecak* to invent a similar scene in a musical drama. Set up the dramatic situation and identify the characters involved, including a group (chorus) and one or two soloists. Create the dialogue (lyrics), then invent the interlocking part for chorus and the solo part(s). Refer to the detailed instructions your teacher will provide. Be prepared to perform your musical scene for the class.

▼*Activity:* **Experience**

Listen to this excerpt from the Balinese music drama *Kecak*, and note the important role the chorus plays in the telling of the story.

Read the story from the *Ramayana*, the great Hindu epic (above).

While you are listening to the scene of Sita's abduction, answer the following questions:

1. Can you distinguish a difference between the narrators, the characters, and the chorus?
2. Are the interlocking kotekan rhythms in the chorus easy or difficult to perform?
3. How does the chorus add to the drama?

The kotekan configuration in the chorus is composed of two rhythmically opposing parts that interlock to create a perpetual flow of sound. The two interlocking parts that form the kotekan are known as the *melos* (maylos, meaning "simple and direct") and the *nyangsi* (yahng-SEE, meaning "differing"), although each part is as rhythmically complex as the other. These negative and positive forces unite to create a continuous current of rhythms that is broken only for phrasing or at the close of an episode. This same principle of kotekan is used in the gamelan orchestra. Balinese performers learn their intricate melodies and rhythms by ear, through repetition and practice. They are not written down.

▼*Activity:* **Master the Principle of Kotekan**

Practice the following rhythms until you can perform them together in interlocking style with accuracy and speed.

Chak-ka-chak,   chak-ka-chak   chak, chak,＿ chak - ka-chak-ka

Chak,   chak-ka-chak,   chak-ka-chak,   chak, chak, chak - ka-

1. Count and clap each of the rhythms until you can perform them securely.
2. While you tap the two beats, chant the rhythms using the words. Practice breathing at the breath mark (**'**). Increase the tempo.
3. Transfer the rhythms to wood blocks and claves, observing the higher and lower pitches as indicated. Start slowly with each line separately, then together. Gradually increase the tempo.
4. Now, decide on your tempo and repeat the four-measure phrase according to the following dynamic pattern (or make up one of your own):

5. For a more complex variation on these rhythms, try performing them in four parts.

Theme and Variations

Composers often base a composition on a theme that is systematically presented in many guises. The theme, or melodic idea, can be borrowed from another composer or newly created. *After it is stated in its clearest and simplest form, the theme is varied in a succession of statements* creating **theme and variations**. The theme can be ornamented, its tempo altered, its harmony changed, its texture transformed, and so forth. There are as many possible variations to a theme as there are different ways to fix a hamburger. Sometimes variations are continuous. At other times they are set off from each other by pauses between them. In both instances, theme and variations achieve unity by basing the whole composition on the same theme and achieve variety by presenting the theme in different treatments.

In 1975 the American composer Frederic Rzewski (CHEFF-ski) (b. 1935), wrote a set of 36 variations for piano entitled *The People United Will Never Be Defeated!* Rzewski used the theme from the Chilean song, *¡El Pueblo Unido Jamas Sera Vencido!* by Sergio Ortega and Quilapayun.

The variations reflect the meaning of the song. There are moments of struggle and defeat, of confidence and victory. The 36 variations are

◀ Composers are not the only artists who create variations on an existing theme. Most contemporary Spanish painters have created variations on Velázquez's painting *Las Meninas* (1656). Pablo Picasso, the great twentieth-century Spanish artist, inspired by the earlier painter's work which he greatly admired, painted a series of 44 variations on this work. Compare Picasso's variation with the work of Velázquez on page 104.

Pablo Picasso. *Las Meninas,* after Velázquez. 1957. Museo Picasso, Barcelona, Spain.

organized into sets of six. The sixth variation of these six sets is in six parts; the first five parts summarize the previous variations of the set, and the sixth provides new or transitional material. The sixth set of variations summarizes all of the preceding variations, ending with a triumphant and inspirational feeling of unity. It has been said that, with each set of six variations, the first five represent the fingers of a hand and the sixth unites them to make a fist.

What holds the work together is the use of one basic theme throughout, but note the variety and contrast that Rzewski achieves.

▼*Activity:* **Detect**

Can you identify a familiar theme even when a composer varies it?

Listen to five variations from *The People United Will Never Be Defeated!,* a set of 36 variations for piano by American composer Frederic Rzewski. To determine how Rzewski varies the theme, follow these steps:

1. Listen again to the original song as sung by Quilapayun to familiarize yourself with the melody. This is what inspired the composer.
2. Follow the musical score below to see how the composer first presents the theme in the opening of his theme and variations. Describe what he has done to the theme here.
3. Now listen to variations 1, 13, 15, and 18. These variations are described on your worksheet but not in the correct order. On a piece of paper, match the variation number with its proper description: A, B, C, or D.
4. Listen to the final statement (variation 36) and write a one-paragraph description of how Rzewski varies the theme to create a dynamic finish.

The People United Will Never Be Defeated!

Frederic Rzewski

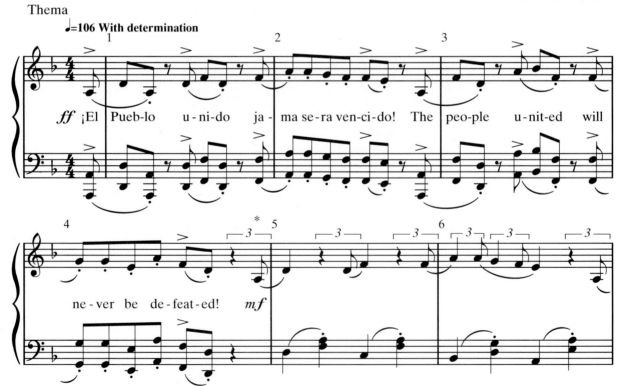

Profile

Arnold Schoenberg
Austrian-born Composer
1874–1951

ARNOLD SCHOENBERG

Arnold Schoenberg was born in Vienna of humble Jewish parents. He began violin lessons at the age of eight and soon took to making musical arrangements. At the age of 16, after the death of his father, he left school and went to work as a bank clerk to help support the family, continuing his education in the evenings. He learned from his friends and taught himself to play cello. He achieved his first success as a composer at the age of 23 with his *String Quartet in D Major*. At 25, he completed his most popular work, the string sextet, *Transfigured Night,* a work descriptive of the deep feelings of a couple who meet on a cold, moonlit night.

Schoenberg sustained himself during many lean years through his masterful teaching of composition. His symphonic tone poems *Pelleas un Melisande* (1903) and *Pierrot Lunaire* (1912), and his early piano, string, and vocal works established his reputation internationally. As his works became increasingly dissonant, the public, while still curious about his work, was often hostile to his music. He invented the method of composition known as serialism in the early 1920s. Among his great accomplishments is the opera *Moses and Aron* (1932).

A rising tide of anti-semitism stirred by Adolf Hitler forced him to leave his position in Berlin in 1933. He and his family migrated to America, settling in Los Angeles where he remained until his death in 1951. His appointment as a professor at the University of Southern California and later at UCLA gave him security, although his works found little audience. His life exemplifies how hard work and extraordinary talent can triumph over the disadvantages of being poor and self-taught. A man of enormous integrity, his innovative spirit took courage and rested on his religious convictions. Great music, he believed, expressed the soul's quest for God.

Twelve-tone Music

Another technique for musical invention and organization is the twelve-tone system. In the early decades of the twentieth century, classical music became less dependent on a specific tonal center such as DO. The major and minor scales that had served as the main tonal materials for music were increasingly overlaid with additional chromatic tones. To enliven musical expression, Claude Debussy (1862–1918) and other composers used clusters of tones, whole-tone scales, and other devices that incorporated all 12 tones of the chromatic scale, not just the eight in the diatonic scale. Still, there was a semblance of a tonal center.

During the second decade of the century, Arnold Schoenberg (1874–1951), an Austrian-born composer, decided to use all 12 tones in his compositions. This new freedom came at a price. Without a tonal center, the traditional sense of tonality was lost. The twelve-tone approach required a method of organizing tones and harmonies. Schoenberg soon set about devising a system of musical composition based on using a series of the 12 semitones that divide the octave.

According to Schoenberg's system, *a composer arranges the 12 pitches in a series,* or **tone row.** The composer can give these tones any order. A note

4: Create a Tone-row Composition

Working individually or in teams of two or three students, use the example of twelve-tone music that you have studied as a model to create a twelve-tone composition of your own. Create your original tone row (O), then write it in retrograde (R), inversion (I), and retrograde inversion (RI). Use these as the building blocks for your composition. Refer to the detailed instructions your teacher will provide. Be prepared to perform your work for the class.

can be repeated immediately, but it cannot be reintroduced again until all 12 tones have been used. The tone row can then be used successively to create melody and simultaneously to create harmony.

The serial or tone-row technique of composition provides the musical material for an entire musical work. The composer manipulates the original row of 12 semitones by transposing it up or down, and by setting it to any rhythm. It can be used in four basic versions:

1. In its original form, designated P (Prime) or O (Original);
2. *Sounded backward* or in **retrograde**, designated R;
3. Turned upside down or "inverted," designated I; and
4. Sounded upside down and backward or in "retrograde inversion," designated RI.

The following example presents the four basic forms of the tone row that Schoenberg used in his *Suite for Piano,* Op. 25, published in 1924:

1. Original Tone Row (O)

2. Retrograde (R)

3. Inversion (I)

4. Retrograde Inversion (RI)

These four basic forms may be transposed so that, in total, each form can be made to sound at 12 different levels (pitches). (Forty-eight forms are, therefore, at a composer's disposal.) In the minuet from his *Suite for Piano,* Schoenberg uses the four basic forms of the tone row notated above, as well as four transposed forms. Two of the transposed forms that are used at the beginning of the trio section of the Minuet movement are presented below. They include the original row transposed up six semitones (designated O_6) and the inversion of the tone row transposed up six semitones (designated I_6):

The *Suite for Piano* that Schoenberg created with this tone row is modeled on dance suites from the time of Bach and Handel. As in a Baroque suite, Schoenberg's suite contains a number of dance movements: prelude, gavotte, intermezzo, minuet, and gigue. However, the expressive effect of twelve-tone or serial technique is very different. Here is the way Schoenberg used the original tone row and its transpositions at the start of the trio section of the minuet:

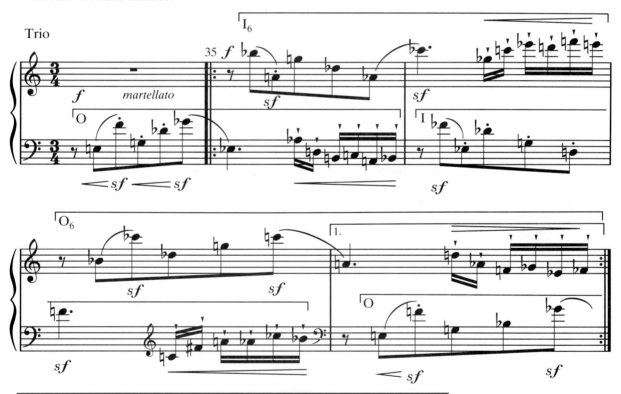

▼Activity: *Try to Hear the Tone Row*

Listen to the minuet from Arnold Schoenberg's *Suite for Piano* and see if you can detect the row.

Study the music (above) to see how the row is used. "O" is the original tone row; "I" is the inverted row. O₆ is the original row transposed up six semitones; and I₆ is the inverted row transposed up six semitones. Now listen to the recording. Can you detect when Schoenberg uses the original row, when he transposes it, inverts it, or uses it in retrograde or in inverted retrograde?

Much of the effect of music composed in the twelve-tone or serial technique is psychological. The system does not negate repetition, but it certainly obscures it. Schoenberg and other composers who championed this system believed that the built-in relationship between the sounds and their fixed patterns of succession are recognized by us subconsciously. The tone row creates a psychological order that our subconscious recognizes, but which our ear may not be able to delineate clearly. It may operate like our "sixth sense"—our ability to sense danger even though it is not readily apparent.

Are You Creative?

Creative people are natural problem solvers. Their answers tend to be unconventional. Instead of thinking convergently, that is, in the customary and expected way, they think divergently, finding different or unusual ways to think and operate. Creative people tend to deviate from the normal or typical in their thinking. They look for new connections, new orders, and new possibilities. They invent.

Artists vary in the degree of their originality. Some prefer to work in the prevailing styles and modes of their day. Others, like Schoenberg, formulate wholly new ways to use sound expressively. When Claude Monet chose to paint haystacks (see page 275)—a scene no other painter at the time would have selected—he found beauty where no one had recognized it before. That kind of thinking is highly valuable. It has permitted the human race to reach beyond and achieve new marvels. Every human being has some sense of creativity. To see how creative you might be, think of the

PEANUTS reprinted by permission of UFS, Inc. Copyright © December 19, 1982 by United Feature Syndicate, Inc.

kind of explanation or description you might attach to a photograph of a man sitting in a reclining seat on an airplane, returning from a business trip or professional conference. Here is the way a very bright high school student described the picture:

> Mr. Smith is on his way home from a successful business trip. He is very happy and he is thinking about his wonderful family and how glad he will be to see them again. He can picture it, about an hour from now, his plane landing at the airport and Mrs. Smith and their three children all there welcoming him home again.

In contrast, here is the way a highly creative high school student described the picture:

> This man is flying back from Reno where he has just won a divorce from his wife. He couldn't stand to live with her anymore, he told the judge, because she wore so much cold cream on her face at night that her head would skid across the pillow and hit him in the head. He is now contemplating a new skid-proof face cream.

Creative people are often unconventional. Their solutions are many times unusual, not the expected. There is an ability to go off in new directions, to "diverge" from the customary and the known. The fantasy is original.

Summary

Composers and performers sometimes rely upon frameworks to help them create musical expressions. For example, there are certain "givens" when one is creating blues: the chord pattern, the number of bars, the structure of the lyrics, the use of blue notes, and so forth. There are strict rules in composing a piece using the tone-row system. There are certain ways one goes about creating a theme and variations, a pop song, a fugue, a march, or any other type of musical composition. These frameworks reduce the number of decisions a composer has to make. They make the composing of music manageable. In a sense, a composer starts by setting boundaries and limitations within which to work, just as a painter starts with a particular size of canvas.

Creating music within these general outlines challenges the mind to its fullest. There is a great deal of figuring out to do. There must be unity and variety, order and emotion, and tension and release. The composer chooses the most appropriate musical means, elements, and form in order to tailor the musical sound to his or her expressive idea. The creative process can take place spontaneously as improvisation, or it can involve hearing the sound in the mind, then producing it or representing it on paper with symbols. The composer speaks directly through sound. Creating music is another way to communicate, another way that human beings comment upon the world and their relation to it.

CHAPTER 17

Creating with Technology

Objectives

By completing this chapter, you will:

- Find out how technology is changing the role of composers and performers.
- Become familiar with how electronic sounds are generated and how they are used for expressive purposes.
- Be able to distinguish between electronically and conventionally produced sounds.
- Learn the history of electronic music and the meaning of its most important terms.
- Become acquainted with the work of some outstanding living arrangers and composers who use technology to create music.

Musical Terms

drum machine
hyperinstruments
MIDI
musique concrète
quantizing
sampling
sequencer
synthesizer
telharmonium

*T*echnology is the place where art meets science. Today, music technology is advancing rapidly, expanding the possibilities of musical expression beyond anything ever dreamed of just a decade or two ago. Music technology has opened a new world of sound. It has already made a major impact on the way we hear and on the way we express and interpret our world. It has given musical creativity a new reach, allowing ordinary people to make music in new ways. It allows us to do with ease what was previously impossible.

Electronic Timbres

Electronically generated sounds are all around us. The invention of new sound technology, particularly the extraordinary developments of the last quarter of the twentieth century, has enabled us to extend the range of musical timbres. The expressive potential of these sounds is infinite and only awaits the imagination of new composers to probe their possibilities. Already there are literally thousands of new musical compositions that owe their existence to this technology.

▼Activity: *Realize the Potential*

Listen to a demonstration of some samples of the variety of sounds and expressive effects that can be created on a synthesizer.

Listen to American composer Wendy Carlos (b. 1939) explain and demonstrate how she made the public conscious of the Moog synthesizer with her 1968 hit recording *Switched-On Bach*, the first classical album to go platinum.

What feats are required to make electronic music expressive and musical in a way similar to music made with acoustic instruments? Discuss such matters as vibrato, the need for overdubbing, touch sensitivity, and the need for taste.

Why is a perfect automated rhythm less exciting than a human's imperfectly performed rhythm?

Most of us are so accustomed to electronic sounds in television commercials, on pop recordings, and in film scores that we may not be able to distinguish these sounds from the more traditional acoustical sources (musical instruments and voices). Although electronic technology has produced hundreds of new timbres, we do not yet have a common language or vocabulary to describe these new sounds. Quite often, however, sounds that are generated electronically deliberately mimic acoustic instruments or human voices and can be labeled accordingly. Often, instruments are electrified—the organ and guitar are common examples. The trick is to get our ears to distinguish sounds that are produced acoustically from those that are produced electronically.

Throughout the world of popular and commercial music, we hear electronic music every day, but we do not always realize how the sound is generated. Can you recognize synthesized sounds when you hear them? For many composers of popular music, the creative combination of synthesized and acoustic (conventional) sounds has become a standard.

▼ *Activity:* **Distinguish**

Can your ears differentiate between acoustic and synthesized instruments in popular music?

Can you distinguish the electronically produced sounds from those produced by conventional instruments when both are combined in the same piece?

Listen to the "Electronic Montage," which consists of musical excerpts, each of which lasts approximately 40 seconds. As you listen, write down on your worksheet the instrumental sounds in each piece that you believe are acoustic and those that are synthesized.

The Beginnings of Electronic Sound

The roots of electronic music go back to the beginning of the twentieth century, when Edison's phonograph, a mechanical invention, was electrified. Here was an electric machine that could reproduce sound. It could perform! Music would never be the same. Electricity was a natural sound producer. Electric motors and generators hummed with discernible pitch. As early as 1900 in the United States, Thaddeus Cahill invented the **telharmonium** (also known as the dynamophone), *a machine that used electrical current to produce sound.* It proved impractical. For one thing, it weighed 200 tons! But the telharmonium showed that electricity could be used to make sound.

In 1923 the Russian, Leon Theremin, introduced the aetherophone (better known as the theremin), an electric instrument that a number of composers incorporated into their music. It had a haunting, vocal-like sound, similar to a musical saw. In France during the same decade, Eduard Coupleux and Joseph Givelet applied the concept of the paper piano roll with its punched holes to control electric oscillators and filters that could create pitch, volume, and timbre. Perhaps the most sophisticated of the early electric instruments was the Hammond organ, which appeared in 1934. There were many other experiments, but most of the electric instruments that were built tried to imitate existing acoustic instruments.

▲ The earliest sound recordings were made by Thomas Edison (right) on a device he designed in 1877. He used a metal cylinder, wrapped in tin foil, that rotated on a long metal screw, which was cranked by hand. Eleven years later, in 1888, on an improved version of the "talking machine," as Edison called his invention, the first recording by a recognized artist was made when Josef Hofmann, at the age of 12, played a brief passage on a piano located in the Edison laboratories.

▲ Artists often incorporate technological developments in their art. French Post-Impressionist Georges Seurat (1859–1891) applied science to the study of color, devising a new method of painting called pointillism. He juxtaposed dots of pure color in such a way that the human eye, viewing them at a distance, blended them so that new colors and forms emerged. In his painting *Sunday Afternoon on the Island of La Grande Jatte,* Seurat uses the technique to picture Sunday strollers in sunlight and shadow at an island park on the Seine River in the outskirts of Paris.

Georges Seurat. *Sunday Afternoon on the Island of La Grande Jatte.* 1884–1886. Oil on canvas. 207.6 x 308 cm. Helen Birch Bartlett Memorial Collection, 1926.224. Copyright 1991, The Art Institute of Chicago, Chicago, Illinois. All Rights Reserved.

Tape Recorder Music

The real development in electronic music began after the Second World War. By then, the tape recorder was perfected. Magnetic tapes could be cut and spliced together, sped up or slowed down, and played backward, making it possible to manipulate the sound, reprocess it, and rerecord it. The potential of the tape recorder as a machine to create music, not merely to reproduce it, was quickly realized.

In 1948, the first electronic music studio was established in Paris by a group of experimenters who called their work **musique concrète.** *The term concrète indicated that the music they constructed consisted of natural sounds— birds and other sounds in nature, and man-made sounds such as sirens and car horns—recorded and manipulated on magnetic tape.* During the 1950s, electronic music studios were established in major cities around the world. One of the earliest (1951) was the Columbia-Princeton Electronic Music Center in New York. Others in Cologne, Tokyo, Milan, and Warsaw, like the Paris studio, were established at major radio stations. Composers in these centers were dedicated pioneers who explored the new electronic medium and established the tape recorder as both a creative device and a performer. These composers dared to make music without using traditional musical instruments. This was revolutionary!

The early experiments were not always greeted enthusiastically. In response to a conference on electronic music in Switzerland in 1955, one newspaper critic wrote: "The sounds range all the way from muted snoring to a howling storm, from the twittering of birds to the chatter of machine guns. But it can hardly be said that this has anything to do with music, all the less so since the poverty of musical thought was manifested with striking impressiveness." The critics were fearful that music would become "the slave of the machine." Then, too, one of the problems for audiences was the static quality of going to a concert and listening to a prerecorded tape. There was none of the usual visual stimuli associated with live musical performance.

In the United States, the first public demonstration of the new medium—tape recorder music—was given by Vladimir Ussachevsky (use-uh-CHEV-ski) in 1952. No matter what his original sound sources—flute, piano, or any other instrument—they were often completely transformed. In the days prior to the existence of the keyboard-controlled, electronic sound-generating devices we now have, the composer had to manipulate the sounds by hand, working with several tape recorders. The composer composed directly on tape, altering sounds and organizing them into expressive compositions.

▼ Pioneering American electronic composers Milton Babbitt (left) and Vladimir Ussachevsky (right) stand with engineer Peter Mauzey in front of the first music synthesizer, the RCA Mark II, at the Columbia-Princeton Electronic Music Center in New York City, c. 1959. To create a sound, the composer set the dials and plugged in the patch chords, then punched the settings into the paper tape, visible in the center and at the left.

In 1960 Ussachevsky (1911–1990) was commissioned to compose an electronic work to commemorate the inventions of Lee De Forrest, inventions that had led to the development of radio. As basic sound material in this work, Ussachevsky used some authentic, wireless spark-generated code signals that he recorded in the Wireless Museum in Trenton, New Jersey. He also included a fragment from Richard Wagner's opera *Parsifal,* which he electronically treated to resemble a shortwave transmission. (*Parsifal* had been the first musical work ever to be broadcast.) The orchestral composition gradually emerges from the montage of wireless signals.

▼*Activity:* **Answer**

Is electronic music—music?

Listen to *Wireless Fantasy* (1960) by American composer Vladimir Ussachevsky and determine whether this has elements that define it as music. Does it have melody, rhythm, dynamics, timbre, harmony, mood, texture, and form?

How is this work descriptive of the period of wireless communication (1899–1925)?

Otto Luening (b. 1900) and Ussachevsky worked together on joint compositions testing the feasibility of combining tape recorder music with a live symphony orchestra. The difficulty was in synchronizing the fixed sounds on tape with musicians performing live. Their *Rhapsodic Variations* (1954) and *A Poem in Cycles and Bells* (1954) left little doubt about the enormous potential of combining the new with the old medium.

At the electronic studios of West German Radio in Cologne, Karlheinz Stockhausen (b. 1928) created musical compositions in the mid-1950s using electronic sounds from oscillators and generators. In those days, producing music by electronic means was highly technical. Stockhausen's mathematical specifications for creating just one minute of music from electronic sources in 1953 filled a one-foot thick stack of 8½ x 11-inch paper covered on both sides. Every aspect of each particular single sound had to be specified! It was a complex, time-consuming, scientific process.

By the 1950s, many musicians as well as most of the public had not yet subscribed to John Cage's belief that all sounds, including noise, have musical potential, depending upon how they are used. People were accustomed to musical sound coming from acoustic sources—musical instruments and the human voice. The Italian composer Ottorino Respighi (ruh-SPEE-gee) (1879–1936) had incorporated a recording of a nightingale in the third movement of his orchestral work *The Pines of Rome* (1924), but after all, this was a bird singing. It was at least musical. What about, however, using other natural sounds? Can music be made from the clatter of garbage cans, the whirling of machines, and the din of car horns?

▼ Activity: **Create and Perform**

Create and perform a composition made from non-acoustic sources of sound.

Suggestions for sounds at hand:

Spinning a coin on a desk	Plucking elastic bands
Ticking clock	Tapping a pencil on a desk
Tapping on a cardboard box	Rolling a marble in a cup
Blowing across bottles of various sizes	Shaking marbles in a closed container
Running water	Dripping water

Look around the classroom and find other objects that can be used to create sound. When you have three sources in mind, use the following procedures:

1. Using a portable cassette tape recorder, record about 20 seconds of each of the three sounds to equal one minute of continuous sound.
2. Extend the sound resources of your composition by using three cassette tape recorders as follows:
   - Tape recorder A: Play your original composition and re-record it on the other two tape recorders according to the following plan.
   - Tape recorder B: Start to record when segment 2 begins on tape recorder A, and record segments 2 and 3. Stop. Rewind tape on tape recorder A, then record segment 1 onto tape recorder B. (The order of the segments on tape recorder B will be 2, 3, 1.)
   - Tape recorder C: Start to record when segment 3 begins on tape recorder A. Stop. Rewind tape on recorder A, then record segments 1 and 2. (Order of segments here will be 3, 1, 2.)
3. Now rewind each tape recorder and then play all three tape recorders at the same time. The student operating each tape recorder may use the volume control on his or her recorder to fade in, fade out, turn volume control rhythmically, and turn volume high to create static.
4. Use a fourth tape recorder to record the composition.
5. Perform your composition for the class. See if your classmates can identify the original sound sources for each of the three segments. Decide which student's composition has the most unique sound sources.

The Synthesizer

A **synthesizer** is *a machine that produces sound electronically.* The first synthesizer, Mark II, was built in the early 1950s by Radio Corporation of America (RCA). Later it was donated to the Columbia-Princeton Electronic Music Center. It was a huge machine—an early computer—covered with dials and switches and filled with 18,000 vacuum tubes, but it allowed a composer to exercise much control over the sounds that were generated. The composer programmed the machine by punching a paper tape with holes that, according to their position, told the machine what to do. The trouble was, it took a genius to understand how to use it.

Electronic technology developed rapidly during the 1960s. Robert Moog and Donald Buchla in the United States and Paul Ketoff in Italy designed synthesizers that replaced the old vacuum tubes with transistors. Moog's

◀ Robert Moog (left), and Keith Emerson of the rock group Emerson, Lake, and Palmer, stand in front of Emerson's custom Moog synthesizer at Rich Stadium in Buffalo, New York, in 1974. Moog, an American engineer and inventor, built many of the early synthesizers, instruments that generated electronically produced sounds.

main contribution was the invention of the voltage-controlled oscillator, a device that allowed the operator to vary the current in order to modify the sound. These early synthesizers permitted the creation and control of all the properties of sound—pitch, envelope (the growth and decay of a tone), amplitude (volume or loudness), timbre, reverberation (repetitions of sound like overlapping echoes), and so forth—through an elaborate system of patch cords, similar to those on early telephone switchboards. The Moog synthesizer soon had a keyboard connected to it that immediately simplified the operation. The first commercial synthesizers were made available to the public in 1964, eliminating the need to rely upon an established studio.

Whereas the early synthesizers required the composer to create and record one sound at a time—a tedious process—the new keyboard models permitted the construction of continuous sound sequences. They could therefore be used to create music in live performance (or in "real time"), not just on tape in a studio. Performers began to use synthesizers in performance. These instruments, however, were monophonic—like the human voice. They permitted only one tone to be generated at a time. Many different melodic lines and timbres could be created, but they had to be recorded separately and then mixed through the process of overdubbing on multi-track taping equipment. This is the way the recording *Switched-On Bach* was created. The process was time-consuming—like creating thousands of tiny colored tiles in many hues and then assembling them into a mosaic.

PROJECT

Choose One of the Following Projects:

A. Analyze Musical Commercials

Based on your knowledge of music technology, listen to three advertisements on television and determine the means (source of sound) for each one. Is the source acoustic? synthesized? or is it a combination of both?

Take notes on the three commercials you analyze, writing down the product advertised and the time and channel of its broadcast. Be prepared to answer both of these questions: **(1)** Which of the three was most effective in promoting the product? Why? **(2)** Which of the three was most creative? Why?

B. Demonstrate Music Technology

Show your musical creativity! If you own a synthesizer, electronic keyboard, drum machine, or some other piece of music technology that allows you to create and perform music, bring it to class to show your classmates. Be prepared to demonstrate several features of your instrument. For example, you might describe and perform rhythm fills and endings, timbre presets, memory functions, sequencing capabilities, pitch manipulation, set time and real time programming, transposition features, customized rhythm patterns, etc.

Prepare a brief lesson plan that outlines the basic points in your presentation. Write out and present to the class a glossary of five of the most important terms or features that you must know if you are going to be creative in using this equipment.

▼*Activity:* **Evaluate**

Which version do you prefer—the original orchestration or the synthesized arrangement?

Listen to and compare the original orchestration of the great classical masterpiece with a synthesized arrangement. For the comparison you do, write evaluative notes in the "timbre," "expressiveness," and "impact" columns on a Judging Quality worksheet.

First movement (*adagio sostenuto*—slow and sustained) from Beethoven's *Moonlight Sonata:*

A. Original for piano (Misha Dichter, pianist)
B. Synthesized transcription (Don Dorsey, synthesist)

After completing the comparison, answer the following questions:

1. How do you suppose the original creator of this composition, Beethoven, would react to the synthesized version?

2. Some people might consider the synthesized version to be a bad joke—a musical distortion of the original. Do you agree? Why or why not?

3. Which version of the composition has the greater musical impact? Why?

4. Which is more creative? Why?

"Pop" Electrified

During the 1960s the pop world eagerly assimilated the new electronic technology. These musicians were flexible and creative. The Hawaiian guitar had been electrified by Leo Fender in 1936, about the same time the standard electric guitar appeared. Now the electric guitar became the focal instrument of rock music. New amplification technology allowed rock musicians to perform outdoors and in stadiums for audiences that numbered in the thousands. As synthesizers became smaller and more manageable, pop musicians everywhere began to use them for both performance and composition.

By the late 1970s and early 1980s, keyboard synthesizers had become a regular fixture in popular music, and so had the wide variety of sounds that these new instruments made possible. Patch cords, now a thing of the past, were replaced by sliders and push buttons. Monophonic synthesizers had been replaced by polyphonic (more than one voice) synthesizers that could play several tones simultaneously. The development of touch-sensitive keyboards gave added control to the performer. Making and using synthesized (electronic) sounds became easy and relatively inexpensive. In fact, the technology itself has prompted the development of two new musical styles: "New Age" and "Space" music.

◀ A master showman and virtuoso guitarist, Jimi Hendrix (1942–1970) experimented with a whole new range of amplified sound effects on his Fender Stratocaster. His rendition of "The Star-Spangled Banner" at Woodstock (1969) has been called by music reviewers, "the most powerful work of American art to deal with the Vietnam War. . . . One man with one guitar said more in three-and-a-half minutes . . . than all the novels, memoirs, and movies put together."

From Analog to Digital

The first commercial synthesizers were "analog" machines. They had moving parts like the hands on a watch. Sound was stored on a magnetic tape that also relied upon mechanical movement. By 1983 microprocessors, or chips, transformed synthesizers from analog to digital. The latter is the same technology that allows a watch to display the time in numbers. Microprocessors are commonplace today in home appliances such as microwave ovens and VCRs. In digital technology, sounds can be stored in the computer in the binary "language" of *1*'s and *0*'s. A compact disk (CD) stores sound in this way rather than by cutting grooves into vinyl that represent the actual vibrations.

This new digital technology has further simplified the process of creating music for both the composer and performer. It gives added flexibility. For example, when sound is stored on tape, increasing the tempo (speeding up the tape) causes the pitch to sound higher. Using digital technology, the tempo can be altered without changing the pitch and vice versa. This is because the sound is not stored as sound but as information (data). Another advantage is that the sound is clearer. The machines, moreover, are compact. One silicon chip that you can barely see now performs the function of 18,000 vacuum tubes!

Computers and Music

The new digital technology is now standard. In 1983 Yamaha introduced the first all-digital commercial synthesizer, its DX-7. The same year, Casio introduced its CZ-101 digital synthesizer—for under $500! Today, other digital synthesizers such as the Roland D-50, the New England Digital Synclavier (base price, over $250,000), the Kurzweil 250 Synthesizer, and the Ensoniq Mirage-DSK sampling keyboard continue the advancement of this technology. These instruments are computers and synthesizers. The combination has greatly simplified the way in which electronic sounds are generated and used for musical purposes.

MIDI

The computer adds another dimension to electronic music making. It can be programmed to react to cues and translate them into musical sounds. These musical signals in computer form are recorded in **MIDI** *(Musical Instrument Digital Interface), a standardized "language" of digital bits that the computer can store.* These bits can be translated into sound when the computer is connected to a music synthesizer (or "synth"), drum machine, or other instrument designed to read MIDI. MIDI is simply an interface or link that allows a performer or composer to connect and synchronize a number of machines and tell them what to do. The Biomuse, for example, uses electrical sensors that are wrapped around the musician's head and forearms to amplify brain and muscle waves. The computer is programmed to convert these waves into sound. It controls the music synthesizer. MIDI software even permits the musical information to be printed out in the form of a notated score. The composer or performer plays a melody or a rhythm; the machinery prints it out. Because the music is in digital form, it can be easily altered in pitch, tempo, volume, and timbre.

Live Performance

Just as a TV broadcast signal needs a television set to translate the signal into a visual image, a computer needs a synth to translate its data into sounds that produce music. One of the problems for popular musicians is duplicating their recordings in live performance. In the recording studio, as many as 24 or more tracks are recorded and mixed. In live performance, the same musicians are limited to the number of parts that can be played with two hands and two feet. With MIDI, however, one musician can link different instruments and synthesizers, and cue different sound sources so that many sounds can be "played" simultaneously—some live, some prerecorded. Parts of the score are stored in offstage computers that are synchronized with the performance and are cued in by the performer. The MIDI controls permit the onstage performers to appear to do more than is humanly possible, but the computers are actually functioning as additional performers.

Electronic music studios now exist in most colleges and universities, and in some high schools. Today, good keyboard synthesizers can be relatively inexpensive. They are rapidly becoming commonplace in the home. Increasingly, the synthesizer is being accepted as a legitimate musical instrument. For many young people, the synthesizer is the first instrument of choice. In the future, no doubt, composers will write for the synthesizer as they have composed in the past for the harpsichord and the piano.

◀ The technology of multitrack recorders allows musicians to electronically orchestrate their creations in a seemingly endless variety of ways. They may choose to emphasize certain instruments or certain passages, achieving different results each time.

Sequencing

The new synths have a built-in memory system so that composers and performers can play back their musical creations. Sequencers have replaced the earlier tape decks. Whereas a tape deck stored the actual music itself, a **sequencer** *stores data about the music.* This is the basic difference between the old analog and the new digital technology. A sequencer greatly simplifies the process of constructing a musical score with many voices (parts) that are synchronized. It allows the composer-performer to become a whole band or orchestra. The various parts are stored on different tracks that can be altered individually. The composer-performer can go back and correct or change individual pitches and rhythms. He or she can reorder the measures, just as sentences or paragraphs might be moved in word processing. Best of all, the revised sound can be retrieved instantaneously and even presented in the form of a printed score. Sequencers facilitate the composing process and make it convenient to retrieve musical information in performance.

Sampled Sounds

The computer permits composers to take small bits of prerecorded sound and manipulate them into musical expression. In the film *Indiana Jones and the Last Crusade,* the adverturesome professor finds himself surrounded by thousands of screeching rats, but the sound actually came from a flock of chickens. The sound of the chickens was sampled and then sped up. **Sampling** is *a recording process that begins with real sounds,* just as the early musique concrète did.

This new technology has many other applications. Composers and performers can now take the sound of a trombone, violin, or any other instrument and create a part for that instrument that can go much higher and lower than the actual instrument. Through sampling, the synthesizer/computer can duplicate real musical timbres with amazing exactness. The reason is very simple: the sound is recorded from the actual instrument. You start with the real sound rather than some electronic simulation of it. Digital recording enhances the process by assuring amazing fidelity. Sampling allows performers to take a real drum stroke and duplicate it playing any rhythm they choose to tap.

Quantizing

The new technology allows composer-performers to synchronize the various parts they compose and perform by **quantizing** the rhythm. *This process corrects and adjusts the rhythm that is performed so that the notes fall precisely on the beat or on even divisions of the beat.* Quantizing is a feature you can apply or not as you decide. You may not want every rhythm exact. It may sound too mechanical and lack the warmth that comes from human imprecision. You may want your music to feel natural.

What Technology Allows Us to Do

Electronics are changing the nature and meaning of composing and performing. Through electronics, composers have a new palette of timbres at their command, but this is just the beginning. Computers enable composers to share the process of creation with the performers or with one or more engineers who manipulate the sounds electronically as they are played or sung. Instead of being a solitary act, composing becomes a group endeavor, and performance, a far more creative process.

Expand Technique and Expression

Today, the electronic keyboard has been given a degree of intelligence that enables the performer to take the performance to wholly new dimensions. A computer accepts the performance information and stores it in its memory, enabling the performer to alter this information in many ways, then play it back. In a very real sense, electronics gives the performer a powerful and versatile helping hand—or 100 hands. With a computer, as many notes at one time can be played as the piano has keys, and they can be played with incredible speed. The performer can exercise a degree of control over dynamics not humanly possible, so that the range of dynamic gradation is multiplied tenfold. With the help of these new technologies, a single performer can become an entire orchestra. That is quite a feat!

Alter and Add Sounds

For his science-fiction opera *Valis* (1987), Tod Machover (MACK-over), a young American composer, uses electronics to create an orchestra out of just two musicians—a keyboard player and a percussionist. In addition to the two instruments, the opera is scored for seven voices, prerecorded tape, and live computer manipulation. Computers analyze the MIDI signals received from the performers and interact with them, altering and adding sounds to create a densely interesting and compelling musical score. The "smart" or "hyper" instruments that the performers feed into can turn chords into a complex filigree of rapid sounds. They can transform a solo singer into a chorus and an instrumentalist into an ensemble of many timbres and textures. They can prolong live tones, or echo them. They can integrate prerecorded rhythms and melodies into the live performance by following the musical score and interacting with it!

Make Prerecorded Parts Responsive

These hyperinstruments even allow for melodic errors and tempo fluctuations in the live performance and adjust their response accordingly. Machover explains that "special extensions to the instruments let the players delicately control and shape a vast sound world." Prior to this development, musicians had to adjust to the rigidity of any prerecorded parts. Now, Machover says, "These computer programs analyze a musician's gestures and performance (e.g., notes played, loudness, aftertouch, etc.) and

▲ A scene from the 1987 Paris premiere of the opera *Valis* by American composer Tod Machover. At the left, one of the singers stands in front of a video wall. At the right, the two live musicians—a keyboard player and a percussionist—create the musical accompaniment using computers that are connected to "smart" or "hyper" instruments.

react immediately, sending MIDI data out to an array of synthesizers, samplers, and sound transformation modules." Computers react intelligently to a live performance and add to it instantaneously.

The Opera, *Valis*

The story of *Valis* is based on a novel of the same name by the American science-fiction writer Philip K. Dick (1926-1982). Dick wrote about a strange experience he had in March 1974 when he claims to have been bathed in a pink light that brought mystical revelations. Most of Dick's novels are explorations of everyday life that are melded with dreams and visions. It is Dick's notion that our inner world of fantasy and spirituality are real and that we must look beyond the face value of events if we want to find the true reality. In the novel, Dick divided himself into two characters, one being Phil Dick, the science-fiction writer; the other Horselover Fat, the weak, unhappy, and neurotic other side of himself.

As the opera opens, Horselover Fat is experiencing an unnerving revelation. In the midst of video monitors, Fat is pierced through the head by a pink laser beam. Based on this experience, Fat thinks that the human mind is like a computer that is not working properly. His various encounters are

Tod Machover
American Composer
1953–

TOD MACHOVER

One of the reasons Tod Machover is so comfortable with technology and music is that his mother was a concert pianist and his father a pioneer in computer graphics. He grew up in an environment that encouraged him to take technology for granted. He learned to play the classics and rock, and he listened to music being reproduced on cassettes and CDs.

No wonder, that as a composer, he relishes trying to bridge the seemingly polar worlds of technology and art, as well as popular and classical musical styles. The main task of the composer, he says, is "to express and communicate something essential about being human." He believes that "technology has to be used to enhance humanity, not to lead us around. We have to use technology to make new expressions possible."

As an inventor, Machover has worked to humanize electronic technology and show how it can be used to create music of dramatic power and emotion. Called "the wunderkind (wonder-child) of the computer-music world," he has helped develop *computer programs that can actually respond to live musicians*. He calls the system that produces this interaction **hyperinstruments**.

Machover is associate professor of music and director of the Experimental Media Facility at Massachusetts Institute of Technology.

---

odd and disconnected. He has strange dreams. Is he having a nervous breakdown? He asks one of the opera's main questions: "How many worlds do we exist in simultaneously?" He fails in a feeble effort to dissuade his friend Gloria from committing suicide. He, too, attempts suicide, but Dr. Stone, a psychiatrist, tells him to believe in his own dream. He writes a journal (his "Exegesis") in which he attempts to explain the universe. Sounds and images flow from his mind uncontrollably. He hears the music of Wagner's opera *Parsifal*, and Phil compares Fat's search for truth to Parsifal's search for the Holy Grail.

Eric and Linda Lampton ("lamp" being a reference to light), two somewhat sinister rock musicians, appear and tell him that the source of his strange experience is Valis, an acronym for Vast Active Living Intelligent System. (Valis represents Dick's belief that there is a single force behind life's seemingly fragmented experiences.) At this point in the opera, the conductor climbs out of the orchestra pit and uses the magic of art and technology—his only language—to sculpt music into the voice of the angel/god/hologram Sophia. It is Sophia who heals Phil/Fat of his duality. Later, she bids him goodbye in a dream—using Gloria's voice.

Valis is the story of painful search and hopeful redemption. It is about synthesis, of bringing strange and seemingly unrelated experiences back together. It is essentially religious. At the end of the opera, Phil/Fat now made whole again and renewed, sits down to await life's next challenge.

To express all the odd and seemingly unrelated events, Machover uses an extraordinary range of music styles—rock, romantic, medieval, serial,

Cooperative Learning

Explain

How can technology be used to expand the expressive capability of musicians and musical instruments?

Listen to the three excerpts from the opera *Valis* by Tod Machover that are explained at the right, then, working in small groups, answer the following questions:

1. What can the performers do that they could not do without technological assistance?
2. Is there variety of timbres? musical styles? tempos? textures? intensities? moods?
3. Are the timbres orchestral imitations?
4. Does this music, much of which is computer generated, have emotional impact?
5. Do you need to know anything about technology to be receptive to this music?

rap, new age, and futuristic "sound poetry." This makes the final synthesis even more powerful. "Above all," the composer says, "I have viewed *Valis* as an opportunity to write the most beautiful music that I could, bringing to life a story that I feel strongly about. I have given free reign to my lyrical impulse. . . . I have tried to develop a rich palette of sonic colors to best shade every nuance of emotion . . ."

You will hear three excerpts from *Valis:*

1. "Lampton Scene" (excerpt). Two rock musicians, Eric and Linda Lampton, are joined on stage by the pianist and percussionist who have been accompanying the opera. They become the two musicians in the Lampton's rock band performing in the atmosphere of a high-tech rock concert. In the presence of Fat, the Lamptons sing about the magic and mystery of Valis, giving Fat his first fascinating, but unclear, description:

    > VALIS.
    > Does it come from the stars?
    > VALIS.
    > This place where we are is one of the stars.
    > Is VALIS a man? Is VALIS a god? Is VALIS a satellite?
    > Or does it destroy?
    > (Vast Active Living Intelligent System.)
    >
    > The Empire never ended,
    > The Buddha is in the park.
    > He lived a long time ago,
    > But he's still alive.
    >
    > VALIS, etc.
    >
    > The mind is ever active,
    > In his crafty designs.
    > It conjures up great plans
    > But is broken.
    >
    > VALIS, etc.

2. "Mini's Solo." Mini, a disabled composer of computer music, uses his hands to sculpt sounds on an invisible instrument. The music here is created from bits of the human voice that are deconstructed at first so as to be unrecognizable. Gradually, the sounds are molded into the singing voice of a young girl, Sophia, who appears on a video monitor. (The next excerpt follows immediately.)

3. "Sophia's Scene" (excerpt). Sophia (angel or hologram?) sings a sermon accompanied by sweet, shimmering synthetic sounds over

long pedal tones. Tones that she sings are prolonged or echoed electronically on-the-spot, giving her an other-worldly presence. Phil/Fat is alone facing her image. He is now one person. She has made him whole again.

Sophia: I can see only one person.
Phil/Fat: Where is the other? You destroyed him?
Sophia: Yes.
Phil/Fat: Why?
Sophia: To make you whole.
Phil/Fat: Are you God?
Sophia: I am what I am.
Phil/Fat: Can you help me?
Sophia: I have already helped you. I have helped you since you were born.
Phil/Fat: I am still afraid. . . .

▼Activity: *Debate*

Is it necessary to have musical knowledge and technique to compose music using a synthesizer and sampling technology?

In groups of four students, divide each group into two teams and choose opposing views of this issue:

Side 1 argues that it is *absolutely essential* to have musical knowledge and technique if you want to compose music using a synthesizer and sampling technology.

Side 2 argues that it *makes little difference* whether one has any musical knowledge and technique when composing with a synthesizer and sampling technology.

Use your analysis of the following two compositions to support your arguments in the debate:

Example 1. Dance music.
Example 2. Jazz tune.

The instrumental parts of both compositions have been created and performed by one individual who plays all the parts on various synthesizers.

Allow 15 minutes for your listening and small group debates.

Effects of the New Technology

A great debate is raging throughout the music world. In its early stages, electronic music was the art of creating and assembling unusual synthetic sounds into musical compositions. Increasingly, synths are being used not so much to create new sounds but to duplicate the familiar acoustic sounds that in the past have been produced exclusively by musical instruments and voices. Sampling and samplers are now making this duplication acutely accurate. The sound is so exact, in fact, that musicians who have spent decades learning to perfect their flute or oboe playing are finding themselves replaced by a sampler, a machine that can play back the actual

Cooperative Learning

Discuss

Working in groups of three or four students, discuss the following: Will technology make conventional musicians and their instruments obsolete?

Musicians have witnessed the loss of jobs due to synthesizers and sequencers. What effect does this have on musicians? on consumers? on our musical tastes? Do these changes represent progress? Will technology invite mistrust between musicians? How fair is it to have one person with a rack of high tech equipment do the work of 4, 20, or even 50 fellow musicians?

sampled sounds of their instrument. A **drum machine**, for example, *has all the sounds of a whole range of percussion instruments stored in its memory, waiting to be applied to any rhythms the operator of the machine might want to perform.* Does the drum machine put *real* drummers out of work?

Sampling has intensified the threat because the sounds of traditional instruments can be reproduced so well. When asked about the use of drum machines in England, drummer Neil Lancaster, says that "the community of drummers has totally collapsed. . . . Amateurs are just sitting there in the [recording] studios and hacking away at these things, and in fact half the time the engineers have to do it, because the guys with the machines don't have a clue how to operate them." Mike Comins, a violinist, says "even though the synthesizer hasn't replaced a symphony orchestra in public or on record, it will have the capability of doing so, and that's frightening." However, he also acknowledges that "it's really kind of fun to listen to Bach played on a synthesizer—but you know it's a synthesizer. [It's not] meant to displace anything."

Derek Austin, a studio synthesist, expresses the other point of view. He says, "A synthesizer is not some glorified electronic box that a scientist invented to put creative artists on the dole. A synthesizer is an instrument, and the people who play it well are musicians. . . ." He does not believe that digital sampling machines will replace orchestral instruments. When a middle C trumpet sample is played up two octaves, he says, "it does not sound like a trumpet hitting a high C." He acknowledges that the problem often boils down to money. Yes, you can create a string wash with a synthesizer, "but if you *really* want to fool the human ear to think you've got a full orchestra, you put six or eight live violins on top as well."

In England, the Musician's Union has succeeded in banning the use of synthesizers to imitate acoustic or percussive instruments. In the United States, the American Federation of Musicians (AFM) has ruled that contracts should "ensure that electronic devices will not be used to replace or reduce the employment of conventional instrumentalists in circumstances where these members may be reasonably expected to be used. However, the electronic devices may be used to produce sounds that cannot be produced by conventional instruments." Such regulations are not easily enforced. On Broadway, for example, synths rather than traditional instruments are being added to orchestras for a fresher sound. Who can say that conventional musicians are being displaced?

Some Limitations

Does technology make the composer's work easier or more difficult? There appear to be two schools of thought regarding the application of music technology. On the one hand, Dominic Milano, editor of *Keyboard* magazine says, "Musician dexterity is still important, but no longer a must. The computer can correct a lot of your errors. The result may not be brilliant noise, but it will be useful noise." On the other hand, composer Wendy Carlos says people who pride themselves on not being able to read music or to play even a simple musical passage without computer corrections (e.g., quantizing rhythms) are both arrogant and ignorant. Creating great music, she says, is difficult and requires "a profound knowledge of many details."

One of the problems with the new machines is that the product is too mechanical, clinical, and purified. The soul has been wrung out of it. The machine rather than the composer seems to dictate the result. When human imagination and creativity take a backseat and the machine rules, the music that is produced tends to be trite and uninteresting. It is a musical cliche—an expression that has been repeated so often that it is boring. Worse, it lacks warmth and emotion. The potential of the new music technology is not realized.

Unquestionably, the new technology makes it possible for people with very little understanding of music to duplicate or create elaborate compositions. The machine makes it easy for anyone. The drawback is that the end products tend to sound monotonously alike, and they often lack the warmth and emotion that are central to any expression we call musical. Technological breakthroughs in music have caused some problems, as any new way of doing anything normally does. However, the potential is enormous. Like Sunday painters, we may soon have a generation of Sunday composers, some of whom may turn out to be the Mozart or Ellington of our time.

Summary

Technology is not meant to relieve us from doing the work of imagining, thinking, creating, and learning. It can facilitate these tasks, but it cannot do them—not yet, perhaps not ever. Technology can provide us with tools that shape and amplify. It is an external resource. It permits us to reach for new worlds of understanding and ability. It provides new ways for us to see and hear who and what we are. Intelligent thinking and planning underlies all musical creation. The magic is in the imagination, not in the technology. The technology should be invisible. It is the vehicle, not the message.

Electronics are extensions of ourselves. They are not replacements. We are using technology to make new expressions possible, but people are still in control and central to the process. Musical performance remains a living art involving live performers. Just as electronic tools provide music with incredible new possibilities, they also pose new problems. The popular musician/composer Sting admits that "one of the problems is that you have this infinite choice, and when you have this infinite choice you have to make decisions."

Some performers who use conventional instruments believe they are being put out of work by synthesizers. Will the keyboard synthesizer replace the piano, the harpsichord, and all the other instruments it can simulate? Or will the synthesizer/computer assume its own independent music-making role, much as the composer Tod Machover uses it? Technology opens the door to a vast and heretofore inaccessible world of musical expression. That is justification enough for whatever adjustments must be made to accommodate it.

CHAPTER 18

Three Musical Creators

Objectives

By completing this chapter, you will:

- Become familiar with a representative sampling of music by three twentieth-century American composers: Aaron Copland, Duke Ellington, and Libby Larsen.
- Learn what makes these composers effective musical communicators.
- Discover the characteristics that make their works American.
- Find out about the lives of these composers and what it takes to be a composer.

Musical Terms

bridge
cadenza
chromatic
composition
creative license
glissandos
swing
swing era

*C*omposing may appear to be an unusual or exotic career, an occupation for a rare few. How many people can you name who make their living partly or wholly from the music they create? There is no doubt that being a composer is a highly specialized profession akin to being a sculptor or painter. You would be wrong, however, if you thought there were very few composers. In truth, there are hundreds of composers at work in the United States, Canada, Mexico, and other countries around the globe.

The Role of the Composer

Almost every university and many colleges have one or several composers on their faculty. Some classical composers attach themselves to major symphony orchestras or opera companies. For example, Shalamit Ran, a professor at the University of Chicago who received the 1991 Pulitzer Prize in Music for her *Symphony*, serves as composer-in-residence for the Chicago Symphony Orchestra. Others, particularly composers who work in the popular field, work independently or combine composing with performing. Stevie Wonder, for example, writes most of the songs he performs.

According to American composer Aaron Copland (1900–1990), composing is the mysterious and challenging process of "exteriorizing inner feelings." What the composer does, he says, is to take what is personal and internal and make a statement of it in sound that is so compelling that listeners and performers can experience what the composer was feeling. Composers learn the art of **composition**, *the craft of putting together sounds to create musical statements that are represented symbolically, usually with the language of notation.* Composition differs from improvisation by giving an account of the musical statement permitting it to be repeated with some degree of exactness. Composers often prepare a written musical score, but their account can also take the form of a tape recording or computer program.

Composers are communicators who use music as their language. To be effective communicators, they must affect their audience. They must be able to convey their meaning so that it is understood and felt by those who hear their work. Like a good speech, their message must be convincing, and it must stir their listeners. They have to know how to use sound as a way to express feeling. In this chapter, you will become acquainted with three American composers, and you will discover what makes them effective musical communicators.

Aaron Copland

Oddly enough, American composer Aaron Copland learned how to write music that is distinctly American in Mexico! He went to Mexico City in 1932 to work with Carlos Chavez (1899–1978), the distinguished Mexican composer and conductor, and was impressed by his respect for and use of Mexican folk music. Copland tried his own hand at using Mexican melodies in his orchestral work *El Sálon México* (1936). Then he set about applying the principles he had learned. During the next decade, he wrote a number of works based on American folk music. He had already experimented with jazz in his *Piano Concerto* (1927). Copland was determined to express his American roots in music, and he succeeded.

▶ Aaron Copland may have been America's most American composer. He composed deliberately and proudly for all people, believing that classical music belonged to everyone.

El Sálon México

Copland's inspiration for *El Sálon México* came from a visit to a nightclub named "Sálon México." "It wasn't the music that I heard there, or the dances, that attracted me so much as the spirit of the place," Copland said. "In some inexplicable way, while milling about in those crowded halls, one really felt a live contact with the Mexican *people*—the electric sense one sometimes gets in far-off places, of suddenly knowing the essence of a people—their humanity, their separate shyness, their dignity and unique charm . . . . At any rate, I soon found myself looking for suitable folk material for *El Sálon México*." He began work on this piece in 1933 and completed it the following year. The orchestration followed in 1936.

▲ The excitement of Mexico City and its people found its way into Aaron Copland's orchestral work *El Sálon México*. He came back to the United States determined to incorporate our American folk music in order to express the spirit of people here.

▼Activity: *Listen and Designate*

Can you identify the order in which Aaron Copland used the Mexican folk melodies and rhythms as you listen to *El Sálon México*?

In preparation for listening, familiarize yourself with the main rhythmic and melodic themes. Perform this melody on a keyboard instrument, xylophone, or other tuned percussion instrument:

Perform the rhythm of this melody.

What are the musical characteristics of these two themes that are typical of the style of Mexican folk music?

Each of the lettered "blocks" on the illustration represents a specific musical event in *El Sálon México*. As you listen, determine the order of the blocks in the composition. Write down the letter of each section in the order in which you hear them. Use the musical descriptors and the musical examples you have performed and analyzed to help make your decisions.

Profile

Aaron Copland
American Composer
1900–1990

AARON COPLAND

Aaron Copland, who made his home in Peekskill, New York, was a composer, author, and in his later years, a conductor. To his credit, he established a style of classical music distinctively American that is recognized and respected around the world. His *Fanfare for the Common Man* ennobles everyday people as only freedom and democracy can. This work, perhaps, represents the purest essence (quintessence) of American musical expression.

Born in Brooklyn of immigrant parents, Copland first studied piano with one of his older sisters. He soon studied with other teachers and began attending concerts regularly. As a teenager, he went on to study music with a private tutor.

In 1921, when he was just 21 years old, he went to Paris and persuaded Nadia Boulanger, the brilliant French musician and teacher, to instruct him in composition. She agreed, and subsequently several generations of American composers followed his example and studied with her.

Despite the fact that he never went to college, he taught at Harvard in 1933 and 1944. His book, *What to Listen for in Music* (1939), was read around the world. He wrote two operas, many symphonic, chamber, and keyboard works, songs, and choral pieces. Many of these works were functional—written for particular occasions. In 1944, he received a Pulitzer Prize for his ballet score *Appalachian Spring*, his most popular work. Copland composed a series of other ballets, among them *Billy the Kid* and *Rodeo*. In 1948 he received an Oscar for his score for the film *The Heiress*, one of eight film scores he composed. He was fond of integrating American folk music into his works. He championed the work of other American composers, particularly Charles Ives, and he served as mentor to many young American composers. In 1964 President Lyndon Johnson awarded Copland our highest civilian award, the Presidential Medal of Freedom.

"Simple Gifts"

Copland, as a young man, was deeply affected by the developments around him. As a young professional in the 1920s and 1930s, he was impressed by the growing popularity of the radio and phonograph. He saw a new audience for music that had grown up around these electronic wonders. He said, "It made no sense to ignore them and to continue writing as if they did not exist. I felt it was worth the effort to see if I couldn't say what I had to say in the simplest possible terms." He wanted to establish a style of musical communication that had wide appeal; he believed that classical music could be enjoyed by everyone.

After his experiences in Mexico, he began to incorporate American folk music into his work. He was always looking for American tunes. One day in a library, he ran across Edward D. Andrews's book of Shaker rituals, songs, and dances entitled *The Gift To Be Simple*. In it he found the melody and words to one of the favorite hymns of this religious sect, "'Tis a Gift to Be Simple." To his credit, he recognized the beauty of this unknown and forgotten song, and he revived it and made it popular around the

'Tis a Gift to Be Simple

American Shaker Tune

world. He used the tune in the closing section of his ballet *Appalachian Spring* and later wrote an arrangement of the song for his first set of *Old American Songs* (1950). He called the song "Simple Gifts"; it might have been a motto for his own life.

Copland had a rare gift in this world of self-promotion and egomania. He was a modest man. He tried to write music that was as ordinary as possible, music that could enchant the listener. He also had a more complex side that led him to compose profound music using the modern idioms of his day, including twelve-tone or serial technique. It was his simpler style, however, that has endeared him to the American public.

▼ Activity: *Perform and Compare*

Sing and perform a simple accompaniment to the Shaker song "'Tis a Gift to Be Simple" and compare your performance to the composed arrangement of the same song by Aaron Copland.

Identify the number of phrases in the song, and decide if the phrases are of equal or unequal length.

Perform this harmonic ostinato as you sing "'Tis a Gift to Be Simple":

Decide what are the folk-like qualities in your performance of "'Tis a Gift to Be Simple."

Listen to Aaron Copland's composed arrangement of "'Tis a Gift to Be Simple" and decide what is similar about the two performances. What is different?

Perform your arrangement of "'Tis a Gift to Be Simple." Notice that the harmonic ostinato sounds on the first beat of each measure. Listen to the Copland arrangement to determine on what beat the chords change in each measure. Can you figure out the pattern of chord changes in Copland's arrangement?

How does Copland's arrangement reflect the influence of classical or "art" music? Does the Copland arrangement of "Simple Gifts" destroy or preserve the folk-like quality of the song? Justify your answer.

Clarinet Concerto

Singlehandedly, Copland pieced together an aural American orchestral quilt that listeners around the world found easily likeable. Some of his works were unashamedly based on American subjects: the ballets *Billy the Kid* (1938) and *Rodeo* (1942), and *Lincoln Portrait* (1942) for narration and orchestra. In some of his works, he combined popular and classical music styles. This is the case with his *Clarinet Concerto* (1947–1948). This work, commissioned by Benny Goodman (1909–1986), one of the great jazz and classical clarinetists, illustrates another of Copland's strengths as a musical communicator—his direct and honest expression of emotion. First and foremost, his music relates to human beings and to life. He believed that one of the great qualities of music was its capacity to "enlarge the sense of who you are and what life is all about."

Copland's *Clarinet Concerto* is in two parts connected by a **cadenza**, *a section designed to show the virtuosity of the soloist.* The first movement, like a slow dance, is lyrical and expressive, almost heartbreaking. It is in simple A B A song form. Jazz elements, first introduced in the cadenza, take over in the fast second movement, a free rondo that ends with an elaborate coda. Copland said that some of the musical material he used "represents an unconscious fusion of elements obviously related to North and South American popular music." The contrasts between slow and fast, gentle and jazzy, classic and popular seem natural and right.

▼Activity: **Listen and Decide**

What characteristics of jazz did Copland use in creating his *Clarinet Concerto*?

Listen to the opening measures. Identify the instruments you hear. Which of the instruments you identified are not usually associated with jazz?

Perform this bass ostinato on a keyboard or tuned percussion instrument:

Clap this over-the-bar-line syncopated pattern:

Clap this rhythmic pattern set in dialogue style:

All of these patterns you have just performed are characteristic of jazz.

Listen to the end section of the concerto and decide how many of the three jazz style techniques you just performed are used in this composition. Identify other musical characteristics associated with jazz that are also used in this concerto.

Would you classify this work as classical music or jazz? Justify your answer.

After the Second World War, Copland's style changed. Like many American composers at that time, he became fascinated by Schoenberg's serial system. His *Piano Fantasy* (1957) and *Connotations for Orchestra* (1962), among other pieces, used this method of composition. Perhaps he realized that he had achieved the American style he had searched for so long, and he took up new challenges. Whatever the case, he left a storehouse of works that are known and loved by a vast American public and another set of more complex works that await the public's discovery.

Duke Ellington

One of America's most original composers, Edward Kennedy ("Duke") Ellington (1899–1974) took jazz and made it a sophisticated art. Previously, jazz had been an informal, improvised group expression. Ellington did what no one had done before. As the leader of his own extraordinary jazz band, he applied the craft of composition, yet accommodated the improvised solos of his individual musicians. He gave jazz form and substance, and timbres it had not known before. By combining his own creativity as composer, pianist, and bandleader with that of his players, he achieved a new level of distinction in jazz.

Ellington brought intellectual depth and originality to everything he created. That immediately set him apart. He was the thinking person's jazz creator. His songs, for example, had a richness and elegance due to their imaginative and colorful harmonies. The melodies of these songs were often generated by these harmonies, not the other way around. In creating his popular songs, Ellington thought harmonically, while most songwriters think melodically. His approach was largely instrumental rather than vocal. As a result, his melodies are often **chromatic**, *incorporating notes that lie outside the regular diatonic scale,* and they contain wide leaps and have angular contours that are difficult to sing and demanding to listen to. Because of this, Ellington's songs—"Satin Doll," "Sophisticated Lady," and "Don't Get Around Much Anymore," to name a few—achieve a special richness.

"It Don't Mean a Thing"

One of his songs, "It Don't Mean a Thing If It Ain't Got That Swing" (1932), anticipated the whole **swing era**, *a period that extended roughly from 1935 to 1945.* Ellington wrote the theme song long before the era started! This was a period when people danced and listened to "big" jazz bands such as the Duke Ellington Orchestra. With its rhythmic energy and swinging beat, this music was made for dancing. Even though many people primarily associate the term "swing" with Benny Goodman, who was known as "The King of Swing," Ellington was probably the first person to use the word in a song. In many ways, this song says what swing is all about. Irving Mills's lyrics try to define it: "It ain't the melody, it ain't the music, there's something else that makes the tune complete." That something else is what Ellington simply called "its rhythmic vitality."

Swing is *a catchy rhythmic feeling that musicians add to the notes.* It is notated one way and played another—a perfect example of the old axiom that you can't make music until you go beyond the notes. This is true of all music, but is well illustrated by swing. Although swing is sometimes improvised by ear, when it is read from a score or "chart," the musicians interpret the notation freely. In classical music, performers refer to this personal touch as "musicality" or "musicianship." In jazz it is called "soul" or "swing."

▼Activity: *Syncopate*

Can you sing with "swing"?

To illustrate, many songs written in "straight" eighth notes are actually "swung" rhythmically in a triplet fashion. For example:

Straight rhythm:

When "swung," sounds like:

Listen to Ella Fitzgerald's rendition of Ellington's song "It Don't Mean a Thing If It Ain't Got That Swing." Note her improvised scat singing. Practice singing along on the highly syncopated "doo wah, doo wah" part of the chorus. It is all on one pitch: B flat.

(doo wah, _ doo wah, doo wah, doo wah, doo wah, _

_ doo wah, doo wah, doo wah,)

You may be able to perform the syncopation from the notation, but be careful that it doesn't become too studied or straight. Is it easier to perform the rhythm by imitation or from the notation? Can you "swing" this rhythmic pattern without looking at the music?

▲ Duke Ellington and his band in 1945. An American bandleader, pianist, and composer, Ellington (at the keyboard) took jazz to new expressive heights. He and his band attained great popularity in the 1940s and they were the first black musicians to perform at New York's Carnegie Hall.

Mood Indigo

Ellington was a ground-breaking musical pioneer. Even early in his career, he was creating jazz compositions for orchestra that were more than merely functional dance pieces. His *Black and Tan Fantasy* (1927), for example, was longer than the usual jazz work. It was meant to be listened to for the feelings it generated. This was one of several compositions dedicated to the dignity and history of African Americans. Later, his work *Black, Brown and Beige* (1943) reached symphonic proportions. His creative powers grew in complexity and finesse.

The Ellington orchestra grew as well. When he first started, Ellington's group sometimes consisted of one or two other musicians. During the early years, from about 1920 to 1927, he used as many or as few musicians as he could round up and afford. These were usually his close friends, and he would often play his gigs as a trio or quartet. Later he was fond of his sextet. In 1927 the group that played at the Cotton Club in New York had ten musicians. This later expanded to 12 musicians in 1930, 14 in 1932, and finally to its fullest size of 19 in 1946. The group varied in size, depending on the situation and the location. One thing remained constant: the orchestra played Ellington's compositions.

Profile

Duke Ellington
American Pianist, Bandleader,
and Composer
1899–1974

DUKE ELLINGTON

Edward Kennedy ("Duke") Ellington was born and raised in Washington, D.C., a city that takes great pride in that fact. In 1974 the Duke Ellington School for the Arts, a performing arts high school, was opened there in his honor.

Always a smart dresser, he was nicknamed "Duke" by his high school friends, and the designation stuck. He was destined to join two other black "royalty" in the jazz world—"King" Oliver and "Count" Basie.

Ellington began to study the piano when he was seven and made his professional debut in 1916, when he was 17, at the time that ragtime was the rage. He was soon organizing bands to play for the many weekend dances in the city. Heeding Fats Waller's advice, he moved his Washington band to New York City in 1923.

By the late 1920s, Ellington and his band were performing at the Cotton Club in Harlem. It was here that he invented the hot "jungle" style of jazz that featured the exotic timbres of "wa-wa" plunger mutes and smooth saxophones set to wild harmonies. The band made over 200 recordings, mostly of music Ellington created.

By 1946, the band consisted of 19 performers, including Ellington at the piano. He composed dozens of popular songs, over 50 film scores, hundreds of instrumental pieces both short and long, many sacred works, and several works for the stage, including the opera *Boola*. He was the first composer to make jazz his creative idiom and to give it form and substance equivalent to any other style of music. He may have composed more than 1,000 compositions!

Ellington was invited to the White House on many occasions both as a performer and as a guest. He made several European tours, one as musical ambassador for the State Department. His concerts at Carnegie Hall were always special occasions. In 1969 he was awarded the Presidential Medal of Freedom.

The changing instrumentation of the Ellington orchestra:

1927 (10)	1930 (12)	1932 (14)
1 trumpet	3 trumpets	3 trumpets
1 trombone	2 trombones	3 trombones
3 reeds (sax/clarinet)	3 reeds	4 reeds
4 rhythm (bass, drums, banjo, with Duke on piano)	4 rhythm	4 rhythm (1 female singer)
1 violin		

In many ways Ellington was an experimenter. He always had his band at hand to try out various musical ideas. He played with different combinations of instruments and invented new sonorities. He tried using the highest and lowest registers of instruments to draw out sounds that were less familiar than those in the comfortable middle range. His excellent musicians gladly took up the challenges he proposed. The band operated as a team. Ellington thought of the musicians as his family, and they had a deep respect for him. They also grew in their own musical ability because he counted on them to add their own creative skill to the whole.

Because his music spoke with a different sound, Ellington's creations rarely became as popular as those of other popular composers of his time— George Gershwin, Irving Berlin, or Cole Porter. His most popular piece was *Mood Indigo* (1930). It was originally written as an instrumental work called "Dreamy Blues" in which he used the instruments in unexpected ways.

▼*Activity:* **Perform**

Can you play the theme and harmonies from *Mood Indigo?*

Look at the first four measures of the famous theme from *Mood Indigo*. How many different pitches does the theme use? Listen to the recording of this popular hit while you follow the four-bar theme. Keep the harmonies (or supporting harmonic color) in your mind's ear.

Working in a small group of three to four students, try to play this theme on any instrument that you can play. Have everyone in your group play the theme in unison.

Now ask someone in your group to play the four-bar theme while the other members play both sets of harmonies below. Which one (No. 1 or 2) comes closer to the harmonic color and mood that Ellington had in mind when he composed this tune?

(1)

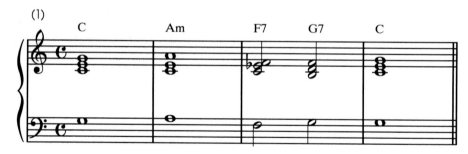

(2)

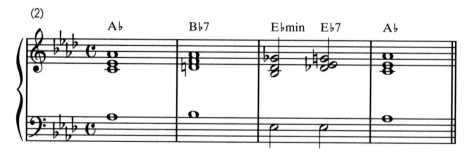

After playing the melody and underlying harmonies, answer these questions:
1. How would you describe the mood of *Mood Indigo?*
2. Do you hear any blue notes in the four-bar theme? If so, where?
3. What color is indigo?

Playing in juxtaposition with a saxophone quartet were vibrato-less muted brass and a clarinet in very low register. In 1931 lyrics by Irving Mills and Albany Bigard were added. The song became a major hit. Here again, it is the creative harmonies that generated an unusual, and very memorable, melody.

Cotton Tail

Ellington reached his creative plateau in the 1940s. His collective approach now included the expert work of Billy Strayhorn, who served as Ellington's arranger and second pianist. Strayhorn joined the band in 1939 and did much of the arranging during the 1940s. One of the great achievements of Ellington and the band was *Cotton Tail* (1940). The piece is a brilliant variation based on the chord changes of George Gershwin's famous song "I Got Rhythm," written ten years earlier (see the chord changes that follow).

Cotton Tail is a trendsetting piece. Prominent American composer and jazz expert Gunther Schuller observes that this work "changed the face of jazz and foretold in many ways where the music's future lay." Both in its conception and performance, it established the big-band style of modern jazz that was to follow. Ellington was clearly ahead of his time.

What made *Cotton Tail* unique? As was usual in jazz, Ellington constructed this piece on an established set of chord changes—in this case, those from "I Got Rhythm"—but he used them in a startlingly new way. He dropped the customary introduction and dived immediately into the melody. Trumpets and saxes announce the theme together in octaves, set against a simple walking bass (see example on page 343). The idea of stating the theme simply and directly at the start became common after this, particularly in the form of jazz known as "bop." Then, too, if you look and listen carefully, Ellington had the courage and imagination to begin the melody on a ninth (C) and *not* on the usual tonic (B♭):

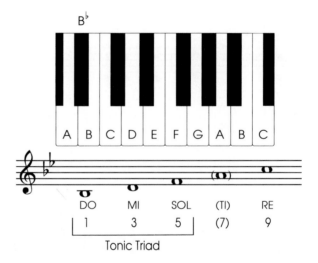

▼Activity: *Find the Bridge*

Can you detect the B section or the "bridge" in a classic saxophone solo?

As an example of Ellington's creative genius, listen to the way he composed *Cotton Tail* using the chord changes in George Gershwin's classic song "I Got Rhythm." The melody of the A theme for *Cotton Tail* is shown on page 343.

In 32-bar song form, the B section in the A A B A structure is known as the **bridge**. You have heard this in Ellington's "I Got it Bad" and several other songs. Ellington uses this form in the 1940 composition *Cotton Tail.* Your challenge is to detect this bridge in the brilliantly improvised tenor sax solo by Ben Webster. (Hint: After 16 bars, the eight-bar bridge is announced by a strong harmonic shift.)

As you listen, follow the notation of Ben Webster's solo that covers two choruses in this work. You will hear the bridge twice. In what measures does the bridge begin? Where does it end? What makes Ben Webster's improvisation so outstanding?

One of the other remarkable achievements of *Cotton Tail* is the improvised tenor sax solo of Ben Webster (1909–1973). This improvisation builds overwhelmingly to the upper reaches of the instrument. It engages us as listeners and carries us along by its spontaneous and virtuosic invention. Schuller calls *Cotton Tail* "creative on all fronts simultaneously"—in melody, harmony, rhythm, orchestration (timbre), texture, and form. In this work Ellington and his entire band speak as one voice, one force.

Ellington was especially adept at devising accompaniments for his players' improvisations. He knew how to use and combine instruments. When he composed, he took into account the virtuosity of his musicians. No wonder they liked him. He gave them a showcase, and he knew how to make them shine. He invited them to enter into the creative process, to feel the spirit of the work, and to add their own skill to it.

Circumstances changed for Ellington around 1950. At that time, his longer compositions were not accepted. His innovative individuality kept him outside the mainstream of jazz. There was a turnover of musicians in his band that caused his creative forces to become unsettled. Nonetheless, his contributions as a composer were indelible. With Ellington, American jazz became the highly respected musical form it is today.

Libby Larsen

As you read this, a great many living American composers, both male and female, are busy composing music. Among the latter is Libby Larsen, a highly talented composer who has written a large body of works in many different genres. Her music is vivid and picturesque—and very American. She enjoys interpreting poetic images, crystallizing them in musical portraits. Her musical works have all the clarity and sparkle of ice sculptures.

Larsen is a product of her age. She accepts the keyboard synthesizer as a legitimate musical instrument and uses electronic sounds comfortably in her scores. She is visually oriented, often incorporating video images and other media effects in her operas. Her music is dramatic and direct in its communication, evoking picturesque images and a wide range of feelings.

"Comin' to Town" from *The Settling Years*

In "Comin' to Town," Larsen connects us with the raw energy of the nineteenth-century pioneers who settled the untamed West. To express their frontier attitude, she began with the poetry of actual pioneers—plainspoken, forthright, and heartfelt. The work comprises three movements. The first, "Comin' to Town," expresses what it must have been like when the cowboys came to town after being out on the range for a time. The second, "Beneath These Alien Stars," describes the great Western expanse:

> The desert wind has waved my hair:
> Desert sands have etched my face,
> And the courage of the mountains
> Has bound me to this place.

The third movement, "A Hoopla," is a celebration describing country fiddling and having a good time. The work is scored for chorus, piano, and woodwind quintet (flute, oboe, B-flat clarinet, horn, and bassoon), and the movements are fast, slow, and fast.

In "Comin' to Town," Larsen takes us back in time to pioneer days by creating a sentiment that is rowdy and raucous. She says, "I've asked for three members of the chorus to double as a 'whooper,' a 'whistler,' and a 'rowdy,' and I've scored them into the piece. The whistler must have a really piercing through-the-teeth whistle, the kind that would have been used on round-up." Larsen adapted the text by Robert V. Carr:

> The boys are comin' to town!
> What does the marshall do?
> He's gone and hid, that's what he did,
> For he knows a thing or two.
>
> The boys are comin' to town!
> What does the dogs all do?
> They hits the trail with a canine wail,
> For they know a thing or two.
>
> The boys are comin to town!
> What does the old town do?
> She goes to bed while they paint her red,
> For she knows a thing or two.

▼Activity: **Figure Out**

What makes Libby Larsen's music so American?

Listen to "Comin' to Town" from *The Settling Years* and make a list of the musical elements that give it a distinctive American flavor.

Try speaking the following rhythm:

Ti - yi - yi - yi - yi - yi - yi - yah.

In the text, what word or words does Larsen choose to create word painting? Word painting is the art of portraying the meaning of a word through sound.

Signal when you hear the music modulate.

Four on the Floor

In *Four on the Floor*, a short work for violin, cello, bass, and piano, Larsen's theme is again American. The title refers to speed—gunning a car in high (or fourth) gear by putting the gas pedal down to the floorboards. Larsen says, "Breakneck is the theme of the piece—an America that is

Profile

Libby Larsen
American Composer
1950 –

LIBBY LARSEN

It is not easy to break down barriers and forge new paths. Libby Larsen defies the idea that composing is a male occupation. "Women and men are socialized differently in our society," she says. "It is very difficult for a man to become a nurse or for a woman to become a composer. We're made to feel that it's unacceptable."

Larsen's determination has won her admiration and acceptance as a composer. She has worked hard. Born in Delaware, she grew up in Minneapolis, studied at the University of Minnesota where she received a Ph.D. in 1978, and continues to live in Minneapolis with her husband and daughter, while spending most of every day composing.

Why did she choose to become a composer? She says, "I wanted to be a composer because I love sound. By giving order to sound, a composer reveals some new understanding of what sound means to us and our lives. Music is a special way of perceiving the world around us in our quiet, private moments."

To those who may aspire to become composers, she has some advice: "There is a difference between aspiring and realizing aspirations. You have to move from dreaming about yourself to acting on your dreams. It can be confusing to know how to make the dream come true. One way is to find someone who has already done it and model yourself after them. If you can't find someone who embodies your dream, then take a chance. Start doing what you want to do and find out about it as you go."

speeding up faster and faster, jazzing into eternity." She has marked quarter notes to be played at 138–144 to the minute!

Four on the Floor, Larsen says, "is inspired by boogie-woogie." After a short three-measure introduction, the boogie beat is set by the piano with its characteristic eight pulses to the measure and the use of triplets (three notes to the beat). Larsen was influenced by the piano styles of Jerry Lee Lewis and Pine Top Smith. The "walking bass" figure in the left hand continues through most of the piece:

▶ Composers work in all kinds of ways. Some compose at the keyboard, others at a desk away from any musical instrument. In the latter case, they invent the music in their heads (audiate) and then write it down. Here Libby Larsen is shown notating her work.

This walking bass figure is repeated later, giving the piece an A B A structure. Toward the end of the piece, after a **glissando**, *a continuous or sliding movement from one pitch to the other*, from high to low on the white keys of the piano, the string instruments invent "ad lib runs, glissandos" that Larsen has indicated by the following "notation":

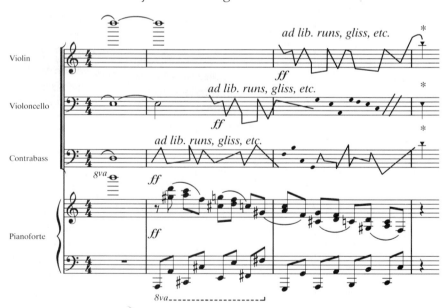

*Play any note you land on. Use marcato at the very least.

Cooperative Learning

Discover

How does Larsen use tempo to give variety and mark the sections of a piece in A B A form?

Listen to *Four on the Floor* and see if you can detect where the tempo changes.

Clue: Listen for a jazzy *pizzicato* (plucked) section for the three string instruments (no piano). When the piano comes in again, there is a new tempo. Is it slower or faster?

Then discuss the following with your classmates: When does the tempo return to what it was at the beginning? Did Larsen take a risk when she asked the performers to invent their own parts? Do you think they realized her intent?

Discuss why Larsen calls this work "a celebration of American music and American musicians."

Here and in some of the following measures, she asks the string players to invent their own parts. The piece comes to a boisterous conclusion.

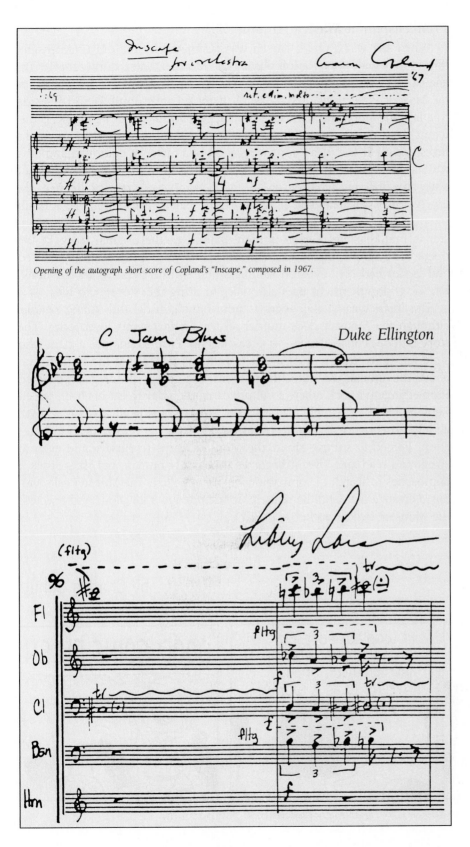

Opening of the autograph short score of Copland's "Inscape," composed in 1967.

◀ Just as each human being has a distinct style of handwriting, each composer has an individual style of writing musical notation. They show their personalities by the way they set their notes on the page.

Frankenstein, a Musical Drama

When she was a child, Larsen was fascinated by the old Frankenstein film (1931) with Boris Karloff playing the Monster. Later, during the 1970s, she came across the original book by Mary Shelley, called *Frankenstein, or the Modern Prometheus* (1816–1817). It took Larsen until 1985 to decide to adapt the story into a musical drama, *Frankenstein*. Her treatment is different from either the book or the film. In the book, the Monster talks incessantly. His last plea—for the creation of a mate "as deformed and horrible as myself"—fills nearly 70 pages! In the film, the Monster does not have any dialogue whatsoever—a good example of **creative license**, *the liberty artists sometimes take in reinterpreting another artist's work.* As a result of such distortions, many people today mistakenly believe that the Monster is Frankenstein! Larsen is more faithful to the original story. In the opera, for example, the Monster speaks, yet its voice is electronically created and performed on keyboard samplers and synthesizers. As in the book, Dr. Victor Frankenstein uses electricity to bring the Monster to life.

The main idea of the opera is not about scaring and killing people, although the Monster does murder all Dr. Frankenstein's loved ones. The story is about consequences. In Greek legend, Prometheus was a giant who stole fire from heaven and gave it to humankind, raising the human race above the animals. As punishment, Zeus, the god of all the gods, chained Prometheus to a rock where a vulture came each day to eat his liver, which Zeus replaced each night. Larsen says, "The Promethean myth is a myth about consequences." Victor creates the Monster but sees it as an evil creation. Forced to survive alone, the Monster learns to survive and even to speak and read and love. It becomes touchingly human, but the people it approaches in search of companionship are repelled. The Monster asks Victor to create a mate, but he refuses. Condemned to a life alone and rejected, the Monster strikes back.

PEANUTS ®   by Charles Schulz

The tragedy is that Victor was not prepared to be responsible for the consequences of his act in creating the Monster. His goal was simply to create the life, not nurture it. When Victor rejects the idea of caring for his Monster by creating a companion for it, he refuses to assume responsibility for the change that he has produced. The Monster then gets even. Larsen says the story of this Monster makes us aware that, as humans, we should "contemplate the consequences of our actions." It is also "a study of those quiet and gentle parts of ourselves that we sacrifice to serve our collective ambition and arrogance."

This story has reverberations today. "If you set change in motion," Larsen says, "you are also responsible for what happens." She explains: "We face that dilemma in our environmental concerns. If we create roadways and cars, we have to be responsible for the greenhouse effect." The story also points out our inclination to misuse technology in the service of personal ambition and ego. So the story of this opera has applications in our own lives, in our own time.

The Music

"One problem with today's opera," Libby Larsen says, "is that there are too many words; they are really plays set to music." She studied screenwriting in order to create an opera that would be "perceived on one level as a cinematic experience." By that she means that visual action is of central importance. Her most radical innovation is in the portrayal of the Monster by a mime and video screens that show what it is seeing, thinking, and feeling.

The opera set—designed in black and white except for the videotape of the Monster—extends outward precariously over the audience. It consists of hanging ropes and ladders, and various constructed levels hidden mysteriously behind scrims. The orchestra consists of 15 performers, including woodwinds (flute, piccolo, oboe, English horn, clarinet and bass clarinet, bassoon and contrabassoon), horn, trumpet, percussion, a string quintet, and keyboards (piano, DX7 Synthesizer, and sampler). The story is told in a prologue and 14 scenes.

Throughout the opera, music joins with the visual action to carry the emotional content of the opera. Here, for example, is Scene 4: The Act in which Victor (Dr. Frankenstein) creates the Monster (stage directions have been shortened):

> *The scene is a dark laboratory, dimly lit. The Monster lies on a table. A large suspended cable with switches that can be reached by rope ladders is connected to the Monster. Victor is hunched over the table working furiously. He checks passages in one of the many books strewn about. There is a knock on an unseen door.*

ELIZABETH: Victor, dear, what are you doing?

VICTOR: Work, Elizabeth, work!

The scene is gruesomely lit. Victor climbs high on the rope ladders and begins to descend.

ELIZABETH: Victor, please, at least take some dinner. If you won't come out, let Henry bring you food.

Victor descends the ladder, looks up, and stops in frustration. The cable connection is coming apart. He climbs to reconnect it. When he reaches the top, he is interrupted by a knock on the door. Elizabeth and Henry have returned.

ELIZABETH and CLERVAL: Victor, come on now. You must eat. Victor, let me in. I have food. Victor, Victor!

A tremendous wind rushes through the open roof door. Victor scurries back down the ladder and approaches the table. Another knock.

CLERVAL: Victor, you can stop now. I believe you. I'm convinced. Now open the door. Victor? Victor!

VICTOR: *(With great irritation)* Go away, both of you. Now!

He looks up. It is lightning. He is exhilarated. He is just about to connect the cable to the Monster when the cable disengages. He scrambles up the ladder with one end of the cable and finally manages to connect it. He scrambles back down, waits for the right bolt of lightning, and connects the cable into the Monster's chest. Silence. We hear only the storm. Victor remains poised over the Monster. Nothing. Then, suddenly, one of the Monster's arms shoots straight up, then drops back. Victor goes back up the ladder and connects another cable. When he starts back down, the ladder breaks. He barely manages to grab a nearby beam. He manages to connect the cable. Still hanging, he waits for a bolt of lightning to send more electricity into the Monster. Silence. More silence. He swings to a nearby pipe and slides down. The Monster lies quietly.

  Victor takes an eye out of a small container and puts it in place. The videotape starts. The image is of a hand backing away from the eye. The videotape is what the Monster sees. He sees Victor.

  The Monster rises. Images of Victor are mixed with other images. The Monster reaches out to touch Victor. Before he makes contact, we see a clear picture on videotape of Victor, terrified. There is the look of a scream. Victor backs away. The Monster tries again. Victor pushes past the Monster and runs from the room leaving the images on the video a muddle of confusion.

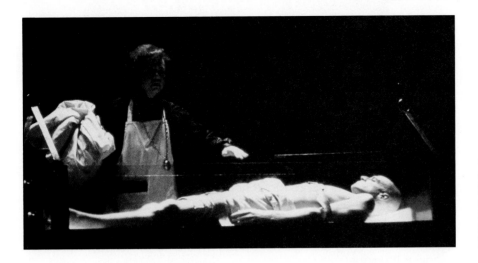

◀ The story of *Frankenstein* is about consequences. Humans need to accept responsibility for their actions. Dr. Frankenstein created the monster, but was so repelled by his creation that he chose not to fulfill his responsibility for its care.

▼ *Activity:* **Answer with Your Ears**

How does Larsen's music in her opera *Frankenstein* help to add atmosphere and activate our imagination?

Listen to Scene 4: The Act, and follow the stage directions and dialogue on pages 351 and 352. What does Larsen do with rhythm, melody, mood, dynamics, timbre, and texture to make the scene and section believable?

Summary

American composers have had a difficult time finding themselves. Should they copy European models? Many did—John Alden Carpenter, Roger Sessions, Walter Piston, and George Rochberg, to name a few. They wrote in what was said to be the "international style," but it was mainly a continuation of the compositional techniques developed in Germany or France. Should American composers develop their own compositional style? Composers such as Edgard Varese, John Cage, Vladimir Ussachevsky, and Elliott Carter went off in their own directions. Or should they strive to establish a distinctly American voice? Charles Ives, George Gershwin, Aaron Copland, Duke Ellington, Leonard Bernstein, and Libby Larsen exemplify this latter approach.

Whatever way our composers have chosen to communicate, something American still comes through. American music is often characterized by a driving rhythmic energy and syncopation, a strong use of percussion and brass, a sense of free expressiveness and invention, a reveling in contrasting timbres, a sense of spaciousness and sweep, and a direct and stirring emotional outpouring. American music blossomed in the twentieth century. In the hands of composers like Aaron Copland, Duke Ellington, and Libby Larsen, American music speaks to all of us. It is egalitarian. It has welcomed women to its ranks both as performers and as composers. Our precious freedom to create, to express, and to communicate—guaranteed by the First Amendment to the United States Constitution—assures American artists a creative environment that is unsurpassed in the entire world.

Apply What You Have Learned
Chapter 15

What musical tools have been used to create vocal and instrumental arrangements of a stock pop tune?

Use the Perceptive Listening Grid to compare and contrast three arranged versions of the same classic love song "What's New?" Work independently and follow the steps below:

1. Listen to the song as it was arranged to be played by Benny Goodman and his band. Make notes about what makes this arrangement distinctive.
2. Listen to the arrangement played by J. J. Johnson on trombone. How is this arrangement different?
3. Listen to the song arrangement performed by Billie Holiday. Again, how is it unique?

Based on your notations on the grid, write a brief (one page) critical essay that describes how music arrangers can use their tools of the trade to become just as creative as composers.

Apply What You Have Learned
Chapter 16

How would you describe the creative process in general and musical creativity in particular?

Discuss the following questions in your small study groups. Take notes on your deliberations. Use your notes and the information in the text to describe the characteristics of musical creativity. Your essay should be two to three pages in length, and it must cite at least one composer and one musical composition.

Discussion Questions

1. Is everyone creative? What are creative people like? How are creative people different from noncreative people?
2. How do teachers usually respond to highly creative students? Why?
3. When someone creates a musical composition or arrangement, what kinds of decisions have to be made?
4. Compare the most and least creative composers you know. How are they similar and different? Is their thinking convergent or divergent?
5. What is the role of the composer in today's world? What is the usefulness of musical expression?

Apply What You Have Learned
Chapter 17

How well do you know your technological terms?

Based on your reading of the text in this unit and on the class demonstrations of music technology, select five terms that you believe should be in the common language of musically informed young adults. Then, write a brief and clear definition for each term. Hand in your list of five definitions. Your teacher will compile from the class a vocabulary list of the most significant technological terms. Identifying the terms on this list will become your end-of-unit exam.

Apply What You Have Learned
Chapter 18

What characteristics make music American?

Pick one piece in this unit that you feel characterizes American music. Write a one-page essay discussing what makes this music American. Cite specific musical events in your selection to support your viewpoint.

▼ American painter Albert Bierstadt (1830–1902) captured the drama and beauty of the western land-scape and pictured the hope and idealism of the early settlers. Even though the realities were less glamorous, Bierstadt presented a vision of Americans—rugged, independent, and courageous— that still lingers today.

Albert Bierstadt. *Emigrants Crossing the Plains.* 1867. National Cowboy Hall of Fame and Western Heritage Center, Oklahoma City, Oklahoma.

Music!...
To Tell the Story of
Our Lives

~

CHAPTER 19

Musical Theater

Objectives

By completing this chapter, you will:

- Be able to relate musical theater to real life experience.
- Know the difference between a drama and a musical.
- Recognize how music sets the atmosphere and the scene.
- Understand how music develops and reveals character.
- Become familiar with the dramatic tools of expression (sets, costumes, lighting, makeup, dialogue, music, etc.).
- Realize that music can add to the emotional impact of theater.

Musical Terms

Broadway musical
librettist
libretto
soliloquy

*S*torytelling may be the oldest art. Humans have been telling tales since they could draw and talk, certainly as far back as the caveman, perhaps earlier. Why do we tell stories? We tell them to share our experiences and learn from them, to try to invent explanations for what we do not understand, to remember what is valuable, and to delight and amuse ourselves. These are some of the reasons we still tell stories to each other today.

The Broadway Musical

When music is added to the drama, the storytelling becomes musical theater. A rock concert with its format of continuous music, singing, costumes, lighting, and movement might be considered to be musical theater, except for one thing—the absence of a coherent story line. Musical theater combines the art of drama with song (and often dance) in order to tell a story with greater emotional impact. When it is used well, music can touch our feelings and intensify the drama. Among the many forms of musical theater are the Broadway musical and opera.

Popular in appeal, the Broadway musical is deliberately brash and commercial—an entertaining way of telling a story with music. Along with jazz, it is an American invention. It is an outgrowth of the minstrel show; the songs, dances, and skits that constituted the early variety shows known as "vaudeville"; and the operettas that were popular during the first three decades of the twentieth century. The world has generally taken a liking to this unique way of telling a story with songs, dancing, costumes, scenery, lighting, and spoken dialogue.

Like opera, the **Broadway musical** is *a dramatic stage form that combines the arts of acting and singing.* Here, however, there is less stylization and more immediate emotional appeal. Like opera, the main vehicle for storytelling is the music. Since opera was considered a bit too stuffy and long-winded for some of the general public, America had to invent its own type of opera, a form that spoke more simply and directly to the people. The answer was the Broadway musical, or what is now called, simply, "the musical."

The style of the musical was established in the 1920s and 1930s by George Gershwin (*Lady, Be Good!*), Jerome Kern (*Show Boat*), and Cole Porter (*Anything Goes*), among others. After the Second World War, it was further developed by Frederick Loewe and Alan Jay Lerner (*My Fair Lady*), Jule Styne (*Gypsy*), Leonard Bernstein (*West Side Story*), and Stephen Sondheim (*A Little Night Music*)—Americans all.

P R O J E C T

Write About a Musical

Select a video or a recording of a Broadway musical and write a short analysis of it considering the following issues:

- What was the inspiration for the musical? a play, an event in history, a folk tradition?
- What is the function of the overture? Does it serve to set the mood of the drama or does it function in a very utilitarian way—to get the audience quiet before the play begins?
- Select a solo or production number from the musical and describe how the music contributes to the emotion and drama of the text.
- What is the relationship between the speaking and the singing parts? Is the story told through the dialogue or the songs, or both? Is there more than one emotional idea or mood projected in the songs?
- How has the use of music (dance, solos, duets, ensemble, instrumental music) enhanced and embodied the meaning of the story?

Carousel

One of America's greatest Broadway musical writing teams was Richard Rodgers and Oscar Hammerstein 2nd, and one of their greatest achievements was the musical, *Carousel*. Like many other Broadway musicals, *Carousel* (1945) was an adaptation of an already existing work, in this case the play *Liliom* by the great European playwright Ferenc Molnár. The story is about a young, shiftless, macho carousel (merry-go-round) barker in Budapest who marries a shy and honest young servant girl. He loses his job, and when he learns that he is about to become a father, he participates in a robbery in order to obtain money to support his family. The robbery attempt fails, and in order to avoid capture by the police, he stabs himself and dies.

Liliom is tried in the Court of Heaven, but refuses to apologize for his actions. The heavenly magistrate knows how Liliom came to beat his wife, plan the robbery, and kill himself. But Liliom is too proud to admit that he really loves his wife and regrets what he has done. He is therefore sentenced to a term of 16 years in the purifying fires of the penitential plains, after which time he will be allowed to return to earth for one day to atone for his sins.

After serving his time, Liliom returns to earth for his day to do his good deed. Dressed as an old beggar, he tries to give his daughter, now 16 years old, a star he has stolen from heaven, but she refuses to take it. Forgetting his situation, he slaps her and is led away. The daughter asks her mother, "Is it possible for someone to hit you—hard like that, real loud and hard—and not hurt you at all?" In the final line of the play, the mother replies "It is possible, dear—that someone may beat you and beat you and beat you—and not hurt you at all."

▶ As creators of musicals, the team of Richard Rodgers and Oscar Hammerstein 2nd was innovative. Instead of the usual overture, they opened *Carousel* with a dance-pantomime. This prologue of actions and gestures introduces the audience to a carnival setting in the late 1800s. The music of "The Carousel Waltz" sweeps the audience up in the nostalgic sound of a calliope.

Profile

Richard Rodgers
Composer
1902–1979

RICHARD RODGERS

Richard Rodgers, composer of some of America's finest musicals, showed remarkable talent when he was very young. At the age of six, he could play the piano by ear and improvise. He studied music but also learned much on his own. Later, he began to compose popular songs while he was studying music at Columbia University.

In 1918 he teamed up with Lorenz Hart, a budding lyricist, who agreed that songs needed better poetry. Soon they were collaborating on the creation of revues and shows. Their unique achievement was a melding of the music with the drama. While operetta plots of that time were daffy, theirs were more serious and real.

Among Rodgers and Hart's most successful works are the musical comedies *On Your Toes* (1936), which includes the ballet sequence "Slaughter on Tenth Avenue"; *Babes in Arms* (1937), with the songs "My Funny Valentine," "The Lady Is a Tramp," and "Johnny One Note"; and *Pal Joey* (1940). Together, they produced nearly 30 musicals.

Following Hart's death in 1943, Rodgers formed a partnership with Oscar Hammerstein 2nd. Their collaboration achieved sensational success with the musical *Oklahoma!* (1943), which won the Pulitzer Prize for drama. Following this, they created *Carousel* (1945); *South Pacific* (1949), which also won a Pulitzer; *The King and I* (1951); and *The Sound of Music* (1959), among others. Rodgers knew how to build a melody and make music uplifting. His colorful harmonies and dance rhythms help to give his music an immediate appeal. *Victory at Sea* (1952) is one of several scores he composed for films and television documentaries.

From Play to Musical

In adapting the play *Liliom* to a musical, Oscar Hammerstein 2nd wrote the book (the story and dialogue) and the lyrics, resetting the action in New England. He was the **librettist**, *the person who writes the text,* also known as the **libretto**, which is *the dialogue and/or lyrics for a musical work.* His partner, Richard Rodgers, composed the finest musical score of his career, surpassing their previous triumph, *Oklahoma!*.

▼*Activity:* **Answer with Your Ears**

How does music help set the scene?

Carousel opens not with the customary overture but with a "prologue" that introduces the audience to the carnival through a ballet-pantomime set to "The Carousel Waltz."
Describe the character of this melody.
What is there about this music that conveys the atmosphere of a carnival?

One of the problems the creators of a musical have to deal with is the transition between dialogue and singing. Although it is natural for characters to speak to one another, when they suddenly break into song, their singing can appear to be very unnatural, if only because it is not something people normally do. The transitions into song, therefore, take careful preparation in order to ease the audience into the music. The less noticeable (smoother) these transitions are, the better.

▶ Julie Jordon meets Billy Bigelow at the carousel where he is the barker, the person hired to attract customers by making loud animated announcements. Unlike the usual romantic hero, he is lazy, vain, and bad tempered. Although she knows Billy's character, Julie sets out to win his affections, determined to change him.

▼ Activity: *Analyze the Transition*

How does the composer make a smooth transition from speech to singing?

Early in *Carousel,* Julie and her friend Carrie Pipperidge are talking about their boyfriends ("beaux"). Their conversation is quietly underscored with music. Soon they are conversing in song in their duet, "You're a Queer One, Julie Jordon."

Are you aware when they move from speech to song?

What makes this duet a conversation set to music?

Sets, costumes, makeup, and lighting are tools of the stage. The musical adds one more: *music*. Rodgers and Hammerstein use music to convey emotion and drama. The addition of music to the dialogue adds to the emotional power. It tells the audience how they are supposed to react and how they should feel. The difference between telling a story with dialogue and telling it with dialogue and music can be startling. Music heightens the emotions making them more obvious, more vivid, and often more intense. Some dramatic stories are told more effectively with music; other, subtler tales are better told with dialogue alone.

▼*Activity:* **Distinguish**

Understand the difference between the play and the musical.

In adapting the play to the musical, both Rodgers and Hammerstein tried to maintain the spirit of the original while they conveyed emotion and drama through the music. To understand the difference between the play and the musical, compare the scene in the play *Liliom*, in which Liliom meets Julie for the first time, with the same scene in the musical, *Carousel.*

Assume the characters and read aloud the parts in the play.

Then learn the musical version that appears on pages 365–376. Girls sing Julie's part, boys sing Billy's. Can you act the scene so that you feel the emotion?

What differences are there between the play and the musical setting?

Excerpt from Act I of *Liliom*

The scene is a lonely place in the park, half hidden by trees and shrubbery, near the amusement park. Center Stage: Under a flowering acacia (uh-KAY-shuh) tree stands a painted wooden bench. From afar, very faintly, comes the music of a calliope. Blending with it are the sounds of human voices, now loud, now soft. It grows progressively darker until the end of the scene. There is no moonlight. In this excerpt, "that Muskat woman" refers to Mrs. Muskat, the woman who owns the carousel and who has fired Liliom from his job as barker.

In the original play, Liliom and Julie have the following conversation at the end of Scene 1.

LILIOM: But you wouldn't dare to marry anyone like me, would you?

JULIE: I know that—that—if I loved anyone—it wouldn't make any difference to me what he—even if I died for it.

LILIOM: But you wouldn't marry a rough guy like me—that is—eh—if you loved me—

JULIE: Yes, I would—if I loved you, Mister Liliom.
[There is a pause.]

LILIOM: *[Whispers.]* Well—you just said—didn't you?—that you don't love me. Well, why don't you go home then?

JULIE: It's too late now, they'd all be asleep.

LILIOM: Locked out?

JULIE: Certainly.
[They are silent a while.]

LILIOM: I think—that even a low-down good-for-nothing—can make a man of himself.

JULIE: Certainly.
[They are silent again.]

LILIOM: Are you hungry?

JULIE: No.
[Another pause. The CALLIOPE stops.]

LILIOM: Suppose—you had some money—and I took it from you?

JULIE: Then you could take it, that's all.

LILIOM: *[After another brief silence.]* All I have to do—is go back to her—that Muskat woman—she'll be glad to get me back—then I'd be earning my wages again.
[She is silent. The twilight folds darker about them.]

JULIE: *[After a pause. Very softly.]* Don't go back—to her—
[Pause.]

LILIOM: There are a lot of acacia trees around here.
[Pause.]

JULIE: Don't go back to her—
[Pause.]

LILIOM: She'd take me back the minute I asked her. I know why—she knows, too—
[Pause.]

JULIE: I can smell them, too—acacia blossoms—

[There is a pause. Some blossoms drift down from the tree-top to the bench. LILIOM picks one up and smells it.]

LILIOM: White acacias!

JULIE: *[After a brief pause.]* The wind brings them down.

[They are silent. The MERRY-GO-ROUND is heard in the distance. There is a long pause before]

THE CURTAIN FALLS

In the musical version, the dialogue is similar in the first meeting between Julie (now cast as a factory worker) and Billy Bigalow (the new name for Liliom), but much of it is underscored with music or sung. Julie and Billy develop their sentiments in the song "If I Loved You." Note that the title of this song comes directly from Julie's line in the original play. The music and the lyrics however, probe more deeply into their characters. The lyrics show how awkward Julie would feel if she were to love Billy. Later, Billy expresses similar feelings about Julie.

Julie and Billy never admit they are in love, but the music lets the audience know they are. In this way, the music heightens the drama. It adds a dimension of emotional feeling that reveals what is going on inside the characters. One of the achievements of *Carousel* is the way in which the musical numbers continue the drama. The story is in the music.

Excerpt from *Carousel,* Act I, Scene 2

Oscar Hammerstein 2nd   Richard Rodgers

girl who don't mar-ry   He's got to be much more   per - tick-ler!

BILLY: Suppose I was to say to you that I'd marry you?

Lento

pp legato

JULIE: You?

BILLY: That scares

you, don't it? You're thinkin' what the cop said.

JULIE: No, I don't pay any mind to what he said.

BILLY:
But you wouldn't marry anyone like me, would you?

JULIE: Yes, I would if I loved you, it wouldn't make
no difference what you did, not even if I died for it.

BILLY: Ah. . . how do you know what you'd do if
you loved me? Or how you'd feel or anythin'?

JULIE: I dunno now
how I know.

BILLY:
Ah—

If   I   loved you,   Words ___ would-n't come ___ in an

eas - y way.   Round   in   cir - cles   I'd   go! _____

cresc.

Long - in' to   tell you, but a - fraid   and   shy,

mf

I'd   let my   gold-en chan-ces   pass   me   by!

Soon you'd leave me Off __ you would go __ in the mist of day,

Nev - er, nev - er to know __

How I loved you If I loved you! __

to Coda ✪ *(second time)*

(They sit in silence, he studies her for a moment, then turns away)
L'istesso tempo

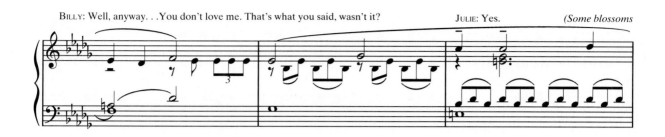

BILLY: Well, anyway. . .You don't love me. That's what you said, wasn't it?   JULIE: Yes.   *(Some blossoms*

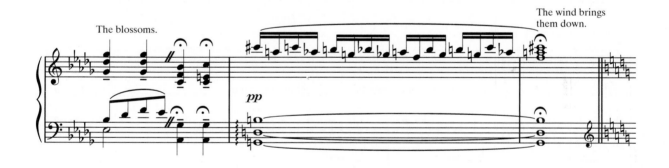

drift down to their feet. Billy picks one up and smells it.)   JULIE: I can smell them, can you?

sempre *pp*

The blossoms.   The wind brings them down.

pp

Moderato con moto   BILLY: *(speaks ad lib.)*   Ain't much wind tonight. Hardly any.   *(sings)*

You   can't   hear a

pp

℗ed.   ✳   *simile*

bout. _____   And I   al-ways say two heads are bet-ter than one, to   fig-ger it   out.

Meno mosso
BILLY: *(speaks)* I don't need you or anyone to help me. I got it figgered out for myself.   We ain't important. What are we? A couple

of specks of nothin'. Look up there.

(sings)
There's a hell - uv-a lot o'   stars   in the sky   And the

sky's   so   big   the sea looks small. _____   And two   lit-tle peo - ple,

BILLY *(sings)*

But some-how I can see Just ex-act-ly how I'd be.

Coda

BILLY: I'm not a feller to marry anybody—even if a girl was foolish enough to want me to, I wouldn't.

JULIE:
Don't worry about it, Billy.

BILLY:
Who's worried?

JULIE:
You're right about there bein' no wind.

The blossoms are jest comin' down by themselves.   Jest their time to, I reckon.

(The music rises ecstatically.)   *(Billy leans down and kisses her gently.)*   End of Scene

Curtain

▲ Most musicals provide the audience with comic relief. In *Carousel* the main story is embellished with a subplot involving Julie's best friend Carrie, who has fallen in love with Mr. Snow, an older man who is a fisherman. Carrie and Mr. Snow are comic characters whose happy relationship contrasts with that of Julie and Billy.

Using Music to Convey Character

In musical theater, music is used to convey character and to make us like and relate to the people in the story. Both the words and the music express and communicate meaning. Most people in the audience get the meaning of the text; they may be less aware that the music is also telling them something. Shortly after their duet "You're a Queer One, Julie Jordan," Carrie sings a solo in which she admits to Julie, her best friend, that she has fallen in love with "Mr. Snow," an unlikely older man who happens to be an overbearing and smelly fisherman. She sings: "The first time

▼*Activity:* **Figure Out**

What kind of a person is Carrie?

As you listen to Carrie sing the song "Mr. Snow," jot down all her characteristics that you discover by what she reveals about herself in the lyrics.

Now consider what the music is telling you about Carrie.

Write the adjectives that best describe the character of the melody in the refrain "When I marry Mr. Snow." How does this melody affect our thoughts about Carrie?

he kissed me the whiff of his clothes knocked me flat on the floor of the room, but now that I love him, my heart's in my nose, and fish is my favorite perfume!" This song is designed to let the audience get to know and like her.

In the play, Liliom is not a very likeable character. He is shiftless and seemingly satisfied not to work. He takes advantage of every free handout. He gambles and keeps bad company. His marriage with Julie is far from ideal. At one point, when Julie asks him why he won't go back to work on the carousel, he hits her. She even has a difficult time telling him that they are going to have a child.

In spite of the fact that Liliom, or Billy in the musical, has never done anything worthwhile, Rodgers and Hammerstein were determined to treat him empathetically: that is, to help the audience project their own personalities into his personality to share his predicament and thus understand him better. They wanted the audience to have some sympathy for Billy. They succeed brilliantly in getting the audience to empathize with him through the "Soliloquy" he sings when he first learns that he is to become a father. The idea of a **soliloquy** (suh-LIL-uh-kwee) is *to have a character reveal his thoughts to the audience, but not to the other characters, by thinking out loud or talking to himself.*

Rodgers and Hammerstein had spent many days talking about this song, what it would be about, who would sing it, and how it would fit into the action. Hammerstein took two full weeks to write the lyrics, but then Rodgers, with his customary speed, completed the music in less than two hours! He had been thinking about this expression of Billy Bigalow's character and knew what it should convey. "Soliloquy" tells the audience that Billy, in spite of his rough edges, has a decent, caring side.

In the same way that "Soliloquy" reveals Billy's character, the song "What's the Use of Wond'rin?" expresses Julie's. In this song, as in Billy's, Julie is thinking out loud about Billy:

> What's the use of wond'rin
> If he's good or if he's bad,
> Or if you like the way he wears his hat?
> Oh, what's the use of wond'rin
> If he's good or if he's bad,
> He's your fella, and you love him
> That's all there is to that.
>
> Common sense may tell you
> That the endin' will be sad,
> And now's the time to break and run away.
> Oh, what's the use of wond'rin
> If the endin' will be sad
> He's your fella, and you love him
> There's nothing more to say.

Cooperative Learning

Listen and Discuss
How does "Soliloquy" show us Billy's good side?

In this soliloquy, Billy is imagining what it will be like to be a father. At first he imagines that his child-to-be is a boy. He is proud of his son "Bill," and he dreams of the fun they will have together. Write down adjectives that describe the character of this section of music.

Then Billy interrupts himself. Suppose Julie has a girl! What would he do then? He'd have to be a real father to a girl. He describes how delicate she will be and how popular she will be with the boys. Write down adjectives that describe the character of this section of music.

Again he interrupts himself. His fragile little girl will go hungry if he continues his shiftless ways. He vows he will do anything to get enough money to bring up his daughter the way she deserves: "I'll make it or steal it or take it—or die."

Write down adjectives that describe the character of this section of music.

Working in small groups, compare your list of adjectives.

Discuss what the music reveals about Billy. Would he make a good father?

Profile

Oscar Hammerstein 2nd
American Librettist and Lyricist
1895–1960

OSCAR HAMMERSTEIN 2ND

Richard Rodgers and Oscar Hammerstein 2nd left an indelible mark on the American musical. Their talents complemented each other in such a way that they were both better because of their association. Like good teamwork in sports, their efforts meshed perfectly so that Hammerstein's book (the story and dialogue of the musical) and lyrics were fully realized in Rodger's musical score.

Hammerstein was an established wordsmith long before his first work with Rodgers. He had written the book, lyrics, or both, for such leading composers as Vincent Youmans (*Wildflower*, 1923), Rudolf Friml (*Rose Marie*, 1924), Sigmund Romberg (*The Desert Song*, 1926), and Jerome Kern (*Show Boat*, 1927). But his long association with Rodgers—from *Oklahoma!* in 1943 to *The Sound of Music* in 1959—made him the most significant author of musicals during this period.

Hammerstein, who has been called "the premier poet of the American musical theater," had an unusual trait that endeared him to people—his modesty. He admitted, for example, that he wrote a "more primitive type of lyric" than some of his contemporaries because of "my shortcomings as a wit and rhymester."

What he may have lacked in crafting clever rhymes and sparkling imagery, Hammerstein made up in other ways. First and foremost, his lyrics are singable because they stress long vowels and comfortable phrases. And his sentiments are direct. His stories made sense, and his songs fit the plot and the character! He made the meaning of a song, and therefore its drama, his focus and in so doing redefined the purpose of lyrics.

Somethin' made him the way that he is
Whether he's false or true.
And somethin' gave him the things that are his
One of those things is you.

In her accepting Billy with all his faults, Julie reveals herself as sweet and totally trusting, but also a bit foolish and naive.

The Message

Rodgers and Hammerstein made the ending of the musical more fitting to their New England setting and a good deal more hopeful than the ending of the play. Rather than end the musical with the touching but still tragic scene at Julie's front porch as in the play, Hammerstein added a brief finale—a graduation scene at the local high school. In his speech to the graduates, one of whom is Louise, Billy's 16-year-old daughter, the town doctor exhorts them to stand on their own two feet. They will come out all right, he says, if they have faith and courage. Rodgers and Hammerstein express this faith consistently in their works. They are not selling religion so much as they are telling people to believe in themselves and in each other.

▶ Years after his death, Billy revisits earth to do a good deed in order to be admitted to heaven. He happens upon his daughter's high school graduation. Louise, now 16, has never been accepted by her peers because of her father's bad reputation. The village doctor tells the graduates not to be held back by their parents' failures. Billy, who is invisible, urges his daughter to believe the doctor, and she does, joining the other graduates in singing "You'll Never Walk Alone." Billy has redeemed himself.

The doctor is reminded of a song he used to sing in school, and soon all the students, except for Billy's daughter Louise, have joined in singing "You'll Never Walk Alone," a song that was first sung to Julie after Billy's death. The lyrics tell us to "walk on, walk on, with hope in your heart, and you'll never walk alone." Rodgers and Hammerstein are saying to the audience that it is hope—being able to hold on to a dream—that will carry us through the dark times. Unseen by the others, Billy takes advantage of his day back on earth to coax his daughter to listen to the words, join in, and believe. Hesitantly at first, then with increasing ardor, she joins in the singing. Still unseen by them, he finally tells Julie: "I love you, Julie, know that I loved you," and Julie, too, joins in. The singing becomes exalted and the show ends with a sense of triumph. Billy has done his good deed.

Coming as it did in 1945, during the last year of the Second World War, *Carousel* raised people's spirits and gave them hope. Its message was that sacrifice is rewarded, that goodness wins out in the end. It was idealistic, perhaps a bit sentimental, but it was and still remains very effective musical theater.

▼*Activity:* **Perform**

Sing the song "You'll Never Walk Alone."

Note how the melody climbs gradually higher. Where is the climax in this song?
What is the range of this song (lowest pitch to highest pitch)?
What makes this song right for the ending of *Carousel*?

You'll Never Walk Alone

Oscar Hammerstein 2nd

Richard Rodgers

Summary

Good oral storytellers know how to create suspense to hold the attention of the audience, how to build the story to a climax and a satisfactory conclusion, and how to use dramatic words and inflections of the voice to create character and feeling. Writers tell tales in the form of short stories and novels. Dramatists create plays. They use the stage to act out their tales to give them greater realism and impact. The arts of theater and film are two of the more elaborate ways we communicate stories; they use actors to "play" the characters in costumes and makeup, with appropriate sets, props, and lighting. Probably the most elaborate form of storytelling is musical theater, a form that encompasses elements of all the others.

Musical theater is a particularly American way of relating a story through drama and music. The Broadway musical, or the musical comedy, is lighthearted entertainment consisting of a story line or plot, usually with some romantic twist, told through dialogue and a series of catchy songs, dances, and ensembles. The American team of Richard Rodgers (music) and Oscar Hammerstein 2nd (book and lyrics) was masterful at creating musicals. As the form has developed to embrace more serious and universal themes, it has been greeted enthusiastically by audiences around the world. People are drawn by the central message of these stories—American optimism—the belief that goodness will triumph over evil.

CHAPTER 20

Opera

Objectives

By completing this chapter, you will:

- Understand how a story is told through the medium of opera.
- Become familiar with one opera (*Carmen*) in detail.
- Recognize how the parts of the opera—overture, recitatives, arias, duets, trios, entr'acte music—all contribute to its total effect.
- Observe how the different timbres of the solo voices add to the interest and overall expression.

Musical Terms

absolute pitch
aria
entr'acte music
grand opera
opéra comique
recitative
seguidilla

New York's Metropolitan Opera celebrated its 100th year in 1983. The celebration saluted a major American cultural institution. Successive waves of immigrants had brought their culture with them—their songs, instruments, and love of music. They wanted America to have symphony orchestras and opera companies, just like their old countries. Even as they moved west during the nineteenth century, the settlers longed for culture. That is why they built opera houses in mining towns like Central City, Colorado.

Opera

Today, there are more than 150 opera companies in the United States with yearly budgets of over $100,000. Together, these companies give well over 10,000 performances of opera each year. And if you do not happen to live in any of those 150 communities or cannot attend productions at Lincoln Center in New York, home of the Metropolitan Opera, you can hear opera by tuning in the Met on your radio on Saturday or seeing one of the "Metropolitan Opera Presents" telecasts over the Public Broadcasting Service (PBS). The radio series that began in 1931 is now broadcast over more than 300 stations. Telecasts began in earnest in 1977 when the technology permitted clarity of pictures without totally relighting the productions.

As a form of storytelling, opera has been around since the early 1600s when Italian composers first tried to combine singing with theater. At first, audiences were excited because they liked the music and stage spectacle. The story or subject matter was less important. These early operas dealt with imaginary or symbolic subjects, often gods and goddesses. They were a celebration of the glories of the past and were performed as entertainments in the courts of nobles. The concept of opera, born in Italy, soon spread throughout Europe, becoming less serious, more public and distinct in national style and character.

Today, a successful opera must achieve dramatic excitement and sustain it throughout. It must have expressive music that reveals and heightens the emotion of the story. The story line or plot must revolve around interesting characters and situations. Costumes, scenery, lighting, and music must combine to dramatize the characters and their predicaments. Achieving this synthesis is a creative process so complex that it is probably equivalent to organizing a voyage to Mars. When an opera is successful, it is therefore a considerable achievement for all of the creators involved.

▲ The Central City (Colorado) Opera House as it looks today. Opened in 1878, it brought culture to this frontier gold-mining town. Although dramas, melodramas, and minstrel shows were the usual fare, the first real opera was presented in 1933. In 1956 the world premiere of *The Ballad of Baby Doe* by American composer Douglas Moore was given here.

Carmen

One of the most successful operas of all time is *Carmen,* the story of a tempestuous gypsy girl and the tragedy caused by her volatile temperament and changeable heart. The story is fast-paced and believable. The characters in the story are all people to whom we can relate. Don José (ho-ZAY), a conventional corporal in the regiment, is corrupted by his own passion. His love for the brusque and free-wheeling Carmen turns into a destructive possessiveness. But Carmen, perhaps the first liberated woman, will not be owned by anyone. Here is the raw material for an intense lovers' quarrel. To make matters worse, Carmen turns her attention to the pompous and heroic matador, Escamillo (es-cah-MEE-yoh), which further infuriates José. To complicate matters, there is Micaëla (mick-eye-AY-la), José's sweet and innocent girlfriend, a direct opposite of Carmen. Then there is the band of gypsy smugglers and Captain Zuniga (zoo-NEE-guh), José's very proper and law-abiding superior. These are all fascinating people who are caught in a web of intrigue.

The work was composed by Georges Bizet (zjorge bee-ZAY), a brilliant French composer of the nineteenth century who lived in Paris for most of his life. The text of the opera—called the libretto—was adopted from a popular French novel by Prosper Mérimée. The tale takes place in Seville (Spain) in 1820. Bizet's vivid orchestral scoring provides splashes of Spanish color to add atmosphere to the story. His music was unusual for its time because it is so integral to the story, moving the action along and fully supporting the drama.

▼Activity: **Answer with Your Ears**

How does Bizet establish the atmosphere for the opera?

As you listen to the Overture to *Carmen,* follow the "map" of the composition. The map uses a different letter for each new melody and the same letter when a melody is repeated.

C - toREadoR
D - fate MotivE
A + B = Bullfight

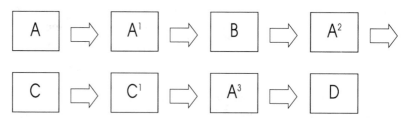

Which section of the music represents the toreador? What in the music tells you?
Which section represents the excitement of the bullfight? What are its characteristics?
Which gives us Carmen's "fate motive"? See the melody on page 388. What clue does it give us about the story? Why does Bizet give us this clue right at the start?
Which section uses full orchestra? Why?

Background

Carmen is an *opéra comique* written for and first performed at the Opéra-Comique theater in Paris. While the name indicates that this should be a comic opera, this is not the case. The fact that the opera is a tragedy was a big part of the controversy that surrounded its premiere.

By definition, an opéra comique was supposed to have some comical moments and, certainly, a happy ending. Given the violence in Bizet's new opera, it is not surprising that the management of the Opéra-Comique theater was horrified. Upon hearing what the composer had created, one of the directors hysterically exclaimed, "Isn't she assassinated by her lover? At the Opéra-Comique! A family theater! A theater for the promotion of marriages! We rent five or six boxes every night for these meetings of young couples. You are going to put our audience to flight. No, it's impossible." He begged Halévy, one of the librettists, to let Carmen live. "Death has never been seen on this stage, do you hear, never!"

Carmen changed all that. After *Carmen,* opéra comique differed from grand opera only in the amount of spoken dialogue. In **grand opera**, *everything is sung;* in **opéra comique** *some of the dialogue is sung, some spoken.* The same thing has happened to the Broadway musical. We no longer maintain that there must be spoken dialogue. Musicals such as *Les Misérables* or *The Phantom of the Opera* are sung throughout. Nor do we call the form "musical comedy," as we used to. Composers simply wanted to be able to use more serious plots, so the label had to be changed. The distinctions have become unimportant. Today there are other versions of *Carmen.* The composer Ernest Guiraud, a friend of Bizet's, revised the dialogue and set it in **recitative**, *a speech-like style of singing,* so that the opera could be sung throughout.

ACT I

When Act I opens, a group of soldiers are lounging in front of the guardhouse watching the people in the square. Soon a relief guard, with Don José and his captain, Zuniga, assumes the watch. At noon, the girls from the cigarette factory pour out into the square. The last to appear is Carmen, the beautiful and brazen gypsy girl, who flirts with Don José and lets him know her thoughts about love. She sings, "If you don't love me, then I love you. If I love you, beware!" She tosses him a flower, and everyone laughs at his embarrassment. The factory bell rings, and the cigarette girls go back to work.

When Micaëla appears, Don José quickly hides the flower. She brings greetings from his mother. She gives him a kiss from her, and he sends one back. Alone, he opens his mother's letter. "Yes," he says, "I'll do what you wish. I'll marry Micaëla."

Suddenly there is a loud noise from the factory. There has been an argument. Captain Zuniga sends Don José and two other guards into the factory. They emerge with Carmen. Don José has caught her with a knife. The women identify her as the culprit. Carmen is insolent. Zuniga tells

---

PROJECT

Critique Two Performances of Carmen's Aria, "Seguidilla"

- Performance No. 1: Carmen is performed by Tatiana Troyanos; conductor is Sir George Solti.
- Performance No. 2: Carmen is performed by Maria Callas; conductor is Georges Prêtre.

In addition to commenting on the criteria listed on the Judging Quality form, try to answer the following questions:

Which performer do you think has the tone quality that best reflects the character of Carmen? Justify your decision.

The "Seguidilla" is based on a Spanish dance rhythm. Which performance do you think captures the spirit of the undanced dance? Why?

Describe the differences in tempo between the two performances. Which tempo best captures the mood of the text? Why?

Don José to tie Carmen's hands while he goes into the guardhouse to make out a warrant for her arrest. Left alone with Don José, Carmen uses her charm to complete her conquest of him. She sings the **aria** *(song)*, "Seguidilla" (seh-gee-DEE-yuh).

In the finale to Act I, Zuniga emerges from the guardhouse and commands Don José to take Carmen to prison. She whispers to José to stay in back of her. She will give him a push to escape. As they walk away, she reminds him, "If I love you, beware!" At the bridge, Carmen pushes José. He falls and she escapes, laughing loudly. The curtain falls.

▼Activity: *Perform*

Learn to play Carmen's "fate motive."

Using the keyboard diagram below, practice playing the "fate motive" from the printed notation.

When you have mastered the pattern, play the first five notes connected as the phrase marking (⌒) indicates, followed by the two Ds performed staccato as the dots indicate. Perform the second line as indicated by the phrase marking. This is one long, connected phrase with a crescendo (gradual increase in intensity) and a diminuendo (gradual decrease in intensity) in the last three measures.

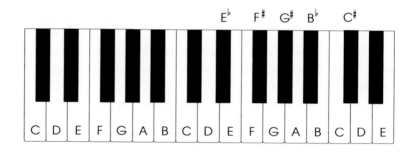

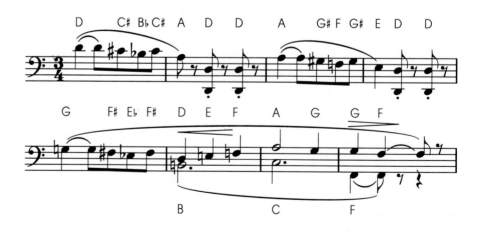

◀ Act I of the opera *Carmen* is set in a public square in Seville in southwest Spain. At noontime the girls from the cigarette factory enter the square to take a break, attracting the attention of the soldiers of the guard who are on duty. The gypsy girl Carmen, played here by mezzo-soprano Adria Firestone in the Houston Grand Opera's 1988 production, flirts with Don José, a corporal, who becomes quite infatuated with her.

▼ Activity: *Discover*

How does Bizet's music carry the story along?

Clap this Spanish dance rhythm known as the seguidilla:

Follow the music and text to the "Seguidilla" to see how the story progresses. A **seguidilla** is *a Spanish dance with many regional variations, or the music for such a dance.* After the introduction by orchestra with flute solo and oom-pah-pah accompaniment, you will hear the following sections:

(A) Carmen sings the seductive melody to the dance rhythm of the seguidilla. She tells Don José, "Near the ramparts of Seville, at my friend Lillas Pastia's tavern, I'm going to dance the seguidilla (a gypsy dance) and drink Manzanilla (a dry sherry)."

(B) To a new melody, Carmen says that she wants company there. She has just showed her lover the door. "All alone, one gets bored. Real pleasures are for two. To keep me company, I would like to take a companion. My heart is free. I have many suitors but they are not to my liking. Who wants my heart? It's there for the taking."

(A) Return to the seguidilla melody: "Near the rampart of Seville," etc.

(C) Don José sings. The style becomes somewhat less melodic and more recitative. He forbids Carmen to talk. She says she is just thinking out loud about a certain officer who loves her. (There are fragments of the seguidilla melody in the flute.) Even though he is only a lowly corporal, she will be happy with him. Don José becomes more impassioned. "If I free you, will you keep your word? If I love you, will you love me?" he asks.

(A) Return of the seguidilla melody. Carmen says yes, and Don José, blinded by his love for her, unties the cord that binds her hands behind her. They will meet later at the tavern.

How has the story progressed? When Carmen begins the aria, she is Don José's prisoner. When the song ends, how has her situation changed?

ACT II

Act II opens with Carmen leading the gypsy girls in a wild dance for the officers of the guard. The setting is Lillas Pastia's tavern. Gypsies accompany the dancing on guitars and tambourine. The plucked strings of the orchestra give the effect of guitars. The music gradually grows faster and more intense. The insistent rhythm drives the dancers into a whirlwind. The chorus of "tra la las" adds to the frenzy, and the full orchestra enters to give the dance a feverish finish.

▼ *Activity:* **Create**

Make up a rhythmic accompaniment to the Gypsy Dance.

Use tambourines, clapping, patting, or other sounds to mark the three basic beats. As the tempo of the music accelerates, speed up the pulse.

Use your accompaniment only when the orchestra plays alone and when the voices sing "tra-la-la." (The dance ceases during the other singing.)

Your parts will move through the following tempos:

Orchestra	*Andantino* (♩ = 100)
First tra-la-la	*A tempo* (♩ = 108)
Second tra-la-la	*A tempo animato* (♩ = 126)
Third tra-la-la	*Piu mosso* (♩ = 138)
Final orchestra	*Presto*

To test your skill, try accompanying on the offbeat. Try half the class on the beat and half on the offbeat.

The tra-la-la section repeats the note E on every beat in the bass throughout, part of the incessant repetition that creates the hypnotic spell of this music. Play the E on the beat.

Captain Zuniga is prominent among the observers, even though the tavern is a meeting place for a gang of gypsy smugglers. In the month that has passed since he ordered Carmen's arrest, he has succumbed to her charms, though she does not hide the fact that she prefers other company. To win a smile from Carmen, Zuniga tells her that her soldier-boyfriend José has been released from prison.

Suddenly the crowd outside shouts greetings to Escamillo, the popular bullfighter. He enters the tavern and sings the "Toreador Song," an aria that reveals his character.

Escamillo, too, makes a play for Carmen's affection, but she tells him he is wasting his time. As the tavern closes, he leaves with the soldiers. Only Carmen and a few of her gypsy friends linger to plan their next smuggling escapade. The girls are delighted to take part, but Carmen excuses herself. She tells them she has fallen in love again, this time with a man who went to prison for helping her.

Profile

GEORGES BIZET

Like many other outstanding composers and musicians, Georges Bizet grew up in a musical family. His mother, an excellent pianist, gave him his first music lessons. No doubt his father, a voice teacher who coached opera singers, encouraged his interest in opera. In this environment, Bizet's musical gifts emerged early, and by the age of ten his **absolute pitch** *(the ability to recognize and reproduce pitches exactly)*, knowledge of harmony, and skill at playing piano won him acceptance as a student at the Paris Conservatoire.

By the age of 17, Bizet had composed his first symphony, and two years later he won the coveted Grand Prix de Rome, a scholarship that enabled him to study musical composition in Rome for four years. At 22, he returned to Paris where he spent the rest of his rather short life supporting himself with a variety of musical "jobs." The most exasperating of these was trying to teach children of little talent to play the piano. At the same time, he continued to pursue a career as a composer by writing operas on commission for the two opera houses in Paris.

But these were not good times for a composer. There was only a small market for new chamber music and none for new French symphonies. The opera houses insisted that composers stick to the narrow conventions of that time and not be too creative. Then, too, opera singers of the day were prima donnas who demanded that composers write music to fit their likes. The composer could exercise little or no control.

It is all the more remarkable, therefore, that Bizet was able to triumph in creating the operatic masterpiece *Carmen*. He died just three months after its premiere in March of 1875.

Georges Bizet
Composer
1838–1875

◀ At a tavern on the outskirts of Seville, Carmen meets the popular bullfighter, Escamillo, and in spite of her love for Don José, her fickle heart is smitten. The scene is Act II of the Seattle Opera's 1987 production of *Carmen*, with Armand Arapian as Escamillo and Isola Jones playing Carmen.

▼*Activity:* **Answer and Perform**

What does the "Toreador Song" tell us about Escamillo?

The full orchestra is used to announce Escamillo's arrival. What feeling does this music convey?

First he sings a toast to the soldiers and the gypsy girls. Then he sings of the crowds that await him, their shouts, and the fame he wins for his courage. Then, boastfully, he sings the refrain "Toreador, en garde!" ("Toreador, on guard!"), and the assembled crowd joins in. As he sings of the dark eyes that watch him in the ring, he looks at Carmen.

What two adjectives best describe both this music and Escamillo?

Learn to sing the "Toreador Song." Practice singing the grace notes and the triplets separately until you have mastered them. Try to give a marchlike snap and vigor to the dotted rhythms.

Can you sing it with the French text?

Toreador Song

Georges Bizet
Translation by Ruth & Thomas Martin

Qu'un œil noir te re - gar - de Et _ que l'a-mour t'at-tend,
Dark eyes watch all a - round _____ And _ love is your re-ward,

To - ré-a - dor, _____ L'a - mour, l'a-mour t'at - tend! _
To - re-a - dor, _____ And _love is your re - ward! _

Hearing Don José's voice offstage, the girls peer out at him approvingly. Can Carmen get him to join their band? To get rid of them, Carmen says she will try. Don José enters and Carmen greets him warmly. She begins to sing and dance for him, as she promised. But in the middle of her dance, a trumpet sounds retreat in the distance, a signal that Don José must report for roll call. When he informs her that he must leave, Carmen gets angry. Go, she tells him, they are waiting for you. So much for your love.

Stung by her taunts, Don José shows Carmen the flower she gave to him before his imprisonment. He tells her in the "Flower Song" how the sweet scent of the dried flower reminded him of her. Then he curses her and questions why destiny has put her in his path, but to no avail. She took possession of his heart. His one hope was to see her again. To sweet harmonies and harp arpeggios in the orchestra, he tells her that he loves her.

Cooperative Learning

Discover Romantic Qualities

What are the qualities that make music romantic?

As you listen to the "Flower Song," make a list of the characteristics of the music that you think help it to "say" its romantic message.

Divide your list into three categories:

1. **The Orchestra** (accompaniment). How does it convey the mood?
2. **The Melody.** What characteristics make it a love song?
3. **The Singing.** How does the tenor who performs the role of Don José express his love by the way he sings? Discuss your observations.

Carmen is not persuaded. "If you loved me, you would come away with me into the mountains," she tells him. "You wouldn't have to obey any officer." Don José wants her love, but not at the price of being a deserter. He begs for her understanding, but she is determined to have her way. "Farewell for ever," she tells him.

Don José is about to storm out when someone knocks. It is Zuniga, captain of his regiment. Spotting Don José, he chides Carmen for wasting her affections on a mere corporal when she could have an officer like himself. He orders Don José to get out. Don José refuses. Zuniga commands him again to leave and again Don José says no. Zuniga strikes him and calls him a scoundrel. Don José seizes his sword. Frenzied music expresses the tension. Carmen, calling Don José a jealous fool, throws herself between them and summons the other gypsies. Rushing to her aid, they seize Zuniga and disarm him.

Carmen informs Zuniga that he must be held captive. The gypsies point their pistols at him and enjoy having the upper hand. They treat Zuniga with mocking politeness. Don José now has no choice. He has disobeyed his commanding officer and has been a party to his entrapment. The gypsies urge him to join with them and enjoy a life that is free. "La liberté!" ("Freedom!") they shout as the curtain falls on Act II.

ACT III

The **entr'acte music**—*light instrumental music that is performed between acts*—suggests the open countryside, the clean mountain air, and the tranquility of nature. This music is in direct contrast to the tense and boisterous music that has just preceded.

▶ The setting for Act III is the gypsy smugglers' hideaway in a wild and rocky mountain pass, as depicted in the 1981 Michigan Opera Theatre (Detroit) Production. It is here that Carmen and her two gypsy friends, Mercedes and Frasquita, tell their fortunes in cards (center left, foreground).

▼Activity: *Perform*

Learn to conduct the entr'acte music to the third act while following the musical map.

Refer to the conducting pattern for 4/4 time on page 125.

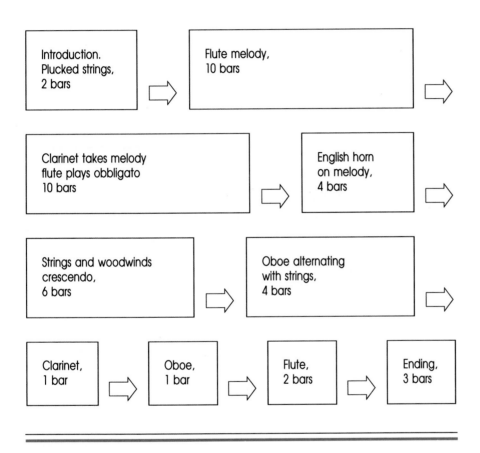

As the curtain rises on a dark, mountainous place, a gypsy smuggler appears on the top of the rocks and gives a signal. Others come down the rocky hillside carrying large bales on their shoulders. Looking down on the village below, Don José recalls his mother. "Then you should go home. The kind of life we lead is not for you," Carmen tells him. At this, Don José's temper flares. Carmen is already growing bored with her half-hearted lover. They quarrel.

Mercedes and Frasquita, Carmen's gypsy girlfriends, spread out cards to tell their fortunes. Lightheartedly, one finds a passionate lover, while the other marries a rich old man who abruptly dies so that she inherits a fortune. Carmen, who has been watching, then asks to see what the cards hold for her. She turns up the cards. Diamonds! Spades! We hear the "fate motive." These are signs of death, and Carmen believes them.

The band of gypsies depart leaving Don José to guard the goods they leave behind. Micaëla creeps up on the camp. She has come to find Don José at the bidding of his dying mother. Fearful of this place, she prays to God to protect her. She catches sight of Don José, but at that moment he raises his carbine and fires in her direction. Micaëla hides behind the rocks, but Don José has not fired at her. It is Escamillo who emerges unharmed and introduces himself. Don José's pleasure at their meeting quickly turns to bitter hatred when Escamillo calmly announces his mission—to meet his sweetheart, Carmen. The two engage in a vicious duel fought with knives. Carmen arrives and intercedes once more, saving Escamillo's life. Gallantly, Escamillo thanks Carmen and invites everyone to the next bullfight in Seville. He leaves the scene defiantly.

▼*Activity:* **Answer with Your Ears**

How does Bizet's music contrast the fortunes?

Listen to the Card Scene, a trio sung by Frasquita, Mercedes, and Carmen.

In the beginning section, sung by Frasquita and Mercedes, how does Bizet tell us that their fortunes are happy?

When Carmen takes the cards, how does Bizet use the orchestra to tell us that her fortune is death ("la mort!")?

Over halting, sustained chords in the orchestra, Carmen sings of her inescapable fate: "You can re-shuffle twenty times, the pitiless card will repeat—Death!" In the orchestra, a turn of four low tones accompanies Carmen's turning of the cards. "Encor!" ("Again!") she says.

Now Frasquita and Mercedes take up their lighthearted fortune-telling, while Carmen sings "Toujours la mort!" ("Always, death!"). Again Mercedes becomes an heiress, again Frasquita finds true love, again Carmen finds death. The trio ends "Encor!"

This trio shows one of the unique characteristics of operatic music—its capacity to contrast different, even opposite, emotions simultaneously. In this case, Carmen's despair contrasts with Mercedes and Frasquita's joyous good fortune.

The smugglers find Micaëla and bring her from her hiding place. She asks Don José to return home, but he is not about to leave Carmen. Then Micaëla reveals that his mother is dying and wants to see him once more. Carmen contemptuously tells him to go. Unable to say no, Don José warns Carmen that he will return, and he swears that nothing but death will ever separate them.

ACT IV

The setting for Act IV is a square in Seville facing the walls of an ancient amphitheater where the bullfights are held. When the curtain rises, we see vendors hawking programs, beverages, and souvenirs. The crowd is excited, anticipating the arrival of the matadors.

▼*Activity:* **Perform**

Learn three of the basic rhythms that give the opening of Act IV color and excitement.

Tap, clap, or use tambourines to perform:

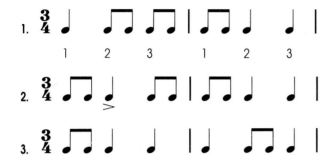

Practice the rhythms so that you can perform them on cue. Divide the class into three groups and perform them together.

Now listen to the chorus that opens Act IV and hold up one, two, or three fingers to indicate the rhythm you are hearing.

Divide the class and perform the rhythms along with the recording as you recognize them.

Rhythm, like melody, can be an organizing device. In this case, it gives infectious character and coloring to the piece throughout.

Directly following this opening, the orchestra announces the bullfighters with the "A" theme that was heard in the Overture. Now the children call, "The Parade! Here they come!" The people in the street salute the brave toreadors. As each one enters proudly with his retinue, they shout cheers and insults. Escamillo, their favorite, enters last with Carmen, radiantly dressed, beside him. The music is a brassy rendition of his Toreador Song, sung by the crowd.

Carmen and Escamillo exchange brief vows of love before he enters the arena. While the crowd moves into the arena, Frasquita and Mercedes approach Carmen and warn her not to stay. Don José is hiding in the crowd. Carmen sees him and tells them she fears no one. They warn her, but she defiantly remains outside the arena alone.

▼*Activity:* **Figure Out**

How does Bizet make Escamillo's entrance more important than the other toreadors?

At the start of each toreador entrance, we hear the orchestra alone on the bullfight theme (A). This is always followed by the reactions of the crowd. Compare those reactions.

Don José appears in a ragged shirt in pitiful contrast to Carmen. Mad with jealousy, guilt, and despair, he makes a last plea to win her. Though he promises not to harm her, horns in the orchestra betray his inner rage. Like a caged animal, the menace in him is about to tear loose.

▼*Activity:* **Challenge**

Follow the libretto to find out how the story ends.

Below is the final scene as it appears in the libretto with the original French as heard on the recording and, next to it, the English translation, line-by-line.

Follow the French text with your ears and eyes while you read the English translation!

Libretto, Finale of Act IV

Don José

Tu ne m'aimes donc plus?	Then you love me no more?
(Carmen is silent and Don José repeats)	
Tu ne m'aimes donc plus?	Then you love me no more?

Carmen

Non, je ne t'aime plus.	No, I no longer love you.

Don José

Mais moi, Carmen, je t'aime encore;	But I, Carmen, I still love you.
Carmen hélas! moi je t'adore.	Carmen, alas, I adore you!

Carmen

A quoi bon tout cela?	What good is all this?
Que de mots superflus!	Useless words!

Don José

Carmen, je t'aime, je t'adore!	Carmen, I love you, I adore you.
Eh bien, s'il le faut, pour te plaire,	Very well, if I must, to please you,
Je resterai bandit, tout ce que tu voudras,	I'll remain a bandit, anything you like.
Tout, tu m'entends, mais ne me quitte pas,	Anything, do you hear me, only don't leave me.
ô ma Carmen,	Oh, my Carmen!
Souviens-toi du passé, nous nous aimions naguère.	Ah, don't you remember the past when we loved each other.

Carmen

Jamais Carmen ne cédera.	Never will Carmen give in.
Libre elle est née et libre elle mourra!	She was born free, and free she will die!

Chorus and Fanfares

(In the arena)	
Viva! la course est belle	Viva! What a fight!
Sur le sable sanglant	On the blood-stained sand
Voyez! Le taureau qu'on harcèle	Look! The angry bull charges!
En bondissant s'élance, Voyez!	They goad the bull, he leaps forward and charges, look!
Frappé juste en plein coeur!	Now he's pierced to the heart!
Voyez! Voyez! Voyez!	Look! Look! Look!
Victoire!	Victory!

▲ In Act IV, set in a public square in Seville at the entrance to the bullfight arena, the love triangle between Carmen, Don José, and Escamillo is finally resolved—tragically. In Michigan Opera Theatre's 1981 production, Don José is played by Barry Busse, Carmen by Victoria Vergara.

(During this chorus, Carmen and Don José have been silent, both listening and hearing the cries of "Victory, victory." Don José does not take his eyes off Carmen. At the end of the chorus, Carmen takes a step toward the bullring.)

Don José
(Placing himself before her)

Où vas-tu? . . .	Where are you going?

Carmen

Laisse-moi!	Let me pass!

Don José

Cet homme qu'on acclame.	That man they're cheering
C'est ton nouvel amant!	is your new lover!

Carmen

Laisse-moi!	Let me pass!

Don José

Sur mon ame.	On my soul,
Tu ne passeras pas.	You will not pass.
Carmen, c'est moi que tu suivras!	Carmen, you will follow me.

Carmen

Laisse-moi, Don José! Je ne te suivrai pas.	Leave me, Don José, I will not follow you.

Don José

Tu vas le retrouver, dis . . . tu l'aimes donc?	You will go to him, tell me . . . do you love him?

Carmen

Je l'aime!	I love him!
Je l'aime et devant la mort même,	I love him, and in the face of death itself,
Je répéterai que je l'aime!	I will repeat that I love him!

Chorus   *(In the arena)*

Vivat! Bravo! Victoire!	Viva! Bravo! Victory!
Frappé juste en plein coeur,	Struck right in the heart,
Le taureau tombe!	the bull falls!
Gloire au torero vainqueur!	Glory to the victorious torero!
Victoire!	Victory!

Don José

Ainsi, le salut de mon âme,	So, I will have lost my soul
Je l'aurai perdu pour que toi,	for you, you wretch, so that
Pour que tu t'en ailles, infâme!	you can go to his arms
Entre ses bras, rire de moi.	and laugh at me.
Non, par le sang, tu n'iras pas,	No, by my blood, you will not go;
Carmen, c'est moi que tu suivras!	Carmen, you're coming with me!

Carmen

Non! non! jamais!	No, no! Never!

Don José

Je suis las de te menacer!	I'm tired of threatening you.

Carmen

Eh bien! frappe-moi donc, où laisse-moi passer!	Well then, strike me now, or let me go!

Chorus   *(Inside the arena)*

Victoire!	Victory!

Don José

Pour la dernière fois, démon,	For the very last time, devil,
Veux-tu me suivre?	will you come with me?

Carmen

Non! non!	No! No!
Cette bague autrefois tu me l'avais donnée,	Here, this ring you once gave me,
Tiens!	take it!
(She flings it at him.)	

Don José   *(Drawing his dagger)*

Eh bien, damnée!	All right, you devil!

(Don José rushes toward Carmen. She attempts to escape, but he catches up with her, stabs her, and she falls as fanfares come from the arena.)

Chorus

Toréador, en garde,	Toreador, on guard,
Et songe bien, oui, songe en combattant	And remember, yes, remember as you fight

| Qu'un œil noir te regarde | That dark eyes are watching you |
| Et que l'amour t'attend. | And that love awaits! |

(Carmen falls and dies. Don José, distracted, falls on his knees beside her as the crowd comes out of the arena.)

Don José

Vous pouvez m'arrêter . . .	You can arrest me . . .
C'est moi qui l'ai tuée!	It is I who have killed her!
O Carmen! ma Carmen adorée!	Carmen! My beloved Carmen!

The Message

The story of *Carmen* is a good example of a "love triangle," a basic plot that can take many forms. In this particular example, two men seek the love of one woman. Don José is a man caught in a fierce internal struggle between the forces of good and evil. His love for Carmen compels him to betray his promise to his mother and sacrifice his loyalty to his country. As Don José's status is reduced from lowly corporal to an outlaw member of a band of gypsies, Carmen's status improves as she becomes the sweetheart of the popular bullfight hero Escamillo. Carmen is more interested in the game of conquering her male idols than in keeping them. She casts Don José aside with contempt, caring nothing for his feelings or the honor he has given up for her. The result is tragic for both of them. His uncontrolled passion and her stubborn selfishness lead to her death and his ruin. The message: the jealousy and madness of rejected love can lead to murder and self-destruction.

Summary

Musical theater can be a powerfully expressive form. By opening a curtain to see ourselves and our human delights and dilemmas, we feel our own human situation more clearly, and we learn to empathize with other humans about their situations. Musical theater gives us a way to dream and listen to our feelings. It is a way that we indulge in our own foibles, laugh at our stupidities, cry for our misfortunes, bask in our loves, and celebrate our triumphs.

More than anything, musical theater lets us feel all the emotions of life. It does not appeal to our intellect as much as to our inner, soulful being. It entreats us to be human. Because it can speak so personally, it can move us as only humans can be moved. It can cause us to feel. It can put us in touch with a most important element of our being—our emotions. That is an essential part of what music communicates and why music is important in our lives.

Film

Objectives

By completing this chapter, you will:
- Understand the development of sound as a part of the storytelling art of motion pictures.
- Understand the role of the film composer and the purposes that music serves in film.
- Become familiar with the work of a number of film composers.
- Be able to select appropriate music to enhance visual images.

Musical Term

background music
dubbing
incidental music
mag track
scoring
soundtrack
source music
spot

*M*usic has been an essential part of motion
pictures from their earliest days. During the silent era
(1896–1927), live music gave the moving images
sound and life. Later, when sound became an integral part
of the motion picture, music added to the dramatic
impact. Like the acting, the sets, and the costumes, it
became an expressive force that enhanced the storytelling.
Should the moviegoer hear a movie score? Yes, being
conscious of the music and responsive to it adds to
the total conception of a film in the same way that
recognizing the technical work of the camera or
knowing the elements of a good story and appreciating
effective acting increase receptivity and understanding.

The Beginnings

Thomas Edison and his assistant William Dickson invented the Kineto-scope in 1889. The Kinetoscope, which contained 50 feet of film, was a simple device that an individual viewer operated by turning a crank. The "peep show" soon became a popular entertainment in the penny arcades of the time. This was the beginning of the motion picture.

In 1896 Edison presented his latest invention, the Vitascope, a machine that projected the Kinetoscope's images on a wall. The Vitascope changed what had been a private experience into a public one. Audiences were soon flocking to storefront "nickelodeons" to enjoy this amazing new novelty. For all the preceding thousands of years of human history, people had never been able to record the way they looked and moved in such a realistic way. And what did they see? The brief films showed circus acts, dances, boxing bouts, comic scenes—snippets of this and that. The flickering scenes were usually accompanied by the unrelenting sound of a piano.

But the novelty of seeing pictures move began to wear thin. The medium had to be used in a new way or the public would lose interest. The cre-ativity of Edwin S. Porter came to the rescue. In 1903 he produced, directed, and wrote *The Great Train Robbery,* an 11-minute film that told a complete and exciting story, the first successful Western. This was the begin-ning of film as an art form, a medium of human expression.

It is important to remember that the images in a film are two dimen-sional. The images on the screen are a theatrically contrived "world" that

**Working alone or
in small groups,
create or select
appropriate music for
a silent film segment.**

Your task in creating an appropriate musical soundtrack is to do one of the following: express the setting and the general mood of the visual images; intensify the drama and impact of the scene; or help to establish the character and give psychological insight.

First, decide what is going on in the segment. What is being expressed? How can music be used to reinforce that expression or to counter it in such a way as *to add a new dimension of meaning?*

Then "orchestrate" the segment. Create a live score using instruments or sounds at hand, or by selecting appropriate recorded sound. Vary the dynamics (louds and softs) and other musical elements to marry the music with the visual images. Try different types of music and discuss the emotional effect. Be prepared to present your interpretation to the class by performing the music or playing your recording.

Discuss and compare the effect of your musical choices and interpretations.

Now watch the segment with its original soundtrack and discuss the effect that the music achieves.

has been edited and spliced together. At first this world was silent. Although the phonograph had been invented by Edison in 1877, there was still no way to coordinate sound and film.

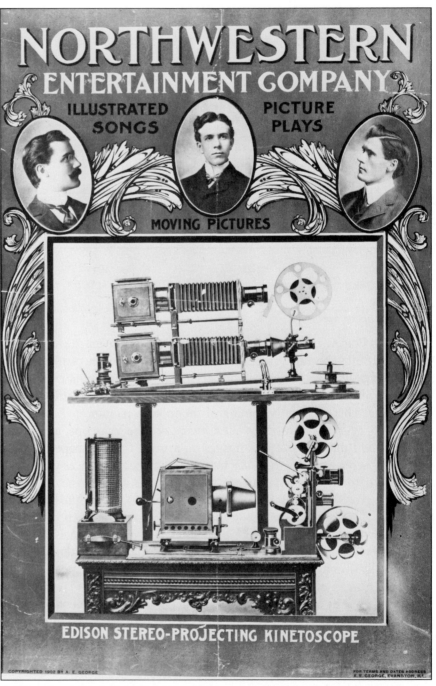

▲ This poster, dating from 1902, shows a later generation of the moving picture machine (also known as the Vitascope) that Thomas Edison (upper right) invented in 1896.

▼*Activity:* **Conjecture**

Where did the idea of using music in films come from?

Listen to the Overture from *A Midsummer Night's Dream* (1826) by Felix Mendelssohn (1809–1847). This was written as incidental music for the Shakespeare play. What is the function of this music when it is played prior to the theatrical performance?

Listen to the Overture from the musical *Mame* (1966) by Jerry Herman (b. 1933). What is the function of the overture in an opera or musical?

Incidental music and overtures had been in vogue long before the advent of films. Can you conjecture (guess, theorize) what influence they might have had on early filmmakers?

Music for Silent Films

There probably never was such a thing as a "silent" film. Long before films had soundtracks, they were accompanied by music. At first, the music was provided by a pianist or an organist in the theater who improvised a musical score on the spot. These musical performers had to watch the screen intently, size up the mood being portrayed on the screen, then quickly adjust the music accordingly. The trick was to marry the image with appropriate mood music. These performers had to have a large repertoire of music of many different moods at their fingertips.

In film, the visual image is dominant. Film takes advantage of the stronger sense of the eye over the ear. Because the visual image is dominant, the music is adjusted to go with it. The character of the music, its form, its length, and its loudness are all adjusted to fit the image. As early

◄ From the beginning, the silent films were accompanied by music. At first a pianist watched the film and played appropriate mood music to accompany the images. The music became increasingly important and elaborate until, in the 1920s, the large theaters in New York, Chicago, and Los Angeles accompanied the silent films with a live symphony orchestra of 80 to 100 musicians.

as 1909, the Edison Company introduced cue sheets to help the musicians plan appropriate music to go with the Edison films. The live music added an immediacy and life to the film that audiences found appealing.

In silent films, music served the practical purpose of covering the clatter of the movie projector, as well as the chatter of audiences and noise from outside the makeshift theaters. Later, the projectors were housed in soundproof booths so that the audience was not distracted by the mechanical noise. New theaters were soundproofed, and audiences became quieter and better behaved. The expressive function of music, far more than its practical value, assured its continued role in the development of the art of film.

Erno Rapée, a pioneer composer of scores for silent films during the 1920s, compiled a book of *Motion Picture Moods for Pianists and Organists* that was published in 1924. The portion of the page pictured here shows a piece he suggested as appropriate for the firefighting scenes that were so popular in silent films. While playing this music, the performer could scan the column along the side of the music to find music suitable to the next mood on the screen.

Hurry No. 2

Otto Langey

Prior to this book, the musicians had to have a vast repertoire of music in many different moods that they played by ear or had committed to memory. Otherwise they had to leaf frantically through a stack of musical scores with one hand while they improvised a transitional passage with the other. The real talent, of course, was being able to match the moods of the music with the visual images as the film went along. These musicians seldom had the opportunity to preview the film in advance, and films changed every few days. Rapée's book gave the musician over 200 themes organized in 52 moods.

▲ During the silent movie era, the Keystone Comedy Company produced a series of films featuring a bungling and inept squad of policemen known as Keystone Kops. Their slapstick comedy, crazy antics, and wild chases were accompanied by wild piano music that added to the humor and excitement of the moment.

▼*Activity:* **Discuss Music for Silent Films**

What was the role of music as it was used to accompany silent films?

Listen to "Hurry No. 2," a piano piece used to accompany fire fighting scenes in silent films, then discuss the following:

1. What makes this music appropriate for a fire fighting scene?
2. What might this music add to the silent visual images?
3. What was the role of music in these early film theaters?

In 1915, the orchestral score to American producer D. W. Griffith's silent film *The Birth of a Nation,* compiled by Joseph Breil and Griffith, showed the possibilities of the aural-visual partnership. Every sound was carefully matched to the visual image. Themes selected from operas and symphonies were combined with original music by Breil, including tom-tom beats that evoked Africa and transitions that connected the various themes. Single-handedly, this film established the symphony orchestra as the ideal sound in the picture palace. At the opening of the film in New York City, the orchestra consisted of 50 musicians.

As silent films became more popular during the 1920s, the live musical accompaniment became more elaborate. The two seemed to prosper together. Music became an important part of the art of film presentation, and as the presentation improved, audiences grew. By the mid-twenties, symphony orchestras of 90 to 100 musicians, along with a "Mighty Wurlitzer" organ, were being used in the large New York theaters to accompany the otherwise silent films. During this period, **scoring** film music—*composing music expressly for the film*—became the standard practice. The composer rather than the performer now assumed responsibility for marrying image with music.

▼Activity: *Find the Answers*

Watch the video excerpt from *Film Scores: The Music of the Movies,* and answer the following questions:

1. What does Bronislaw Kaper's music add to the scene in the film *The Stranger* (1946) in which Loretta Young climbs the tower?
2. Why was music added to silent films?
3. What makes motion pictures an art of many arts?

The silent motion picture brought a wholly new musical medium into existence. Although film music was new, it was an extension of a very old tradition. Dramatic presentations had often used "incidental" music at the start and during scene changes. (The term **incidental music** refers to *music that occurs in connection with, but is less important than, the drama it serves.*) This music established the general mood of the play, much as overtures and entr'acte music do.

There is evidence that Greek dramas were presented with musical interludes. Medieval religious dramas that related the biblical stories to audiences who were illiterate and, therefore, unable to read the scriptures, used music as a part of the storytelling. In the seventeenth century, Shakespeare's dramas were often accompanied by incidental music. Film music operates in much the same way. Like program music and music for opera and ballet, it is music in the service of telling, showing, and feeling.

The "Talkies"

Edison and other inventors worked many years to find a way to synchronize sound with the motion picture. While sound reproduction existed as a separate device, no way had been found to synchronize the sound with moving images. How could motion picture images and the sounds that went with them be recorded and reproduced together? That problem was mind-boggling.

The first attempt at synchronizing sound and image was accomplished through a phonographic machine called the Vitaphone. It was used to create the first talking film, *The Jazz Singer* (1927, Warner). Audiences were stunned to see Al Jolson actually singing, dancing, and speaking. His voice was synchronized exactly to his movements as he played the piano and sang. Here for the first time was an image of real life captured and immortalized. In "talking" films, the lifelike presence of sounds and dialogue helped to create a sense of realism. But the Vitaphone process took careful coordination during each showing. It was not a satisfactory solution.

The answer was the film **soundtrack**, *a strip along the film to the side of the visual image that contained visual representations of the sound* (an alternative to the grooves in a record or the electronic signals on a compact disk) that could be retranslated into sound by the mechanism in the motion picture projector.

◀ Al Jolson actually sang to his mother (played by Eugenie Besserer) in the first talking film, *The Jazz Singer*, in 1927. Images and sound were synchronized by the newly developed Vitaphone sound-on-disk system. Although the film contained only four talking or singing sequences, it was a smash hit, and people wanted more.

▶ The splendid atmospheric movie palaces that were built across America during the 1920s gave the art of the motion picture respectability. The Ohio Theater in Columbus, built in 1928 and meticulously restored, shows the Spanish Baroque-style opulence and craftsmanship that made going to the movies a fantasy. Designed by Thomas Lamb, it lives on today as a performing arts center.

When the soundtrack was invented in the late 1920s, there was no way to include musical background. It was several years before the soundtrack for speaking could be overlaid with continuous musical background. Therefore, the early sound films still had live music provided in the theater. At first, only the talk was recorded on the soundtrack—hence the name "talkies." By 1933, improvements in technology permitted the background music to be included on the soundtrack along with the voices and other sounds. Now music did not have to be used throughout the film as a way to fill the vast silence. It could be used when it was needed.

The Process

Certain steps must be followed when a composer creates music for a film. First, the composer views the film after it has been edited and is considered to be in its final form or "cut." Then there is a discussion with the producer and director to **spot** the music: that is, *to determine which scenes should have music.* This may take several screenings. Good film music is used sparingly.

Since a film is usually near completion at the time it is scored, there is very limited time for a composer to complete the scoring. Composers generally view all the sequences in a film that are to be scored to get a feel for them before they begin sketching musical ideas. Film composers must write rapidly. They must be versatile in expressing a range of moods. Amazingly, film composer Max Steiner wrote the three hours and 45 minutes of original music for *Gone With the Wind* (1939, MGM/UA), plus the score to another film, and supervised the recording of both, all within the space of four weeks.

After the film has been scored, the music is recorded while the conductor watches the filmed sequence. This assures that the music will be synchronized with the images as the composer intended. Usually, the composer conducts the recording session. The music is recorded on magnetic track or **mag track** that is *the same as 35mm film, except that it is coated with an oxide surface like sound tape.* Mag track has four sprocket holes per frame like optical film so that it moves at exactly the same rate of speed— 24 frames per second.

The final step in the process is **dubbing**, *putting all the elements of sound—dialogue, sound effects, and music—onto one soundtrack.* During this process, the sound level of the music is adjusted to the other sounds. Sometimes in the dubbing process some music is almost lost, because it is treated as mere background. Film music should be a carefully crafted element that is integral to the total artistic statement of the picture. It is an important part of the whole.

Adding to the Meaning

Composers of film music must also know their craft and be able to come up with inventive musical solutions. Film composer Ernest Gold says that good film scoring "is not a duplication of what is seen." The music must put a quality in the picture that was not there before. He gives this illustration: A man is refused a job and walks back to his apartment in a New York slum. You see his despair. You know what has happened, but how does he feel? The music could play to his emotion, conveying the feeling of despair. Far better, Gold says, the composer could play rock 'n' roll on a radio in one of the apartments the man passes. In this way the music comments on the indifference of the neighbors to his plight. That solution is more powerful, more telling. It is also more imaginative. It goes beyond merely copying what is seen.

Why Music in Films?

Like the settings, acting, make-up, costumes, lighting, camera work, and editing, film music is one element of the storytelling process. In both musical theater and films, music supports and reinforces the dramatic action. However, there is a basic difference between music as it is used to tell a story in musical theater and music as it is used as "background" in films. The difference is the less dominant role music usually plays in films, but to call all film music "background music" is misleading. True, film music serves the visual event, but it is not always subservient to it. At times it may take over as the primary focus. At other times, it is not supposed to distract the viewer or draw undue attention to itself. This does not mean that viewers should close their ears to the music. Although the music is often supportive and not dominant, hearing the music and understanding its function can help the viewer to react to it and get its message.

In film, music adds feeling to the action. It reinforces and enhances the pictorial mood, helping audiences to become more emotionally involved in what they are seeing. If it is right, that is, if it is well-married to the image, music wins us over. It helps us accept the fantasy of what is playing before us, in a word, to *dream*. It makes the two-dimensional facsimile of reality on the screen appear more believable. Even visions and flashbacks—interruptions in the continuity of a story to portray some inner thought or earlier episode—are accepted as real, although we know that this is not the case in actual life.

Like easy listening music on a car radio or in a shopping mall, the background music in a film creates an environment. Its effect can be hypnotic. It can tie the visual and aural senses together in one state. It can help make the moving images expressive and, therefore, artful. The meaning of music, however, depends on cultural conditioning. It is possible, therefore, that the musical background of an American film with American music might have to be altered if the film were, say, translated into Chinese or vice versa.

A Film Composer Speaks

by Aaron Copland, American composer

The next time you settle yourself comfortably into a seat at the neighborhood picture house don't forget to take off your ear-muffs. . . . Millions of moviegoers take the musical accompaniment to a dramatic film so much for granted that five minutes after the termination of a picture they couldn't tell you whether they had heard music or not. . . . But it's the spectator, so absorbed in the dramatic action that he fails to take in the background music, who wants to know whether he is missing anything. The answer is bound up with the degree of your general musical perception. It is the degree to which you are aurally minded that will determine how much pleasure you may derive by absorbing the background musical accompaniment as an integral part of the combined impression made by the film.

◄ The film *Amadeus* (1984), winner of eight Academy Awards, featured the life and music of Wolfgang Amadeus Mozart. Much of the music in this film is on-screen. Here Mozart, played by Tom Hulce, conducts a performance of one of his works for the king of Austria and members of the court.

The Purposes

Film music serves a number of purposes. In a musical film, it is a central part of the storytelling. In *Saturday Night Fever* (1977, Paramount), for example, John Travolta and Karen Gorney dance to music that is an integral part of the visual telling of the story. Similarly, the film *Amadeus* (1984, Thorn EMI), which relates the crippling rivalry between composers Antonio Salieri and Wolfgang Amadeus Mozart, has a considerable amount of music as part of the plot and dramatic action.

In most films, however, music assumes a less prominent role. It may be purely **background music**—meaning not that it is unimportant, but that it is *off the screen*. Then, too, it may be a part of the action on the screen, such as the music that is playing on a car radio while a character is driving. In these films music serves three main purposes: to establish mood, to enhance the drama, and to give the film continuity.

Music Establishes the Basic Mood

More, perhaps, than any of the other film elements, music points out clearly the time and place and the feeling of what the story is about. Music accomplishes this by conveying a particular mood. Knowing that music can evoke its time and culture, film composers deliberately use this capacity to suggest, say, Elizabethan England, or America in the 1920s.

Music also evokes the spirit of the picture. It shows an audience the essence of what the film is—its heart. It may do this by announcing the film's essential theme—majestic, tragic, comic, heartfelt, homespun, frightening, religious, or so on. It works in much the same way as an overture in a musical or incidental music in a play. Music reassures the audience that they are in tune with the images, that they are getting the message.

▼*Activity:* **Answer with Your Ears**

Determine the basic mood and spirit of the film by listening to the music that opens it (without the visual images).

You will hear musical examples that are used in the opening of a motion picture to set the mood of the film. In each case, try to characterize the music with descriptive words selected from the following list (or think up your own):

happy	Roman Empire	horns
serious	mid-1700s	out-of-tune piano
urgent	late 1800s	orchestral
majestic	the future	chimes
exciting	lively	harpsichord
lofty	heroic	religious
dramatic	comic	spacious
stately	romantic	

Now watch the opening of the film. How correct were your choices? How well does the music support and enhance the visual image?

Music Enhances the Drama

If music can establish the general setting and mood of the film, it can also enhance the drama. In a mystery, music can add to the suspense. In a story that tugs at the heart-strings, music can add to the emotional intensity, and in a comedy, music can add a lighthearted touch.

Music also enhances the drama in three quite specific ways. Used well, it helps establish character, it gives psychological insight that conveys the intent of a particular character or the meaning of an event, and it intensifies the drama and adds to the impact.

Music helps establish character. By adding an aura of feeling around a player, music can reveal the nature of that person, much as it does in musical theater. It can suggest the affection of one character for another, even if they do not actually embrace on the screen. It can also convey what is going on in the mind of a character, even though it may not show on the face.

Music helps the viewer attach certain emotions to people and events as they recur throughout a film story. Like the "hook" that organizes a pop tune, or the melodic motive that recurs and gives coherence to most classical music, musical themes in film are repeated to recall important associations. When such themes recur, they are like memory asserting itself. Themes are reminiscent. They help us remember what has happened earlier in the film. By attaching the theme to a character, situation, or object when it is introduced, we tend to set up an association that the theme recalls when it is replayed.

Some films—*Superman* and *Gone With the Wind* are good examples—have a central musical theme that is attached to a character and follows that person throughout. In his score for *Superman* (1978, Warner), composer John Williams created a main title theme that we immediately identify with the hero:

Similarly, the "Tara" theme by composer Max Steiner in *Gone With the Wind* establishes Scarlett's love for the land and the strength that she derives from it. Steiner gave this theme many different orchestrations and tempos in the film to convey Scarlett's different moods. The film is based on Margaret Mitchell's novel about life in the South during the American Civil War.

▼ *Activity:* **Judge**

What qualities make the theme music right to represent Superman and Scarlett?

A. Listen to the main title theme composer John Williams created for *Superman* and write down qualities of the (1) melody, (2) rhythm, and (3) orchestration that convey the idea of Superman. Is this melody (above) *conjunct* (moving from one scale degree to the next) or *disjunct* (moving by intervals larger than a second)?

Try chanting this rhythm while you tap the steady beat:

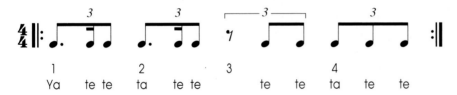

B. How does Scarlett O'Hara's music in the film *Gone With the Wind* convey her character and mood?

When Scarlett (Vivien Leigh) returns to the plantation to find it in shambles, the "Tara" theme conveys her feelings. What does it tell us and how?

At the end of the film, Scarlett's child has died and her husband Rhett Butler (Clark Gable) has left her. She realizes too late that she loves him. Again the "Tara" theme enters to tell us how she reacts. What does it tell us and how?

Compare: How does Scarlett's music compare with Superman's? What are the differences that make each theme work? Are there any similarities?

Music gives psychological insight. As viewers of a film, we generally accept the unreality of film background music. We seldom ask where the background music is coming from. Viewers accept the music on a psychological level. It is part of the unreality that puts us in the frame of mind to accept the fantasy of what we are viewing. Music adds to the

▶ Superman, played by Christopher Reeve, uses his heat vision in the 1978 film about this famed comic-book hero. The music in this film composed by John Williams enhances the drama by telling the audience how to react emotionally to what is on the screen.

psychological impact, whether it is offscreen (background) or is a part of the on-screen action. In either case it functions to complement the action and reinforce its emotional intent.

In *Platoon* (1986, Hemdale), Oliver Stone's film about the Vietnam War, *Adagio for Strings* by American composer Samuel Barber (1910–1981) is used as background music in a number of scenes. The music is particularly appropriate for the scene in which American soldiers enter a Vietnamese village, interrogate the villagers, and burn their houses. Scored for stringed instruments, the music gives a heart-wrenching feeling of sadness. There is a notable use of dissonance in this music—tones that conflict and are close, creating a sense of anguish and tension.

▼ Activity: *Answer and Perform*

What qualities in this music make it work well with this scene?

The scene is the burning of the village from *Platoon*, Oliver Stone's film about the Vietnam War. The music is American composer Samuel Barber's *Adagio for Strings*, which he composed in 1938.

As you listen, describe on paper the characteristics of this preexistent music that make it a good choice as background for this scene. Discuss the emotional intent.

Learn to sing this melody (right) expressively using the syllable *oo. Cantando* (kahn-TAHN-do) means to sing in a smooth and flowing manner. Is this melody conjunct or disjunct?

How does dissonance in this work add to the emotional effect?

Profile

Samuel Barber
American Composer
1910–1981

SAMUEL BARBER

American composer Samuel Barber was born in West Chester, Pennsylvania in 1910, and displayed musical talent at a very early age. He entered the Curtis Institute of Music in Philadelphia in 1924 at the age of 14 and graduated in 1932. During his eight years at Curtis, he received a thorough education in many aspects of music, but it was Barber's skill as a composer that stood out. Barber was awarded many prizes, including the Prix de Rome in 1935, which allowed him to compose at the American Academy in Rome. He also received the Pulitzer Prize in 1958 for his opera *Vanessa* and again in 1963 for his *Piano Concerto.* Among the influential conductors who introduced his works was Arturo Toscanini who gave the first performance of the *Adagio for Strings*, an orchestral transcription Barber made of the second movement of his *String Quartet.*

While other twentieth-century composers were experimenting with alternatives to the traditional tonal system, Barber found success with a lyric and dramatic style based upon harmony from the late nineteenth century. Like Johannes Brahms, Barber did not create any new style or technique. Instead, he wrote beautiful pieces that bore his own personal style. "I write what I feel," he stated. "It is said that I have no style at all but that doesn't matter. I just go on doing my thing. I believe this takes a certain courage." Some of his popular works include *Dover Beach, Prayers of Kierkegaard,* and *Knoxville: Summer of 1915.*

Adagio for Strings, Op. 11

Samuel Barber

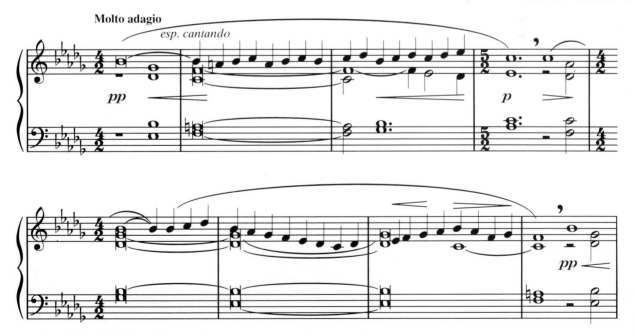

Music is also used to tell viewers what is going on inside a character—what a character is thinking and feeling. As in real life, our inner thoughts are not always revealed by our facial expression or actions. We may be looking one way but thinking something quite different. Music can let the viewer inside the mind of a character to see and feel the inner truth. In this way, too, it gives psychological insight.

The film *A Place in the Sun* (1952, Paramount) tells the story of George Eastman (played by Montgomery Clift), a poor boy driven by the lure of wealth to reach for a more glamorous life. He falls in love simultaneously with Alice Trip (Shelley Winters), a factory girl, and with Angela Vickers (Elizabeth Taylor), a wealthy socialite. When his relationship with the factory girl threatens to stop him from becoming a rich and respected gentleman, he finds himself in a difficult predicament.

In the climactic scene, George is called away from his visit at Angela's summer home on the lake by Alice who threatens to "tell all" if he doesn't marry her. She is carrying his child. Reluctantly, he meets her at the depot. The office of the Justice of the Peace is closed because it is Labor Day. George suggests they make the best of it and head for the lodge on the lake. Halfway there, he stops the car and rents a boat to row the rest of the way. George knows that Alice cannot swim. Composer Franz Waxman's music tells us what George is thinking:

Music	*Action*
The music is tranquil.	They float through the silent wilderness.
The sound of a loon.	Signal of darkness.
The music thumps.	George's heartbeat. He stares at Alice, threateningly. She speaks of the possibilities of their life together. "Only there's going to be more than two of us, isn't there?" she asks.
The music swells to climactic chords.	George has thoughts about Alice. Then he becomes sorry he has treated her badly. "I'm not afraid of being poor," Alice says.
The music is anguished, tense.	"Stop it!" he yells. "Do you wish that I was dead?" she asks. "No, I didn't. Leave me alone." "Poor George, I know it isn't easy. I shouldn't have said that," she says

and stands up in the back of the boat to move up toward him. George shouts a warning, but it is too late. The boat capsizes.

The music soars with crashing chords.

Tragedy has struck.

Sometimes music is a deliberate part of the action on the screen. The characters might be in a night club, for example, while a singer is entertaining. Such **source music**, that is, *music that comes from a visible source such as a radio or a dance band,* also creates mood for the scene. Source music (on-screen), like background music (off-screen), can also reveal what is going on in the mind of a character on camera.

In the film *The Year of Living Dangerously* (1982, MGM), a drama of explosive passions and conflict set in Indonesia, the photographer Billy Quan (Linda Hunt) plays Richard Strauss's song "September" from the *Four Last Songs* (*Vier letzte Lieder,* 1949) on the phonograph for the newsman Gary Hamilton (Mel Gibson). "Listen to this, guy," Billy says very simply. When the romantic music floods over him, Gary's eyes wander the walls looking at all of Billy's photographs. He spots Jill, and the camera zooms in. The music alone reveals his unspoken thoughts.

▼*Activity:* **Compare**

How do George's off-screen music in *A Place in the Sun* and Gary's on-screen music in *The Year of Living Dangerously* compare in their effectiveness in telling us what these men are thinking?

Watch the climactic scene from the film *A Place in the Sun* in which Alice drowns, first with no sound, then with the sound. How does the music let us know what is going on in George's mind?

In the film, *The Year of Living Dangerously,* watch the scene in which Billy plays music for Gary, and the camera zooms in as he spots Jill's photograph on the wall. What does the music tell you that Gary feels about Jill?

Is this source music (on-screen) as effective as George's background music (off-screen)?

Music intensifies the drama. Music sets us up for the action and deepens our emotional involvement. It adds to the impact of dramatic events. It may foreshadow a sinister event by announcing a threatening mood. It may increase our excitement by helping to drive the pace of the action forward. It may give an emotional charge to what is happening. In these ways, music can trigger our anticipation, heighten our sense of suspense, urge our emotional reaction, and strengthen the climactic moments.

Cooperative Learning

Perform

To what effect does composer Giorgio Moroder use the ostinato pattern in the opening of the film *Midnight Express*?

Working in small groups, learn to perform the ostinato pattern (right).

Discussion: What makes the ostinato pattern appropriate for a chase? What does it suggest about life in prison?

In the "chase" that opens the film *Midnight Express* (1978, Columbia), composer Giorgio Moroder uses this ostinato pattern almost throughout:

An offbeat drum gives urgency and added character to this largely electronic score. This is the true story of a 22-year-old American named Billy Hayes who was subjected to the horrors of a Turkish prison during a lengthy imprisonment, beyond the power of the U.S. government or his parents. Hayes not only survived, but he also triumphed.

▲ The burning of Atlanta and the flight of Scarlett O'Hara and Rhett Butler is one of many memorable scenes in the American film classic *Gone With the Wind* (1939), set during the Civil War. In his musical score, composer Max Steiner uses a symphony orchestra to intensify the emotions and give the film a sense of continuity.

Music Gives a Film Continuity

Music is often used to give a film coherence, a sense that it is one continuous, unified flow of action from beginning to end. This quality of connectedness between the beginning, the middle, and the end is conveyed partly by the consistency in the style of music. The return of the opening theme at the end of the film is a commonly used device to tie the film into one statement. In *High Noon* (1952, Republic), for example, the return of the tom-tom at the end of the film ties the end to the beginning. The "Tara" theme in *Gone With the Wind* at the beginning and end is another example. A consistency in the style of the music gives the film a feeling that it is cut from one piece of cloth. At the end of a film, music can also give a sense of finality. We know it is over by the event that is pictured and also by the conclusion that the music reaches.

▼*Activity:* **Challenge**

How does film composer Bernard Herrmann use music to create suspense and horror?

Watch the film *Psycho* (1960, Universal) from beginning to end. While you are watching, write brief descriptions about the music that you hear during the following scenes:

1. "Prelude"—The opening with the titles.
2. "Temptation"—The money is on the bed, and Marion wonders if she should take it to the bank or not.
3. "Flight"—Marion is driving away and is seen by her boss.
4. "The Rainstorm"—Marion hears voices, then sees the lights of the Bates Motel
5. "The Madhouse"—Norman says, "You mean a madhouse?"
6. "The Peephole"—Norman watches Marion through the wall.
7. "Finale"—the famous murder scene in the shower. Later, face-to-face with the killer (Norman dressed as his mother).
8. The chord at the end.

How does the music establish a sense of continuity and coherence?

Summary

In films, music adds to the meaning of the visual image in several important ways. The mood of the music helps to establish the spirit of the film. By touching our feelings, music enhances the dramatic effect of a film by sharpening character, giving us psychological insight, and intensifying our emotional reactions. Music also gives a film continuity, making us feel that the film is one statement from beginning to end.

Music adds to a film's meaning and impact. It is one of the ways that a film conveys its message. Change the music, and we alter that meaning and impact. Music does this in spite of the fact that, alone, it is not as specific as dialogue in what it says. It is one of the expressive forces that make the cinematic image a commanding storytelling medium.

Apply What You Have Learned
Chapters 19 and 20

Make a list of the similarities and differences between the Broadway musical and opera. To discover what is alike and different about these musical forms, compare what you have learned about the Broadway musical *Carousel* with what you have learned about the opera *Carmen*.

For example, one similarity is that both generally include dance. One difference is that the Broadway musical is usually performed in a theater, while an opera generally requires a larger stage, usually an opera house. How many other similarities and differences can you find?

▲ Today, the differences in style between a musical and an opera are becoming less distinct. In the musical *Sunday in the Park with George*, for example, American composer Stephen Sondheim dispenses with spoken dialogue, preferring to set the text to continuous music throughout as in grand opera. Look at the painting on page 313. This work, executed during 1884–1886 by pointillist Georges Seurat, is a good example of how one type of fine art influences another. Notice how well the set designer captured the detail and the feeling of Seurat's piece.

Apply What You Have Learned
Chapter 21

Critique the music and the roles it plays in the film of your choice.

Watch the entire film, then address the following questions:

What is the basic style of the music?

What is the source or sources of musical timbres in the film—vocal, instrumental, electronic, or a combination? (Identify the voices and instruments that are used.)

Is the music primarily background (offscreen) or source (onscreen) music, or is there some of both? (Give examples by describing specific scenes.)

Write an analysis of how music is used, or not used, in each of the following basic roles:

1. To establish the basic mood of the film
2. To enhance the drama
   a. Establish character
   b. Give psychological insight
   c. Intensify the drama
3. To give the film continuity

Is the music appropriate and effective? Why or why not?

▼ The Indiana Jones films are a good illustration of how musical themes for the movies often become better known than the films for which they were written. Below, Harrison Ford investigates a crypt in *Indiana Jones and the Last Crusade.* Can you name any other musical themes from the movies or television that you recognize almost immediately?

Music!...
To Characterize
The Age

~

Chapter 22
Music of Our Generation

Chapter 23
Music of Previous Generations

Chapter 24
Jazz

Music of Our Generation

Objectives

By completing this chapter, you will:

- Become knowledgeable about the musical characteristics of some of today's popular and classical styles.
- Discover how the increasing visualization, urbanization, and globalization of culture affect current musical trends.
- Understand how the addition of visual elements can alter your musical perceptions.
- Become acquainted with the styles of New Romanticism and minimalism.
- View music as a reflection of its time and its society.

Musical Terms

minimalism
New Age
New Romanticism
program music

*T*oday's music reflects today's people. Our music mirrors our time. Social trends have a direct bearing on the music we create and the music we embrace. Musical creation is not haphazard. It relates to the way we think and the way we live. As our ways of thinking and working have changed, so has our music. The music of our generation directly reflects the trends of contemporary civilization. Like the world in which we live, music has become more visual, urban, and global. Our music reinforces, interprets, and clarifies these trends. When viewed from this larger perspective, we can better understand the music of today.

Culture as More Visual

Since the advent of motion pictures and television, especially the latter, people have become more visually oriented. We now take in enormous quantities of information through our eyes (often in combination with our ears). Today, the old saying "seeing is believing" has flooded our world with advertising designed to captivate the eye. Prior to television, radio dramas forced listeners to envision the characters and scenery from clues in the script. People created worlds in their imagination. They added their own reality to the story by completing the missing pieces. In contrast, television dramas create the settings, the costumes, and the characters for the eyes so that the viewer does not have to invent them. Because all the details are provided, our imagination is not called into play. It is the difference between reading a novel and seeing a motion picture.

Music Videos

Popular music is becoming increasingly visual. Music videos became popular in the United States in 1981 as a way to advertise popular artists and their new releases. These videos are round-the-clock commercials that begin and end with product information, including the name of the artist and album. Music videos soon became art forms in and of themselves and established a market of their own. Today, cable television's MTV literally defines youth culture. These videos not only advertise a new CD but also compete with it. Young people can buy either the audio or video version of any release.

PROJECT

Analyze Music Videos

Watch at least three different music videos on either broadcast or video tape. Write down the name of the artist and the title of the song and categorize the video according to its basic type: performance, dance, story, or fantasy. Then jot down all the aspects of each video that show imagination. Finally, try to determine how these visual features affect the musical impact of the song. Bring your completed list to class as preparation for a discussion of musical videos with your classmates.

▶ At its start during the early 1970s, the American rock group Aerosmith was criticized for imitating the Rolling Stones, but original material created mostly by Steve Tyler (vocals) and Joe Perry (guitar) soon made their early albums go platinum by selling one million copies. In the late 1970s, the band lost two of its members, but the original group was later reformed and made a triumphant comeback in 1987 on tour with their new album *Permanent Vacation.*

This new world of music visualization has altered our perceptions. What we see has a powerful impact on how we think about and respond to a song. The usual music video averages about four minutes in length, the standard for a popular song. These videos convey information that we do not get by hearing a recording of the same work. When we listen to music treated visually, we accept someone else's imagination in place of our own. We then associate these visual images with the sound whenever we hear it. Although listening to a recording can stimulate our imagination, watching a music video tends to have the opposite effect. The visual interpretation becomes indelible, obliterating any need for us to exercise our own imagination. Now, popular artists have to give as much attention to the camera as they do the microphone.

One of the most widely recognized and influential early music videos was Michael Jackson's *Thriller* from his 1983 record album of the same name. This video helped to set a standard for popular music videos for the remainder of the decade. Four main types of music videos were developed:

- Performance videos that present the artist in the format of a concert.
- Dance videos that present the music largely in a dance format.
- Story videos that may or may not have a direct relationship with the lyrics.
- Fantasy videos that rely heavily on computerized manipulation of visual images that may or may not relate to the music.

▼*Activity:* **Imagine**

To what extent do visual images change our perception of a musical composition?

Listen carefully to a musical composition and imagine what visual images you might use if you were to produce a music video of this performance. Which of the four main types of music videos would be appropriate here? Will your visuals interpret the lyrics? To what extent will you feature the performer?

Working with other students, create a "storyboard" for your video—a plan for how the music and visual elements will mesh. Outline your concept in two columns with music cues (or lyrics) on the left and visual images on the right.

Compare the concept your video design team has developed with other concepts developed in your class. Finally, view the commercial video of this song. How closely does it match your ideas?

Today, concerts of pop music often add a video dimension. On their world tours, rock groups such as Ireland's U2 create an audiovisual experience for their stadium audiences. Complex technology comprising video walls, mega screens, and random satellite transmissions overlays the live audio elements with images and text. Just as background music in films enhances the visual images, background images in stadium concerts illuminate the music, interpreting it and extending its meaning. The result is rock theater, a multimedia extravaganza. Bassist Adam Clayton says, "There is a video generation out there now and video is a part of music whether you like it or not."

Culture As More Urban

During the twentieth century, increasing numbers of people have moved into urban and suburban environments. Because large numbers of people live so close together, a new lifestyle has developed. It is intense, impersonal (anonymous), complex, and varied. Compared to the simple life in rural areas or in small towns, urban living provides more choices. There are more options not just because of different people's interests but also because there are sufficient numbers of people to support a variety of enterprises. These alternatives are necessary in order to serve a varied population. The result is a vibrant and exciting culture but also one that is sometimes divisive and unruly. Cities offer people operatic, symphonic, choral, and chamber music, but they also serve many other musical tastes.

Urbanization has produced its own music. There are about as many different kinds of music as there are distinguishable groups of people. Music has always served specialized audiences, but now the social layers have multiplied, and musical styles address the subdivisions of society by age, ethnicity, class, and education. Popular music, especially, comprises a broad mix of different genres. Just as there are frictions between elements within the society, there are sometimes frictions between their favored types of music.

Rhythm and Blues

In the 1950s and 1960s the blues shed some of their rural and country roots to enter the mainstream of musical expression. They were refurbished in more sophisticated, urban clothing—elaborate arrangements and forms, more instruments and voices, a greater variety of rhythms, and sometimes more elaborate improvisations. Rhythm and blues, or R & B, transformed the blues to appeal to a wider audience. This was the popular music of African Americans that evolved into "soul" music in the 1970s. R & B is ensemble music, generally with a raw, sometimes shouted, vocal melody and a strong offbeat rhythmic drive supplied by a rhythm section consisting of a drum set, bass, keyboard, and/or electric guitar. Other instruments, sometimes including a hard-edged tenor saxophone and backup vocalists, support the harmony and supply riffs and responsive fillers. The lyrics, too, were liberated, sometimes relating to traditional blues subject matter, but more often following the prevailing "pop" style. R & B singers moaned and groaned, sighed and cried.

▶ American guitarist, vocalist, and composer B. B. King (left) is a master of the blues in all its applications— urban, rural, country, rock, and pop. His form of R&B has influenced many other musicians. Here he performs with the late guitarist Stevie Ray Vaughn (c. 1956–1990). King has recorded more than 55 albums and won five Grammy Awards.

B. B. King (b. 1925) is one of the giants of R & B. King, who was born on a cotton plantation in the Mississippi Delta, acquired the initials "B. B." from his billing on a Memphis radio station as the "Blues Boy from Beale Street." King has taken the blues around the world believing passionately that this music reflects the history of black Americans—not only the pain and misery, but also the love and triumphs. He sings in a natural "pop" voice and uses his guitar ("Lucille") to fill in the breathing spaces in each line of the lyrics, trading back and forth between the emotional vocal and the improvised wailing instrumental response. His blues style has commanded a substantial interracial following.

▼Activity: *Analyze*

How were the traditional blues urbanized?

Listen to "Go On" performed by B. B. King and determine what makes this music different from traditional blues.

Discuss such matters as:

- The instruments and voices that are used.
- The form of the piece.
- The rhyme scheme. (You will recall that the rhyme scheme in the blues is a simple couplet in which the first line is repeated.)
- What makes it more sophisticated than a traditional blues?
- What keeps it related to blues?

Rock

After the Second World War, the migration of southern blacks to northern cities brought a new musical influence to the urban culture. The younger generation was no longer entranced by the sweetness of Tin Pan Alley songs or the polished singing of Frank Sinatra and Perry Como. The younger generation was attracted to rhythm and blues and began to tune in to it on the radio. These lyrics were earthier and so was the singing. There was more energy in the rhythm, induced by heavy accents on the upbeats (2 and 4). Rock 'n' roll emerged full-blown in 1955 with Bill Haley's recording of "Rock Around the Clock," even though the name rock 'n' roll had been coined by disc jockey Alan Freed in 1951.

During the 1960s this early style of rock 'n' roll dominated the popular music scene around the world and spawned many offshoots. It became increasingly electrified and amplified. The electric guitar became the central instrument. Soon many styles were encompassed under the banner "rock," including rockabilly, hard rock, soul-rock, punk, heavy metal, new wave, syntho-rock, jazz-rock fusion, and so on. Rock music has now become so mainstream that some classical composers are weaving elements of it into their symphonic works, and some rock composers have taken to writing symphonically. This kind of musical mating or "crossover" can

► After the breakup of the Beatles, English composer, singer, and bass player, Paul McCartney, shown here at the drums, formed his own group, Wings, in 1971. Just as the Beatles were pioneers in bringing classical elements into rock, McCartney has continued to forge new musical territory, moving away from hard rock, particularly on his solo albums. A versatile musician, he composed the classically styled *Liverpool Oratorio* in 1991.

Cooperative Learning

Listen and Perform

How authentically can you perform an original rap?

To prepare yourself for creating your own rap, listen to the rap tune "Know How" by Young M. C. and answer these questions:

1. What is the basic purpose of this rap?
2. Who is the intended audience for this rap?
3. Was this rap written or improvised?
4. How often do the words rhyme throughout most of the piece?
5. What is this rap about?

Working in small groups, recite the rap lyrics written by Kenneth Banks that your teacher will distribute. Figure out how the rhythm of the words might go. Then, using instruments of your choice, create a rap accompaniment for your performance. Compare interpretations with your classmates.

debase both styles, or it can result in something quite fresh. You will have the opportunity to explore the blending of different styles in Chapter 26.

Rock music is now in its fourth decade. It suffers at times from copycat musicians who repeat by formula what others have invented before them. Is this a signal that rock 'n' roll is dying? Music critic Greil Marcus says that as a cultural force, rock music "no longer seems to mean anything." Still, it commands new audiences among this generation who find in it honest reflections—some disconcerting, some reassuring—of the world around them. Rock music will be explored further in Chapter 25.

Rap

Urban African-American youth have invented their own music. One example is rap, an energetic and talky form of accompanied "song" that reports on the harsh realities of urban America. Rap music gives voice to disenfranchised black youth—those whom society has seemingly left by the wayside. Some rap lyrics have been attacked as obscene, bigoted, and socially irresponsible. In 1990, the 2 Live Crew's *As Nasty as They Wanna Be* became the first piece of recorded music to be declared obscene in a U.S. District Court. This led to the arrest of several record retailers and members of the group. It also fueled the controversy over labeling albums that contain explicit lyrics.

Not all rap lyrics are socially irresponsible. Kris Parker, better known as KRS-One (meaning "Knowledge Reigns Supreme Over Nearly Everyone"), creates raps that argue against injustice, racism, drugs, and police brutality and at the same time chide his audience to overcome everyday obstacles and give their attention to education. In a *Washington Post* interview, Parker said, "Every generation comes along and brings with it *its* music, and this is the music of this newest generation."

Rap is the equivalent of a musical newspaper. It can be improvised but often is not. It is aggressive, often rebellious, music with confrontational lyrics that address the hard, street-smart realities of life in urban ghettos. In its lyrics, rap is highly visual, presenting vivid graphic images. The language is the vernacular of ordinary people.

◀ Rap artists such as Kris Parker (left), better known as KRS-1, consider their work to be poetry. Many of them write the poems first, then assemble the music around the words. Parker says, "Poetry is the language of the imagination." Rap artistry often addresses the moral dilemmas faced by today's youth.

Country and Western

Not all of today's music targets a youthful audience. From its roots in the folk tradition and its early designation as "hillbilly" music, American country and western music has grown into a well-established genre as popular with city dwellers, or more so, as it is with country folk. The simplicity of the music and the homespun lyrics may hold special appeal to the urban population because they are nostalgic reminders of a simpler lifestyle for which many city people yearn. Country and western lyrics pose basic questions and clear-cut solutions. The "twang" of the vocal color and the guitar accompaniment immediately define the style. Some of the best guitar players of all types are in the field of country music, but the instrument that most characterizes the style is the pedal steel (or Hawaiian) guitar. The music brings us back to our rural roots and the time when life was not so complex and perplexing.

► Country singer Reba McEntire sings her Oscar-nominated song, "I'm Checkin' Out" at the Academy Awards in 1991. Country music has now entered the mainstream, commanding a national audience and a following around the world.

▼Activity: *Answer with Your Ears*

What are the characteristics that make country and western music so appealing?

Listen to the singer on the audio example and take notes to answer the following questions:

1. What tells you that this is a country and western song?
2. Which of the three types of love song is this (lost love, longing for love, or celebration of love)? What is it about?
3. Can you describe the vocal style?
4. What instruments do you hear?
5. How do you think this music is used?

Salsa

Today's ethnic urban mix of people has embraced a wide variety of musical styles, many of which derive from international sources. Some of these styles are the result of a fusion of different ethnic elements. Reggae, for example, is a Jamaican popular music infused with elements of rock 'n' roll and calypso. Similarly, salsa is a dance music of Cuban origin that borrows rhythms, harmonies, and improvisatory elements from jazz and from Puerto Rican and South American music. In salsa, the fusion of these components has produced a Latin jazz sound that is distinctive in itself. The form is sectional, and the polyrhythms give the music a particularly "catchy" feeling that made it popular in New York and Miami night clubs. The following layered Latin rhythms can be heard in "Descarga—Yema Ya," an example of this music:

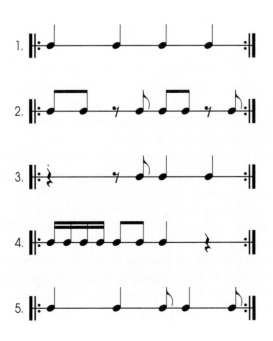

▼*Activity:* **Identify the Difference**

Can you identify the musical characteristics of "Descarga—Yema Ya" that are Latin in style and those that derive from jazz?

Perform the layered Latin-style rhythmic patterns on page 435. Decide which percussion instruments you think sound the best on each rhythmic pattern. Perform all the patterns together.

Follow the musical events in "Descarga—Yema Ya." Check next to each whether the influence is from Latin music, jazz, or both. Check which of the events exhibit organized form and which exhibit free form. Which of the events is the longest?

Which events could be accompanied by the Latin-style rhythmic patterns you learned? Why is this urban music?

Culture As More Global

There seem to be as many styles of urban music as there are different people living in our cities. The advancements in communications worldwide have created the first human inklings of a global community.

The first music to reach this global audience, accessible within most cultures, is American pop. Prior to electronic reproduction, music was confined to specific locales and societies. For better or worse, if there is a common denominator of world taste, American popular music seems to be it. Electronic communication has made the commercial reach of this music literally stretch around the world. The range of our pop styles seems to offer something to everybody. Perhaps the international makeup of American culture makes our music speak with a universal voice.

The human race appears to be moving in two conflicting directions at the same time. On the one hand, we are seeing ourselves as one gigantic family on a fragile planet, all dependent on each other for survival. On the other hand, we are recognizing and asserting our tribal differences. While we are becoming more interdependent and universally minded on some matters, we are proclaiming our independence and singularity on others. These trends are two sides of the same coin. We balance our increasing collectivity with an assertion of individuality. As the world grows ever more democratized, differences are recognized.

Music is also universal and singular. Styles serve the global audience as well as the tastes of individual audiences. The arts are eclectic: they often draw their inspiration from a variety of sources and serve many tastes and interests. There is a definite trend to democratize music so that it has the widest possible appeal and is accessible to all people. Multiple influences are combined to create new styles that speak to new audiences.

One of the recent trends in popular music is a revival of *a cappella* singing. The group Take 6, for example, sings complex jazzy arrangements with a passion usually reserved for gospel music. These six men vary their sound with intricate rhythms, up-tempo vocal acrobatics, fresh harmonies,

▲ The picture above was taken during the Moscow Peace Festival in 1989. Music has long been a force for change. In recent years, musicians around the world have made an effort to raise the moral consciousness of society through concerts, albums, and music videos.

a solid bass, and percussive vocal effects. Bobby McFerrin sometimes sings all the parts of his songs himself, over-recording them to create the sound of an instrumental accompaniment. One of the best-known international a cappella groups is Ladysmith Black Mambazo, but there are many other groups, both male and female.

▼*Activity:* **Detect**

Can you find the common links in the four different songs?

Listen to the montage of four different songs. Each one lasts approximately 40 seconds. Become a "song detective," taking notes on each example. Try to gather enough evidence so you can answer the following questions:

1. What are three elements all four songs have in common?
2. Which example sounds most unusual in comparison to the others? Why?
3. Which pairs of examples sound most alike? Why?
4. Which example sounds the oldest? Which sounds newest? Why?
5. This music came from three different continents: can you name them?
6. What different styles of music are represented in these songs?

New Romanticism

Classical music, too, has been energized with a will to reach new audiences. Whereas much of the classical music of the mid-twentieth century appealed to a small select (some would say "elitist") audience, classical music is now trying to reach out to attract a wider public. Many of today's classical composers are setting out to write music that is intensely emotional. The self-indulgence that was passed off as self-expression has been replaced by a more urgent drive for communication. Some composers have traded in the tone row and serialism for **New Romanticism**, *a genuine tonal melody wrapped in exotic textures and timbres*. They like intense drama, splashy effects, virtuoso fireworks, and colossal climaxes. Most of all, they want audiences to react. This new musical attitude has been labeled New Romanticism, but it is definitely a product of the new age of communication.

To be certain they achieve strong meaning and reaction, New Romantic composers sometimes lean on literary subjects. American composer David Del Tredici (b. 1937), for example, has been inspired for more than a decade by the poetry in Lewis Carroll's *Alice in Wonderland*. He has created *Child Alice* (1980), a massive evening-long musical composition that depicts the dramatic contrasts of mood in the poem that is the preface to Carroll's novel *Through the Looking Glass* (1872). Del Tredici's music—a type of program music—was awarded the Pulitzer Prize in 1980.

Although descriptive music probably has existed as long as humans have been creating music, the term program music was invented by the Hungarian composer, Franz Liszt (1811–1886). Liszt coined the term **program music** to describe *instrumental compositions that attempt to convey a specific idea without using lyrics*. Such works enable a composer to express something beyond the music itself. These "extramusical" ideas are often provided by the composer in the form of an explanatory note or a program that accompanies the score.

John Corigliano (b. 1938) is another contemporary American composer who is determined to communicate with his audience. *Newsweek* magazine called his opera, *The Ghosts of Versailles* (1991), "a triumph." His *Symphony No. 1*, an impassioned response to the AIDS crisis, earned him the 1991 Grawemeyer Award, and his score for the film *Altered States* earned him both Grammy and Academy Award nominations. His works capture attention and hold it because of his ability to combine many different compositional procedures to attain exceptionally vivid contrasts and expressive power. His *Pied Piper Fantasy* (1979–1982), a concerto for flute and orchestra, was inspired by Robert Browning's poem, *The Pied Piper of Hamelin*. Although this is Corigliano's first work to have a programmatic outline, the work is a fine example of his brilliance in using the orchestra as an expressive vehicle. The concerto is divided into seven sections based on events in the story. In Browning's legend, the town of Hamelin was overrun with rats. The piper played his flute to charm the rats and lead them to destruction. In Browning's words, this is how the rats took over Hamelin:

> Rats! They fought the dogs, and killed the cats,
> And bit the babies in their cradles,
> And ate the cheeses out of the vats,
> And licked the soup from the cook's own ladles,
> Split open the kegs of salted sprats,

Made nests inside men's Sunday hats,
And even spoiled the women's chats,
By drowning their speaking
With shrieking and squeaking
In fifty different sharps and flats.

▼Activity: *Evaluate and Compare*

How does classical music of our time embody the expressive and communicative dimensions of Romantic music?

Turn back to Chapter 9, pages 141–145 and make a list of the musical characteristics of the Romantic period (c. 1825–1910).

Listen to two short movements from John Corigliano's *Pied Piper Fantasy* and characterize this music according to mood, timbre, dynamics, contrasts, and other qualities. How does the mood change? What parts of the story might the composer be expressing?

What characteristics in the music suggest that the rats became hypnotized by the piper's song?

How does this music embody musical principles of the Romantic period? How does it embody musical principles of our own time?

◄ Contemporary composer John Corigliano is pictured here in the lobby of the Metropolitan Opera House in New York. His opera, *The Ghosts of Versailles*, debuted there on December 19, 1992. This was the opera company's first opera premiere in 25 seasons. Corigliano's interest in composing developed in part because his father served as concertmaster of the New York Philharmonic for 23 years.

Profile

Philip Glass
American Composer
1937–

PHILIP GLASS

Philip Glass is one of the most innovative and prolific composers in North America today. Glass combines Indian, African, classical, and modern elements to create a distinctive style, free of most European tradition. His music, which has been heard through ensemble performance, dance company collaborations, and film scores, is particularly known for its manipulation of rhythmic units in a repetitive context and over a static harmony.

Glass has composed several operas, among them *Einstein on the Beach* (1975-1976), *Satyagraha* (1980), and *Akhnaten* (1983). Inspired by his intellectual, political, and spiritual heroes, Glass has updated the traditional operatic genre to include modern styles and themes. Unfortunately, the staggering cost of producing an opera has limited his activity in the field.

Born in Baltimore in 1937, Glass studied music at the Peabody Conservatory in Baltimore before receiving a scholarship to New York's Juilliard School of Music. There, he was exposed to writers of the beat generation, bop musicians, and alternative theater, in addition to being educated in the conventional forms of music. After earning a master's degree, Glass went to Paris where he honed his technique with Nadia Boulanger, the great French musician and teacher (1887–1979), and also worked with Ravi Shankar (b. 1920), Indian sitar player and composer. Glass now lives in Nova Scotia, Canada, with his family.

Minimalism

During the mid-twentieth century, classical music faced a crisis. The twelve-tone or serial music that was being written appealed to a very small audience of connoisseurs—people who had expert knowledge and highly specialized tastes. Many composers, particularly those who were affiliated with a college or university base, wrote for a small discerning audience. The public for new classical music had dwindled to the point where it was almost nonexistent.

Along came Philip Glass. His studies of music left him dissatisfied. The new music was either too complex or, in the case of John Cage's chance music, too vague and indeterminate. Glass wanted to find a new path for musical expression. His studies in Paris in 1966 with Ravi Shankar, the Indian composer and sitar player, helped him find it. He became fascinated by the rhythms in Indian music and began to compose in ways that explored the interplay and repetitions of simple rhythms and minimal melodies and harmonies. Glass's music, which has also been influenced by the insistent and repetitious rhythms of rock music, has been called "minimalist." The instrumentation of his touring ensemble resembles that of a rock group, and he has established a sizable, mostly young, audience. Other composers, among them Steve Reich (b. 1936) and Terry Riley (b. 1935), have used minimalist techniques. **Minimalism,** *tonal music that stresses the element of repetition with changes that are dictated by a rule or system,* is clearly an American invention, attracting audiences in Europe and elsewhere.

One of the ways that contemporary composers have won the interest and following of new and younger audiences is to use real events as their subject matter. The titles of recently composed operas reveal this attempt to relate to today's interests and concerns: *The Death of Klinghoffer; Nixon in China; The Manson Family;* and *X: The Life and Times of Malcolm X.* These works are dramatized portraits inspired by newspaper headlines.

Glass has led the way in making music relevant to today. His operas explore global themes—political and social events that have affected humanity. *Satyagraha,* for example, tells the story of Mahatma Gandhi's invention of passive (or nonviolent) resistance. The subject of his orchestral work *Koyaanisqatsi* is respect for nature. The title is a Hopi Indian term meaning "life out of balance," and the subject is nature's desecration.

"Islands," one of the movements of *Glassworks* (1977), illustrates the simplicity of musical materials that is typical of minimalism. Glass says that this work "was intended to introduce my music to a more general audience than had been familiar with it up to then." The tone colors accumulate gradually while the motives are repeated over and over again, but in slightly altered versions. The first ostinato-like motive is introduced by slowly undulating violas:

Glass then adds a static, sustained melody above this ostinato pattern, played first by clarinet, then joined by saxophone:

The combination of these rather simple resources creates an atmosphere that evokes the stark simple beauty of an island.

▼*Activity:* **Perform and Experience**

Who is the audience for this "post-modern" music?

Using keyboard or tuned percussion, perform the fluctuating rhythmic and melodic patterns in "Islands" (page 441) from *Glassworks* by American composer Philip Glass (b. 1937).

Listen to the recording and try to identify the two basic musical ideas—the ostinato-like pattern and the higher, long-noted melody. Can you play along?

As you listen to the entire composition, you will hear the ostinato rhythms and melody repeat as they modulate to new tonal centers. How else does Glass create variety within all the repetition? What happens to the texture?

Point out when these two musical ideas change register; that is, when the ostinato pattern moves to the high register and the long-noted melody shifts to the low register.

Describe the expressive and psychological effect of minimalist music.

How does Glass end the composition?

New Age

It has been said that describing the style of New Age music is like trying to nail Jell-O to a wall. Yet most record stores have a section for New Age music, and over 200 New Age radio stations have sprung up across the country. More than 50 record companies in the United States, Europe, and Asia now specialize in this music that has commanded its own category at the Grammy Awards since 1987. Today, New Age music generates upwards of $100 million in sales a year as it continues to increase in popularity. But is this music a distinct musical genre or is it, like rock, an amalgamation of many styles?

New Age music presents an alternative to the hard-driving, up-tempo, vocal music that usually tops the popular music charts. It appeals to people who want to shut out the abrasive discords of modern life. It is tranquil and pastoral. **New Age** music is *instrumental music produced by musicians who have combined characteristics of classical and popular music, as well as a wide variety of other cultures, particularly Eastern, to produce a hybrid music that is intimate, peaceful, calming, and meditative.* Largely improvised, it often incorporates actual sounds from nature. It borrows its hypnotic repetitions and subtle rhythmic mutations from minimalism. The music often suggests visual images. Guitarist William Ackerman, one of the earliest exponents of the style, calls it "a varied landscape of emotion." Its detractors have labeled it "aural wallpaper," "audio Teflon," and "yuppie Muzak." New Age is sometimes referred to as "easy listening" music.

Styles of music continue to evolve. Old styles give impetus to new ones. Some, like rock and reggae, have become international, appealing to many, but certainly not all, people around the world. Dance music, which avoids the language barrier inherent in vocal music, crosses cultural borders most easily. But American popular vocal music may help to account for the acceptance of English as the preferred second language around the world.

▼*Activity:* **Evaluate**

What are the distinguishing features of New Age music?

Listen to the musical example, "Lullaby from the Great Mother Whale for the Baby Seal Pups" by the Paul Winter Consort, and write down its musical characteristics.

Using your notes, evaluate this piece. What is there about it that is intriguing? Speculate about the uses of this music. Do you know anyone who is a New Age enthusiast? Some people regard this as "elevator music." In what ways might this label be appropriate?

*S*ummary

Our music mirrors us. It emerges from the social fabric of our culture to speak directly to all our differences. Taken piecemeal, it can be narrow in scope and limited in how well it reflects us. Taken collectively, it provides a fairly accurate picture of American life today. As our culture has become more visual, so too has our music. As we have become more urbanized, our music has changed to serve the dynamic juxtaposition of different ethnic groups, classes, and lifestyles that abound in our cities. As our culture has become more global, our music has absorbed and combined musical elements from many cultures. Popular and classical music have both reached out to communicate to a broader public, particularly the younger generation, in all its variety.

Our music is becoming more democratized. In the vast diversity of its styles it tries to accommodate everybody. The conglomeration of people has produced an abundance of musical styles. No group seems to be left out. There is something for everybody, and people generally seek out their own musical common denominator. It is a paradox of today's music that it reflects our narrow and separate individualities and, at the same time, our broad and cosmopolitan oneness.

CHAPTER 23

Music of Previous Generations

Objectives

By completing this chapter, you will:

- Learn to recognize the style of music in the Renaissance, the Baroque, and the Classical periods.
- Be able to delineate the characteristics of these styles.
- Become acquainted with some of the compositions of composers Michael Praetorius, Thomas Weelkes, Claudio Monteverdi, Jean-Philippe Rameau, Antonio Vivaldi, Wolfgang Amadeus Mozart, and Franz Joseph Haydn.
- Understand the process involved in the evolution of musical styles.
- Understand the relationship and interplay between polyphony and homophony.
- See the connection between the way people think and live, and the kind of music they create.

Musical Terms

concerto grosso
continuo
madrigals
terraced dynamics
tutti

*M*usic evokes its time. Each epoch seems to
have a particular character—a way of thinking, acting,
and living that affects the taste and style of that day.
The arts record these attitudes and outlooks. They are
indelible imprints of their age. That is why we can live
and breathe history through the architecture, drawings,
paintings, literature, and music that artists, writers, and
musicians create. When we hear the music of a
particular historic period, we can begin to experience
the feeling and style of that time. Music becomes a very
tangible way to touch and be touched by our human
heritage. It puts us in contact with those who lived
before us. In the preceding chapter you caught a
glimpse of how music reflects our own times.
Here you will see how it characterizes other times.

Renaissance

One of the greatest flowerings of art, literature, and learning of all time
occurred in Europe during the fifteenth and sixteenth centuries. The rediscovered classical ideals of the ancient Greeks inspired a rebirth and revival
of human creativity. The change in thinking began in Italy and spread gradually northward through Europe, awakening a new spirit that overtook the
age. That new spirit marked the transition from the medieval world to the
modern. Much of our thinking today is rooted in the remarkable achievements during the Renaissance.

The Renaissance was a time of brilliant accomplishments in literature,
science, and the arts. In Italy, economic expansion brought contact with
other cultures and a flourishing urban vibrancy. The Medici family in Florence, the doges in Venice, and the popes in Rome, among others, became
patrons of the arts. During the Renaissance secularism asserted itself.
Humanism—the emphasis on human values and capabilities—moved
society away from the pervasive authority of the church that had dominated life during medieval times. There was a conscious return to the classical ideals of ancient Greece. Human possibilities were exemplified by
Leonardo da Vinci, a universal genius as talented and creative in science
as in the arts. This was the age of the artists Michelangelo, Raphael, Titian,
and Tintoretto.

The Rise of Instrumental Music

In music secular subjects assumed a place alongside the sacred music that had formerly commanded so much attention. Italian composers wrote sacred motets and secular **madrigals**, *nonreligious vocal works in several parts (usually five)*. They asserted their sense of harmony in direct competition with the counterpoint that had long dominated music. In Renaissance music, for the first time, the horizontal (polyphonic) and vertical (homophonic) aspects were balanced. Music was no longer primarily vocal. Instrumental music was given greater emphasis and began to flower. It no longer merely supported the voices. Instruments were given their own parts!

The great German composer Michael Praetorius (c. 1571–1621) was a church musician who wrote many sacred hymns, motets, and songs as well as secular madrigals, songs, and dance pieces. His instrumental music shows the new independence that instruments were given in the late Renaissance. In his "Bourrée," from *Terpsichore* (1612), for example, he used the tempo, meter, and character of a traditional French dance in a quick duple meter to create a purely instrumental expression. For contrast, he delighted in using loud oboe-like double-reed instruments called shawms, soft flutelike recorders, and reedy and nasal krummhorns.

▼Activity: *Experience*

What is the style of the new instrumental music in the late Renaissance?

Listen to the "Bourrée" from *Terpsichore* (1612), a collection of instrumental French dances, by the German composer Michael Praetorius.

- Describe the tempo and metric organization of the music.
- Describe how contrast is achieved in the music.
- How is the music organized? Are there sections? Is there any repetition? Perform the melodic and rhythmic accompaniment to the "Bourrée."

Word Painting

With humanism came a greater interest in the text and its meaning. During the Middle Ages it was common for several texts to be set to music simultaneously, the polyphonic treatment making it difficult to follow any one of them. In the sixteenth century, composers discovered that music could portray human emotions, not just express religious texts. To explore the new phenomenon, composers tied music more closely to poetry. Although the focus had previously been on the form of the text, its meaning now took center stage. In their madrigals Renaissance composers expressed the meaning of the text musically by coloring words with new harmonies and chromaticism. They used the device of word painting—making their music portray the literal meaning of the words of the text and making certain that the counterpoint did not confuse the meaning even when there were four or more parts.

The English composer Thomas Weelkes (1575–1623) wrote both sacred and secular music, but he is clearly one of the great composers of madrigals. He is one of a number of English composers who adopted the Italian style. His music is ordered through repetition of sections and by imitation between the parts. His six-voice madrigal, "As Vesta Was Descending" (1601), demonstrates how he used music to convey shades of meaning in the text. Even though the subject matter is about goddesses, the music is not stuffy. These goddesses had human feelings. After all the serious music of the Middle Ages, Renaissance composers were actually having fun.

▲ In Italy at the beginning of the fifteenth century, the prosperous merchant city of Florence showed the world a new way to live. Tradesmen and craftsmen built a flourishing city-state, replacing the old monumental Gothic architecture with buildings of a smaller, more human scale. In his Pazzi Chapel (built c. 1429–1433), architect Filippo Brunelleschi demonstrated this new Renaissance style. The curved Roman arch, the mathematically spaced classical columns, the neatly treated flat surfaces, the balance of vertical and horizontal elements, and the overall symmetry of the design show a new sense of geometrical clarity, unity, and logic. Renaissance music exhibits similar characteristics.

Filippo Brunelleschi. Pazzi Chapel. Begun c. 1440. Santa Croce, Florence, Italy.

As Vesta Was Descending

As Vesta was from Latmos hill descending,
she spied a maiden queen the same ascending,
attended on by all the shepherds swain,
to whom Diana's darlings came running down amain.
First two by two
then three by three together,
leaving their goddess all alone, hasted thither,
and mingling with the shepherds of her train
with mirthful tunes her presence entertain.
Then sang the shepherds and nymphs of Diana
Long live fair Oriana!

▼*Activity:* **Investigate**

How did composers treat the relationship between words and music during the Renaissance?

Listen to the madrigal "As Vesta Was Descending" by Thomas Weelkes while you follow the text. What is it about?

- Describe the mood of the music and the text. What musical characteristics helped you make your decision?
- How did Weelkes paint the meaning of the text in his music?
- Follow the text while you identify the correct musical description.
- Is the word painting in the madrigal obvious or subtle? Why?

Baroque

The term "baroque" derived from a French word for an imperfect or irregular pearl. The term describes a way of thinking that reached beyond the classical Greek ideals of perfect circles, squares, and triangles, of symmetrical organization, and of clear, simple, and highly ordered statements. Why not ovals and curved lines and highly embellished and ornamented melodies? Baroque artists burst out of the confines of four-square thinking. Two and two became five! These people saw beauty and emotion in the imperfect shapes and forms that abound in the real world. They relaxed the "laws" of expression and tried letting go of their emotions. Baroque composers continued the exploitation of emotions in music, but now they did it with greater drama and freedom.

The Beginning of Opera

The great Italian composer Claudio Monteverdi (1567–1643) was one of the first composers to infuse the meaning of the text with feeling. During the Baroque period, composers found that their music could represent

◀ The Baroque style was exuberant and emotional. The restraint and simplicity of the Renaissance style was replaced by heavy ornamentation, exaggerated emotion, and vivid movement. Spanish architect José Benito de Churriguera's ornate altarpiece for the church of San Esteban, Salamanca (1693) shows this extravagant style. More than 90 feet (27 meters) high, the twisted and garlanded columns, set at alternating depths in over-rich abundance, writhe upwards dramatically.

José de Churriguera. Altarpiece. 1693. San Esteban, Salamanca, Spain.

and contrast basic emotional states: sorrow, fear, love, anger, and other "affections," as they were called. These were the passions—psychological states that could be represented in music. The main purpose of Baroque music was to move the affections by sustaining and contrasting them.

In their attempt to portray human emotions in sound, Baroque composers established states of feeling that were rather fixed and that shifted abruptly. Each section of a work maintained a single mood throughout. Rhythms and melodies in the section, based on one or two short motives, retained a consistent character. They used **terraced dynamics**, *calling for different sections of a movement to be performed at different, and contrasting, dynamic levels.* They were further contrasted by altering that character to create a definite change in mood.

▲ Many early musical works have been lost. One of the earliest operas that is still performed today is *Orfeo* (1607) by the Italian composer Claudio Monteverdi (1567–1643). Of the many operas he composed, only three survive. His music is inventive and touching. Monteverdi was musical director at St. Mark's in Venice from 1613 until his death.

The Baroque period in music developed around 1600, reached its apex, and ended with the death of Johann Sebastian Bach in 1750. While Bach expended his genius in taking the old contrapuntal style to its final, glorious heights, other composers explored simpler and less regimented schemes of expression. The solo voice was recognized as the best means for communicating the meaning of a text. While polyphony remained important, and composers continued to create complex textures in which each part has its own independent melody, a new style was emerging that was quite different. Composers experimented with assigning melody to one voice rather than keeping all the voices equally busy. Instrumental accompaniments were simplified to support the voice with a solid bass and chords. This **continuo** or thoroughbass—named because it sounded continously throughout—*usually consisted of a harpsichord that sounded the chords and elaborated upon them and a viola da gamba (a low, bowed string instrument) that reinforced the bass line.* (The delicate sound of the harpsichord could not by itself emphasize the bass line sufficiently.) Composers left it up to the harpsichord continuo player to fill out the inner parts by improvising within the chord patterns that were specified. The outer voices were thereby emphasized. The melody in the upper voice was supported by the constantly moving bass line. Harmonies changed rapidly. Composers were now generating music vertically as well as horizontally.

These developments set the stage for opera, which made its first appearance around 1600. In order to dramatize a story through music, the characters had to speak for themselves and convey emotion at the same time. The idea of a solo voice supported by accompaniment was absolutely essential. So was the development of "recitative," a way of speaking musically. Recitative is a combination of singing and speaking. It mimics the inflections of speech but uses melody and rhythm as a way to give the words emotional meaning. The events of the story are told through recitatives. In contrast, the singing of an aria is more sustained. It marks a pause in the storytelling while a character reacts to the events.

One of the earliest operas is Monteverdi's *Orfeo* (1607). The story of this ancient Greek tragedy relates Orpheus's descent into Hell to retrieve his dead bride Eurydice from the powers of the underworld. He pleads his case so convincingly in song that he is permitted to lead her out, but with one condition. He must not look back to see if she is following or he will lose her again. Orpheus does look back. He loses Eurydice, but the god Apollo comes to his rescue and takes him to a cloud where he can look down upon Eurydice forevermore.

Monteverdi scored the opera for soloists, chorus, and orchestra. The highly expressive music of *Orfeo* consists of recitatives, arias, madrigals, and orchestral music—all the prevailing forms of the day. The music succeeds in depicting real human character and passions. The melodious recitative "Tu se' morta" ("You are dead") conveys grief with a melody and rhythm that follows the natural inflection of the text. There are climaxes on high notes on the words *rimango* (remain), *stelle* (star), and *sole* (sun) that give the singer opportunities to express emotion. High notes convey excitement and grief; low tones despair and death. As in his madrigals, Monteverdi uses word painting; for example, he sets the word *stelle* (star) on the highest note and *profondi abissi* (profound abysses) and *morte* (death) on the lowest. There are built-in pauses for breathing that remind us of speech.

Tu se' morta	**You are dead**
Tu se' morta, se' morta, mia vita,	You are dead, dead my darling
ed io respiro? Tu se' da me partita,	And I live; you have left me,
se' da me partita per mai più,	You have left me forever,
mai più non tornare, ed io rimango?	Never to return and I remain—
Nò, nò che se i versi alcuna cosa ponno,	No, no, if verses have any power,
N'andro sicuro a' più profondi abissi,	I shall go boldly to the deepest abysses,
e intenerito il cor del rè dell'ombre,	And have melted the heart of the queen of shadows,
meco trarotti a riverder le stelle,	Will bring you with me to see the stars,
o se ciò negherammi empio destino,	Or if cruel fate will deny me this,
rimarro teco in compagnia di morte!	I will remain with you in the company of death,
Addio terra, addio cielo, e sole, addio.	Farewell earth, farewell sky, and sun, farewell.

▼Activity: *Compare*

How did composers in the Baroque treat the relationship between words and music differently from composers in the Renaissance?

Follow the English translation of the Italian text as you listen to the recitative "Tu se' morta" ("You are dead") from the opera *Orfeo* by Claudio Monteverdi. Be prepared to describe the feelings about which Orfeo is singing.

Compare "Tu se' morta" with "As Vesta Was Descending":

1. How many voices are singing?
2. What instruments can you identify?
3. Which composition is homophonic? polyphonic?
4. Which composer has set the words of the text much like the speech of an actor in a play?
5. Which setting of text makes the meaning of the words clearer? Why?

Harmonic Foundations

The French composer and theorist Jean-Philippe Rameau (1683–1764) invented the names of the basic harmonies: tonic, dominant, subdominant, and so forth. Although composers were now using these harmonies, they had not explained their relationships scientifically. The way these harmonies progressed or functioned in homophonic music was now formulized. The principles of chord movement were clarified and codified (explained systematically).

Rameau derived his melody from the harmony. Baroque composers began to think in terms of chords, not just melodies. The long reign (some would say tyranny) of counterpoint came to an end. The harmonic foundation of music became its fundamental expressive force. Like many composers in the Baroque, Rameau composed instrumental suites comprising stylized dances. During this period, dance rhythms permeated music of all kinds.

▼*Activity:* **Speculate**

Why did Baroque composers favor a single melody supported by chords over the complex contrapuntal music of the past?

Is Jean-Philippe Rameau's composition "Tambourin" for solo harpsichord contrapuntal or homophonic? What musical characteristics give the music its expressive force?

Identify the form of the composition. How is contrast achieved in this composition? How would you describe the melody in the opening and closing sections of the composition?

What percussion instrument is Rameau attempting to suggest in sound?

The Concerto

In Italy, the Baroque was the age of the great violin makers—Nicolò Amati (1596–1684), Antonio Stradivari (1644–1737), and Giuseppe Guarneri (1698–1744)—and of great string music. Baroque composers wrote for strings with the intensity that Renaissance composers wrote for voices. In instrumental music, the suite, the sonata, the concerto, and the sinfonia, a forerunner of the Classical symphony, were invented. Composers became increasingly interested in exploiting contrasts of timbre, especially in their instrumental works. In the new *concertato* style, solo parts alternated with a group of instruments.

Undoubtedly, the Italian composer Antonio Vivaldi (1678–1741) was the greatest creator of concertos. He wrote more than 500 of them! Vivaldi established the favored three movement scheme: fast, slow, fast. Most of his concertos are for a solo instrument—chiefly violin—and orchestra. He also composed solo concertos for most of the instruments of his time, including bassoon, recorder, and mandolin—double concertos for two solo instruments, and even ensemble concertos that contrasted a group of solo instruments with the orchestra. In the **concerto grosso** ("grand" concerto)

PROJECT

Understand the Baroque Concerto

Determine how the Italian Baroque composer Antonio Vivaldi used the concerto as a dramatic and expressive form. Listen to "Spring" (first movement) from *The Four Seasons* and distinguish the interplay of *tutti* and solo sections. Arrange the blocks in the order in which you hear them. Before you listen again, decide which blocks are similar. Which programmatic descriptions refer to spring?

Describe the sound of the Baroque orchestra. What instruments were used in this work? Describe the relationship between the soloist and the accompanying orchestra. How does Vivaldi employ dynamics as a dramatic device? What gives this work a powerful sense of unity? variety?

Profile

Antonio Vivaldi
Italian Composer
1678–1741

ANTONIO VIVALDI

Antonio Vivaldi was a composer who lived in Venice during the Baroque era. Born in 1678, young Vivaldi studied to be a priest, but he also became an accomplished violinist and harpsichordist. When, for reasons not entirely known, Vivaldi left the ministry, he was appointed in 1703 to be the director of music at the Pio Ospedale della Pietà. The Pietà was devoted to the care of orphaned girls, and Vivaldi provided musical training to those who showed aptitude. Their performances were a high point of the social season in Venice, so it was necessary to have a competent teacher and composer in charge. For nearly 40 years, Vivaldi wrote many different kinds of musical works suited to all the festivals and occasions at the Pietà. His success and popularity led to outside commissions and to the publication of his pieces outside of Italy which, at the time, was quite an honor. One of his most influential publications, *L'estro armonico*, a collection of violin concertos, so impressed J. S. Bach that he transcribed several of them for keyboard.

From 1718 on, Vivaldi traveled widely, composing operas and concertos for various European courts. A skillful orchestrator, Vivaldi was as successful at composing for instruments as for voices. Unfortunately, much of his prolific output has been lost because many of these works existed only in manuscript form. His surviving orchestral works display Vivaldi's skillful and widely copied treatment of the contrast between solo musician and the orchestra. His best-known work, *The Four Seasons*, is a programmatic masterpiece that captures the individual moods of the seasons, an extraordinary achievement in his time.

there is *contrast between ripieno (full or tutti) sections for a small string orchestra and concertino sections for a group of soloists.* The ripieno had the simpler parts and were usually assigned an easily remembered theme or refrain—a *ritornello*—that is repeated. The soloist had the more difficult part. The whole idea of a concerto was the give-and-take—the dramatic tension—between these forces. The "argument" or contest between soloist and orchestra come to a resolution at the end.

The most celebrated of Vivaldi's concertos are those that comprise *The Four Seasons* (1725). The descriptive title indicates a programmatic approach. Vivaldi tried to characterize the four seasons and named the concertos accordingly: "Spring," "Summer," "Autumn," and "Winter." In addition, he introduced each work with a sonnet. The music can be quite descriptive. In the second (slow) movement of the "Spring" concerto, for example, the solo violin portrays a sleeping shepherd while the orchestral violins imitate a murmuring brook and a viola depicts a restless sheepdog. These works have been called a "miracle of tone-painting," but Vivaldi was not a slave to his literary ideas. The work is scored for solo violin and a small string orchestra with harpsichord (continuo). These concertos are masterpieces of Baroque musical style: virtuoso figuration, elaborate motivic invention, ornamented melody, rhythmic vitality, harmonic clarity, and a clear sense of form. They add up to exuberant expression.

Classical

Even before J. S. Bach died, his sons were exploring simpler ways to express themselves musically than the complex, contrapuntal style of their father. They thought that polyphony was too complicated, too cerebral, too unnatural. They resorted to the ideals of classical antiquity—once again. The excavations of Pompeii in 1763 turned attention back to the ancients.

▶ The French painter Jacques-Louis David (1748–1825) returned to classical ideals. He showed this new spirit in his *Oath of the Horatii* (1786). Three simple Roman arches frame the figures. In the center stands Horatius Proclus dedicating the swords of his three sons. While their sisters grieve at the right, the young men swear to defend the Roman republic. The heroic theme and political message is strengthened by the carefully balanced order, the stark handling of light and shadow, and the clarity of the contours and modeling. Everything is controlled; nothing is extraneous.

Jacques-Louis David. *The Oath of the Horatii.* 1786. Toledo Museum of Art, Toledo, Ohio.

The Beginnings

Like any new generation, Bach's children saw the world differently from their parents. They aspired to a simpler, more natural form of musical expression. They found the affections of Baroque music too artificial. After all, human emotions are in a constant state of transition. Why shouldn't music convey this continuous flux of feeling? Wilhelm Friedemann Bach (1710–1784), Carl Philipp Emanuel (C. P. E.) Bach (1714–1788), and their brother Johann Christian Bach (1735–1782) followed these new instincts and helped establish the new style.

In music, stylistic changes develop gradually. During periods of transition from one major style to another (for example, Renaissance to Baroque or Baroque to Classical), elements of the old style and new style usually exist side by side. You have already heard some examples. The German composer Michael Praetorius spanned the late Renaissance and early Baroque. His music shows stylistic features of both periods. At the same time that J. S. Bach was summing up the contrapuntal style of the Baroque, George Frideric Handel (1685–1759) was emphasizing melody and harmony.

The mature musical style of the Classical period (c. 1725–1810) can be heard in the works of the greatest composers of the era—Franz Joseph Haydn (1732–1809), Wolfgang Amadeus Mozart (1756–1791), and Ludwig van Beethoven (1770–1827) in his early years. The concertos of Mozart provide a good example of mature Classical style. The overall plan of these works, which are of remarkable invention, is the same as Vivaldi's concerti: three movements in fast, slow, fast order. But there the resemblance ends. Mozart's orchestra is bigger. To Vivaldi's strings he adds woodwinds, trumpets, horns, and timpani. He also uses the orchestra differently, often blending it with the solo parts, rather than alternating *tutti* with solo sections. **Tutti** indicates *a section in which all the instruments and/or voices perform together.* Instead of melodies created from short motives, there are fully developed themes. Within movements contrasts of emotions are created by continual changes of instrumental timbres and dynamics. Polyphony is re-employed as an element of the basically homophonic texture.

▼ Activity: **Tell the Difference**

How do Baroque and Classical concertos differ?

Compare the first movement of Vivaldi's "Spring" concerto with the second movement of Wolfgang Amadeus Mozart's Piano Concerto No. 21. The following questions should help:

1. How are the two orchestras different?
2. Which concerto has more "songlike" melodies?
3. Which concerto exhibits the most dramatic and stark contrasts of dynamics, texture, and density?
4. How does the role of soloist and the accompaniment differ in the two concertos?
5. Which concerto uses the more subtle dynamic shading?
6. Which concerto do you think would be more difficult to perform? Why?

A Simpler, Clearer Art

In the eighteenth century, an avid new and influential middle class established a market for music and the other arts. This was the beginning of public concerts. Concertos and sonatas became popular with this new public as vehicles to showcase musical skill. Audiences liked instrumental soloists to display their technique in the same way that singers did in opera. The rise of the middle class was a result of the enormous scientific and intellectual advances of the preceding century that perpetuated a belief in natural law and human progress. This new way of thinking—The Enlightenment or The Age of Reason—favored common sense, equal rights, and faith in the individual. This was the time of the American Declaration of Independence and the creation of the United States Constitution and the Bill of Rights.

In accordance with the scientific thinking of the time, music had to be easily understood and ordered. Classical art was a people's art, dignified and free of complexities. It had to be instantly appealing, natural, universal, and noble. Whereas the Baroque had been grand, intricate, and sometimes pompous, the new music was given a simpler and more direct expression. Instead of the motivic phrases of the Baroque, Classical composers gave balance to their melodies by organizing them in regular two- or four-measure antecedent and consequent (or question-and-answer) phrases, sometimes with an extension. Here are two examples from the opera *Don Giovanni* ("Don Juan") by Mozart:

Antecedent

Consequent

Antecedent

Consequent (with extension)

Classical Opera

Mozart's operas are about human beings. The stories are logical, and characters are delineated musically. Melodies are developed to give the characters greater depth of emotion. Rhythm follows the natural accentuation of the words of the text. Different instrumental timbres in the orchestra produce a variety of moods. The harmonic language is expanded, and dynamics are used expressively. The bass is slowed down and so are the chord changes. Forms satisfy dramatic needs. Homophony reigns, absorbing polyphonic elements as expression calls for them.

In the opera *Don Giovanni* (1787), Mozart took musical Classicism to its heights. This is the story of a scoundrel and his punishment. Don Giovanni is a nobleman whose notorious and deceitful conquests of women finally catch up with him. When he tries to seduce Donna Anna, her father, a Commandant, tries to defend her honor. The old man challenges the Don to a fight and is killed. Donna Anna swears to avenge her father's death. In the final act the statue of the Commandant returns as a ghost, stomping into the Don's banquet and asking him to mend his ways. The Don refuses. Suddenly, flames engulf the Don, the earth opens, and he is dragged unrepenting to hell.

In Scene 3 of Act 1, the nobleman's decidedly "un-noble" character with women is revealed. Don Giovanni and his friend Leporello happen upon Zerlina and Masetto, two peasants celebrating their engagement. Left alone with Zerlina, Don Giovanni flatters her with a promise of marriage. They sing a duet in which Zerlina is torn by temptation and forced to choose between her fiancé, Masetto, and the nobleman, Don Giovanni, who is making advances:

Giovanni

La ci darem la mano,	There we'll join hands and
La mi dirai di si!	you'll say "yes!"
Vedi, non é lontano;	Look, it isn't far;
partiam, ben mio, da qui!	let's be off from here, my love!

Zerlina

Vorrei, e non vorrei;	I want to, and I don't;
Mi trema un poco il cor.	my heart is beating faster.
Felice, é ver sarei,	It's true I should be happy,
ma puó burlarmi ancor.	but he could be deceiving me.

Giovanni

Vieni mio bel diletto!	Come, my pretty delight!

Zerlina

Mi fa pietà Masetto!	I'm sorry for Masetto!

Giovanni

Io cangieró tua sorte!	I'll change your whole fortune!

▲ In this scene from the San Francisco Opera's 1968 production of *Don Giovanni* by Wolfgang Amadeus Mozart, the nobleman Don Giovanni, played by Cesare Siepi, flatters Zerlina (Jeannette Pilou) with a promise of marriage he has no intention of keeping. She is torn by temptation, being engaged to a peasant man but drawn by the attentions of a man who is rich and famous.

Zerlina
Presto, non son piú forte!   Oh, quick, I'm weakening!

Giovanni
Vieni! Vieni!   Come, oh, come!
La ci darem la mano,   There we'll join hands,

Zerlina
Vorrei e non vorrei;   I want to, and I don't;

Giovanni
La mi dirai di sí!   There you'll say "yes!"

Zerlina
Mi trema un poco il cor . . .   My heart is beating faster . . .

Giovanni
Vieni mio bel diletto!   Come my pretty delight!

Zerlina
Mi fa pietá Masetto.   I'm sorry for Masetto.

Giovanni
Io cangieró tua sorte.   I'll change your fortune completely.

Zerlina
Presto, non son piú forte!   Oh, quick, I'm weakening!

Giovanni
Andiam! Andiam!   Let's go! Let's go!

Zerlina
Andiam!   Yes, let's go!

Giovanni and Zerlina
Andiam, andiam mio bene,   Let's go, let's go my precious
A ristorar le pene   to soothe the pains
D'un innoccente amor!   of innocent love!

▼ *Activity:* ***Be the Critic!***

How did composers in the Classical period treat the relationship between words and music differently from the way composers treated it in the Baroque? Which is more effective?

Follow the English translation as you focus on Mozart's duet "La ci darem la mano" ("There we'll join hands") from the opera *Don Giovanni.*

Compare the antecedent and consequent phrases sung by Zerlina to the two phrases sung by Don Giovanni (see notation on page 456).

Learn to play these opening phrases on a keyboard instrument.

How are they similar, how are they different, and why? Which phrases end on a strong, tonic cadence?

Describe the dramatic change that takes place in the music when the Don and Zerlina begin singing at the same time. How does the change reinforce the meaning of the text?

How does this operatic music differ from Monteverdi's?

The Development of the Symphony

The symphony came of age as a major instrumental musical form during the Classical period. Its beginnings can be traced to the Italian opera overture or *sinfonia.* As soon as these sinfonias were performed separately from the opera, they assumed a life of their own. When composers began to write pieces just for orchestra, they borrowed the form of the sonata with its several contrasting movements. One of the early symphonists in Italy was Giovanni Sammartini (1700–1775) who composed more than 70 symphonies. In Mannheim, a cultural center in southwest Germany, Johann Stamitz (1717–1757), the director of the court orchestra, wrote symphonies in four movements with a minuet for the third. The first movement was in sonata form.

The first truly great composer of symphonies was Franz Joseph Haydn who wrote more than 100. In his hands the symphony became a powerful new vehicle of human expression. Haydn's reputation grew, and he was invited to England in 1791 and 1794 to conduct performances of his music, including a dozen new symphonies (numbers 93–104) that he composed for his visits. In creating the "London" symphonies, he gave his utmost, not wanting to disappoint the discerning English audiences. In these, his final symphonies, Haydn achieves order, expressivity, and a noble simplicity. There are fiery rhythms, unusual modulations, and intriguing contrapuntal interplay of melodic motives.

▼Activity: **Discover!**

How did Franz Joseph Haydn create music that embodies classical order?

Listen to the opening section of the second movement of Haydn's Symphony No. 101 in D, "The Clock," and answer the following questions:

1. What is the meter? tempo?
2. How many measures of the "clock" rhythm are present before the main theme enters?
3. What instrument plays the main theme?
4. Listen again and count the number of measures of both presentations of the main theme in the violins. Are both presentations of the theme of equal length?
5. What is the form of this movement?
6. How is a sense of unity achieved?
7. How is contrast accomplished?
8. What in the music suggests that Haydn had a sense of humor?

Composers in the eighteenth century almost always wrote their works for specific occasions. As is the case today, composers depended upon a system of patronage for their livelihood. Many eighteenth-century composers were employed in one of the many courts of the nobility where they composed under contract. Some composers held musical posts in churches while others taught privately or in schools. They wrote on commission, often dedicating a work to the patron who paid for it. Music publishing, which started in the Renaissance, flourished in the Baroque and Classical periods, providing composers with another source of income. During this time, music evolved into a major cultural force. There was a constant demand for new works.

Profile

Franz Joseph Haydn
Austrian Composer
1732–1809

FRANZ JOSEPH HAYDN

Like most people who achieve success, Franz Joseph Haydn succeeded through hard work and good fortune. He was born into a musical family of modest means. His parents, both amateur musicians, taught him to play musical instruments and to sing. A relative helped him attain a position as chorister in Vienna at the age of eight. He remained in Vienna for 20 years, becoming a seasoned musician by attending to his own education.

Haydn met many important people during these years, and he began to compose. In his late twenties, he was taken into the service of Prince Paul Anton Esterhazy, one of the wealthiest patrons of the arts. Haydn enjoyed 30 years in his employment, which provided ideal circumstances for him to develop and mature as a composer. The prince had a theater for opera, an orchestra of 25 skilled musicians, and a dozen talented singers. It was Haydn's job to write all the music the prince demanded, to conduct the performances, manage the musicians, and organize musical entertainments. Although he was a taskmaster, the prince became a great champion of Haydn's work.

Performances for the many distinguished guests that visited the Esterhazy estate spread Haydn's fame. By the time he was in his forties, he was receiving commissions from all over Europe to compose all types of music. During his lifetime, Haydn wrote an astounding number of works, including 104 symphonies, 83 string quartets, 52 piano sonatas, scores of chamber works for many different instrumental combinations, 23 operas, as well as cantatas, masses, and other church music. His oratorios *The Creation* and *The Seasons* retain a place in today's standard repertoire.

Haydn brought the symphony to life and made it a magnificent form of musical expression. In the process, he established the Classical style.

Summary

Much of the history of the human race can be traced from the alternation between periods of Classicism and Romanticism. There appears to be a natural tension between ideal beauty and sensuousness, between the head and the heart, and between thought and emotion that can be traced back to the Greeks and the Romans who also went through periods of stressing one style, then the other. The human race is a balancing act, hovering between a choice of one or the other mode to guide human affairs. Changes represented by the different musical styles of the Renaissance, Baroque, and Classical periods are a study of these reversals.

Music defines its time, and the times circumscribe the music. How people think and live affects the way they compose and perform. Music characterizes its age. At any one point in human history, people are reacting in different ways to the forces of life around them. Some take a conservative, some a progressive view. Composers choose to write in the old well-worn style or in the new emerging style. A momentum gathers that makes one style dominant. But there are always alternatives nipping at the edges. These are the prospects that keep cultures moving and changing. That is the excitement of knowing how people were creating and performing in previous generations. Our own twentieth-century music emerges from the same forces.

CHAPTER 24

Jazz

Objectives

By completing this chapter, you will:

- Learn about the beginnings of jazz.
- Become acquainted with the early contributions of Jelly Roll Morton, Fletcher Henderson, and Louis Armstrong.
- Be able to distinguish between the many styles of jazz such as Dixieland, small band jazz, swing, bebop, and fusion.
- Become familiar with some of the repertoire of classic jazz.
- Find out about the contributions of other jazz performers such as Charlie Parker and Dizzy Gillespie and what made them so great.

Musical Terms

bop
break
Dorian mode
fusion
scat singing

*J*azz is America's musical gift to the world. This unique invention, born in New Orleans and bred largely in Memphis, St. Louis, Chicago, and New York, is still alive and kicking and going on almost 100 years old. Without doubt, it is the most original and influential music to emerge from the American continent—so far.

The Beginnings

The roots of jazz in and around New Orleans extend back into the second half of the nineteenth century, perhaps earlier. Brass bands, made up of free blacks, played there during the War of 1812. These bands had a way of cutting loose with the rhythms. During this period, blacks participated in a rich, expressive music of their own. In churches they sang spirituals. Outside they sang work songs and the blues, and played dance tunes. All this music issued from the same deep sentiments, born of poverty in the Mississippi Delta and years of bondage. It was not just frivolous entertainment; it was real and basic human expression.

While spirituals and blues had some influence on the development of ragtime and jazz, the New Orleans brass bands and the minstrel bands of the period seem to have been their most direct ancestors. These bands used the classical instruments of the day—trumpets, trombones, clarinets, saxophones, and drums. Jazz seems to have evolved slowly from many sources, the term itself being applied later after the creation was full-blown.

Ferdinand "Jelly Roll" Morton (1885-1941) was one of the key figures in the early jazz movement in New Orleans. Jazz expert Gunther Schuller calls him "the first great [jazz] composer," recognizing that jazz performers were necessarily creators through their improvisations. Morton was a pianist and bandleader who helped bring together many of the varied African-American musical elements that were the building blocks of early jazz. In particular he perfected the New Orleans jazz style that featured a unique blend of polyphonic improvisations. The music had a highly contrapuntal texture in which a melody would be stated by a trumpet (or in the early years, a cornet), and at the same time, countermelodies would be improvised on the trombone and clarinet.

Morton was a creole musician who was not shy about self-promotion. His personal card stated: "Jelly Roll Morton: Inventor of Jazz & Stomps, World's Greatest Hot Tune Writer." He displayed his status with a diamond imbedded in one of his front teeth! Even if his claims were exaggerated, Morton's improvisations at the piano, his use of blue notes, jazz harmonies,

PROJECT

Survey the Public About Jazz

Working in small groups, find out how much the people in your community know about jazz. Each group is to conduct five-minute interviews of 10 to 12 persons using the Jazz Interview form. Compile your results and be prepared to report in class with answers to the following questions:

- What style of jazz are these people most familiar with?
- Is their knowledge of jazz excellent, good, or poor?
- What age group knew the most about jazz? the least? Why?
- How do you account for these answers?

and a looser beat did establish a Dixieland style of music. During the first decade of the century, he broke out of the confines of ragtime, creating a music that expressed a wider range of emotions. Morton claimed to have begun using the term "jazz" in 1902 as a way to distinguish this style from ragtime.

As a musician, Morton exhibited unusual versatility and a preference for music that spoke from the heart. *Jelly Roll Blues,* one of his first compositions, shows the style of this early jazz. His music was less stiff and more spontaneous than the prevailing ragtime. He and his group—Jelly Roll Morton and His Red Hot Peppers—introduced a swinging drive. He explained his use of a broader dynamic range this way: "If a glass of water is full, you can't add any more water, but if you have half a glass, you can always put more water in it—and jazz music is based on the same principles." His musicians did not just play loudly. They held back so that they could give their all in a rousing finale. This technique is exemplified in his recording of his "Black Bottom Stomp" (1926).

The Jazz Age

Jazz was finding its dancing feet in the early decades of the century. It was an earthy urban music that invited people to celebrate themselves. During the First World War musicians went north from New Orleans up the Mississippi seeking work in Memphis, St. Louis, and Chicago. This new sound drew a wider audience, including the white cornetist Bix Beiderbecke, one of the most creative jazz musicians of the 1920s. The style of music was New Orleans Dixieland jazz, and the bands were small with little, if any, duplication of instruments.

During the Roaring Twenties—the Jazz Age—teenage youths shocked their parents by dancing to the Charleston and the Black Bottom. Jelly Roll Morton's "Black Bottom Stomp" is typical of this new rhythmic urgency. Jazz is primarily a rhythmic feeling that is induced by combining the steady beat with rhythms that play around and tease it. Soloists improvised melodies rhythmically, shifting accents to the weak beats and emphasizing syncopation and offbeats. The custom of clapping on the offbeats (2 and 4) sets up this competition with the strong beats (1 and 3). The rhythm of jazz —certainly one of its most "telling" characteristics—is actually polyrhythmic. The crossrhythms and crossaccents—the juxtaposition of two or more different rhythms—give the music its compelling propulsion. According to Gunther Schuller, the rhythm of jazz is really a stylization and simplification of the complex polyphonic rhythms found in African music to make them fit into the steadily recurring rhythmic patterns of so much European classical music. Jazz was the result of this accommodation.

Among the many distinguishing features of Dixieland jazz is its marchlike feeling and reliance on 2/4 meter. Dixieland features a "front line" of instruments: trumpet, clarinet, and trombone. (These instruments attained their position in the New Orleans marching bands.) Cordophones such as

Cooperative Learning

Figure Out

How many jazz musicians play "Black Bottom Stomp" by Jelly Roll Morton and His Red Hot Peppers?

As you listen to this example of early jazz from New Orleans, try to identify how many performers make up Morton's Red Hot Peppers. The best way to do this is to write down all the instruments you hear being played. (Here are two hints: Morton himself plays piano on "Black Bottom Stomp," and there is only one player per instrument in the remainder of the band.) Complete this activity with one of your classmates.

Once you have identified the instruments, try to answer the following questions:

1. There are three main improvised solo sections in this piece. Can you name them in order?

2. There are four very short "breaks" in this piece. (A "break" is a measure or two where everyone stops except the soloist.) Can you name the breaks by instrument in the order they are played? (Hint: one of these short breaks is played by two instruments; another occurs in the middle of one of the three solo sections.)

Now that you have figured out the ensemble makeup and the location of the solos and breaks, listen again for Jelly Roll's characteristic New Orleans improvised counterpoint. These are the roots of Dixieland.

▲ The Crescent City Joymakers perform their brand of Dixieland Jazz at New Orleans' Preservation Hall in 1982, preserving a musical tradition that started there early in the century. How many instruments can you identify?

banjos and mandolins were often included in these early ensembles. In the interweaving of various lines, the melody or lead line is meant to stand out and the others are supposed to be less forward and obvious. There is a definite distinction between foreground and background. In polyphonic music with several different parts sounding simultaneously, there is a need to give the music focus.

Among the distinctive traits of early jazz was the "stride" piano style of Eubie Blake, James P. Johnson, and Earl Hines. It was built on a steady, "oom-pa," time-keeping left-hand bass, against which the right hand shifted the accents as it embellished the tune. A good stride pianist could imitate the entire band. The early stride pianists were influential in carving out an important place for the piano in jazz. In turn, their work influenced successive generations of pianists. Thomas "Fats" Waller, Art Tatum, and Thelonious Monk followed in their footsteps, taking jazz piano into all the prevailing new styles.

The art of jazz often involves taking an existing song and embellishing its melody. This was very characteristic of the Dixieland jazz bands. They favored the technique of short improvised "riffs" or "licks" in a call-and-response format, a form which derived from spirituals and work songs. The tune "When the Saints Go Marchin' In" lends itself very well to this type of improvisation. The Preservation Hall Jazz Band epitomizes the New Orleans Dixieland style. This is polyphony with a beat!

▼*Activity:* **Improvise**

Can you find four appropriate places for a responsive improvisation in the Dixieland classic "When the Saints Go Marchin' In"?

Before you listen, sing the tune "straight"—just as it is printed. As you sing, see if you can determine where it would be suitable and musically interesting to add an improvised "lick."

Try first to *tap* out the rhythms of your improvisations in the places where you think they will fit. Then, sing your improvisations. You may use actual words (derived from the lyrics) or scat syllables (nonsense words such as "doo wah, do wee.")

Now listen to the Preservation Hall Jazz Band play this tune. Although they are improvising primarily on instruments, keep an ear out for the similarities between the improvisational *ideas* in the band and your own improvised musical ideas.

When the Saints Go Marching In

Negro Spiritual

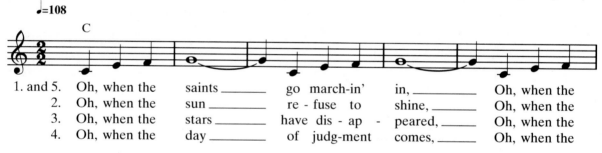

1. and 5. Oh, when the   saints _____ go march-in' in, _____ Oh, when the
2. Oh, when the   sun _____ re-fuse to shine, _____ Oh, when the
3. Oh, when the   stars _____ have dis-ap - peared, _____ Oh, when the
4. Oh, when the   day _____ of judg-ment comes, _____ Oh, when the

saints   go   march - in'   in, _____
sun   re - fuse   to   shine, _____   Oh Lord, I   want   to   be   in that
stars   have   dis - ap -   peared, _____
day   of   judg - ment   comes, _____

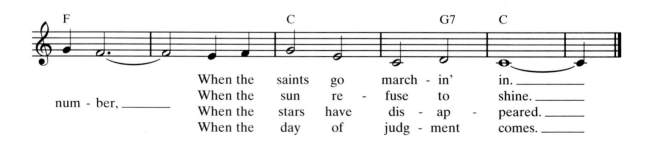

num - ber, _____

When the   saints   go   march - in'   in. _____
When the   sun   re - fuse   to   shine. _____
When the   stars   have   dis - ap -   peared. _____
When the   day   of   judg - ment   comes. _____

The Emergence of Swing

Fletcher Henderson (1897-1952) played a pivotal role in the development of the swinging jazz band. He was a pioneering bandleader, composer, and arranger. During the 1930s, other bands adopted the basic Henderson style as their model; however, Henderson established it first. Toward the end of the Roaring Twenties, a new type of jazz was emerging in his band—swing. Although his music was not fully developed swing, it certainly contained the roots of it.

Henderson led the field. He enlarged the band and established the instrumentation that became standard. There were three sections: a brass section consisting of three trumpets and two trombones (later three), a reed section consisting of three or four saxes (these players could double on clarinets), and a rhythm section consisting of drums, piano, guitar, and double bass. His arrangements used a call-and-response form in which the various sections of the orchestra took turns speaking to each other. (The violin has never won a regular place in jazz.) Henderson treated the various instrumental sections separately. There was an emphasis on solo playing underscored by arranged accompaniments. Solos alternated with the larger ensemble. This "antiphonal" style became the trademark of swing bands. Consequently, jazz music evolved into a sectional form.

▼ Composer/arranger and pianist Fletcher Henderson (1897–1952), an important pioneer of big-band jazz, led his own orchestra during the 1920s and the 1930s. He is credited with inventing the structure of the big band with its sectional instrumentation. Fletcher's years as chief arranger for the Benny Goodman Orchestra helped that group attain its notable popularity.

▼*Activity:* **Distinguish the Sections**

Can you hear the various sections that make up the overall form of a jazz tune?

Listen to the recording of Fletcher Henderson's classic dance tune, the "Henderson Stomp." After an eight-measure introduction, try to figure out the precise length of each thematic section. This means you must concentrate and count measures aurally. You will be successful if you count measures in a meter of two rather than four. The secret to this problem may be found in counting the length of the stride piano solo by the great Fats Waller, a member of Henderson's band.

Extra challenge: In what year do you suppose the Fletcher Henderson band made this recording? (Hint: It was only a year after Louis Armstrong left the band to move to Chicago and begin his work with his "Hot Five" group.)

▶ In the mid-1920s, the great jazz trumpeter Louis Armstrong (seated at the keyboard) made musical history leading his Hot Five—the brothers Johnny and Warren Dodds, Kid Ory, and Lil Hardin Armstrong, his wife. Recordings he made with the Hot Five (1925–1927) and later with the Hot Seven (1927) set new standards for jazz solo virtuosity.

Louis Armstrong, one of the giants of jazz, trumpeted his way out of New Orleans into international stardom. His was a prodigious talent that took the trumpet to new heights of musical expression. Armstrong's playing was unique and masterful. He gave a different emphasis to the rhythm with well-placed, subtle accents that swung. Even though he played third trumpet in the Henderson band, his way of playing influenced the way every other musician in the band (and many others who heard him) played.

Jazz experts Gunther Schuller and Martin Williams give Armstrong credit for turning the Henderson band, and those that copied it, into swing bands. They call him a "major innovative figure in American music" and give him credit for creating swing. According to them, "Armstrong's main effect was that he introduced new ways of syncopation, a new rhythmic feel, a new

Profile

Louis "Satchmo" Armstrong
American Jazz Trumpeter
and Entertainer
1901-1971

LOUIS "SATCHMO" ARMSTRONG

This extraordinarily talented musician was introduced to the bugle and cornet at the age of 14 at the New Orleans' Colored Waifs' Home. For Louis Armstrong, the trumpet became his ticket from poverty to riches. He had an intuitive genius for making the instrument say more than it ever had before.

His early mentor in New Orleans was Joe "King" Oliver, the cornet-playing leader of the Creole Jazz Band. At 23, Armstrong was invited to join Oliver and his band in Chicago. With this band he made the first recordings of authentic jazz and exhibited his virtuosity as a jazz soloist. Lil Hardin, the pianist with the band, became his second wife in 1924. Through her prodding he left Oliver and joined the New York-based Fletcher Henderson Band, the best black orchestra of the time. His sensational improvised solos astounded his fellow musicians and set a new standard for jazz performance on any instrument.

To his big, warm trumpet sound, thrilling explosions in the high register, and brilliant improvisations, he added scat singing and "jive" vocals sung with his inimitable raspy but tender voice. He had a gentle way, a ready sense of humor, a broad grin, and a winning personality that audiences loved. He was the first to learn to swing, and the world followed in his footsteps.

---

kind of momentum to the music. The musicians, and eventually the audiences, needed a new name for it. The name was *swing*. The term swing refers to the special rhythmic character that jazz musicians add to the music.

Singlehandedly, Armstrong established the standard for solo jazz artistry. His facility on trumpet was phenomenal. He had a warm vibrato and an easy, full-bodied tone throughout the range of the instrument. Vocally, he complemented his instrumental improvisations with spontaneous singing on nonsense syllables. This **scat singing**—*a form of vocal improvisation*—became a characteristic that many jazz singers adopted. They would sing a chorus straight, then follow it with an improvised scat chorus. Scat singing became a form of creative expression in jazz, but the singing, too, was different—more rhythmic and hard-edged than the prevailing gentle and mellow crooning of the time.

During the 1920s, jazz evolved into a sectional form with the full ensemble alternating with solo sections. If the jazz composition was built on a blues tune, it might be segmented into 12- or 16-bar sections. Many of the tunes that were created maintained a basic 32-bar length. When an instrument improvised a chorus, it was usually 32 bars long, often including a two-bar break just before the next 32-bar section began. These short **breaks** were *cadenza-like improvisations by an instrumentalist or singer that were inserted between the ensemble passages*. Being able to distinguish these breaks allows the listener to anticipate the beginning of a new 32-bar section. The breaks added an interesting textural variety to the composition.

Among Armstrong's many great performances and creations is "Hotter Than That" (1927), a brilliant example of the new style of "hot" jazz. This work was composed by Lil Hardin Armstrong, the pianist in the Hot Seven band and Armstrong's wife. In the A^3 section, guitarist Lonnie Johnson maintains the steady 4/4 pulse while Armstrong improvises vocally in what is essentially a 3/4 rhythm. The performances throughout are improvisational within the format of a fairly strict sectional structure:

Hotter Than That

Sections	Performers	Length
Intro	Everyone	8 bars
A^1*	Trumpet & rhythm Clarinet Break (2)	32 bars
A^2*	Clarinet & rhythm Vocal Break (2)	32 bars
A^3*	Voice & guitar	32 bars
B	Voice/guitar duet**	16 bars
C	Piano interlude	4 bars
A^4	Trombone & rhythm (14) Trumpet Break (2)	16 bars
B	Everyone (14) Guitar Break (2)	16 bars
Coda	Trumpet (2) / Guitar (2)	4 bars

*There are also 2-bar breaks in these sections just ahead of the second 16 bars.

**Alternating 2-bar breaks.

From *Early Jazz: Its Roots and Musical Development* by Gunther Schuller. Copyright © 1968 by Oxford University Press, Inc. Reprinted By Permission. All Rights Reserved.

▼Activity: *Detect*

Can you hear and identify improvisation in Louis Armstrong's performance of "Hotter Than That"?

Follow the sectionalized analysis map (above) as you listen to this 1927 masterpiece. The first time you listen, make a list of all the sections in which you hear improvisation. In particular, note Armstrong's musical genius during both his trumpet and scat singing solos.

During a second listening, make a list of all the sections in which you hear breaks. (These are similar to the breaks in Jelly Roll Morton's "Black Bottom Stomp.")

Discuss: Why do this group and this piece represent the 1920s concept of "hot" jazz?

The Big Band Era

The Wall Street crash of 1929 led to the Great Depression of the 1930s that began in the United States and spread abroad. Many people lost their fortunes. Jobs were scarce and unemployment high. Survival was difficult. It was a time when people turned to motion pictures and music to lift their spirits. These were years when people drew together, and the Second World War united Americans as they had never been before. At its best, swing reflected this cohesiveness in its ensemble—musicians and dancers caught up totally by the beat. Radio spread the joy across the country.

The big band era began in earnest in the mid-1930s and went on to the end of the 1940s, a period of about 15 years. Swing, we should not forget, was primarily dance music. Teenage youth abandoned the serene fox trots and waltzes of their parents in favor of the frantic gyrations of the jitterbug and the lindy hop. The two-beat of early jazz gradually gave way to a solid four. The beats were now evenly accented and of equal value. Swing was a technique that could be applied to just about any existing piece of music. Jazz performers could translate a tune into the style of the moment.

First and foremost, the bands of the 1930s were dance orchestras, not jazz bands. The tunes that were best for dancing often became the popular, commercial successes. Compared with the best of the jazz that was produced by these bands, much of this music was mediocre. The need to make a living caused many jazz artists to compromise their art for the sake of commercial success.

◀ Bandleader, arranger, and clarinetist Woody Herman (1916–1987) and his Thundering Herd rode the crest of jazz through most of its manifestations from 1936 well into the 1980s. The popularity of the band was assured in 1939 with the million-selling recording, "Woodchopper's Ball."

Cooperative Learning

Debate

Which reed instrument is better suited to the performance of improvised jazz solos—the clarinet or saxophone?

While the clarinet enjoyed a prominent role during the early history of jazz, the saxophone became the favored reed instrument during the later swing era. Why did this happen? Was it just a trend?

Which of these two reed instruments would you argue is better for improvised jazz solos? In groups of three or four students, choose an instrument (clarinet or sax) and prepare to debate this issue. All of your information must be gathered by listening carefully to two different swing hits: "China Boy" featuring Benny Goodman (clarinet) and his trio, and "Cherokee" featuring Lester Young (tenor sax) and the Count Basie Orchestra.

Before you begin, it is important to note that both soloists are considered by jazz critics and historians to be among the finest musicians ever to have played these reed instruments. They are virtuosos. Also, the tunes were recorded within a year of one another (1938 and 1937 respectively) and both are composed in the standard A A B A song form. Finally, each features extensive improvisation on familiar melodies.

Start your debates after listening and taking notes. When you have concluded, answer this question: Why are these versions of "China Boy" and "Cherokee" classified as swing?

The best of the swing bands—those of Jimmy Lunceford, Fletcher Henderson, Count Basie, and Duke Ellington—were black, but there were many excellent white bands as well, among them, those of Tommy Dorsey, Benny Goodman, Woody Herman, Harry James, Stan Kenton, and Glenn Miller. Although it originated in black culture, swing was not wholly black music. The genre is defined not by color but by the artistic excellence of many fine performers and creators, both black and white, who contributed to its development. It is a travesty that in its early days, the recording industry, owned by whites, did not give black bands the visibility they deserved.

By the beginning of the swing era, around 1935, the saxophone had replaced the clarinet as the reed instrument of choice for solo jazz work. The one clarinetist who stayed very much in the forefront of jazz, however, was Benny Goodman. He was known as a virtuoso clarinet performer. Like Wynton Marsalis today, his broad musical education permitted him to play the classical literature as well as jazz. His big band was highly successful. In fact, he became known as the "King of Swing"—an unfortunate label because it suggested that other great bandleaders were somehow less competent. As an artist, Goodman could take almost any tune and polish it into a miniature gem; he was among the best.

As the saxophone began to define the swing era, many exceptional sax soloists began to set new standards for tonal beauty, technical wizardry, and improvisational creativity. According to jazz critic Grover Sales, "The saxophones became dominant jazz instruments because musicians sensed they were akin to the human voice and that you could make these instruments *sing.*" The saxophone gradually established itself as a jazz instrument largely in the hands of Coleman Hawkins (1904-1969). He demonstrated how his tenor sax could negotiate solos, and his influence helped to establish the sax section in the swing bands.

Count Basie's nine-piece band honed its style in Kansas City, where jazz and dance melded artfully. These musicians knew how to swing, and the band had a rhythm section—guitar, bass, and drums—that urged the musicians on. Basie's piano filled in and kept the rhythm swinging. The lead tenor saxophonist with the Count Basie Orchestra during the 1930s was one of the all-time great sax players—Lester Young. While Coleman Hawkins had established the tenor saxophone as a gutsy robust instrument, Young showed its lyrical and subtle richness. His playing became the model for other jazz musicians, including the incomparable Charlie Parker. Young inspired most of the artists that dominated jazz in the early 1950s, showing them a new sensitivity and artistry.

The 1940s and Bebop

Right after the Second World War, interest in jazz intensified. While big band jazz was becoming a formula, another style was emerging. Some of the younger jazz musicians wanted the freedom to create outside the confines of swing. This new style—called "bop" or "bebop"—was invented in

Benny Goodman
American Clarinetist and
Swing Band Director
1909-1986

BENNY GOODMAN

Like Louis Armstrong, Benny Goodman used his musical instrument as an opportunity. His poor Russian-Jewish family did not deter him from becoming a child virtuoso on clarinet. He took lessons at the local synagogue and played in the band at Jane Addams's Hull House. Later he studied privately with a member of the Chicago Symphony Orchestra.

When he was 16, he joined the Ben Pollack band in Los Angeles and three years later went with them to New York, which became his home base. In 1934, at the age of 25, he formed his own band and hired Fletcher Henderson as his chief arranger. Due largely to the depression, Henderson had been forced to disband his own orchestra earlier that year. Henderson's arrangements were responsible for establishing the character of the Goodman band—and much of its success. Goodman's band was featured on the Saturday evening coast-to-coast radio show, *Let's Dance*, causing a national craze for jitterbugging among young people.

Goodman was as competent at playing the classics as jazz. He set standards of excellence in both worlds. He was the first jazz artist to establish an equally successful parallel career as a concert artist. He commissioned contemporary composers Aaron Copland and Paul Hindemith to write clarinet concertos for him, and he appeared as a soloist with all the major American symphony orchestras.

Goodman ran a well-disciplined and musical swing ensemble. His band's performance at the Palomar Ballroom in Los Angeles in August 1935 is often cited as the beginning of the swing era. In 1936 Goodman established his trio, the first interracial musical group, with Gene Krupa on drums and Teddy Wilson on piano. He later expanded it to a quartet and subsequently a septet. In 1949 he disbanded his orchestra, marking the end of the swing era.

Harlem jam sessions that took jazz back to a small combo. **Bop**, *a complex and sophisticated type of improvised jazz, was an art for listening rather than dancing.* It was a reaction against the rigid conventions of swing. The jazz world was suddenly split into two camps: swing versus bop.

Trumpeter John Birks "Dizzy" Gillespie and alto saxophonist Charlie "Yardbird" Parker led this new movement and changed the face of jazz in the 1940s. They introduced melodic and harmonic innovations that established the style of contemporary jazz. These pioneers gave bop the sophistication of classical chamber music. Melodies became more chromatic. Harmonies and rhythms became far more complex. Beats were often doubled from four to eight, and constantly shifting accents created intricate polyrhythms. There were rapid tempos and dazzling technical displays but, at the same time, a seething soulfulness. Improvisations on the lips of these masterful musicians became more complex, dissonant, and daring. Parker's brilliance as an improviser was not measured just by the notes he could spin, but with the blues he could wrap them in. His bop could be melancholic. Through his improvisation a tune was transformed into a higher state—a reincarnation through invention.

I Got Rhythm

Words by Ira Gershwin

Music by George Gershwin

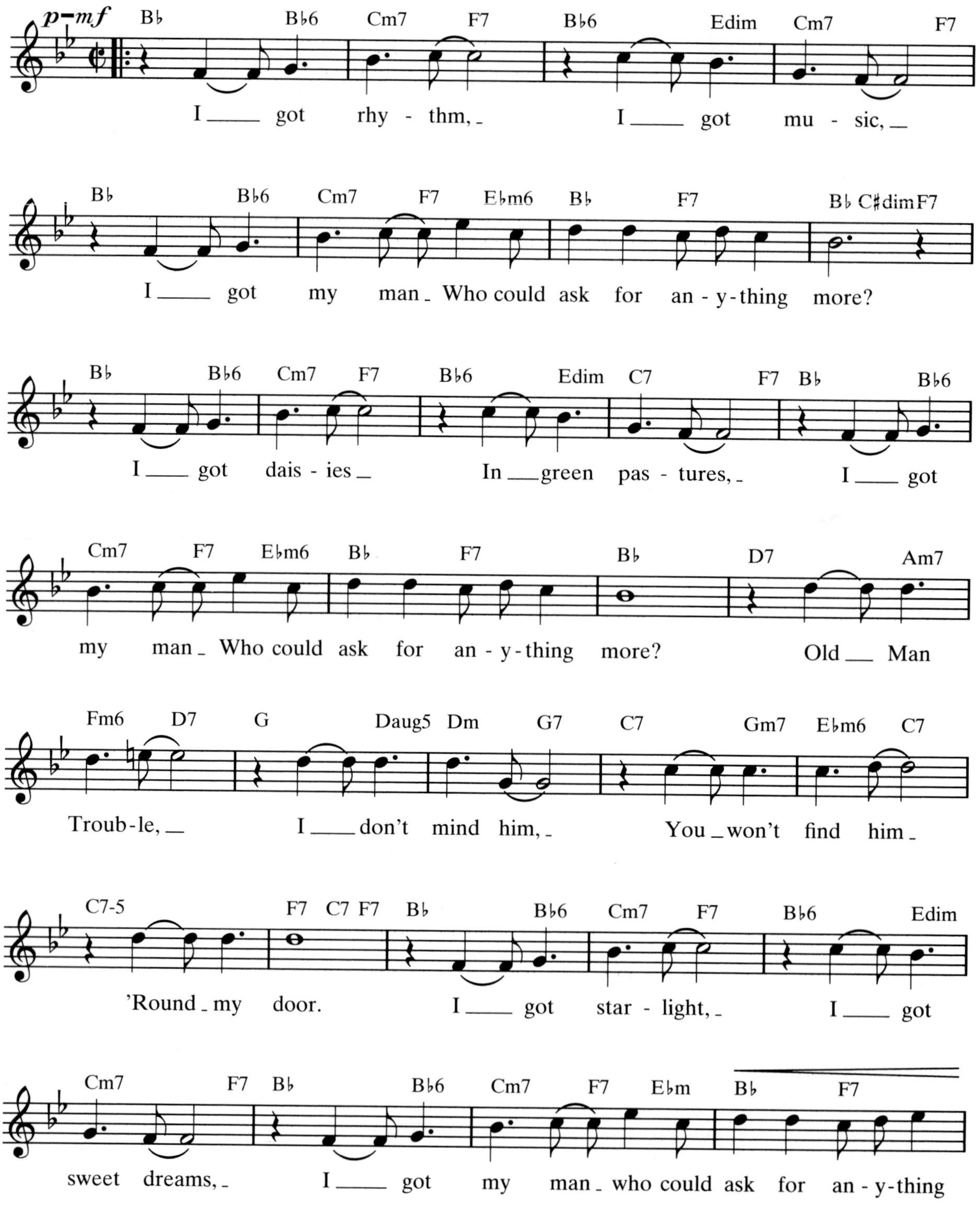

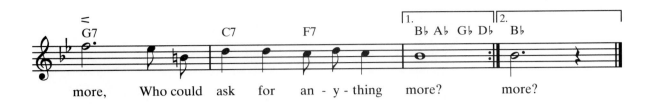

Bebop or "modern jazz" was a more intimate art than the big band jazz. Jazz artists realized that what they were doing and saying went deeper than just easy entertainment or music for dancing. They could be profound and virtuosic, subtle and sophisticated, sensitive and expressive. With bebop jazz declared itself an art and the performers, artists. One of the goals of these beboppers was to see how far they could stretch a musical composition while still maintaining its basic formal structure. Fast and creatively complex improvisation became the highest form of art. Together Parker and Gillespie expanded the language of jazz, and other musicians studied their innovations and learned from them.

▼Activity: *Perform*

Can you sing the melody of "I Got Rhythm" while you listen to two different jazz tunes?

To compare the complex and intricate improvisational style of bebop with the more dancelike feeling of swing, listen to two recordings based on George Gershwin's "I Got Rhythm." First, listen to Duke Ellington's *Cotton Tail* (1940) with its tenor sax solo performed by Ben Webster. (You previously studied this tune and Webster's brilliant improvisation in Chapter 18.) Then listen to "Shaw 'Nuff" (1945) by alto saxophonist Charlie Parker and trumpeter Dizzy Gillespie. While you listen to each tune, try to sing Gershwin's famous melody.

In which composition does the improvisation seem more "far out"? In which is it more difficult to stay true to the original melody?

Based on these performing and listening experiences, how would you describe the difference between bebop and swing?

▲ Alto saxophonist Charlie "Bird" Parker (1920–1955, left) was one of the greatest bebop soloists and improvisers, having a brilliant technique, magnificent tone, swinging rhythmic drive, emotional force, and most importantly, an incredible imagination. His 1945 collaboration with Dizzy Gillespie (1917–1993, right) produced some of the finest jazz music of the period.

Although jazz is largely an instrumental expression, there have been a number of outstanding jazz singers, beginning with Louis Armstrong and Billie Holiday and continuing later with such greats as Sarah Vaughn and Ella Fitzgerald. Jazz singers developed many of the techniques of the jazz instrumentalist—a natural brassy tone, a rhythmic delivery, and the ability to improvise. Jazz is not a simple art. It takes considerable practice and an excellent ear.

The term "jazz" gradually became the umbrella label for a number of styles—"swing" in the 1930s, "bebop" in the 1940s, "cool," "progressive," or "hard bop" in the 1950s, and "fusion" in the 1960s and 1970s. From

▶ With her rich contralto voice, singer Ella Fitzgerald (b. 1918) has become well known for her scat singing—vocal inventions that are the counterpart of instrumental jazz improvisations. Her finest work can be heard in her renderings of popular standards such as "Lady Be Good" and "How High the Moon."

ragtime, blues, and early jazz to the swing era and the bebop period, the jazz scene absorbed many dramatic and creative new directions. The new styles generally emerged even though the old style was still popular. Inevitably, there was a time when the old and new styles existed side by side. That is why the dating of these styles can appear to be confusing, and there is disagreement among the experts as to when these styles began and ended. In most cases there was a transition period during which the old style was waning while the new style was establishing itself and taking over.

You probably can easily distinguish ragtime from Dixieland or tell the difference between swing and bebop. Through all these stylistic changes, however, many of the basic musical forms and performance values (e.g., 12-bar blues and 32-bar A A B A song form, improvisation, syncopation, and the basic instrumentation of brass, saxophone, and rhythm) remained constant. It is the consistency of these "basics" that solidifies the musical linkage between all the evolving styles within the broad history of jazz.

The 1950s and Cool Jazz

Change often stems from dissatisfaction. That was the case again in the 1950s when there was a reaction against the complexity of bebop. The white reaction to bebop was a revival of older forms of jazz—Dixieland, ragtime, and the jazz style of King Oliver. The black reaction was a return to blues dressed up with a danceable beat, a style called "rhythm and blues." Still another reaction was the invention of a simpler style through the use of different modes—musical scales other than the major and minor.

One of the leading players of this "modal jazz" was trumpeter Miles Davis (1926–1991). Another innovator during this time period was the great jazz pianist Thelonious Monk (1917–1982). Davis and Monk are legends to millions of "hip" jazz fans.

Jazz now took a turn at being cerebral. The emotional intensity of bop was cast aside. Stan Getz, Miles Davis, Stan Kenton, Bill Evans, Dave Brubeck, Woody Herman, George Shearing, and Gerry Mulligan expanded the language of jazz technically. In the 1950s "progressive" or "cool" jazz, which incorporated a simpler melody and rhythm than bop, flourished chiefly on the West Coast. Sonny Rollins and John Coltrane led a wave of "hard bop." The 1950s was a time of diverse styles and rapid changes. Jazz was transforming itself once more.

The Miles Davis Sextet in the late 1950s included alto saxist Cannonball Adderley, pianist Bill Evans, and alto (later soprano) saxophonist John Coltrane. The Sextet was the principle jazz group of that time, producing influential albums such as *Miles Davis + 19* (1958) and *Kind of Blue* (1959). Davis's style of playing was restrained and moody, and it was copied endlessly. These albums brought a new public to jazz. The tune "All Blues" on the latter album is a 12-bar blues set in the **Dorian mode**, *a scale with the pattern of whole-step, half, whole, whole, whole, half, and whole.*

▼Activity: *Test Your Knowledge*

Can you identify traditional forms used in the "new" jazz of the 1950s?

The test: You will hear a composition performed by each of these jazz greats. Pianist Thelonious Monk plays his 1954 version of the classic song "Smoke Gets in Your Eyes," and trumpeter Miles Davis plays his almost entirely improvised tune "All Blues." The test here is simple. Listen carefully to the musical repetition and contrast in both examples and write down the form of each.

Lesson Extension: The influential "All Blues" with Davis and John Coltrane uses the Dorian mode beginning on G. Musicians call this "G Dorian," and it is an easy scale to play. The notes in the scale are G A B♭ C D E F G. You may want to play the following patterns along with the recording, then improvise some new ideas by using either set of just three notes.

Jazz took a back seat during the rock explosion of the 1960s and 1970s. This was a time of experimentation and of looking for new beginnings. There were attempts at collective improvisation. The "free jazz" of Ornette Coleman stretched expression to its ultimate limits, making music that was atonal and intellectualized. New structures were tried that broke away from reliance on repetition of a given harmonic pattern. There were experiments with different tempos and mixed meters, with new textures and densities, and with the use of timbres from other cultures. One of the briefer experiments in jazz was the concept that Gunther Schuller called "third-stream" music—a fusion of jazz with the techniques of Western art music. Jazz presented itself in many guises.

In the 1960s, Miles Davis and others managed to merge rock with jazz. This *jazz-rock combination*, called **fusion**, introduced electronic keyboards to jazz. The synthesizer was invited to become a jazz instrument. Musicians such as Herbie Hancock continue in this fusion vein today, relying heavily on technology. For purists, the problem is that fusion rather handily obscures two fundamental pillars of jazz: basic forms and improvisation. But jazz is still reinventing itself.

▼*Activity:* **Decide**

What makes this music a fusion of jazz and rock?

Listen to the fusion hit "Birdland" (1977), performed by Joe Zawinul and his five-member group, Weather Report. Do you hear a guitar—or is it a synthesizer?

Make a list of the qualities of this music that derive from rock and those that reflect jazz. Is it more rock, or more jazz?

▶ Two visual trademarks for which Dizzy Gillespie was noted were his "chipmunk-pouch" facial appearance when playing and the bent bell on his trumpet. He was featured in medical journals because his cheeks were so unusual. The bent bell on the trumpet came about when a friend accidentally stepped on it, bending it out of shape. Gillespie tried playing it and found that he liked the sound much better after the accident, so he chose to keep it that way.

◀ Tenor (and soprano) saxophonist John Coltrane (1926–1967) crafted his art while performing with Dizzy Gillespie, Miles Davis, and Thelonious Monk. His recordings from 1959 to 1965 demonstrate his majestic tone and emotional power. He continued to experiment, spending his final years exploring the free jazz of Ornette Coleman.

In jazz today, there is a simultaneous diversity of styles, all legitimate and acceptable. One style no longer dominates. In fact, almost all the jazz styles of the past remain current today. In the 1990s there is a trend of going back to acoustic jazz that has a bebop flavor. This jazz reflects a deep reverence for the creative and technical genius of Armstrong and Parker more than anyone else. The emphasis is on being moved by brilliant improvisation. As was true from the 1940s on, this music demonstrates that jazz is a vehicle for some of the most inspired and artistic creation imaginable.

Summary

The most original, influential, and American of all our music is jazz. It is one of the great contributions of African Americans to Western civilization. When Africans were uprooted and brought to the New World as slaves, their musical culture met head on with the European-based culture already here. Soon southern blacks were playing all the new instruments—cornets (trumpets), clarinets, trombones, saxophones, banjos and guitars, and doing so with the spontaneity, pizazz, and rhythmic sense that reflected their African heritage. They made the most of these new musical resources, and the result was a wholly original expression—jazz.

Taken as a whole, jazz is largely an up-tune, but its expressive range is as broad as its many styles. Tracing the evolution of this new musical species is difficult. It appears to have made its first recognizable appearance in New Orleans in the early years of the twentieth century. It spread quickly to other urban centers and spawned generations of musicians, both black and white, and a whole series of styles—Dixieland, small-band jazz, swing, bebop, free jazz, and fusion, among others. Today, jazz is an important part of every American's musical heritage, a unique and splendid art that reveals the vitality and the variety of our collective being.

Apply What You Have Learned
Chapter 22

Read the August 27, 1990 editorial from *The Washington Post* (below) and write an essay that addresses the following questions:

How can certain types of music be used to attract and repel people? Focusing on one of the musical styles referred to in the editorial, mention specific characteristics that would appeal to some people and offend others.

Easy Listening

Music continues to be the psychic battleground on which the fiercest campaigns of intergenerational culture war are waged. Forget the Beatles, forget the Stones, forget 2 Live Crew: this time, the aggression is going the other way—and classical and country-and-western are the chosen weapons. The Associated Press reports a widening circle of 7-Elevens and other convenience stores in the Pacific Northwest have begun to deal with the problem of disorderly young customers "hanging out" by filling the parking lots with music these customers can't stand: for instance, recordings of Mantovani and of Perry Como. The mastermind of the policy, a "loss prevention manager" for the Southland Corp. that owns the 7-Eleven chain, explains that he got the idea when he noticed his teenaged son fleeing the house whenever he played the '60s songs that are now referred to as "classic rock."

If this is the direct-mail philosophy played out in a weird new dimension, it nonetheless seems to work quite nicely. In Tillicum, near Seattle, a convenience store called Hoagy's Corner is blaring a country-and-western radio station in its parking lot to keep young GIs from two nearby military bases from sitting around too long in the parking lot with their own car radios on loud. (The country-and-western isn't so audible from inside the store, so the GIs still make their purchases, and the neighboring stores have nothing but praise for the selections.) Some 7-Elevens across the border in western Canada have cut down on loitering by playing Petula Clark or even Mozart.

A bemused representative of Muzak Inc., the corporation with perhaps the best handle on how to tailor one's piped-in music to attract a specific audience, calls this the perfect reverse of normal music-customer relations: "Usually you choose your music with an eye to the sort of customers you want to attract; why not for the sort of customers you want to repel?" Muzak is based in Seattle, but its representatives hasten to note that their own product, which they refer to as "environmental music," is not being utilized in this undertaking. We don't know if they should consider it a compliment, however. Going to piped-out Muzak in this particular war of nerves would probably be considered an unfair escalation, the moral equivalent of going nuclear.

Apply What You Have Learned
Chapter 23

Can you classify musical compositions according to their stylistic periods?

Listen to three selections representing the Renaissance, Baroque, and Classical styles. Write down the period each work represents and justify your choice of classification by relating what you know about the characteristics of each style.

Apply What You Have Learned
Chapter 24

Which of the following great jazz recordings would you recommend to a friend who asked your advice about contemporary jazz?

Listen to two performances of Ray Noble's song "Cherokee": one by the great jazz trumpeter, Clifford Brown (1930–1956), the other by the young jazz trumpet phenomenon, Marlon Jordan. Then write a letter to a close friend recommending only one of these two recordings. Pick the one you like better and give good reasons why it is your preference. Follow these steps:

1. As you listen to the performances, follow the sheet music of "Cherokee," the tune (in A A B A song form) that both Brown and Jordan use as the basis for their improvisational interpretations.
2. Notice how each man moves away rhythmically and melodically from the basic theme. As you listen, jot down notes that will help you evaluate the performances and decide on your preference.
3. Although both recordings feature virtuosos, pick the one you would recommend and describe your own level of understanding.

Cherokee

Ray Noble

Music!...
To Share
Our Humanity

~

Chapter 25
Folk, Popular, and Classical

Chapter 26
Styles Influencing Styles

Chapter 27
A Unique Record of Humankind

Folk, Popular, and Classical

Objectives

By completing this chapter, you will:

- Review how you can get the most out of new music you listen to.
- Realize that you can value many kinds of music for many different reasons.
- Recognize the basic differences between folk, popular, and classical music.
- Understand that the music of other cultures is not all folk music.
- Learn that we all have a responsibility to respect differences in musical tastes.

Musical Terms

folk music
genre
popular music

$\mathcal{L}$ike all the arts, music serves as a window on the
world, presenting us with insights that reinforce, clarify,
or challenge our perceptions. Each of us, as a listener or
a performer, engages with music to derive some kind
of satisfaction. The knowledge we bring to music—
our own familiarity with this communication system—
helps us to understand it. We must know the "language"
of music in order to be able to enjoy its revelations.
One way we learn this language is to grow up with it.
We hear the music around us, become accustomed to it,
and gradually come to understand it. The society we
live in conditions us to its musical traditions.

Unlocking Musical Meaning

Music is not one language but many. Although the music of different
societies serves many of the same purposes, the musical elements and
practices of making music often differ in the extreme. Music that is different from the music we grew up with poses difficulties, but they are not
insurmountable. We have to familiarize ourselves with the musical system
and, if the music is from a different culture, with the forms music takes
in that society.

In this section, you will be asked to put the knowledge you have
acquired to work and to come to terms with a broader vision of musical
styles. The music of the world can generally be classified as folk, popular,
or classical. All of the many different styles of music that you have studied fall into these broad categories. All of these styles have something to
say, but their messages are received with different degrees of difficulty. Some
give us their meaning with relative ease. Popular music is generally presented in a simple and direct form that speaks to us immediately. That is
what makes it popular or of mass appeal. Folk music may be simple or
difficult to understand, depending on our familiarity with the particular
tradition. Other music may require serious effort in order for the meanings to be unlocked. We have to study classical music and unfamiliar music
from other cultures in order to understand them. New music, or music
that is different from any we have heard, poses the greatest challenge. If
we are willing to listen several times and put some effort into it, we may
be treated to some new revelation. We have to communicate with the music
before it can communicate with us.

▼*Activity:* **Refine Your Approach**

What processes are involved in learning to perceive and react to a new musical composition?

Before you hear "The Pines of the Appian Way" from *The Pines of Rome* by Ottorino Respighi (1879–1936), ask yourself the following questions:

1. What image comes to mind when you read the title?
2. Have you ever heard of the composer? Speculate about his nationality.

   Now listen to the work.

3. Was your reaction to the work different from the image that came to your mind when you read the title?
4. In listening, did you put to work some of the new musical perceptions that you have acquired?
5. What other knowledge might help you understand this work?
6. Would knowing more about the composer help?

Before you hear this work again, go to the library and investigate the composer. Write a report that answers the following questions: (a) Where did Respighi live? (b) Did he study with other composers? (c) What other works did he compose? (d) What is the style of his music? (e) What other works that you have studied are similar in style? Come to class ready to share your insights.

Now listen to the work again, putting your musical perceptions to work as well as the knowledge you have acquired. How does this affect your reaction?

Discuss what makes one musical work so readily understandable and others more difficult to grasp. What should you do to make a musical work more understandable?

Why We Value Music

Throughout this text, you have listened to and studied many different kinds of music concurrently. The juxtaposition of these different styles was deliberate, so that you could see how various kinds of music address many of the same general social themes and purposes, achieve unity and variety, and touch us emotionally. It would be a mistake, however, to think that all music is of the same or equal value. We can treasure music for its simple emotional directness, its subtle profundity, its mysteriousness, its spirituality, its compelling fascination, or for many other reasons. We can savor a work because of its particular musical qualities or because of the way it serves a special purpose or function.

There are reasons for the variety of musical styles. Music plays different social roles. It relates to us as human beings in a specific way and usually in a specific environment. It reveals certain aspects of life and not others. Each **genre**, or *style of music* does something different—and often better than—some other style. Each is necessary because no one style of music can say everything or serve all the functions required of music. These stylistic differences are important and complementary. They permit music to speak across the entire population and to serve broad, comprehensive purposes. Music should be valued accordingly.

◀ The Philadelphia Symphony Orchestra is one of the 250 fully professional symphony orchestras in the United States that perform for upwards of 27 million audience members each year. (That's not counting the people who hear them on radio or recordings.) In addition, there are roughly 1,400 student, amateur, or semi-professional orchestras that perform for thousands more. The sound of a live symphony orchestra can be an exciting and emotionally overpowering sonic experience, and the more you know about music, the more you will respond to it.

▼Activity: *Show Your Wisdom*

What are the reasons people value a wide variety of musical styles and genres?

Listen to the following examples. Decide why each musical example is regarded as significant and important for the society in which it functions as a mode of expression. Focus on musical descriptors to validate your responses. Draw upon the musical knowledge and understanding you have acquired.

Title	Source/Composer
"Gloria in excelsis Deo" from the *Missa Solemnis*	Ludwig van Beethoven
"Ay te dejo en San Antonio"	Flaco Jimenez
Piano Concerto No. 2	Sergei Rachmaninoff
Liberty Fanfare	John Williams
"Hush, Hush, Somebody's Callin' Mah Name"	(traditional) Spiritual

Can one person value all these different types of music?

Distinguishing Styles

Categorizing music is a tricky business. There are no easy definitions or answers. There are many styles of folk, popular, and classical music in our own society and in other societies around the world. These terms are big catchalls that are convenient to use in general ways. But as soon as we look (and listen) more carefully, we find that the definitions do not always suffice to describe the reality of the music itself. This is a major reason for inventing names to distinguish specific styles within the large categories: hard rock, heavy metal, folk rock, country rock, and so forth.

Still, these designations—folk, popular, and classical—delineate and define large bodies of music. They distinguish fundamental differences. Knowing the meaning of these terms and applying them with care helps us understand and communicate. Yet these labels are sometimes used derogatorily. The term "classical" is used to mean "stuffy," the label "folk," to imply "simplistic," and the term "popular," to suggest trivial and unimportant. The terms are used to pit one kind of music against another: popular versus classical or vice versa. Such misuses have been blamed on a disease called "hardening of the categories." We shall look at these broad genres of music one more time, now that we have experienced different examples of them. The object is to make certain that their real meaning is clear.

Popular Music

The idea of popular music developed with the rise of the middle class during the nineteenth century in Europe and America. Prior to this time, music was usually associated with the church or the aristocracy: the courts of Europe and those who had position and wealth. The folk and dance music of the people (and let us not forget that the commoners always had their own forms of music making) was not considered to be at the center of musical culture. Their music was not written down or given serious study.

As the growth of industrialization brought prosperity to greater numbers of people, the expanding urban middle class embraced its own musical culture. What appealed to them was music they could readily understand, music that was relatively simple in construction and easy to perform. This new popular music was made widely available through published sheet music and, later on, through recordings and broadcasting. In the 1960s, inexpensive portable radios and record players permitted young people to make this music a passionate avocation. Today, the term "popular" has often become synonymous with "commercial," and some composers write strictly to meet the demands of the marketplace and instant appeal.

The Style

Popular music generally refers to *relatively short works with a prominent melody and a simple chordal accompaniment.* Often the work is sung. In the nineteenth century, popular music originated in minstrel shows and other popular entertainments, and even included some folk music and "light" classical music. It was music that met the tastes and interests of the broader public. Popular music served to raise the morale of the growing industrial population who had little access to concert halls.

During the first half of the twentieth century, popular music came from operettas, vaudeville, and Broadway revues and musicals. It was the ever-present dance music of the day. When sound was introduced to motion pictures in the 1930s, films became a rich source of popular music. Today in the United States, popular music is everywhere—in dance halls, on radio and television, in theaters and concert halls, in stadium concerts, in films, and on recordings. It is the mainstream musical culture of American democracy.

Over the years, popular music has taken its blows. As recently as 1991, Gerald Early, professor of English and African-American Studies at Washington University in St. Louis, said of it: "American popular music thumbs its nose at the respectability of art while yearning for nothing but that respectability. This contradiction is the source of its strengths, and of its imbecility, its cheapness, its nonsense, its incivility, its disregard of taste." Although popular music may be relatively simple, it is not necessarily shallow. It can be entertaining, and it can be serious. The intent is almost always pleasurable. Fortunately, a number of highly inventive composers have brought particular distinction to American popular culture.

◀ It is often difficult to specifically categorize musicians or the type of music they produce, and Jerry Jeff Walker (b. 1942) provides a good example. Although he started as a guitarist and folk singer, he has dabbled in folk-rock, country, and pop. His song, "Mr. Bojangles," composed in 1968, became established as an American pop classic when Sammy Davis, Jr. began performing it regularly as part of his repertoire.

Mr. Bojangles

By Jerry Jeff Walker

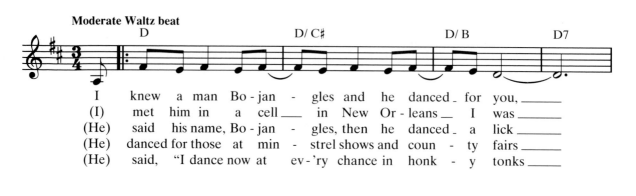

Moderate Waltz beat

I	knew a man Bo-jan - gles and he danced_ for you, _____
(I)	met him in a cell___ in New Or - leans __ I was _____
(He)	said his name, Bo-jan - gles, then he danced_ a lick _____
(He)	danced for those at min - strel shows and coun - ty fairs _____
(He)	said, "I dance now at ev-'ry chance in honk - y tonks _____

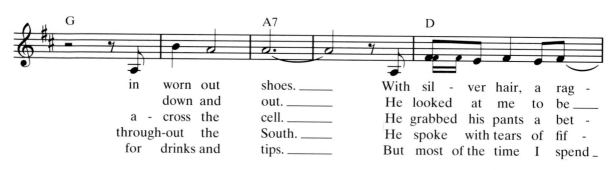

in	worn out	shoes. _____	With sil - ver hair, a rag -
down and	out. _____	He looked at me to be ___
a - cross the	cell. _____	He grabbed his pants a bet -
through-out the	South. _____	He spoke with tears of fif -
for drinks and	tips. _____	But most of the time I spend_

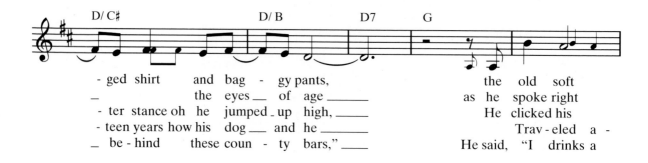

- ged shirt and bag - gy pants,	the old soft
_ the eyes __ of age _____	as he spoke right
- ter stance oh he jumped_ up high, _____	He clicked his
- teen years how his dog __ and he _____	Trav - eled a -
_ be - hind these coun - ty bars," ____	He said, "I drinks a

shoe. _____	He jumped so high,	jumped _____ so
out. _____	He talked of life,	talked _____ of
heels. _____	He let go a laugh,	let _____ go __ a
bout. _____	His dog up and died,	he _____ up __ and
bit." _____	He shook his head	and as he shook his

Folk Music

Folk music was *the first popular music. It is generally uncomplicated, and it speaks to us directly of everyday matters.* The indigenous music of the world evokes the heart and soul and the lifestyle of the people from which it comes. It evokes the human qualities of those people. It speaks directly to us of the simple pleasures of life and of life's foibles and difficulties.

Folk songs often do more than tell stories; they espouse a cause. Music can give a cause more immediacy, vitality, and impact. Some folk songs have a "message" and are specifically created to publicize or criticize a controversial political or social issue. These issues are important to the people singing and listening to them. Such music is socially conscious. It may

▲ In 1931, some 10,000 miners went on strike in West Virginia, demanding better working conditions. Striking miners and symphathizers march along the road near their homes from which they have been evicted. It was the cause of these union workers that inspired the creation of songs such as "Which Side Are You On?"

make a case for caring about people in need, or our environment, or an endangered species of animal. It may issue some form of political statement of protest. The feature that these songs share is the expression of a longed for ideal (such as civil rights) on the part of the creators, singers, and listeners. These are songs of struggle that help us to react to the world around us.

The struggle of working men and women to gain fairer wages and working conditions is one of the oldest civil rights campaigns in our country. From the period following the Civil War, in the late 1800s, until the present, workers have sought to organize themselves into unions (such as the American Federation of Labor) as a way of protecting themselves against exploitation and bad economic conditions. Miners have a long history of protest and struggle to improve their working conditions. In 1931 Florence Reece, the wife of a Kentucky coal miner, wrote the words to the song "Which Side Are You On?" to bring the miners together to join the union. The melody was originally an old hymn tune, but the lyrics have an almost militant edge. This is an example of folk music.

Which Side Are You On?

Words by Florence Reece

Music: Old hymn tune
Arranged by Waldemar Hille

My daddy was a miner, and I'm a miner's son
And I'll stick with the union, till every battle's won . . .
They say in Harlan County, there are no neutrals there
You'll either be a union man, or a thug for J.H. Blair.

Oh, workers, can you stand it? Oh, tell me how you can.
Will you be a lousy scab, or will you be a man?
Don't scab for the bosses, don't listen to their lies.
Us poor folks haven't got a chance, unless we organize . . .

▼Activity: **Discuss**

How does "Which Side Are You On?" reflect a sense of struggle?

Listen to the Weavers sing "Which Side Are You On?" Discuss and debate the following questions:

1. How would you answer this question yourself?
2. How might this question polarize a community?
3. Which verses could be sung about any union?
4. Without changing the chorus, for what other social issues could this song be adapted?
5. What qualities make this a folk song?

We distinguish folk music as music that has been handed down by the aural/oral tradition. We do not usually know the composer. Indeed, there are many composers, because successive performers created their own versions. They altered the melody, rhythm, harmony, dynamics, and/or lyrics—the character—to suit their own musical technique, taste, message, and purpose. Folk music is music that people feel they can make their own. Nowadays, the transmission of music is accomplished largely through technology—via recordings and printed scores. Passing a song on from one person to another is still practiced, but largely in rural areas.

▼Activity: **Distinguish**

Can you define the differences between popular music and folk music?

Listen to one example in each of these musical genres (popular and folk) as the basis for writing two short paragraphs about each category. Listen carefully and apply what you have learned about analyzing musical genres. The challenge is to write accurate descriptive definitions of both popular and folk music—*without* comparing the two examples in your definitions. Cite as many characteristics as you can.

After writing your paragraphs, be prepared to answer the following questions:

1. What are the greatest similarities between folk and popular music?
2. What are the greatest differences between these two categories?
3. Would you classify either one of these two pieces as rock music? Why or why not?

Ethnic Folk Music

People who share a common culture, ancestry, and language also generally share a common music. Ethnic folk music reflects this ethnicity, even when the group is a small (but distinct) part of the larger heterogeneous (varied) population. Americans of Puerto Rican extraction, for example, share a musical tradition called *musica jíbara* (MOO-see-kah HEE-bah-rah), the jíbaros being the farmers, fishermen, and laborers who developed their own unique culture. This is music of the people. Wherever Puerto Ricans live, you are apt to find them enjoying traditional musica jíbara.

This music requires the skills of both the musician and poet. The typical jíbara musical ensemble, called *conjunto* jíbaro (kohn-HOON-toh), centers upon a *cuatro* (KWAH-troh), a uniquely shaped guitar with ten metal strings, that plays the melody, accompanied by a guitar, guiro (WEE-roh—a gourd rasp), and often bongos. But the focus of attention is on the solo singer. The songs consist of a series of ten-line poetic stanzas called *décimas* (DEH-see-mahs). Each line of the décima must be eight syllables long and fit into a fixed rhyme scheme: A B B A A C C D D C. The singer is as much a poet as a singer!

In some cases décimas are improvised on the spot—no easy feat. The text may discuss current events such as a hurricane, relate Biblical stories, or report on everyday situations. A poet/singer might be hired to perform at a birthday party to sing improvised décimas about the person celebrating, the guests, or other lighthearted topics.

The singer Enrique Galarza composed the décimas of "Mi triste lamento" ("My sad lament") to express his feelings of sadness about his loss of skill at improvising décimas. He says that all he has left is his "amor a la canción" (love of song). In this song, he mentions the *pie forzado* (pee-EH for-SAH-doh), literally the "forced foot of poetry," a reference to the fixed last line of each décima (or stanza) that adds to the challenge of improvisation.

P R O J E C T

Find Your Musical Roots

Find out if there is a tradition of ethnic or folk music in your community. You may have parents or grandparents or elders in your community who came to the United States from another country. Do they recall any storytelling songs (ballads or narrative songs) that are a special part of their heritage? If so, try one of the following:

1. See if the person will permit you to make a tape recording of the song. Find out on what occasions the song was sung and the social reason for the song's existence.

2. Write down the words of the song. Does the song have a message? Does it tell a story? What is it about? Does it refer to a specific historical event? Prepare a report for the class.

◀ A Puerto Rican décima singer performs at a birthday celebration at a small country store in Orocovis, Puerto Rico.

▼*Activity:* **Find Out**

Do all four décimas of "Mi triste lamento" ("My sad lament") adhere to the typical décima rhyme scheme of A B B A A C C D D C?

Listen to this traditional Puerto Rican song-story which comprises a series of ten-line poetic stanzas called décimas and check the rhyme scheme of each décima or stanza to see if it complies with the pattern.

Does each décima (stanza) have the same melody?

Why is improvising décimas so challenging?

What is there about the instrumental part of the music that allows the meaning of the text to be heard?

How does this ethnic music define Puerto Ricans and their culture? What does it tell us about them?

▶ Elvis Presley (1935–1977), the king of rock 'n' roll, was a singer, guitarist, composer, and actor. In 1956, his first major hit "Heartbreak Hotel," one of many that followed, helped to establish rock 'n' roll as the dominant form of popular music. Today his legend lives on, and Graceland, his home in Memphis, Tennessee, continues to be visited by his fans.

Rock Music

Like every major musical genre, rock music consists of many individual styles. The music of the Jefferson Airplane, the Beatles, the Rolling Stones, the Who, Led Zeppelin, and other groups is not alike, even though there is a common spirit. Rock music emerged in response to social and political events in the 1950s and early 1960s. The civil rights movement in the United States was trying to correct decades of repression and persecution. At the same time, people rebelled against the social mores and rigidity of the 1950s. They sought a new openness and personal liberation. Music became one of the centerpieces of this largely youthful rebellion.

The first artist to bring rock 'n' roll to a broad public was Elvis Presley (1935–1977). Born in Mississippi, Presley was influenced by gospel music, rhythm and blues, and country music. He blended these black and white musical influences to help create the style known as rock 'n' roll in the mid-1950s. His first major hit was "Heartbreak Hotel" (1956). From then on, he had a succession of hits, and he commanded a large audience of faithful fans. He constituted a major threat to the establishment singers such as Bing Crosby and Frank Sinatra, who could not and would not sing this new style of music. Presley is the only singer whose popularity rivaled that of the Beatles, and they admired his work and were greatly influenced by him. He is the most important performer of the rock 'n' roll era.

The music itself took advantage of the new possibilities afforded by electronic amplification and distortion. Musicians burst out of the confines and constraints of the prevailing popular forms. They experimented with freer forms, new harmonies, driving rhythms that emphasized the second and fourth beats, and different timbres. The lyrics were sometimes political, sometimes very personal and poetic. The electric guitar became the main musical instrument. There were distinctive soloists: Janis Joplin, Bob Dylan, Jimi Hendrix, and Jim Morrison, among others.

The Beatles were pacesetters. Their music was highly original, artful, and expressive. Their four-piece ensemble consisted of the standard lead (or solo) guitar, rhythm guitar, bass guitar, and drums, but later they supplemented their sound with sitar and violins. They took advantage of the creative possibilities afforded by the development of multiple track tape recording. They recorded different tracks and then overlaid the sounds to create textures of considerable sophistication and complexity—effects they could not reproduce in live performance.

Country Music

Soon after radio broadcasting was started in the United States in 1920, country music was being sent over the airwaves throughout the rural areas of the South. This was the music of the isolated populations in the hilly regions of the rural South and West. Urban populations had little taste or liking for it. They thought of it as hillbilly music. Country music then was a mixture. It consisted of narrative ballads; lively instrumental dance music

▲ For many years, The Oak Ridge Boys, who now prefer to be called The Oaks, were one of the top groups in gospel music. However, in 1975 they decided to move into the country music genre and within three years they won the first of many Country Music Association awards.

played on the fiddle, guitar, and banjo; and religious music in the form of hymns and gospel tunes that were highly emotional and personal. Much of this music reflected the Scottish traditions that immigrants had brought to this country. The music was homespun and largely amateur. It was the antithesis of European art music.

Today country and western music is a popular style of American music. How did it happen? In the 1920s, the new southern and western radio stations began to showcase their local country performers. Public interest was aroused. Barn dance programs soon became the rage. Americans everywhere took to square dancing, and country music was "in." A whole recording industry arose in Nashville and elsewhere to exploit this new public interest. By the mid-1930s, cowboy singers such as Gene Autry became folk heroes through their films and recordings. Nashville's Grand Ole Opry became an American musical institution, and broadcasts from there helped to establish country music as a major and respectable form of American musical entertainment. Country and western music continues to evoke the simplicity of rural life. Although it is now broader in style and message, and somewhat more sophisticated than in earlier days, styles such as bluegrass maintain the integrity of the folk tradition.

Classical Music

Not all classical music is great. Not all classical or so-called art music is profound. Length and complexity do not automatically make music better. At its best, however, there are moments of extraordinary revelation in classical music that enlighten our humanity. The mystery and meaning of life is probed. The human spirit is revealed, rejuvenated, and replenished. The classical music of the ages can put us in touch with the accumulated wisdom and insight that preceded us. That is why we call some music and art "classic." It continues to relate to the here and now. The reason we call Shakespeare's plays "classics" is that they continue to speak to our concerns today. This is true of classical music as well. It reaches out across the ages to say something important to us now.

Like the genres of popular and folk music, the genre of classical music consists of not one style but many. In spite of the individual styles it encompasses—Renaissance, Baroque, Classical, Romantic, and Modern—its broad characteristics clearly distinguish it from other major musical genres such as folk and popular.

▼ At the age of ten years, Mozart is captured in this painting by French artist Ollivier Michel Barthelemy (1712–1784), as he plays for the aristocracy while they enjoy an afternoon tea. While Mozart's music is of the Classic period or style, many of his compositions are regarded as *classic*—pieces that reach across the centuries to touch us deeply and speak to our concerns today.

Ollivier Michel Barthelemy. *Le thé à l'Anglaise au Temple Chez le Prince de Conti.* 1766. Louvre, Paris, France.

▲ Pianist Eugene Istomin came to national attention at the age of 17, when, as a result of winning both the Leventritt and Philadelphia Orchestra Youth awards, he made professional debuts in the same year with the Philadelphia and the New York Philharmonic orchestras. He was the first American musician to give concerts in both Cairo and Tel Aviv after the signing of the Israeli-Egyptian Peace Treaty. He has also given recitals in Tokyo, Seoul, Hong Kong, and Taipei.

▼Activity: **Explain**

What are the basic differences between classical and popular music?

Compare the following compositions: "My Funny Valentine" by Richard Rodgers, and the fourth movement of the *Ninth Symphony* by Ludwig van Beethoven.

Use the following criteria to make your comparison:

- Text/message.
- Vocal style.
- Timbre/instrumentation.
- Degree of complexity.
- Intended audience.

Write a short paragraph focusing on the following:

1. What are the most obvious differences between these compositions?
2. What are the similarities?
3. What are the differences in the technical demands on the composer and performers?
4. Is one of the compositions "better" music than the other one?

Classical Traditions Elsewhere

The music of other cultures is often miscategorized as folk music. The traditional music of India, Egypt, Indonesia, and China, for example, has been handed down aurally over many decades, or even centuries, and no one knows who created it. These are folk characteristics. At the same time, however, this music has characteristics that are decidedly classical. It is often highly complex and deals with profound subject matter. It is an art with a difficult technique that can be mastered only with years of effort. It is sometimes considered to be the highest art of that culture. In such cases, the categorizing of music as "folk" or "classical" is misleading. This music seems to carve out a middle ground between the two. Our labels for music are inexact. We therefore have to be careful how we use and apply them.

Just as American musical culture spans folk, popular, and classical styles, other cultures embrace a variety of styles. Mexico, for example, has a strong folk tradition that includes mariachi, but it also has a classical tradition with composers as world famous as Carlos Chavez (1899–1978). In the twentieth century, many nations around the world have been influenced by our Western system—politically, economically, and culturally. It is important to remember that what you have learned in this course is only the beginning of an understanding of the world of music. One course cannot provide all the answers, all the insights. The great door to musical understanding has been opened, but many adventures still await you on the other side.

We may never be able to hear or understand the music of another culture in the same way as a person from that culture does; however, we can derive pleasure from it and some sense of its emotional impact. To do so we must spend time with the music and try to understand the tradition behind it. We have to avoid dismissing this music by assigning it a derogatory label that stereotypes it as unworthy of our interest. Even the term "folk" can be a put-down, depending on how we use it.

▼Activity: **Discuss**

Is the traditional music of other countries simple folk music?

Listen to the excerpt from the Balinese music drama *Kecak* (keh-CHAK) that you heard in Chapter 16. This is the scene of "Sita's Abduction" (see page 297).

1. Is this music simple or complex? How do you know?
2. Can this music be learned quickly or does it take considerable time and effort to learn? How do you know?
3. Is this music easy or difficult to perform? Why?
4. Is the subject matter simple or profound?
5. How would you label this type of traditional music—as folk, popular, or classical? Why?

All the Music for All the People

Democracy begs the question: Can we have quantity and quality at the same time? The French observer Alexis de Tocqueville thought not. In 1835, after a year of travel in the U.S., he wrote in his book *Democracy in America:* "Is it your object to refine the habits, embellish the manners, and cultivate the arts, to promote the love of poetry, beauty, and glory? . . . If you believe such to be the principal object of society, avoid the government of a democracy, for it would not lead you with certainty to the goal." In the production of goods, America has shown that quality and quantity need not conflict. The fact that a product is made widely available does not mean that it is necessarily shoddy. We have made the visual arts and music accessible to all through inexpensive reproductions, including recordings. The commercial mass market manages to produce for a variety of tastes and does not cater just to the lowest common denominator, although the latter often commands the most attention.

America is a pluralistic society that is held together by a belief in freedom, opportunity to work and acquire, and a culture borne of commerce and industry. Music expresses our similarities and differences as a nation comprising many ethnic groups. It represents and interprets the many worlds of our composite nature. Through music, we acknowledge that as human beings we are not just cold brains and logic but also emotional, caring persons who dream, hope, fear, and suffer.

As Americans, we are free to place ourselves in the smaller or the larger world in which we exist. We can be a Korean, an Asian American, an American, or all three. Our musical choices reflect the way we view ourselves socially. If we are Mexican American, we can listen only to Mexican music, to a mixture of Mexican and American music, or to all the different kinds of music that comprise American culture. Technology has made all music accessible to all people. One no longer has to be rich to be able to have access to opera and symphonic music. We live in a pluralistic society. We can enjoy it all.

Music: Where and When?

Music can be used indiscriminately and inappropriately. It can be made so pervasive in our lives that it becomes tiresome. We shut it out. When music is constant over long periods, it can become annoying. We may end up treating it with indifference or even hostility. Music requires its counterpart—silence—in order to be special. We must have the right kind of music in the right circumstances. Then it can speak to us with its full intent and impact.

Music making (and listening) depend upon certain conditions. Primitive people do not make music when they are hungry. According to ethnomusicologist John Blacking, the forces of self-preservation tend to separate people from each other. Only after self-preservation is assured do they restore their sense of community. Then they rebalance their lives by placing the self back into its social context. They make music together. They have the time and the energy to tend to their spirit.

In our busy, high-tech world, the conditions for using and enjoying music are sometimes haphazard. We cannot always control them. Electronics have advantages and disadvantages. They permit us to have music any time, whether we want it or not, whether it is appropriate or inappropriate. They also allow music—often the wrong kind of music—to invade our privacy in food stores, elevators, on the telephone, and at other times and other places.

Ann Landers

Dear Ann Landers:

I love and appreciate good music but spare me the stuff that is piped into every bank, doctor's and dentist's office, store, restaurant, beauty parlor, mall etc. There is no escaping the merciless din. It's even in the elevators. We have no choice and are forced to listen to what somebody else enjoys. I hope the store managers will take note because I have walked out of several shops when I could no longer stand the racket. Where are my rights to a little peace and quiet? Companies pay good money for this so-called entertainment. What a waste.

What is wrong with our culture that we cannot go anywhere—and I mean anywhere—without being entertained? What does this say about us? Please respond in print. It's time someone spoke up.—Anybody, Anywhere, U.S.A.

Reproduced by permission from Ann Landers's and Creators' Syndicate. *The Washington Post,* August 9, 1991.

▼Activity: *Offer Your Advice*

When does music become "noise pollution?"

Read the letter Ann Landers published in her advice column in August of 1991. Do you agree or disagree with the writer?

Instructions:

1. Working on your own, jot down notes that support your viewpoint. Take a definite stand (agree or disagree) and outline the arguments you would make in response.

2. Next, bring your notes to a small group of three or four classmates. Compare your viewpoints and discuss the different arguments each person made on his or her own. Answer the following questions in your discussion group:

   - Can you think of a time when you were genuinely bothered by music over which you had no control? Why? Did the style of the music have anything to do with your reaction?
   - Can you think of a time when you actually liked the music you heard in some public place? Why? What was the music?
   - When is piped-in music or forced listening appropriate? Where or when is it inappropriate?
   - Is it one's civic responsibility to respect the privacy and musical tastes of others?

3. After concluding your discussion, return to individual work and write your advice in response to this letter. Summarize your opinion. Write clearly and persuasively. Be prepared to turn in your paper.

▲ Above is a photo of a sign in the parking lot of Porky's Bar-B-Que in Pine Mountain, Georgia. Who do you think the owners had in mind?

Summary

Thanks to recorded sound, all the styles of music are available to us. No one in the United States has to be stuck in a musical ghetto—whether that narrowly focused style is hard rock, rap, folk, or classical music. The wonder of American democracy with technological communication at everyone's fingertips is the possibility it provides for all of us to spread our wings. We can cast off restrictions and choose to be part of the culture around us. We can embrace the wider world of music in all its wondrous manifestations. We can like various kinds of music for different reasons. We can use music to reach beyond emptiness and trivia and trashiness to cherish the higher values of our humanness—love for other people, respect for those who are different from us, beauty in all things, the triumph of the human spirit, and other moral values.

This is not to say that all dance music is equally good, or that dance music is as good as classical music, or that classical music is better than popular music. We can still discriminate within the types. We can still have our likes and dislikes. We can recognize that we are probably not going to want to dance to Beethoven, nor can we hope to probe the more mysterious realms of our being through a popular dance tune. We can choose music for entertainment, and we can choose it for its profound emotional insight. We do not have to limit ourselves to one or the other. We can have it all. The wider our choice, the more that music will reflect our mental and emotional life in all of its vast diversity.

CHAPTER 26

Styles Influencing Styles

Objectives

By completing this chapter, you will:

- Find out how different styles of music can affect each other.
- Discover how music in one culture is influenced by the music of another.
- Learn how a rhythm in South Africa is transported and transformed into the Cuban cha-cha, and early American rock 'n' roll.
- Familiarize yourself with the work of American composers Louis Moreau Gottschalk, George Gershwin, and John Lewis.
- Become acquainted with the music of composers Antonín Dvořák, Claude Debussy, Igor Stravinsky, Modest Mussorgsky, and Heitor Villa-Lobos.

Musical Terms

acculturation
clave
crossover
pentatonic scale
time line

$\mathcal{M}$usic has a good deal of influence on itself,
and this works in a number of different ways.
Sometimes, for example, the music of one culture
will affect the music of another. An American classical
piece, for example, might incorporate Latin rhythms.
One example you are familiar with is Aaron Copland's
El Sálon México. Cross-cultural influences can be even
more sweeping as, for example, when the Japanese
adopted Western symphonic music. Most Japanese cities
of any size have a symphony orchestra that performs a
largely Western repertoire—Mozart, Beethoven, Brahms,
and so on. This is cultural adoption and absorption
on a grand scale. The Japanese have become
so Westernized that they now export classical
artists who perform around the world.

Influences from One Musical Style to Another

Not all influences of music upon itself are of this magnitude, but they are always of consequence. The blending of styles, however modest, is significant. As traditions are adapted and transformed, the resulting music exhibits a different character.

Folk to Classical

Folk songs have served as a major source of inspiration for classical composers. During the nineteenth century, many composers expressed their nationalism by incorporating their country's folk music in their compositions. Some accomplished this by imitating folk music; others actually incorporated the tunes. In Norway, for example, Edvard Grieg (1843–1907) was one of the first composers to cultivate the rhythmic and melodic flavor of native (Norwegian) folk songs in his works. Following this same path, the Finnish composer Jean Sibelius (1865–1957) created melodic patterns that were characteristic of Finnish folk music. In Hungary, both Béla Bartók (1881–1945) and Zoltán Kodály (1882–1967) collected Slavic folk songs and were influenced by them. Bartók often evoked this Slavic feeling in his music, while Kodály quoted these folk songs directly. All these composers were considered "nationalistic" because their music deliberately reflected and asserted their culture.

Profile

Louis Moreau Gottschalk
American Pianist and Composer
1829–1869

LOUIS MOREAU GOTTSCHALK

No matter where he performed in the world, Louis Gottschalk wowed his audiences. He was charming and friendly and his many trips abroad spread goodwill, particularly to the Latin American people. This American pianist was a virtuoso performer and the first solo musician from America to become world renowned. Today he is an all but forgotten, highly gifted American composer who deserves to be rediscovered.

Born in New Orleans, Gottschalk could pick out tunes on the piano when he was only four. He was sent to Paris to study when he was 11 but was refused admittance to the Paris Conservatory because, according to Gottschalk's own notes, "America was only a country of steam engines."

Even at 11, Gottschalk was not a person to be discouraged. He studied privately in Paris and made his debut there at the age of 16. Both Frédéric Chopin and Hector Berlioz, highly regarded composers of the day, praised his pianistic ability which was often compared with the brilliant playing of Franz Liszt.

In his many original musical works, Gottschalk was a pioneer in incorporating native folk song materials. Because of this, his music is uniquely American, and he deserves to be recognized as our first nationalistic composer. John Doyle, an expert on Gottschalk says, "ironically, the Bohemian composer Antonín Dvořák is credited for turning the attention of Americans to their native music many years after Gottschalk's earlier example."

▶ In his work, *Trio*, American painter Ben Shahn (1898–1969) visualizes an unlikely musical ensemble. He is expressing the social themes of equality and integration. The house painter (left) playing the violin, the worker (center) playing guitar and harmonica, and the classical musician playing cello, join together to create a harmonious mix of styles.

Ben Shahn. *Trio.* 1944. Private collection, New Jersey.

One of the earliest composers to incorporate native folk themes in his work was an American. Louis Moreau Gottschalk (1829–1869), a composer and pianist, composed *The Banjo,* Op. 15 around 1854–1855. This piano work has been called "one of Gottschalk's most virile compositions." It uses themes common to the spiritual "Roll, Jordan, Roll" and Stephen Foster's "Camptown Races." The piece was written by Gottschalk for his New Orleans concerts of 1855. It is a clever imitation of the banjo that was popular in the minstrel shows of the period.

To add to its folklike flavor, Gottschalk used a five-note, or pentatonic, scale in *The Banjo.* The **pentatonic** scale is *any scale that is made up of five tones within the octave.* It therefore has many forms because there are many choices. Although much of the music we hear is based on the diatonic (or major) scale, the pentatonic scale is very common, particularly in folk music.

▼ *Activity:* **Detect**

Hear how the American composer and pianist Louis Moreau Gottschalk incorporated the flavor of American folk music in ***The Banjo.***

Sing, play, or hum the melody of Stephen Foster's song, "Camptown Races," a folklike tune that was very popular at the time Gottschalk composed *The Banjo.*

Camptown Races

Stephen Foster, 1850

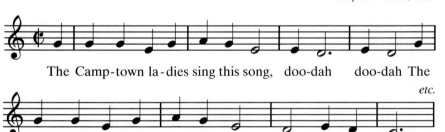

The Camp-town la-dies sing this song, doo-dah doo-dah The

etc.

Camp-town race-track five miles long, oh doo-dah day,

Listen to *The Banjo* to determine how Gottschalk imitated this folk instrument on the piano and how he evoked the melody of "Camptown Races," particularly the "doo-dahs."
Why does Gottschalk's music sound so American?
What other American composers incorporated folk music in their works?

Jazz to Classical

Classical music has also been influenced by jazz, particularly during the first part of the twentieth century when jazz was making its way around the world as a new form of musical expression. The French composer Claude Debussy (1862–1918) heard American ragtime music at the turn

---

Learn to play and sing a pentatonic (five-tone) scale.

The five black keys on the piano form a pentatonic scale. Working in small groups, play and sing this scale both upwards and downwards:

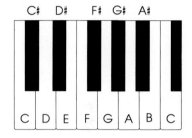

Transpose each of these five tones down one-half step so you can play this same pentatonic scale on the white keys:

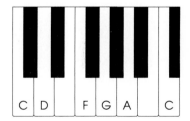

To compare this pentatonic scale with the seven-tone diatonic scale (DO, RE, MI, etc.), play the diatonic (major) scale on all the white keys from C to C. What tones of the diatonic scale are missing from this pentatonic scale? What is the pattern in steps (intervals) between the successive tones? Discuss your answers.

of the century, perhaps at the Paris Exposition in 1900. Ragtime gradually became popular in the bistros of Paris where people danced to its lively beat. France has had a long love affair with American jazz, one that has been revived in the 1990s. In 1991 the French government bestowed on American jazz trumpeter Miles Davis its highest distinction—the French Legion of Honor. Debussy, too, was taken in by this new, daring rhythmic wildness, and he mimicked ragtime in some of his works. One example is his "Golliwogg's Cake-Walk" from the *Children's Corner Suite* for piano (1908). This was not ragtime as Scott Joplin had created it, but it was definitely influenced by Joplin's use of syncopation.

American popular music, in particular the music of African Americans, has made a strong impression on composers around the world. Many, like the Russian Igor Stravinsky (1882–1971), incorporated some element of it in their work. Stravinsky lived in Paris from 1911 until the First World War broke out in 1914, when he moved to Switzerland for the duration of the war. In keeping with the shortages and poverty that many people

▶ Russian composer, Igor Stravinsky (right), one of the masters of modern music, works with musicians on the interpretation of one of his works. Although Russian subjects dominated his early creations, the composer became fascinated and inspired by French and American music, absorbing these influences into his music. Stravinsky spent the last 32 years of his long life in the United States. He became an American citizen in 1945.

Profile

Claude Debussy
French Composer
1862–1918

CLAUDE DEBUSSY

Some composers play a transitional role between one period and another. Claude Debussy was such a figure. Although he grew up in the Romantic Age when the Germanic style of Richard Wagner dominated musical composition, he sought his own very different sound. In this sense he was revolutionary.

Debussy's prodigious talent won him many awards, including the coveted Prix de Rome (1884) which permitted him to study in Italy. He had been admitted to the Paris Conservatory at the age of ten!

His compositions were the musical counterpart of the French poetry and Impressionistic painting of that time—fluid, colorful, and atmospheric. The titles of his works reveal the feelings he portrayed. His most well-known piano work is *Moonlight* (*Clair de lune*). His works for orchestra include *Prelude to "The Afternoon of a Faun," Clouds, Festivals, Nocturnes,* and *The Sea* (*La Mer*), among many others.

Debussy is credited today for being the creator and foremost exponent of the musical style known as Impressionism, in spite of his protests about the application of that term to his work. The new style he established had an important effect. It freed music to explore new avenues such as exotic scales, parallel intervals and harmonies, delicate timbres and textures, subtle moods, and rhythms and forms that evolve almost improvisationally. By breaking many of the established rules, Debussy prepared the world for the modern expression of the twentieth century.

▼*Activity:* **Answer with Your Ears**

How did American ragtime music influence Claude Debussy?

Listen to the "Maple Leaf Rag" and review the musical characteristics of ragtime.

Half the class should tap the steady duple beat, while the other half taps the following melodic rhythm of "Golliwogg's Cake-Walk" from Debussy's *Children's Corner Suite* (1908):

Now tap along with the recording while you decide which characteristics of ragtime Debussy used here.

What is the main difference in the way Joplin and Debussy treat the steady beat?

As part of the fun, Debussy mocks the dramatic, Romantic style of Richard Wagner by introducing a melodic motive from his opera *Tristan und Isolde*:

How does Debussy let you know he is not being dramatic and serious himself?

suffered during the war, he developed the idea of economy in the use of musical resources. This idea was in direct opposition to the post-Romantic inclination toward the end of the nineteenth and beginning of the twentieth century to inflate everything—the length of musical forms, the number of performers, and the bigness of the sound.

To show this new approach, he wrote a musical stage play, *L' Histoire du Soldat* (1918), for seven instruments and narrator. Following this same reasoning, on Armistice Day (November 11) that same year, he composed a work for just 11 instruments that he called *Ragtime*, a piece inspired by the popular American dance. As you might imagine, it is joyous, celebratory music to mark the end of the First World War. With this work, Stravinsky, whose compositions are full of dance rhythms, followed a tradition of bringing a popular dance form into the concert hall, just as composers had used the minuet, gavotte, waltz, and other dances before him.

▼*Activity:* **Figure Out**

How did Igor Stravinsky introduce a form of popular music into the concert hall?

Listen to Stravinsky's *Ragtime* for eleven instruments and write a paragraph or two describing the fusion of the two styles of music—classical and popular. You may wish to use the following questions as points of discussion:

1. Name some of the instruments you hear in this composition. Are these instruments usually associated with popular or classical music?
2. What characteristics of the popular style does Stravinsky incorporate?
3. What characteristics of classical music does Stravinsky use?
4. Where might Stravinsky have heard ragtime? Why do you think he chose to base his composition on this style of American music?

Classical to Pop

Sometimes classical music influences popular music. This is more common than you might suppose. For example, classical melodies are often popularized. The pop composer takes the main theme of Tchaikovsky's Piano Concerto No. 1, sets words to it, gives it a popular treatment and it becomes "Tonight We Love."

Whole Broadway shows have been created by these means. The musical *Song of Norway* was based on the music of Norwegian composer Edvard Grieg. *Kismet* (1953) used popularized versions of the melodies of the Russian composer Alexander Borodin (1833–1887) as the basis for its score.

As you learned in Chapter 24, jazz musicians frequently base their improvisations on the themes of other composers. Occasionally, the original themes are taken from classical sources. One of the masters of this type of improvisation is John Lewis (b. 1920), who for nearly 30 years has been the pianist for the Modern Jazz Quartet. He is also a prolific composer and a fine classical pianist. He has recorded an entire album based on the music

◀ The Modern Jazz Quartet, shown here in 1961, presents jazz as a serious art form worthy of tuxedos and concert halls. As leader and pianist, John Lewis is as adept at classical music as he is at jazz, and he mixes the two styles freely.

of J. S. Bach. One of these tunes, entitled "One Diamond," starts with the beginning of Bach's Prelude 16 in G Minor from Book 1 of *The Well-Tempered Clavier*. Very gradually, he moves into a jazz improvisation based on Bach's contrapuntal piece.

Musical styles have been influencing one another for centuries. One example is the transformation of Hans Leo Hassler's seventeenth-century secular song, "My peace of mind is shattered (by a tender maiden's charms)," into J. S. Bach's eighteenth-century sacred chorale, "O Sacred Head, Now Wounded." In 1973, Paul Simon continued the tradition by using this same melody in his composition "American Tune" as a setting for the words: "Many is the time I've been mistaken, and many times confused," making it secular again.

This trading back and forth between styles is common practice for a very good reason. These "parodies" of songs are adaptations that keep the creative fountain flowing. Musicians, like architects and actors, get inspiration from each other. One of the serious problems that afflicts commercial music is the tendency to imitate the popular fad of the moment. Sometimes there is little real innovation or originality. Groups tend to sound a great deal like each other. For the popular artist who wants to create an individual sound, classical music can sometimes provide a fresh approach. On the record jacket for his 1985 hit album, *The Dream of the Blue Turtles*, the rock star Sting acknowledges that he borrowed the theme for his song "Russians" from the classical Russian composer Sergei Prokofiev (1891–1953). Prokofiev created this theme in 1934 for his orchestral work,

Cooperative Learning

Pinpoint
Can you identify the precise moment when John Lewis changes styles?

Listen to the first few minutes of John Lewis's "One Diamond." At some point in this piece he gradually changes styles, going from J. S. Bach's contrapuntal, Baroque sound to a more contemporary style. Your job is to listen for both styles and pinpoint the exact place (the minute and second) where the change occurs.

Work with a friend and follow a watch or clock that has a second hand or a digital indication of minutes and seconds. Write down the exact time at which you hear a stylistic change. Can you identify the two different styles? How did you know that a change in styles had occurred? You may need to listen to the work more than once.

Cooperative Learning

Critique

Write a two-page paper that compares four versions of Mussorgsky's work.

In teams of two or three, listen to four different versions of "The Great Gate of Kiev" from *Pictures at an Exhibition:* (1) piano, (2) orchestral, (3) electronic, and (4) brass ensemble. As you listen, write down terms that describe and characterize the musical impact of each version. Using this list, compare notes with your teammates and elect one team member to draft a short paragraph describing each version, making comparisons among them. What do three of these versions have in common?

In a final paragraph, explain which version the team likes best and why. Knowing that the original composition was written for piano, how do the other three arrangements help to popularize this work? Try to justify your team's preference by referring to the musical elements: the appropriateness of the tone color, interpretation, and expressiveness.

Compare your team's opinions with other teams in the class. Do others agree with you? How do they substantiate their preference?

▶ One fine example of the crossover from classical to pop is the 1991 Academy Award winning popular musical score to Walt Disney Pictures' *Beauty and the Beast,* music by Alan Menken, lyrics by Howard Ashman. In the opening music in the film, Menken borrowed his underlying theme from "Aquarium," the seventh movement of French composer Camille Saint-Saëns' *Carnival of the Animals* (1886).

The Lieutenant Kije Suite, Opus 60. In the Evaluation for Chapter 9 on page 168, you learned that the singer/pianist Eric Carmen borrowed the theme from the first movement of Sergei Rachmaninoff's Piano Concerto No. 2 as the basis for his popular hit, "All By Myself."

It is not unusual for classical music to be popularized—made more appealing through an arrangement, orchestration, or adaptation. Consider, for example, the way that Modest Mussorgsky's "The Great Gate of Kiev" from *Pictures at an Exhibition* (1873) has been popularized during the past 100 years. This work has become a favorite of many musicians, including pop groups. It was written in memory of one of Mussorgsky's friends, Victor Hartmann, an artist whose paintings inspired the composer. Like many other programmatic works, *Pictures* is in several sections. In this case, Mussorgsky walks the listener through an art gallery where a number of Hartmann's paintings are displayed. The composer uses a "Promenade" theme to depict himself walking between pictures:

(The original is in B♭.)

With its shifting rhythm, the theme is a bit awkward, suggesting, perhaps, Mussorgsky's own uneven gait. Although the theme is presented in a different color and character each time it appears, it serves as a connecting and unifying element between the sections and is heard in the finale, "The Great Gate of Kiev." The sections of this program suite portray ten different paintings in the gallery, and Mussorgsky took his inspiration directly from them, often in surprising ways.

Mussorgsky originally wrote this program suite for piano. His own musical training, like that of many of today's rock musicians, was limited. He

simply did not have sufficient skill to score the work for an orchestra. Consequently, the work has been arranged for orchestra by other composers. The most memorable and familiar orchestral version is by Maurice Ravel (1875–1937).

Popular artists of our own time have found Mussorgsky's work so appealing that they have arranged it for their own performances. For example, the rock group Emerson, Lake, and Palmer arranged several movements from *Pictures* in the early 1970s. Later in that decade, Tomita, a Japanese musician well known for his electronic transcriptions, arranged the work for synthesizers.

Influences from One Culture to Another

As transportation and communication systems speed up and reach into even the remotest regions, the world seems to become smaller. Today, any part of the globe is accessible within a single day's journey. Peoples and cultures that were separated by many months of travel just a few decades ago are now almost instantly present at the other end of a telephone, radio signal, or fax machine. Electronic communication invades and obliterates human isolation, assuring contact with other cultures.

Although many societies existed in almost total isolation at the beginning of the twentieth century, very few do today. This awareness of each other has made people conscious of different ways of living. Lifestyles are imported and exported. For better or worse, American popular music provides an excellent example of how a particular form of contemporary expression can encircle the world.

When two or more cultures exist in proximity, there is apt to be some exchange between them. Some traits of one will be adopted by the other, and vice versa. In anthropology, the study of cultures, this process is known as **acculturation**, *the mutual influence of different cultures in close contact.* Examples are common, particularly in music.

Antonín Dvořák (1841–1904), a Czech composer, traveled to the United States for the first time in 1892. He had accepted a two-year appointment as director of the National Conservatory of Music in New York City. Dvořák was already well known for establishing a distinct Czech national music by embracing elements of Czech folk song style in his works, particularly in his Slavonic dances and rhapsodies. During his stay in the United States (1892–1895), he produced his most frequently performed composition, The Symphony No. 9 in E Minor, Op. 95 (*From the New World*) (1893). In it he incorporated references to the Negro spirituals that he heard here. Dvořák was as interested in the music of black Americans as he was in his own Czech folk music. He even went so far as to invite Harry T. Burleigh, a student at the conservatory, to sing spirituals for him. Although he said that the title, *From the New World,* simply meant "impressions and greetings from the New World," he captured the flavor and spirit of the spiritual in the work.

PROJECT

Create a Composition

Create your own popular composition based on a classical theme. Working alone or in small groups, study the promenade theme from Mussorgsky's *Pictures at an Exhibition* (p. 512) and learn how it is put together and how to perform it. First, determine where Mussorgsky placed his bar line to divide this 11-beat melody into two measures (with an accent on the first beat in the second bar). Label the meter signature of *each* measure. Now learn to perform and conduct this famous theme.

Why does it *not* have the feeling of a popular theme? What would give it that feeling? Your assignment is to adapt this tune, altering the rhythm, creating words, adding to the melody, or otherwise using it as the basis for creating your own popular work. Now that you know the melody well, try some of the following techniques to adapt this music for your own song. Some possibilities:

- Write words to this melody line.
- Alter the rhythm of the melody.
- Extend the melody and lyrics to create a song using a verse-chorus format, or an A B A structure.
- Plan a place for vocal or instrumental improvisation.
- Add a strong rhythmic accompaniment.
- Try to chord your melody and create your own accompaniment.

Make sure you specify details such as instruments, tempo, dynamics, and number of performers. Once your composition takes shape, rehearse it so you can perform it for the class.

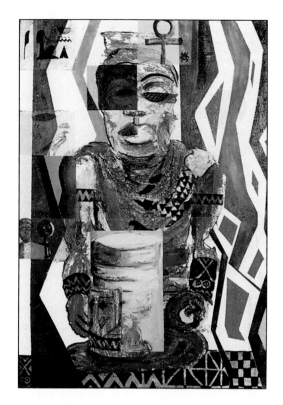

▲ Characteristics of African art and music have been adopted and adapted by European and American artists. The angular and geometric forms of African sculpture (left) that can be seen in this work from Gabon in West Central Africa influenced European artists in the early part of the twentieth century, helping them to develop the style called Cubism. In the painting on the right, titled *Influence,* contemporary artist Herbert Andrew Williams (b. 1973) captures the spirit of the African art of his ancestors as well as the feeling of Cubism.

(Left) Primitive. Figure, Reliquary. African, Gabon, Kota. c. 1800–1900. The Metropolitan Museum of Art, New York, New York. Purchase, 1983. (1983.18). (Right) Herbert Andrew Williams. *Influence.* 1992. Statesboro, Georgia. Private Collection.

Dvořák's use of American folk music in a classical composition started a controversy that lasted for years. Suddenly, American composers became aware that it was possible to create their own nationalistic music based on black, Native American, and other folk sources.

However, they had to learn their lesson from a foreigner rather than from the American composer Louis Moreau Gottschalk, who had used the same techniques! Dvořák encouraged this development as a way for American composers to free themselves from European models and establish their own style of American music. Some composers embraced the idea; others fought it as a homogenization that would corrupt and destroy both styles of music. The American public had no difficulty with the idea as it was exemplified in this work; they claimed Dvořák's symphony as their own.

Dvořák did not lose his Czech identity by incorporating the feeling of the American spiritual into his symphony. It is still essentially a Czech work. By reaching outside his own familiar territory, he enriched his musical expression. Sometimes, however, the original culture is abandoned in the process. When a young musician in Indonesia hears a recording of Wynton Marsalis playing jazz, he just might aspire to play the same way. He could decide to lay aside his own gamelan music and instruments and take up trumpet and Western music instead. If such acculturation becomes widespread, it can overrun a culture and obliterate it. One's own indigenous culture can be lost.

From the New World
Largo Theme

Antonín Dvořák

Nobody Knows the Trouble I've Seen

Traditional Negro Spiritual

▼*Activity:* **Put Your Skill and Knowledge to Use**

How was Antonín Dvořák's compositional style in the largo theme from the second movement of his Symphony No. 9 in E Minor (*From the New World*) influenced by the character and pathos of the black spiritual?

Perform the spiritual "Nobody Knows the Trouble I've Seen." Be sure to focus on the tempo, dynamics, and relationship between the words and the music.

What are the musical characteristics of this spiritual that are usually associated with folk music?

Learn to play or hum Dvořák's theme from the second movement of *From the New World* symphony. What does this melody have in common with the spiritual "Nobody Knows the Trouble I've Seen"?

Listen to the opening section of the second movement. The melody begins after the chords in the orchestra. Can you identify the instrument that plays this melody?

Listen to the entire movement and analyze the form. How is contrast achieved? How is unity achieved? Which sections sound the most folklike? How did you determine this?

Crossover

Fortunately, in music, acculturation is not usually total or exclusive. Usually some characteristics rub off; others do not. There are influences that alter the music in certain ways but not in every way. The alterations that are induced by the other culture can be very exciting. They can add new life and vitality to a staid tradition.

The sharing of musical ideas across cultures happens in many ways. In music, ideas are borrowed quite freely. Generally this is a harmless, invigorating indulgence. As humans, we tend to copy what we like and what moves us. New styles often overturn previous styles. Sometimes, however, there is a **crossover**, *a merging of styles*. This is how new styles such as "country-rock," "blue-bop," (an amalgam of bebop and bluegrass), and "fusion," to name a few, were developed.

From Europe to Africa

The centuries-old contact of Africans with Europeans and with Christian culture is reflected in African music. By the early 1900s, choirs of mixed voices and the use of the Tonic Sol-fa system were established traditions in some African churches, schools, and communities. The dense (thick) musical texture that results from this multipart organization is now a dominant characteristic of South African Nguni vocal music. African composers do not view these elements as weeds that will kill or endanger their own traditions. The music of South Africa retains a number of characteristics that are typically African. The European elements are viewed as additional resources that provide an expanded range of musical choices.

The Protest Song in South Africa

Perhaps no other country in the world has used music so effectively as a means to communicate dissent than South Africa, where music serves as a powerful vehicle of protest against racial injustice. In 1886, when the largest gold strike ever recorded was made there, mine workers came into the country from many places in Africa and throughout the world. The population of South Africa is one of the world's most complex mixes of ethnic and racial types. Four racial categories are recognized in the population of more than 30 million: *Whites* of European descent, *Coloreds* of mixed origin, *Asians* mostly of Indian ancestry, and *Blacks* of African descent. Blacks are subdivided into six major groups—Nguni (which includes the Zulu); Xhosa; Ndbele; North Sotho, South Sotho, Tswana; Tsonga or Shangaan; and Venda.

For many decades, the official policy of the social system was *apartheid* (a-PAR-tate), an Afrikaans term for separateness or racial segregation. When the Afrikaner Nationalist Party won electoral victory in 1948, apartheid was soon enshrined in hundreds of laws. These laws restricted ownership of land according to race, provided for segregation of public facilities by race, assured lower quality education for non-whites, and made non-whites permanent residents of "independent" homelands, whether or not they had ever been there. Thanks to the resistance of the South African people and the sanctions of the international community, apartheid is now being dismantled. Nelson Mandela is the foremost leader of the struggle for liberation in South Africa.

The Music

Blacks have demonstrated their resistance to apartheid with protests and civil disobedience and through artistic expression. Songs, dances, plays, and other art works are proving to be an effective means of exposing cruelty. In South Africa today, culture and politics can no longer be separated. Of all these artistic expressions, music has played the most pivotal role. South African musicians have become the most outspoken critics of the system, chroniclers of the people's suffering, and uncompromising fighters for a new, democratic, and nonracial nation.

South African music has established a worldwide reputation because of its powerful message, its vast array of styles, and its excellent creators and performers. Its effectiveness has caused the Pretoria government to force musical artists into exile and to make it illegal for their music to be aired on radio or even to be listened to privately. Miriam Makeba, Abdullah Ibrahim (Dollar Brand), Hugh Masekela, Jonas Gwangwa, and Julian Bahula are just a few of the many superb, internationally acclaimed artists who were exiled. Their efforts have succeeded in reducing censorship. Most of these artists are now free to return home. Artists around the world have repeatedly voiced their sympathy and support for the plight of the South African people.

"Sobashiya" (soh-bah-SHE-ya) is a freedom or protest song that means "we will leave" in Zulu. It is performed by Amandla (a-MAN-dlha), the cultural group of the African National Congress. Amandla is the Zulu term for power. The meaning is "power to the people," the basic demand of the oppressed majority. This musical ensemble, founded in 1978, comprises exiles from virtually all ethnic groups. It performs the best music, dance, poetry, and theater of the South African peoples. The group is directed by John M. Gwangwa, probably best known in the United States for his musical score for the film *Cry Freedom.*

The song expresses the determination of people who have no choice but to leave the country and join the liberation movements abroad.

Sobashiya	We Will Leave
(S = soloist; C = chorus)	
Zulu text:	English translation by
	Thami Makwakwa:
1. (Verse)	
S: Sobahizy abazali ekhaya	We will leave our parents
C: Saphuma, sangena kwamanye amazwe	We will leave for other countries
(Refrain)	
S: Kwamanye amazwe	For other countries
C: Lapho kungazi khona uBaba noMama	Where our parents don't even know
Silandeli nkululeko.	In Search of Freedom
2. (Verse)	
S: Sithi salani, salani, salani ekhaya	Stay well at home
C: Sesi ngena kwamanye amazwe	We're now entering other countries
(Refrain, as above)	
3. (Verse)	
S: Sobashiya aBafowetu	We left our brother
C: Saphuma sangena kwamanye amazwe	We left for other countries
(Refrain, as above)	

Sequence of the repetitions is 1, 2, 3, 2, 1, 2

The tune of this song is traditional, but the arrangement is modern. The most obvious outside influence is the arrangement of the voices in soprano, alto, tenor, and bass parts, no doubt an adoption of the format of the Christian hymn or chorale with its chords and cadences.

Sobashiya

Amandla, South Africa

▼ *Activity:* **Determine**

What are the African and non-African characteristics of this music?

Listen to the South African protest song "Sobashiya" ("We Will Leave") as sung by Amandla. Note the following musical characteristics:

1. The multi-part organization of the chorus into soprano, alto, tenor, and bass parts (like a hymn).
2. The use of call-and-response or "antiphonal" (alternating) style, marked by the independence of the solo and choral parts.
3. The use of polyrhythm or polymeter:

Melody (triple)

Foot stamping (duple)

4. The extensive use of repetition (with slight variations in the solo part dictated in part by the text).

Which of the above characteristics were adopted, which are African in their origins? Aside from the text, what makes this music work as a protest song?

From Africa to the Americas

West African music has had enormous influence on our popular musical styles. Between the fifteenth and nineteenth centuries, some 10 million Africans were uprooted from their culture and brought to the new world as slaves. Their descendants in North America, the Caribbean, and South America forged new traditions with double roots: one side drew upon the cultures of Europe (English, French, Spanish, and Portuguese), and the other side fed upon a rich variety of African traditions. Because these Africans had come largely from central and western Africa, the musical traits of these regions were evident in African-American music. The threads of continuity include leader-and-chorus (also called call-and-response) singing, the use of repetition as a unifying principle, the combination of relatively simple rhythms to create complex polyrhythms, an emphasis on percussive sounds and dense textures, and highly developed forms of improvisation.

The Time Line

In much West African drumming there is a **time line**, or *a basic rhythmic pattern that provides the foundation for the complex rhythms played by multiple drums.* This pattern or time line is asymmetrical; it is made up of two different halves. Frequently, the pattern is played on an iron bell, struck wooden sticks, or some other instrument that makes a loud enough sound to penetrate the thick, sonic texture that is created when multiple drummers play interlocking patterns.

◀ *Swing Low, Sweet Chariot* (c. 1939) by African-American painter William H. Johnson (1901–1970) visualizes the Negro spiritual of the same name. While a band of angels (with wings) sways like a gospel choir, God's chariot swings low and carries the soul of the slave over the Jordan river (the Atlantic Ocean) to home (heaven or Africa). The repetition of the angels contrasted with the lone foreground figure, along with their asymmetrical placement, suggests the polyrhythms of African music.

William H. Johnson, *Swing Low, Sweet Chariot.* c. 1939. National Museum of American Art, Smithsonian Institution, Washington, D.C.

▼ *Activity:* **Perform**

Learn to play the time line pattern and recognize it by ear.

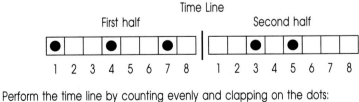

Perform the time line by counting evenly and clapping on the dots:

Listen to *gome* (GO-may) drumming performed by the Ga people of the West African country of Ghana. The time line, played on clapped wooden sticks, begins the recorded example. Tap along, keeping the time line steady as the master drummer improvises.

▶ The African dance group, Teye Sa Thiosanne Ban, toured the United States in 1992, bringing their culture to audiences here. Such cultural exchanges are common today among most of the countries of the world. They help cultural influences to flow both ways, and they help people to develop respect for cultures different from their own.

The time line is important as an organizing ostinato. It helps all the musicians stay together. In African drumming, the musicians have to be able to perform their own rhythms while they hear all the others. Their attention must be divided among the various parts without losing their focus. This is why the time line is so important. Even very experienced drummers use it to reorient themselves if they lose their place during a particularly tricky improvisation. Because the time line is asymmetrical, it is easy to hear which half of the 16-beat pattern is being played and to reenter the flow of the music.

This time line pattern in West African music has influenced the rhythms in the Cuban cha-cha, in Latin jazz, and in rhythm and blues, among other African-American musical styles. *In Afro-Cuban music, the time line is called* **clave** (KLAH-vay), *a word that also refers to two round wooden sticks that are* *struck together to produce the pattern.* The clave rhythm has influenced popular music in many parts of Latin America. It is also the basis for the pattern called "hambone" that is common in the music of the Mississippi Delta and in other African-American folk music styles. It is an excellent example of how different musical cultures have borrowed from each other, yet in each case, the pattern appears in its own very different musical and cultural context. It provides a link back to its origins.

▼*Activity:* **Recognize**

Try to hear the clave pattern in each of the two musical examples and tap along with them.

1. In this Afro-Cuban cha-cha, the clave pattern is the reverse:

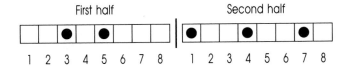

First half   Second half

1 2 3 4 5 6 7 8   1 2 3 4 5 6 7 8

This pattern is called the *reverso* ("reverse") or *2-3 clave*, in contrast to the *primero* ("first") or *3-2 clave* you learned in the previous activity. Try to maintain the pattern as other percussion instruments enter and add layers of rhythmic complexity.

2. In this early rock 'n' roll piece, recorded in 1955 by Elias McDaniel (Bo Diddley), you will hear a rhythmic pattern called "hambone" that is closely related to the West African time line and the Cuban clave. The pattern, which is elaborated by the drummer on the tom-tom and by Bo Diddley on the guitar, is common in the music of the Mississippi Delta where Diddley was born. Can you hear it and tap along?

The Blending of Styles

Today, classical music also continues to be enriched by cultural exchange. As composers absorb ideas from other cultures, they tend to establish new communicative musical "languages." Often, classical composers are inspired by the work of other classical composers. This is the case with the Brazilian composer Heitor Villa-Lobos (1887–1959), who as a young man, fell in love with the music of J. S. Bach. It was Bach's music that led him to compose a series of nine works he called *Bachianas Brasileiras*, a series of dialogues between Bach and Brazil. Each of the works sets up a contrast between elements of Baroque and Brazilian musical styles.

The *Bachianas Brasileiras No. 5*, scored for soprano and eight violoncellos, is the most celebrated work in the series. Here the contrasting pairs are Aria (Cantilena) and Dance (Martelo). In the first section, Villa-Lobos combines the formality of a Bach aria with the Brazilian *modinha* (mo-DEEN-huh), a lyrical and sentimental song. The first part of the composition is a vocalise for soprano—an aria without a text!

Profile

George Gershwin
American Composer
1898–1937

GEORGE GERSHWIN

In spite of his short life—not quite 39 years—George Gershwin left an indelible mark on American music. Born and reared in Brooklyn of immigrant parents, Gershwin's talent as a pianist appeared early. By the age of 16 he was hired in music stores to improvise arrangements of the latest tunes. This was the way sheet music was sold in the early decades of the century.

He wrote his first hit, the song "Swanee," at the age of 19. It sold over a million copies and brought him early recognition. He was soon writing a string of Broadway musicals—*Lady Be Good* (1924), *Oh Kay!* (1926), *Strike Up the Band!* (1927), *Funny Face* (1927), *Girl Crazy* (1930), *Of Thee I Sing* (1931), which won him a Pulitzer Prize, and many others. In most of his songs, he teamed up with his brother Ira, who wrote the lyrics.

His music possesses an infectious rhythm derived largely from the popular jazz of the day, which he applied to his songs with great originality. Later in his life, he moved to Hollywood where he wrote scores for a number of films. His gift for writing memorable melodies never failed him.

In spite of his scant musical education, Gershwin's musical ambitions stretched well beyond songwriting. He composed *Rhapsody in Blue* for piano and jazz band in 1924. *An American in Paris*, a work for orchestra, followed in 1928, and *Porgy and Bess*, undoubtedly the most American of all operas, was premiered in 1935. When it was learned that he was suffering from a brain tumor, President Franklin D. Roosevelt tried to find a doctor to save him but to no avail. His death at such a young age robbed American music of one of its great geniuses.

▼*Activity:* **Listen Perceptively**

Can you distinguish the different musical styles that the Brazilian composer Heitor Villa-Lobos brought together in the "Aria" from his *Bachianas Brasileiras No. 5*?

What elements of Baroque musical style—the style of J. S. Bach—did he copy?
What elements of Brazilian musical style does his music evoke?
Does this type of interplay between two cultures help or hinder the music?

Like their European counterparts, American classical composers were impressed by the new music called jazz, impressed enough to integrate some of its basic characteristics into their music. George Gershwin (1898–1937) went to Harlem nightclubs and was so impressed by the vitality of this new music that he incorporated some of its features into many of his works. Gershwin extended the borders of musical style. He created a hybrid form of musical communication that combines and merges elements of both classical and popular music. His *Rhapsody in Blue*, an extended work for piano and orchestra, was premiered in New York in 1924 with Paul Whiteman's jazz orchestra and the composer at the piano. In this work the worlds of classical and popular music met on congenial terms. Gershwin's aim was to show people that jazz could be just as respectable as classical music.

▼*Activity:* **Test Your Knowledge**

How did George Gershwin (1898–1937) merge popular musical expression with traditional forms of art music?

Listen to the opening of Gershwin's *Rhapsody in Blue* and make two lists—one of the musical characteristics that are classical, the other of the characteristics that are related to jazz or popular music.

Clues: Consider the following: Instrumentation (timbre); size of the orchestra; rhythm; melody; harmony; use of dynamics; and overall feeling.

How would you classify this composition? Jazz? Classical music? How did you arrive at your answer?

Today composers and performers continue to mix and merge different stylistic influences. Why? Because the combining of styles gives new vitality to musical communication. Musical styles influence each other because musicians are fascinated by the new sounds that they hear. They are continually borrowing and absorbing these new sounds and blending them with, or discarding, the old sounds in order to create new expressions that are fresh and vibrant. Stylistic amalgamation is one of the ways musical creators reach out to embrace the world around them.

§ummary

In our global society, music absorbs and reflects unique sounds from many different cultures. The music of the world is becoming increasingly homogenized. As cassette players, CDs, and broadcasting have made all kinds of music accessible to people everywhere, musical styles have tended to blur. Culture may be America's biggest export. American popular music has traversed the globe, influencing music in many other cultures. You can hear Janet Jackson and the Oak Ridge Boys in Bangkok, Berlin, Buenos Aires, Baghdad, Bogotá, and Bombay. The music of these seemingly faraway places can also be heard here. These sonic influences are persuasive, altering musical tastes, and changing our musical preferences.

Musical styles are continually being modified. One of the ways music evolves is through a blending of different styles. This occurs when the musician or composer views different musical styles as opportunities rather than as barriers. When musicians become explorers they combine styles to create their own individual sound. This is one of the fundamental ways that music evolves. In a very real sense, this is the way music epitomizes the breaking down of boundaries, the reconciliation of incompatibles, and the fusion of differences. These are important concepts in a world prone to conflict.

CHAPTER 27

A Unique Record of Humankind

Objectives

By completing this chapter, you will:

- See how your tastes have changed over the term of this course.
- Understand how music establishes a sense of time and place.
- Understand how music expresses our humanity.
- View music as a fundamental means of human communication.
- Realize how much you have learned about musical styles and being able to recognize them.

*N*one of us can escape the mystery of human life.
What is the purpose of our existence? Music
commands our attention because it is one of the languages
of civilization through which we connect with other
human beings—those around us, those who came
before us, and those who will come after us. In many
ways, music serves as humanity's memory, stirring
our feelings today as it stirred others' yesterday,
decades ago, or even in centuries past. Feelings are at the
core of our existence. They radiate the life within us.

Music Is Human Communication

Music turns the beat of the human heart into a drum, and the feelings of human experience into a melody. Just as a drawing captures the rhythm of the hand, music captures the pulse and the passion of its creator. It represents the essence of the person who created it, and because of our human sameness, the essence of all people. This human essence is given representation in sound so that it can be relived and shared. Music permits us to express and communicate our emotional reality. It is an extension of our being and, at the same time, a representation of it.

Musical communication may be more important to us than we have yet recognized. In America, our sense of community depends on our establishing linkages across our many ethnic and racial differences. Music is one of the splendid connectors between different peoples and cultures. It is a way for America to speak to itself in all its different guises. It is a way for Americans to attain a feeling of unity and cohesiveness—of oneness.

▼*Activity:* **Radio Scan**

How have your musical tastes changed?

Early in this course, you listened to ten brief musical selections as if you were scanning a variety of radio stations. The idea was to indicate your reactions to each musical example by writing down how long you would want to listen to the music playing on those stations.

Now that this course is nearing completion, listen to these same selections again and indicate how many minutes or seconds you would want to stay tuned-in to each musical example. When you have finished, compare these results with your first reactions. Have your musical tastes and interests changed? Has learning more about music helped you to be open to a broader range of music?

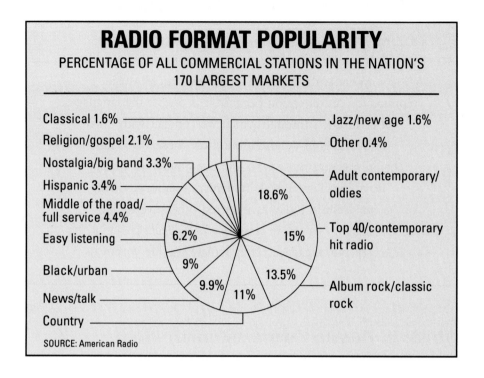

RADIO FORMAT POPULARITY
PERCENTAGE OF ALL COMMERCIAL STATIONS IN THE NATION'S 170 LARGEST MARKETS

Classical 1.6%
Religion/gospel 2.1%
Nostalgia/big band 3.3%
Hispanic 3.4%
Middle of the road/full service 4.4%
Easy listening
Black/urban
News/talk
Country

Jazz/new age 1.6%
Other 0.4%
Adult contemporary/oldies
Top 40/contemporary hit radio
Album rock/classic rock

18.6%
15%
13.5%
11%
9.9%
9%
6.2%

SOURCE: American Radio

Establishing Connections

Humans await a message from the stars. If there are other living creatures out there, they may choose some form of music as their first means of making contact. The film *Close Encounters of the Third Kind* suggests just such a scenario. When the spaceship from outer space lands on Earth, the message it broadcasts is musical:

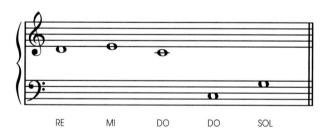

RE   MI   DO   DO   SOL

Through the arts we can make connections with other people and with our own inner being. To be willing to listen to music that is different from what we know is to begin to open ourselves to human differences as well. The idea is not just to tolerate what is alien to our comfort sphere, but also to accept. Acceptance calls for a deeper understanding and commitment. Tolerance does not reach out and embrace, acceptance does.

As social animals, it is our nature to seek alliances. We want to establish contact with other creatures. If there are other forms of consciousness in the universe, we want to make connections with them. Will we, however, be able to communicate? Words may not suffice. Some sort of sign language may prove more effective. So might pictures or music. Sharing our music is like baring our souls, our feelings, our spirit. Music offers another form of basic communication. It gets right to the core of our humanness.

If other creatures out there in the vastness of the universe have their own forms of music, then we cannot be so far apart. Sharing the sound-scapes we have invented breaks through some of the barriers of fear and distrust. Music could provide a possible basis for the beginning of an alliance based on one form of intellectual and emotional understanding. It provides a way for us to see something of ourselves in other creatures and they in us. It is not by happenstance that our discovery of the songs of the whales, and being able to record and hear them, coincides with world-wide efforts to "Save the Whales." Their songs helped to give us empathy for these magnificent creatures.

When we deal with the minds of others—human or animal—we are necessarily dealing with degrees of consciousness. One of the most impressive feats of the human mind is its capacity and determination to understand itself and the farthest reaches of the universe. There may be minds somewhere out in the universe that have intelligence far superior to our own. These beings might possess a far greater understanding of the meaning of their own lives and the nature of the universe and their place in it. It is conceivable that their physics and mathematics might be so astonishing and fantastic that they would be unintelligible to us. Their insight may so eclipse ours that our greatest attainments would appear primitive by comparison. If so, they will have enormous advantages over us.

Cooperative Learning

Figure Out

How can music connect people who do not otherwise relate?

Watch the short film *Caesura* by Frank Kerr, then write an essay on how music was able to bridge the hostility between these two men. Were any words spoken? Did they need to be? Could words have accomplished the same thing? Why can music work this way? Share your ideas in discussion.

◀ Music can bring people of all kinds together. It is one of the main ways that we make connections with other human beings. Because it reaches inside us to express our being and our humanness, it could serve as an important link between humans and extraterrestrial beings, if such beings exist.

▶ One of the two Voyager spacecraft that were launched in 1977, shown as it would appear to an alien spacecraft approaching it a billion years from now in interstellar space. The recording of Earth's music is centered on the side panel. For a close-up of this recording, see the photograph on the next page.

If the social, emotional, and intuitive insights of aliens are as remarkable as their scientific knowledge, then we could hope to establish bonds based on mutual trust, respect, cooperation, even true admiration and affection. Empathy for other creatures depends upon being in tune with our own feelings so that we can understand the feelings of others. This scenario provides a good reason why we might be wise to develop the capacities of our senses as well as our minds. In the long run, our sensibilities may play as large a part in our survival as our intellect.

Voyager and Its Music

Launched by the United States in 1977, the Voyager 1 and Voyager 2 robot spacecraft completed the first human reconnaissance of the planets in our solar system. They explored Jupiter and Saturn, then went on to visit Uranus and Neptune. Both spacecraft are now continuing on their long journey to the stars, and both are still transmitting data back to Earth. The Voyager spacecrafts are now traveling at the rate of a million miles a day! Even at this rate, it will take them 20,000 years to break entirely free of the gravitational shackles of the sun. Then they embark on phase two of their mission: possible contact with an extraterrestrial civilization.

Affixed to the outside of each spacecraft is a gold-coated copper phonograph record encased in a mirrored aluminum jacket containing selected examples of the Earth's music. Carl Sagan of Cornell University, who serves as Distinguished Visiting Scientist at the National Aeronautics and Space Administration's Jet Propulsion Laboratory in California, wanted to include music because "there is much more to human beings than perceiving and thinking. We are feeling creatures." He views the inclusion of music as "a creditable attempt to convey human emotions."

What music should be included? Two criteria for choosing the music were established: (1) the selections should represent a wide range of cultures, not just music familiar to the society that launched the spacecraft; and (2) every selection should touch both the mind and the heart. The result was 90 minutes of the Earth's greatest musical hits—Eastern and Western, classical and folk, including a Navajo night chant, a Pygmy girl's initiation song, a Peruvian wedding song, a Japanese piece for *shakuhachi*, Bach, Beethoven, Mozart, Stravinsky, Louis Armstrong, and Chuck Berry. Also included on the recording are greetings in 55 human languages and one whale language; a 12-minute essay of the sounds of Planet Earth, including a baby's cry and a kiss; and 118 pictures, digitally encoded, that reveal our science, our civilization, and ourselves.

▼*Activity:* **Analyze**

How well does the music included on the Voyager recording represent the variety and the depth of the world's music?

Look at the list of 27 musical works on page 532 that were included on the recording attached to the Voyager spacecraft. To analyze the list, answer the following questions:

1. What balance was achieved between classical, popular, and folk music?
2. What balance is there between the old and the new?
3. Is the entire world represented or only a small part of it?
4. What is the balance between works that are relatively simple and works that are complex?
5. How much music of Americans is included?

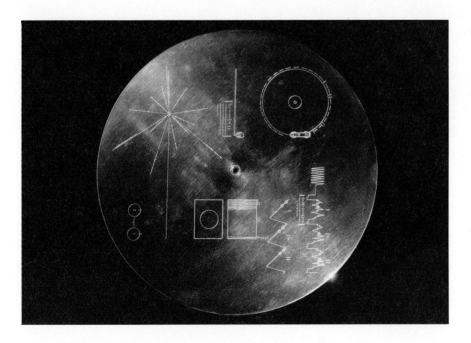

◀ The Voyager recording, enclosed in this golden, mirrored jacket, is mounted on the outside of the spacecraft along with a stylus and cartridge. Among its contents are almost 90 minutes of Earth's greatest music. Like a bottle with a note inside, tossed into the ocean, the recording carries news of our existence to the cosmos.

The Music on Voyager

1. Bach, Brandenburg Concerto No. 2 in F, First Movement, Munich Bach Orchestra, Karl Richter, Conductor.

2. Java, court gamelan, "Kinds of Flowers," recorded by Robert Brown.

3. Senegal, percussion, recorded by Charles Duvelle.

4. Zaire, Pygmy girls' initiation song, recorded by Colin Turnbull.

5. Australia, Aborigine songs, "Morning Star" and "Devil Bird," recorded by Sandra LeBrun Holmes.

6. Mexico, "El Cascabel," performed by Lorenzo Barcelata and the Mariachi México.

7. "Johnny B. Goode," written and performed by Chuck Berry.

8. New Guinea, men's house song, recorded by Robert MacLennan.

9. Japan, shakuhachi, "Cranes in Their Nest," performed by Coro Yamaguchi.

10. Bach, "Gavotte en rondeaux" from the Partita No. 3 in E Major for Violin, performed by Arthur Grumiaux.

11. Mozart, *The Magic Flute,* "Queen of the Night" aria, No. 14. Edda Moset, soprano. Bavarian State Opera, Munich, Wolfgang Sawallisch, conductor.

12. Georgian S. S. R., chorus, "Tchakrulo," collected by Radio Moscow.

13. Peru, panpipes and drum, collected by Casa de la Cultura, Lima.

14. "Melancholy Blues," performed by Louis Armstrong and his Hot Seven.

15. Azerbaijan S. S. R., bagpipes, recorded by Radio Moscow.

16. Stravinsky, *Rite of Spring,* "Sacrificial Dance," Columbia Symphony Orchestra, Igor Stravinsky, conductor.

17. Bach, *The Well-Tempered Clavier,* Book 2, Prelude and Fugue in C, No. 1. Glenn Gould, piano.

18. Beethoven, Fifth Symphony, First Movement, the Philharmonia Orchestra, Otto Klemperer, conductor.

19. Bulgaria, "Izlel je Delyo Hagdutin," sung by Valya Balkanska.

20. Navajo Indians, "Night Chant," recorded by Willard Rhodes.

21. Holborne, *Paeans, Galliards, Almains and Other Short Aires,* "The Fairie Round," performed by David Munrow and the Early Music Consort of London.

22. Solomon Islands, panpipes, collected by the Solomon Islands Broadcasting Service.

23. Peru, wedding song, recorded by John Cohen.

24. China, ch'in, "Flowing Streams," performed by Kuan P'ing-hu.

25. India, raga, "Jaat Kahan Ho," sung by Surshri Kesar Bai Kerkar.

26. "Dark Was the Night," written and performed by Blind Willie Johnson.

27. Beethoven, String Quartet No. 13 in B flat Major, Opus 130, Cavatina, performed by the Budapest String Quartet.

The hope is that somewhere out there in the vastness of space, a sufficiently advanced civilization will intercept the spacecraft and be able to decipher the messages on the recording. Voyager will provide these beings with news of our existence. Visual instructions for playing the record are included. Sagan points out that "Even quite optimistic estimates place the nearest civilization at a few hundred light-years, where a light-year is almost six trillion miles. It would take our present spacecraft some tens of thousands of years to go the distance to the nearest star, and several tens of millions of years to travel this estimated distance to the nearest other civilization."

PROJECT

Select the Music for the Next Voyager Mission

Working in small groups, create your own list of the world's music to be included on the next interstellar spacecraft mission to the cosmos. Write down your set of criteria for deciding what you will include. Limit yourself to 15 works. Select your music primarily from the music you have studied in this course, but pick out *at least one* work from your own collection that reflects the best example of a new style that has emerged since the original 1977 launch. Justify every piece you include, based on what it might tell some extraterrestrial being about us as humans. When you are finished, share your list with one other group and determine how much your lists differ and agree. Listen to the five selections that appear most often on all the lists. Discuss the various reasons behind the choices of these five examples. Is there a consensus in the class on the selection criteria?

▲ Above is a view of the moon and the earth as it might appear from the Voyager spacecraft as it sped outward into the universe to explore the planets and then interstellar space.

▲ What we consider beautiful varies from culture to culture as well as from one historical period to another and is often reflected in the arts. Here are pretty faces from (clockwise from top left) Kenya, India, Mexico, the United States, the Netherlands, and Japan. The ideals of visual beauty differ, just as they do in music. However, if we open the doors to new sounds and new experiences, we often develop appreciation for that which we originally viewed as foreign and strange.

Music Expresses Our Humanity

Music permits us to relate to other people and their lifestyle in a highly personal, emotional way. Through music, we can feel the way they feel. There is a near miracle here, because as soon as we have a glimpse of other people's humanity, we have crossed the cultural chasm that separates us. We must remember that intellect alone seldom connects us to other people; feelings do. Once we achieve empathy for others, we have acquired the basis of respect. It is respect for other people that provides the basis for any worthwhile relationship across cultures. You do not have to like the music of other people; you should, however, strive to respect it. If we respect what people have been able to create, then we can appreciate the people.

Because the music of a people gives such a clear representation of their essence, it provides a powerful means for understanding them. Music can help to lift the veil of ignorance that sometimes stands between people who differ in race, ethnicity, religion, economic well-being, and lifestyle. If we accept their music and have some understanding of it, we have established a way to relate. As their music moves us and ours moves them, we share our humanity. We cross the boundaries and obliterate the walls of prejudice, hostility, and misunderstanding that so often persist among peoples.

America is a microcosm of the world. Our population is the world in miniature—a cross-section of all the world's people. That is the great and exciting experiment that is America. But the challenge is to embrace our differences and to find the ways to link arms in spite of (and because of) them. Music is a bridge. It is a fundamental human connector. Its power is that it can join us not just intellectually but also empathetically and emotionally. Feelings are the basis of any real attachment we have for others. Music presents us with a stream of sounds that we can equate with our lives. By putting us in touch with our emotional fiber, it communicates with our essence, drawing us into its fold, arousing our expectations and satisfying them. We do not just perceive it, we live it.

The arts are the way we say our humanity, the way we express our being, the way we see our individuality and our commonality. Music gives shape to the feeling of human experience. It is one way in which we express our insight and wisdom about our emotional and spiritual being. In studying how music is used by humans to serve their human needs, we see how similar those needs are. As humans we have a need to define who we are, to move and perform, to express ourselves, to communicate, to celebrate, to commemorate our dead, to create, to tell stories of our lives, to characterize our time, to understand life's meaning, and to share our humanity. All humans use music to express these needs, but they express them differently.

▼*Activity:* **Determine the Place**

How do musical characteristics and style convey a sense of "place"?

Listen to examples of music that you have studied. On the basis of each work's musical character, determine its geographic "home" or origin. If it helps, refer to the map on pages 540–541. Be ready to justify your decisions musically.

Music Expresses Our Differences—and Similarities

The means of musical communication are infinite. These differences, which are sometimes extreme, prevail in every society. Music is valued by people everywhere—but not the same music. Nor are cultures as monolithic, that is to say, as unified in tastes as we might like to believe. While there are common threads in all cultures—values and lifestyles that are representative, and this is true of music—there are also tastes that are uncommon. These dissonances keep cultures vibrant and moving. Differences excite. They stimulate. They cause us to rethink, to reevaluate, and to change. That is why the juxtaposition of diverse peoples creates a dynamic society. This is the great strength of America. Yet as America becomes increasingly diverse, there are people who choose retrenchment in racial and ethnic enclaves and resistance to intracultural exchange. They honor just their own music.

▶ In his rapid pencil sketch entitled *Study for the Black Countess* (c. 1880), the French artist Henri de Toulouse-Lautrec (1864–1901) captures the elegance of Paris in the late nineteenth century. We are there. As in music, we come into intimate contact with the artist's presence, his sense of discovery, his passion, and his time and place. The vague, unfinished quality invites us to use our own imagination to complete the work—to see what we want to see. Can you hear the galloping hooves? Can you feel the spontaneity of the artist's hand, frozen in the act of creation?

Henri de Toulouse-Lautrec, French, 1864–1901. *Toulouse-Lautrec Sketchbook: La Comtesse Noir*. Graphite on ivory wove paper. 1880. 16 x 25.6 cm. The Art Institute of Chicago, Chicago, Illinois. All Rights Reserved. Robert Alexander Waller Collection, 1949. 80 leaf 4 recto.

People's musical tastes are often more varied than we might suppose. African Americans, for example, do not all like or understand jazz to the same degree. Some prefer rap, some classical music. White Americans exhibit a similar range of tastes. So do people in Canada, Mexico, Egypt, Japan, Germany, and other countries in which communications media bring music of the outside world to the doorstep. The world is still very large in spite of our easy access to so much of it, and musical tastes range far and wide. We have to be cautious about stereotyping people musically— pigeon-holing them with labels that are too general to be fair and accurate.

Bringing People Together

Still, as humans, we are not all that different. What we think and feel is not vastly unlike what most other people think and feel. Our problems, our inner doubts, our hurts and hopes, our feelings of defeat and inferiority, our successes and failures, our pleasures and pain are similar to what all people experience. Music lets us know that we are not alone in our feelings. It tells us how commonplace these inner states really are. By coming to know that our spirit is shared by others, music bonds us to a community of other human beings. That is enormously comforting. Music is salve for our singular vulnerability, and our sense of aloneness. It reinforces our need for joy, sharing, and belonging. Most importantly, it puts us in touch with the universal humanness within us.

If music can bring all kinds of people together by uniting them in spirit and feeling, it surely has a role to play in world peace. Any force that can bring people together, cross cultural boundaries, and break through cultural centrism and isolation should be valued highly in today's world. Technological advancements continue to bring the people of the world into closer proximity. We live in an age of immediate contact with people across the entire world, yet contact alone does not assure understanding. We need to rely upon the arts to help us facilitate the human communication process. For many years, cultural exchanges between different countries have been recognized by governments as a way to open the doors to human understanding. Such exchanges acknowledge that the arts are one of the great treasures of the human race through which we define ourselves, our world, and our era.

▼Activity: *Determine the Time*

Can you place a musical composition or style in its proper era?

Listen again to the following musical examples that you have studied. Evaluate the musical characteristics and designate where the composition would best be placed on a time line. Be ready to justify your decision musically.

1. The Third Movement—Minuetto from Symphony No. 40 by W. A. Mozart
2. "Maple Leaf Rag" by Scott Joplin
3. "Alleluia, *Vidimus Stellam*" (Chant)
4. "Siegfried's Funeral Music" from *The Twilight of the Gods* by Richard Wagner
5. "As Vesta Was Descending" by Thomas Weelkes
6. "China Boy" performed by the Benny Goodman Trio
7. "Mini's Solo" from *Valis* by Tod Machover
8. Toccata and Fugue in D Minor by J. S. Bach

How does music convey its era?

Summary

Music in all its vast variety speaks the heart of humankind. It is one of the clearest ways we represent and communicate our humanity. It is the means we use to convey our emotional reactions to the people and the life around us. Music permits us to express who we are and what we feel about the world we live in. With it we establish our identity as a people living in a particular place at a particular time. Music puts us in touch with our own humanness and with the humanness of other people. By probing the mysteries of our existence—our uncertainties, our hungers, our excitements, our dreams—music provides a portrait of our inner being. That is its mission—and its power. That is why it is such an important means of communication within and between all human societies and why, too, it provides us with the promising possibility of communicating with alien life forms.

In a world of cold technology, facts, and information, music brings us back to our basic humanness. It is one of the fundamental ways we have invented to search for life's meaning and to express our human essence in this world. It is a main means of caring for and preserving the life of our spirit. Through music we can find our roots as global human beings—members of the human race. We can stretch ourselves to be bigger, to be more, to realize our fullest human possibilities. In these ways, music gives balance to our existence and helps our humanity survive. The real wonder of it all is that these rewards can be ours for a lifetime.

Apply What You Have Learned
Chapter 25

How would you categorize these five musical compositions?

Listen carefully to each example and place it in the category you believe is most fitting: (a) Folk; (b) Popular; (c) Jazz; (d) Classical; and (e) Rock.

After you have completed your worksheet, reflect on how you would answer the following questions and prepare to take part in a lively class discussion:

1. What is the arguably correct answer for each example?
2. Why might someone who knows very little about music confuse these different styles?
3. Do you see any problem with generalizing about stylistic categorizations of music? If so, what are some of the issues that arise?

Apply What You Have Learned
Chapter 26

Artists of all kinds are inspired by cultures other than their own. Shortly after the French composer Georges Bizet captured the sound of Spanish music in his opera *Carmen* (1874), American painter John Singer Sargent, also living in Paris at that time, painted *El Jaleo* (1882) featuring a Spanish gypsy dancer (see page 539). Sargent was inspired by his visit to Spain and perhaps by the wave of interest in Bizet's opera. Similarly, the American composer Aaron Copland was inspired to compose *El Sálon México* based on his experience of and admiration for Mexican culture.

Choose one of the following subjects and write a research paper. Your task is to discover the cultural influences that inspired the composer by reading and by listening to appropriate musical examples:

A. The influence of Slavic folk songs on the music of Hungarian classical composer Zoltán Kodály (1882–1967). (Possible work to study: Hary János Suite, 1927.)
B. The influence of the music of other cultures on the music of American popular musician Paul Simon. (Possible albums to study: *Graceland* (1986) or *Rhythm of the Saints* (1990).)
C. The influence of jazz and Negro folk idioms on the music of black American composer William Grant Still (1895–1978). (Possible work to study: *Afro-American Symphony*, 1930.)

Apply What You Have Learned
Chapter 27

How broad has your aural knowledge of musical styles become?

In the activity called Musical Style Check on page 8, you were asked: "How familiar are you with the many styles of music heard daily in the United States?" Listen again to all 20 of the original musical examples, and try to identify them with 100 percent accuracy.

If you completed all the chapters in the text, then you have studied each of these musical pieces. Your greater awareness of musical style and the vocabulary you have learned should enable you to earn a high score this time around. You may be surprised at how well you do!

▲ Artists sometimes try to capture the essence of another culture. For example, American artist John Singer Sargent (1856–1925) painted *El Jaleo* (1882), a large painting depicting a Spanish dancer and the musicians accompanying her. In 1879 he visited Spain and saw the famous dance, *jaleo de jerez*. He captures the impassioned performance with the energy and spontaneity of his brush work.

John Singer Sargent. *El Jaleo.* 1882. Isabella Stewart Gardner Museum, Boston, Massachusetts.

WORLD MAP

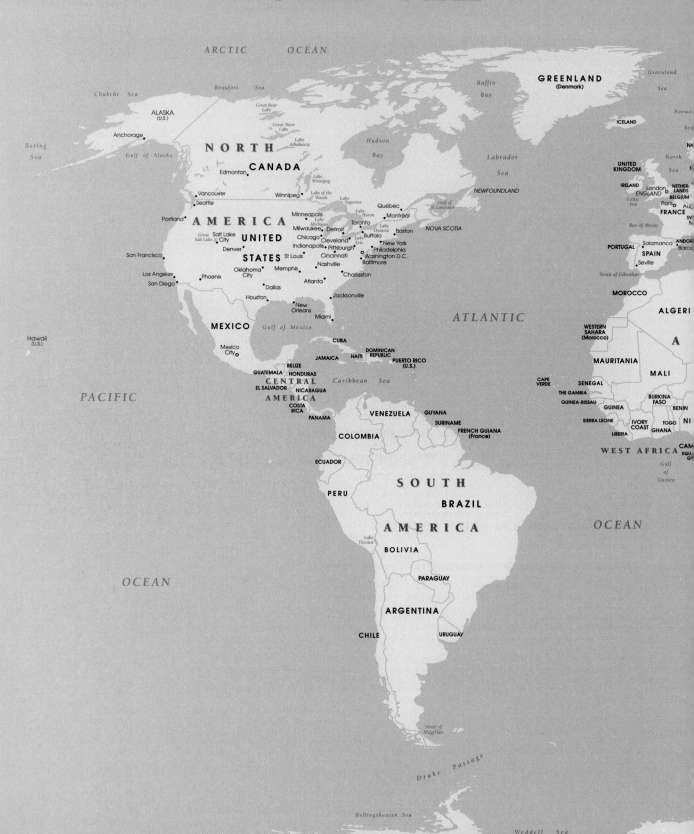

ARCTIC OCEAN

Chukchi Sea

Beaufort Sea

GREENLAND
(Denmark)

Greenland Sea

ALASKA
(U.S.)

Great Bear Lake

Baffin Bay

ICELAND

Norwe Se

Bering Sea

Anchorage

Great Slave Lake

Hudson Bay

Labrador Sea

NORTH

Gulf of Alaska

CANADA

Lake Athabasca

NEWFOUNDLAND

UNITED KINGDOM

North Se

Edmonton

Lake Winnipeg

Vancouver
Seattle

Winnipeg

Lake of the Woods

Québec

Montréal

Gulf of St Lawrence

AMERICA

Portland

Lake Superior

Lake Huron

Toronto

NOVA SCOTIA

IRELAND London **NETHER-LANDS**
ENGLAND
Paris **Au** **BELGIUM**
FRANCE

Celtic Sea

Great Salt Lake

Salt Lake City

UNITED

Minneapolis
Lake Michigan
Milwaukee

Detroit

Lake Ontario
Buffalo

Boston

San Francisco

Denver

Chicago
Cleveland
Indianapolis

Lake Erie
Pittsburgh

New York
Philadelphia

Bay of Biscay

PORTUGAL

Salamanca

SPAIN

ANDO

STATES

St Louis

Cincinnati

Washington D.C.
Baltimore

FRANCE
PORTUGAL
Seville

Barce

Los Angeles

Oklahoma City

Memphis

Nashville

Strait of Gibraltar

San Diego

Phoenix

Dallas

Atlanta

Charleston

MOROCCO

Houston

Jacksonville

ALGERI

Hawaii
(U.S.)

MEXICO

New Orleans

Miami

ATLANTIC

WESTERN SAHARA
(Morocco)

A

Gulf of Mexico

Mexico City

CUBA

DOMINICAN REPUBLIC

MAURITANIA

MALI

JAMAICA

HAITI

PUERTO RICO
(U.S.)

GUATEMALA

BELIZE

CAPE VERDE

SENEGAL

CENTRAL

HONDURAS

Caribbean Sea

THE GAMBIA

BURKINA FASO

PACIFIC

EL SALVADOR

NICARAGUA

GUINEA-BISSAU

GUINEA

BENIN

AMERICA

COSTA RICA

VENEZUELA

GUYANA

SIERRA LEONE

IVORY COAST

TOGO

NI

PANAMA

SURINAME

LIBERIA

GHANA

COLOMBIA

FRENCH GUIANA
(France)

WEST AFRICA

CAM
EQU.
G

ECUADOR

Gulf of Guinea

PERU

SOUTH

BRAZIL

OCEAN

AMERICA

Lake Titicaca

BOLIVIA

OCEAN

PARAGUAY

ARGENTINA

CHILE

URUGUAY

Strait of Magellan

Drake Passage

Bellingshausen Sea

Weddell Sea

Ross Sea

ARCTIC   OCEAN

Barents   Sea   *Kara   Sea*   *Laptev   Sea*   *East   Siberian   Sea*

FINLAND   *Bering   Sea*
Lake *Lake*
Ladoga *Onega*
ESTONIA   •St Petersburg
ATVIA   A S I A
THUANIA   •Moscow   *Sea of Okhotsk*
AND   BELARUS   RUSSIA
E U R O P E   JAPAN
•Kiev   *Sea of*
VAKIA UKRAINE   KAZAKHSTAN   MONGOLIA   NORTH   *Japan*
ARY Budapest   MOLDOVA   KOREA
NIA ROMANIA   *Sea of*   *Lake*   SOUTH   •Tokyo   PACIFIC
UGO. BULGARIA   *Azov*   *Aral*   *Balkhash*   Beijing   KOREA
MAC.   *Black Sea*   *Sea*   UZBEKISTAN   KYRGYZSTAN   (Peking)•
BANIA   GEORGIA   *Caspian*   OCEAN
GREECE   ARMENIA AZERBAIJAN   TURKMENISTAN TAJIKISTAN   C H I N A
ranean TURKEY   *Sea*   TAIWAN
N CYPRUS SYRIA IRAQ   AFGHANISTAN   *TIBET*
Sea CYPRUS LEBANON •Damascus   *South*   *Philippine*
ISRAEL   MIDDLE   KUWAIT   NEPAL   *China*   *Sea*
YA JORDAN   EAST   BAHRAIN *Persian Gulf* PAKISTAN   BHUTAN   LAOS   *Sea*
EGYPT   QATAR   BANGLADESH   PHILIPPINES
Red   SAUDI   U.A.E.   I N D I A   MYANMAR
ICA *Sea*   ARABIA   *Arabian*   THAILAND
CHAD   OMAN   *Sea*   *Bay*   CAMBODIA VIETNAM
ERITREA YEMEN   *of*
SUDAN   DJIBOUTI *Gulf of Aden*   *Bengal*   BRUNEI
Lake   ETHIOPIA   SRI   MALAYSIA
CENTRAL *Turkana*   LANKA
AFRICAN *Lake*
REPUBLIC *Albert*   SOMALIA   *SUMATRA*   *BORNEO*
GO   UGANDA KENYA   *CELEBES*   NEW GUINEA
RWANDA *Lake*   PAPUA
ZAIRE BURUNDI *Victoria*   I N D I A N   I N D O N E S I A   NEW
Lake   GUINEA
Tanganyika TANZANIA   *JAVA* *BALI*   SOLOMON
GOLA   ISLANDS
ZAMBIA   MALAWI *Lake*
Lake   *Malawi*   O C E A N   *Coral Sea*
Kariba   MADAGASCAR
BIA ZIMBABWE MOZAMBIQUE
BOTSWANA   A U S T R A L I A

SWAZILAND
SOUTH   LESOTHO
AFRICA   *Great Australian Bight*   *Tasman*
Sea

NEW
ZEALAND

A N T A R C T I C A   *Ross*
Sea

Glossary

A

absolute music music without extra-musical associations, as opposed to program music

absolute pitch the ability to recognize and reproduce pitches exactly

a cappella unaccompanied vocal music

accelerando (aht-cheh-leh-RAHN-doh) a gradual increase in tempo; growing gradually faster

accent the emphasis placed on a beat

accidentals sharp, flat, or naturals occurring outside of the given key signature within a composition

acculturation the mutual influence of different cultures in close contact

adagio (ah-DAHJ-ee-oh) slow tempo, but not as slow as largo

aerophones instruments that produce sound by a vibrating column of air including wind instruments such as woodwinds and brass and reed instruments such as the accordion and the organ

affections cataloged feelings used during the Baroque period

aleatory music music in which composers deliberately leave parts of the composition and performance undetermined; see also chance music

allegretto a little slower than allegro

allegro fast and lively tempo

alto the lowest female register; see also contralto

andante moderately slow; a walking tempo

andantino a little faster than andante

animato with spirit

antecedent term for the question half of a melodic phrase

anthropologist a scientist who studies the physical and cultural characteristics and social customs of a group of people

antiphonal describing musical groups that perform alternately in a call-and-response manner

aria a song for a solo singer and orchestra, usually in an opera, oratorio, or cantata

arpeggio (ahr-PEJ-ee-oh) a broken chord whose pitches are heard successively

arrangement an adaptation of a composition from one medium to another

arranger one who reworks preexistent musical material

articulation clarity and distinct rendition in musical performance

a tempo a return to the preceding rate of speed

atonal, atonality absence of tonality or of a tonal center

audiation the skill of being able to hear, think, or imagine music in your head

authenticity performing music as nearly as possible in the way it was performed at the time it was created

B

backbeat in popular music, accents on beats 2 and 4 that answer the normal accents on 1 and 3

background music film music with no visual or logical source

band a large instrumental ensemble consisting primarily or solely of wind and percussion instruments

baritone the male voice between bass and the tenor

bar line vertical dividing line between measures on the musical staff

Baroque stylistic period of music between c. 1600 and c. 1750

bass the low male voice; the lowest instrument in the violin family, also called contrabass

bass clef F clef that indicates the placement of F below Middle C

basso continuo bass line and accompanying chords for keyboard instruments, used extensively in the Baroque period

basso profundo the lowest of men's voices

beat steady recurring pulse; a unit of time

bebop see bop

bel canto Italian vocal technique of the eighteenth century with emphasis on beauty of sound and brilliance of performance

binary form a two-part form

bluegrass a type of American country music that uses acoustic instruments

blues a form of African-American folk music expressing frustration, ordeal, and hope

blue tones lowered third and seventh degrees of the major scale (and sometimes the fifth) often used in popular music and jazz

book the story and the dialogue of a musical

bop a complex and sophisticated type of improvised jazz, intended for listening rather than dancing; also called bebop

bourrée (BU-ray) A French seventeenth century dance usually in quick duple meter with a single upbeat

brass wind instruments that derive their sound from vibrations transmitted through cup-shaped mouthpieces, including the trumpet, French horn, trombone, and tuba

break a cadenza-like improvisation by a jazz instrumentalist or singer that is inserted between ensemble passages

bridge a connective part of a composition; a support to raise the strings from the soundboard

Broadway musical a dramatic stage form that combines the art forms of design, dance, costuming, acting, and singing

bugaku danced portions of Japanese gagaku; see also gagaku

C

cadence a breathing break; punctuation or termination of a musical phrase

cadenza a solo section in an improvisatory style, usually near the end of the piece, giving the performer a chance to exhibit technical mastery

cakewalk an exuberant dance with syncopated rhythms that may represent an early form of jazz

call and response a song style that follows a simple question-and-answer pattern in which a soloist leads and a group responds

calypso folk-style music from the Caribbean Islands

canción (cahn-see-OHN) ***ranchera*** a popular type of Mexican song, usually in AAB form, performed by mariachi bands

canon a musical form that uses exact imitation; melody performed similarly to a round

cantata a sectional composition for solo voice, a combination of solo voices, and/or chorus with instrumental accompaniment

chaconne (shah-KOHN) continuous variations based on an underlying repeated harmonic progression

chamber music music played by small groups, such as a string quartet or a piano trio

chance music music in which aspects such as melody, rhythm, dynamics, timbre, and form are left wholly or partly to the discretion and creativity of the performer; *see also* aleatory

chart jazz score, often abbreviated

chorale hymn tune; a hymn melody of the German Protestant church usually harmonized for singing by a congregation

chorale prelude a composition serving as an introduction to the singing by a congregation

chord simultaneous combination of at least three different pitches

chordophones instruments that produce their sound through the vibration of strings by being bowed, plucked, or struck

chromatic incorporating tones foreign to the diatonic scale; indicated by a sharp (♯), flat (♭), natural (♮), double sharp (×), or double flat (♭♭)

chromatic scale a scale consisting of successive half steps

classical music a style of art music of any culture distinguished from folk, jazz, or popular music; European music of the Classical period, composed from about 1750 to 1825

clave an Afro-Cuban rhythm; also, the two round wooden sticks struck together to produce the pattern

clef symbol indicating pitch designations for the lines and spaces of the staff

coda a short concluding section; of a musical composition, designed to convey a sense of finality

coloratura a rapid scale, arpeggio, trill, or similar virtuosic passage, particularly in vocal melodies of eighteenth- and nineteenth-century operatic arias; a soprano who performs such passages

complete cadence cadence that terminates on the tonic triad, with the tonic tone appearing as both the highest and lowest pitch

composer a person who creates musical works

composition a musical work; the craft of putting together sounds to create a musical work

concertino the section of a Baroque concerto played by a small group of soloists

concerto a composition usually written in three sections or movements featuring the interplay between one or more soloists and an orchestra

concerto grosso a work in which there is a contrast between ripieno (full or tutti) sections for a small string orchestra and concertino sections for more than one soloist or a small group of soloists

conductor the director of the orchestra, choir, or other performing group

conjunct melody employing successive pitches of the scale; stepwise movement

consequent term for the answer of a melodic phrase

consonance absence of tension or discord in music

contemporary music or art that is current; also, composers who lived during the same historical periods as each other are known as contemporaries

continuo a Baroque musical accompaniment consisting of a harpsichord sounding the chords and a viola da gamba (a low, bowed string instrument) that reinforces the continuous bass line

contour the shape of a melody or its rise and fall

contralto the lowest female voice; *see also* alto

contrapuntal in the style of counterpoint; the combining of melodic lines

cool jazz jazz style of the 1950s

counterpoint the technique of combining melodic lines to create a polyphonic texture

countersubject a secondary melodic pattern used at the same time as the principal subject

countertenor the highest male register; a mature male voice of light quality that sings in the female pitch range

country and western a style of American popular music from the rural South and West that usually refers to commonplace subjects in the lyrics

creative license the liberty artists take when reinterpreting another artist's work

crescendo (kreh-SHEN-doh) to gradually become louder: (<)

crossover a merging of styles

culture the customs, ideas, tastes, and beliefs acquired from a person's background; the sum total of one's lifestyle

D

decibel unit for measuring volume of sound

decrescendo (day-kreh-SHEN-doh) to gradually become softer: (>)

descriptive music another name for program music; music that represents images, stories, or poetic ideas

development the section of the sonata form in which thematic reworkings and modifications occur

diatonic the tones of a major or minor scale

diminuendo a gradual decrease in the loudness of a sound; decrescendo

disjunct melody formed by leaps rather than by steps

dissonance discord in music, suggesting a state of tension or "seeking"

dodecaphony twelve-tone music

dominant the fifth pitch of a diatonic scale; the chord built on the fifth degree of the diatonic scale

Dorian mode a scale with the pattern of whole-step, half, whole, whole, whole, half, and whole

downbeat the accented first beat in a measure

drone a long sustained note, usually in the lower part

drum machine a machine that has all the sounds of a whole range of percussion instruments stored in its memory, waiting to be applied to any rhythms its operator might want to perform

dubbing putting all the elements of sound—dialogue, sound effects, and music—onto one soundtrack

duet composition for two performers

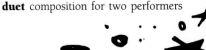

duple beats grouped into sets of two (strong-weak)

dynamics the volume of sound, the loudness or softness of a musical passage

E

electrophones instruments that produce sounds from electricity

electronic music music generated or altered by electronic means

ensemble a group of musicians performing together; the quality of togetherness

entr'acte music light instrumental music that is performed between acts of a staged production

episode a section of a fugue in which the subject or main theme is not heard; a connective passage

ethnomusicologist a professional who studies the music and musical practice of a particular culture or cultures

exposition the opening section of a sonata form, in which the main thematic material is given its first complete statement

extramusical the idea that inspires a programmatic piece of music

F

"felt" time the time that music appears to carve out for itself; one's subjective sense of time, in contrast to time measured by real, or clock time

fermata a hold (⌒)

finale concluding movement or passage in a musical work

flat symbol that lowers a pitch by one half step: (♭)

folk music uncomplicated music that speaks directly of everyday matters; the first popular music

form musical design, incorporating repetition and contrast, unity, and variety

forte loud

fortissimo very loud

free-form jazz jazz of recent times that does not use a set tune as the basis of improvisation, but rather allows the performers to interact and to generate their own composition

fugue a polyphonic composition consisting of a series of successive melody imitations; *see also* imitation

fundamental the main pitch from which the harmonics of the overtone series are generated

fusion a jazz and rock combination

G

gagaku literally, elegant music; Japanese orchestral music (sometimes with singing) that is used at imperial court ceremonies and at temples and shrines; *see also bugaku*

gamelan the centerpiece of Balinese music; an ensemble of 25 performers or more who play on metallophones of several sizes and pitches, gongs of different sizes, cymbals, drums, a flute, and sometimes a simple string instrument

genre a general type or kind of music

gig an engagement to perform music, especially jazz

glissando a continuous or sliding movement from one pitch to the other

gospel a type of religious folk or popular music sung largely in black churches

grand opera nineteenth-century opera that became somewhat grandiose in design, incorporating a large orchestra, continuous singing, ballet, and a large cast

Grand Staff the combined treble and bass staffs

ground bass an underlying musical phrase repeated as a bass line, over which melodic variations occur, as in a *passacaglia; see also passacaglia*

H

half cadence see incomplete cadence

half step the closest pitch above or below any given pitch on the keyboard, such as C to C# or F to E

harmonic series barely audible tones generated by the vibration of a fundamental sound

harmonics a series of tones generated by the fundamental tone; *see* partial

harmonizing the ability to invent on the spot a vocal line that will complement a melody

harmony vertical blocks of different tones that sound simultaneously; a progression of chords

heterophony musical texture that occurs when performers sing or play the same melody simultaneously, but in different ways

homophonic a texture in which a melodic line is supported by chords; *see also* harmony

homophony a style of musical texture in which a single melody is supported by chordal accompaniment

hook the generally repeated musical motive that accompanies the words to the title of a popular song

hymn a strophic song sung within a religious service by the congregation

hyperinstruments "smart" instruments that, with the help of computers, respond to live musicians

I

idée fixe (EE-day FEEKS) term used by Berlioz for a recurring theme used in all the movements of one of his program symphonies

idiophones wood or metal percussion instruments that produce sound by being struck, scraped, or shaken

imitation the restatement in succession of identical or nearly identical musical material in two or more parts

Impressionism a French style of atmospheric music created by Claude Debussy in the late nineteenth century as a reaction against the overblown emotion of Romantic music

improvisation spontaneous musical invention, commonly associated with jazz

incidental music music that occurs in connection with a drama

incomplete cadence a resting point at the end of a musical phrase that does not sound finished, because the pause is on the dominant seventh chord; a half cadence marking a midpoint within a larger musical thought

indeterminance term referring to music that has elements of chance or a great deal of freedom

intensity degree of loudness; dynamics

interlocking rhythms a principle of Balinese music in which the parts intermingle to create a complex texture; *see also kotekan*

interval the distance in pitch between two tones

inversion arranging the tones of a chord in an order different from the way they are derived; performing a melody by turning the contour upside down

J

jazz a style of American dance music originated in the South by black Americans; it is characterized by strong, prominent meter, improvisation, and dotted or syncopated patterns

jitterbug a fast dance of the 1940s to swing music

K

Kecak (keh-CHAK) a Balinese musical theater work based on the Hindu epic, *Ramayana*

key the basic scale and tonality of a composition

keynote the tonic pitch; number one of the scale

key signature designation of sharps or flats at the beginning of a composition to indicate its basic scale and tonality

kotekan (ko-TEH-kahn) the Balinese term for interlocking rhythms; *see also* interlocking rhythms

kritis (KRI-tees) Hindu religious songs sung in praise of a particular god or gods

L

Lali a warrior dance of west central Africa

largo very slow

legato a smooth articulation of a series of tones, each connected to the next

lento slow

librettist the author of the libretto

libretto the complete book of words for an opera, oratorio, or cantata

lied a German art song (plural, *lieder*)

lyricist the writer of lyrics, particularly for popular songs

lyrics the words of a song

M

madrigal a nonreligious vocal form in several parts, popular in the Renaissance

mag track music recorded on film coated with an oxide surface, like sound tape

major scale scale built on the formula of two whole steps, one half step, three whole steps, one half step

major triad three tones that form a major third (bottom) and a minor third (top), such as C E G; in a major key, the tonic, subdominant, and dominant chords are all major triads

mambo an Afro-Cuban dance in syncopated 4/4 time with heavy accents on 2 and 4

march music with a steady beat in 2/4, 4/4, or 6/8 time, suitable for a parade or procession

mariachi a Mexican instrumental ensemble consisting of violin, trumpet, and various guitars

Mass the primary liturgical service of the Roman Catholic church and the music written for it

measure the division of beats into set groups; a measure is denoted by a bar line

melismatic a melody in which each syllable of text is set to several pitches

melody a logical succession of musical tones

membranophones instruments that produce sound by striking or rubbing a skin or membrane stretched across a resonating air chamber

mestizo mixed culture

meter a rhythmic measure of a certain number of beats

mezzo medium

mezzo forte medium loud (mf)

mezzo piano medium soft (mp)

mezzo-soprano the intermediate female voice; one who sings in the lower part of the soprano range

MIDI Musical Instrument Digital Interface; a standardized "language" of digital bits that the computer can store

minimalism a repetitive type of twentieth-century music in which a motive or motives are repeated

extensively according to a system or set of rules

minor scale scale built on the formula of one whole step, one half step, two whole steps, one half step, two whole steps

minor triad three tones that form a minor third (bottom) and a major third (top), such as C E flat G; in a minor key, the tonic, subdominant, and dominant triads are minor, although the dominant is frequently altered to make it a major triad

minuet a slow and traditional French dance in triple meter, probably originating as a country dance

mixed meter changing meter

mode diatonic scale other than major or minor, especially the Dorian, Phrygian, Lydian, and Mixolydian, used extensively during the Middle Ages and Renaissance

moderato moderate tempo

modulation the changing from one key to another within a composition

monophonic a musical texture having a single melodic line with no accompaniment; monophony

monophony a style of musical texture consisting of a single melody without accompaniment

motive a short, distinctive musical pattern or figure, often used by composers as a building block

movement one part of a larger composition that is relatively complete and independent, much like one chapter of a novel; symphonies and sonatas are often cast in three or four movements that are contrasted by tempo and meter

musical expression the particular feeling conveyed by a performance

musical style the distinct manner or character of musical expression

music critic a person who judges the quality of musical performances

music drama Wagnerian approach to grand opera that uses continuous singing, orchestral commentary, leitmotifs, and plots derived from Teutonic mythology

musique concrète a system of electronic composition in which natural sounds are taped, edited, and shaped into a composition recorded on magnetic tape

N

national anthem a song of praise or devotion towards a country

natural a mark that cancels out a sharp or a flat: (♮)

neumes marks over words used to indicate the direction of the melodic line in plainsong or Gregorian chants

New Age a contemporary type of meditative, mostly instrumental, music

New Romanticism a communicative style of contemporary classical music that relies on dramatic effects

O

obbligato a subordinate melody above a main melody

octave an interval of eight pitch names, such as C to the next C above or below; a distance of twelve half steps

offbeat emphasis of the weak beats in a measure

opera a staged drama that is predominantly sung, most often with orchestral accompaniment

opéra comique a Baroque opera in which some dialogue is sung and some is spoken

opus work; a number indicating the order in which works were composed

oratorio a large vocal work that is similar in musical construction to an opera, but is neither staged nor acted out

orchestration the process of scoring for an orchestra

organum an application of part singing in Gregorian chant in which a second melody (vox organalis) was added to the existing plainsong (vox principalis); although its earliest form was parallel organum, it eventually developed into free and melismatic organum; *see also* parallel organum

ostinato a rhythmic or melodic passage that is repeated continuously

overtone one of a series of faint higher tones that are generated when any one tone is sounded

overture an extended orchestral introduction to an opera, ballet, or similar type of musical presentation

P

parallel organum an early type of polyphonic music (ninth and tenth century) in which the voices move together note-for-note at the interval of a fourth, but begin and end on the same pitch

partial a harmonic generated by a fundamental tone; *see* overtone

passacaglia (pahs-ah-KAL-yeh) continuous variations on a bass melody; *see also* ground bass

passing tone nonharmonic tone that literally moves between two chordal tones

Peking opera the most well-known regional type of Chinese musical theater

pentatonic scale any five-tone scale

perceptive listening the ability to discern musical characteristics

percussion instruments that derive their sound from being shook or struck, including drums, cymbals, triangles, xylophones, gongs, chimes, and rattles

perfect cadence a conclusive dominant-to-tonic chordal progression marking the end of a musical idea; *also called* authentic cadence

phrase a complete musical idea, comparable to a sentence

pianissimo very soft (pp)

piano soft (p)

pitch the highness or lowness of sound determined by its frequency of vibration

pivot chord chord that is common to two tonalities or keys and is used as the basis of modulating from one to the other

pizzicato playing string instruments by plucking with the fingers rather than bowing

plainsong a religious melody of early Christianity; Gregorian chant

polka a rapid dance in duple meter

polychoral music antiphonal music for two or more groups

polyphonic music a texture in which several melodies sound at the same time

polyphony the simultaneous combination of different melodies and rhythms

polyrhythms a combination of two or more contrasting rhythmic patterns played at the same time

popular music

popular music American music that has wide appeal, is immediately communicative and relatively short

prepared piano the alteration of a traditional piano's timbre by the insertion of various objects among and between the strings, as invented by John Cage

presto very fast; faster than allegro

prima donna the principal female singer in an opera; a feisty, conceited opera star

primary chord the tonic, subdominant or dominant chords of a major or minor key; I, IV, and V chords

program music a piece of instrumental music associated with a story or other extramusical idea

program symphony a symphony with a program, as composed by Berlioz or Liszt

pulse the steady beat

Q

qawwali (kha-WAA-lee) a type of religious music of Pakistan and India

quantizing the process of electronic synchronization of the rhythm

quartet a combination of four voices or instruments; also music written for such an ensemble

quintet a combination of five voices or instruments, for example a woodwind quintet; also music for such an ensemble

R

raga Indian melodic material; a traditional melodic pattern or mode, or the improvisation based on it

ragtime a style of American popular music, often for piano, in which the syncopated melody conflicts with the steady 2/4 or 4/4 rhythm

range distance between the highest and lowest pitches used in a melody, that is, its outer limits

rap a highly rhythmic, talky form of contemporary popular, largely black, music

recapitulation the section of a sonata form that is basically a repetition of the exposition (main thematic material)

recitative a speech-like style of singing used in opera, oratorio, and cantata

refrain a chorus (melody and text) that is repeated at intervals in a song, especially following each verse

reggae a popular musical style mixing African and Caribbean rhythms created by Jamaican musicians

register the high, middle, or low section of the vocal or instrumental range

Renaissance the period in Western Europe from c. 1400-1600; the style of music of this period

repertoire an inventory of compositions mastered and performed by a musician; also the historical listing of similar pieces in any one period

Requiem Mass funeral Mass or Mass for the dead

resolution in harmonic analysis, the succession of a dissonant sound to a consonant sound

retrograde the backwards sounding of a musical rhythm or melody

retrograde-inversion the backwards and upside down sounding of a musical idea

rhumba a ballroom dance that imitates the Afro-Cuban rumba; *see also* rumba

rhythm combinations of long and short sounds that convey a sense of movement

rhythm and blues (R & B) a style of American popular music that combines blues harmonies and rhythm with gospel-like vocals in up tempo

rhythm cycle a fixed number of beats in a series that repeats itself over and over, particularly in Arabian and Indian music

riff jazz ostinato

ripieno the orchestral sections of a Baroque concerto

ritardando the gradual slowing of tempo; abbreviated as rit; *also called* ritard

ritornello a refrain-like repeated section in a Baroque concerto

rock a style of popular music of American origin in the mid-1950s that featured guitar and a driving rhythm with accents on the offbeats; *also called* rock 'n' roll

Romantic music music of the nineteenth century that stressed the expression of feeling

Romantic period an era spanning from c. 1825 to 1910 in which composers were inspired to express their inner feelings

rondeau a fixed poetic form of the thirteenth century that alternates repetitions of the main theme with two or more contrasting sections

rondo an instrumental form based on an alternation between a repeated (or recurring) section and contrasting episodes

root the pitch which is the foundation or building block of a chord

round a composition in which the same melody is started at different times and sounded together; *also called* canon

rubato "robbed time"; the free treatment of meter in performance

rumba an Afro-Cuban popular dance; *see also* rhumba

S

sacred of or dealing with religious music; *see* secular

salsa a type of Latin American dance music of Afro-Cuban and Puerto Rican origins

samba (SAHM-bah) an Afro-Brazilian dance in duple time that is faster and jazzier than the tango

sampled sounds prerecorded bits of sound that are reprocessed

sampling a recording process that begins with real sounds

sarabande a seventeenth and eighteenth century dance in stately triple meter with an accent on beat two

scale a sequence of tones arranged in rising pitches

scat singing style of vocal jazz improvisation in which nonsense syllables are used to imitate the sound of an instrument

scherzo a movement, usually the third, of sonatas, symphonies, and quartets, introduced by Beethoven to replace the minuet

score a notation showing all the parts of a musical composition, aligned vertically on staves one above the other

scoring composing music expressly for a film

secular music without religious associations; *see* sacred

seguidilla a Spanish dance with many regional variations, or the music for such a dance

sequence repetition of a melodic idea or phrase at a higher or lower pitch level

sequencer a digital playback system

serialism use of a set sequence of pitches as the basis for a musical composition, such as the ordering of the twelve chromatic tones, which are then transposed, inverted, presented in retrograde, and so on

sharp a symbol that raises a pitch by one half step: (#)

solfège (sohl-FEZH) a method of sight reading, using the syllables "DO, RE, MI, FA, SOL, LA, TI, DO"

solmization a system of sight singing by syllables

solo composition for one performer

sonata a composition for a solo instrument, or instruments with accompaniment, which consists of three or four large sections called movements

sonata-allegro form a large A-B-A form consisting of three sections: exposition, development, and recapitulation

son jarocho (SOHN hah-ROH-choh) a traditional Mexican song

song form ternary form in ABA

sonority the degree of resonance or blend of sound

soprano the highest female voice

soul music a form of rhythm and blues

soundtrack a strip along the film to the side of the visual image that contains visual representations of sound

source music film music that comes from a visual (on-camera) source

spiritual a religious song of the American Negro; also Negro spiritual

spot to determine which scenes in a film should have music

staccato played in a detached manner, as opposed to legato

staff a set of five lines and four spaces on which music is notated

stanza the verse of a text

stretto a polyphonic texture in which the imitating voices overlap, creating a heightened sense of drama

string quartet an ensemble of four stringed instruments including two violins, a viola, and a cello; also music performed by the ensemble

strophic the repetition of music for each new verse in a song

style the particular character of a musical work, a performance, or a historical period

subdominant fourth pitch of a diatonic scale as well as the triad built upon that pitch

subject the principal musical idea, synonymous with the theme but usually applied only to the main melody of a fugue

swing a type of Big Band jazz of the late 1930s and 1940s

swing era a period that extended roughly from 1935 to 1945

syllabic a melodic setting in which each syllable of text is sung to one pitch

symphonic poem a piece of orchestral program music in one long movement; *also called* tone poem

symphony an extended work in several movements, for orchestra; also an orchestra configured to perform symphonic music

syncopation deliberate shifts of accent so that a melody goes against the steady beat, conflicts with it, and tries to upset the steady pulse

synthesizer an electronic instrument for the production of sound

T

tala (TAH-lah) an Indian time cycle

tango an Argentinean dance in 2/4 or 4/4 time with long, gliding steps

technique the mechanical (motor) skill required to play an instrument or sing

telharmonium a machine that used electrical current to produce sound

tempo the pace with which music moves, based on the speed of the underlying beat

tenor a high pitched male voice

ternary a three-part form, such as ABA

terraced dynamics the layering of dynamic levels within a Baroque composition; change occurring without gradual transition

tessitura the general range of a voice part, considering the commonly used pitches not the lowest and highest extremes

texture the character of the different layers of horizontal and vertical sounds

theme a melody that assumes importance in the development of a composition because of its central and continued use

theme and variations a musical form in which a theme is stated, then varied in a succession of statements; variations may be sectional or continuous

through-composed a setting of text in which different music is provided for each stanza of the poem

timbre the distinctive tone quality of a sound

time line a two-bar repeating asymmetrical rhythmic pattern that originated in Africa and has influenced popular music in the Americas

tintal a popular 16-beat rhythmic cycle in the music of India

toccata keyboard piece (usually) that displays the performer's manual dexterity, typically in one movement

tonality a feeling in melody and harmony that one pitch, the tonic, is the pulling force or center

tone poem *see* symphonic poem

tone row an ordering of the 12 pitches of the chromatic scale in a series that forms the basic material for a musical composition; *see also* twelve-tone music

tonic first pitch of a diatonic scale or the triad built on such a pitch

transcription an arrangement of a piece of music for an instrument, voice, or ensemble other than that for which it was originally written

transpose to move a whole piece, or a section of a piece, or a twelve-tone series, from one pitch level to another

treble clef a sign (𝄞) on a staff indicating the tone G above middle C

tremolo an effect found in string or keyboard music that involves the quick repetition of one or two pitches; in singing it refers to excessive use of vibrato

triads a chord of three tones consisting of a root, a third, and a fifth

trio a work or movement for three voices or instruments

triplet three notes performed in the time of two

troubadour a minstrel of noble birth in southern France, Spain, and Italy during the eleventh to thirteenth centuries; *see also trouvère*

trouvère a minstrel in northern France during the Middle Ages; *see also* troubador

tutti all; everyone together

twelve-bar blues jazz form based on three phrases of four measures each in 4/4 time, using a set progression of I, IV, and V chords, often with added 7ths

twelve-tone music twentieth-century system of writing music in which the twelve tones of the chromatic scale are arranged into a series (number 1 to 12), and subsequently used as the basis of melodic and harmonic variation

U

upbeat a weak beat preceding the downbeat

V

verse a line of metrical writing or a stanza

vibrato a slight wavering or pulsating of a tone in singing or playing an instrument

virtuoso a performer of extraordinary technical and expressive capabilities

vocal range the highest and lowest pitches one can sing

W

waltz a nineteenth-century dance in triple meter

whole-step distance of two half steps in the same direction, such as between C and D or E and F sharp

whole-tone scale scale in which all intervals are whole steps, such as C, D, E, F sharp, G sharp, A sharp, C

word painting a musical illustration of the meaning of a word or a short verbal phrase

Z

zydeco the music of black Creoles that originated in south Louisiana

Artists and Their Works

Composers, Musicians, and Their Works

Index

Acknowledgements

PHOTOGRAPHY CREDITS   Cover: Clockwise from left to right. David Young-Wolff/Photo Edit; Chad Ehlers/Photo Network; Richard Hirschl; Kevin Roznowski; Bill Ross/Westlight; Deborah Davi/Photo Edit.

AP/Wide World Photos 312, 439; Art Resource 506b; Craig Aurness/Westlight 55, 71tl; Cradoc Bagshaw/Westlight 330; David Ball/The Stock Market 534tc; Moles Beck/LGI Photo Agency 110; Ian Berry/Magnum Photos 109; Bettman 13, 35, 46, 52, 61, 64, 65, 71bl, br, 105b, 107, 111, 139, 143, 193, 195, 225, 241, 242, 254(2), 280, 285, 294, 305, 332, 334, 340, 361, 379, 391t, 404, 405, 434, 450, 453, 462, 467, 468, 469, 471, 473, 475, 479, 492, 496, 506t, 508, 511; Allen Birnback/Westlight 11b; Greg Booth 41, 42, 45; Brown Brothers 48, 59, 84, 101, 103, 105t, 145, 161, 211, 257, 262, 341, 417, 461, 509, 524; Dan Bryant 235; Syndey Byrd 11t, 17, 28c, 212, 247, 291, 430, 465; Robert Cahen 83t/b, 240, 458; Jim Caldwell/ Houston Grand Opera 197, 358, 362, 377, 380, 389; Central City Opera 386; Gordon Clark 108; Columbia Artists Management Inc. 500; Columbia University Electric Music Center 314; Crane School of Music/Potsdam College of the State University of New York 222; Cris Cuffaro/Visages 272; Culver Pictures 402, 407, 409; Deborah Davis/Photo Edit 268; © The Walt Disney Company 512; Larry D. Doell/The Stock Market 534bc; Zoe Dominic Photography 82b; Thomas A. Dorsey 214; Chad Ehlers/Photo Network 27; Zviki Eshet/The Stock Market 534bc; Hans Fahrmeyer/LGI Photo Agency 476; Foto Marburg/Art Resource, NY 258; Charles Fowler 25, 136, 206, 250, 503; David R. Frazier Photolibrary, Inc. 7, 8, 14, 32, 151; Tony Freeman/Photo Edit 244, 529; Carol Friedman/Sony Classical 504; Giraudon/Art Resource, NY 9, 499; Glencoe Stock 420; Globe Photos 53, 413, 416, 423, 478, 489; Greater Miami Opera 384; Gilbert M. Grosvenor/National Geographic 298; E. Hartman/Magnum Photos 99; Dallas & John Heaton/Westlight 180, 248; Walter Hodges/Westlight 4; Richard Hutchings/ Photo Edit 2; Jet Propulsion Laboratories 531; Jive Records 433; Winnie Klotz/Metropolitan Opera Association 82t, 83tr; LGI Photo Agency 498; Robert Landau/Westlight 198; Elliott Landy/Image Works 319; Libby Larson 347, 348, 353; Carol Leigh/Photo Network 172; Brian Leng/Westlight 266; Library of Congress 122, 188; R. Ian Lloyd/Westlight 163; Matthew Neal McVay/Seattle Opera 391b; © 1992 MTV Networks 426, 428, 432, 437; Carl Machover 324; Linda Matlow/Pix International 90; Peter Menzel 310, 325; J. Messerschmidt/Westlight 137; Metropolitan Opera 82r; Michigan Opera Theatre 394, 399; Antonia Minnecola 102; Miss America Pageant 534br; Jack Mitchell 62; Robert Moog 317; NASA 530; New York Public Library 360; The Ohio Theatre 410; Chuck O'Rear/Westlight 333; Kingsavanh Patthamavong 113; Jim Pickerell/Westlight iiib, 281; Todd Powell/Photo Network 132; Richard Price/Westlight 76; John Rainer/Red Willow Songs 115; Jim Richardson/ Westlight 128; M. Roessler/H. Armstrong Roberts 534tl; Bill Ross/Westlight iv, 29t, 74, 146; Kevin Roznowski 112; Nicolas Sapieha/Art Resource, NY 447; Scala/Art Resource, NY 121, 200, 449, 454; Peter Schaaf/Boston Symphony Orchestra 92; Dan Sheehy/National Endowment for the Arts 23, 495; Rhoda Sidney/Photo Edit 205; Solaris, NY 57, 226; Kim Steele 487; Gene Stein/Westlight 21; William Grant Still Music 68; Steve Strickland/Westlight 29b; Superstock 28t/b, 36, 142r, 160; Martha Swope Photography Inc. 60, 71tr, 81, 194, 356, 422, 440, 444; Vestax Musical Electronics Corp. 321; Luis Villota/The Stock Market 534tr; William Warfield 83bl; Bob Waterman/Westlight 1; Ron Watts/Westlight 50, 413, 416; Dana C. White/Dana White Productions 30, 72, 170, 286, 289; James Woodard Associates/Photo Network 484; Mike Yamashita/Westlight iiit, 24, 130, 202, 220; David Young-Wolff/Photo Edit 482, 522; Jack Zehrt/FPG International 533; Anna E. Zuckerman/Photo Edit 526; Jim Zuckerman/Westlight 142L.

REPRINT CREDITS   The following material has been reprinted by permission. International Copyrights Secured. All Rights Reserved. P. 176–177, "You are the Sunshine of My Life," by Stevie Wonder. Copyright ©1972 Jobete Music, Co. Inc. and Black Bull Music, Inc. Used by permission of CPP/Belwin, Inc., Miami, FL. International Copyright Secured. Made in U.S.A. All Rights Reserved. P. 189, lyric for "Prendes i Garde" from *The European Musical Heritage.* Copyright ©1987 McGraw-Hill; P. 196, lyric for "Bess, You Is My Woman," from *Porgy and Bess,* George Gershwin, Ira Gershwin, and DuBose Heyward. Copyright ©1935 Chappell & Co. (Renewed); P. 219, "Heaven on Their Minds," from *Jesus Christ, Superstar.* Words by Tim Rice. Music by Andrew Lloyd Webber. Copyright ©1969 by Leeds Music Limited, London, England. Sole Selling Agent Leeds Music Corporation, 1755 Broadway, New York, NY 10019. MCA Music Publishing; P. 231, Civil War Soldier Quote from *And the Band Played On,* by Carolyn Bryant. Copyright © Smithsonian Institution Traveling Exhibition Service (SITE); P. 243, Gerald Abraham, 1812 Criticism, from *The Music of Tchaikovsky.* Copyright ©1946 W.W. Norton & Company, Inc.; P. 249, excerpt from *A House in Bali,* by Colin McPhee. Copyright ©1987 Oxford University Press; P. 277, 278, Berlioz quotes from *The New Oxford Companion to Music, Volume 2.* Copyright ©1983 Oxford University Press; P. 307, Five Measures of the Trio Section from *Suite for Piano,* by Arnold Schoenberg. Copyright © Belmont Music Publishers; P. 308, "The Highly Intelligent and the Highly Creative Adolescent," by J.W. Getzels and P.W. Jackson in *Scientific Creativity: Its Recognition and Development,* C.W. Taylor and F. Benson, ed., Copyright ©1975 Krieger Publishing; P. 323–327, *Valis* excerpts and Tod Machover quotes, printed by permission, Bridge Records, Inc., from the CD recording of *Valis,* BCD 9007; P. 328, excerpts from "The Great Synthesizer Debate," by Bob Doerschuk, *Keyboard,* December, 1983. Copyright ©1983 Miller Freeman, Inc.; P. 343 "Cotton-tail," from *The Swing Era,* by Gunther Schuller. Copyright ©1946. Renewed 1968. Robbins Music Corporation. Rights Assigned to EMI Catalogue Partnership. All Rights Administered by EMI Robbins Catalog Inc.; P. 332–338, Copland quotes from *Aaron Copland: 1900–1942,* by Aaron Copland. Copyright ©1984 Aaron Copland and Vivian Perlis. Reprinted by permission of St. Martin's Press Inc.; P. 347–353, Libby Larsen material copyright by Libby Larsen; P. 501, *Democracy in America, Volume 1,* by Alexis de Tocqueville. Copyright ©1965 Arlington House.